NEGIMA!? NEO

MAGISTER NEGI MAGI

3

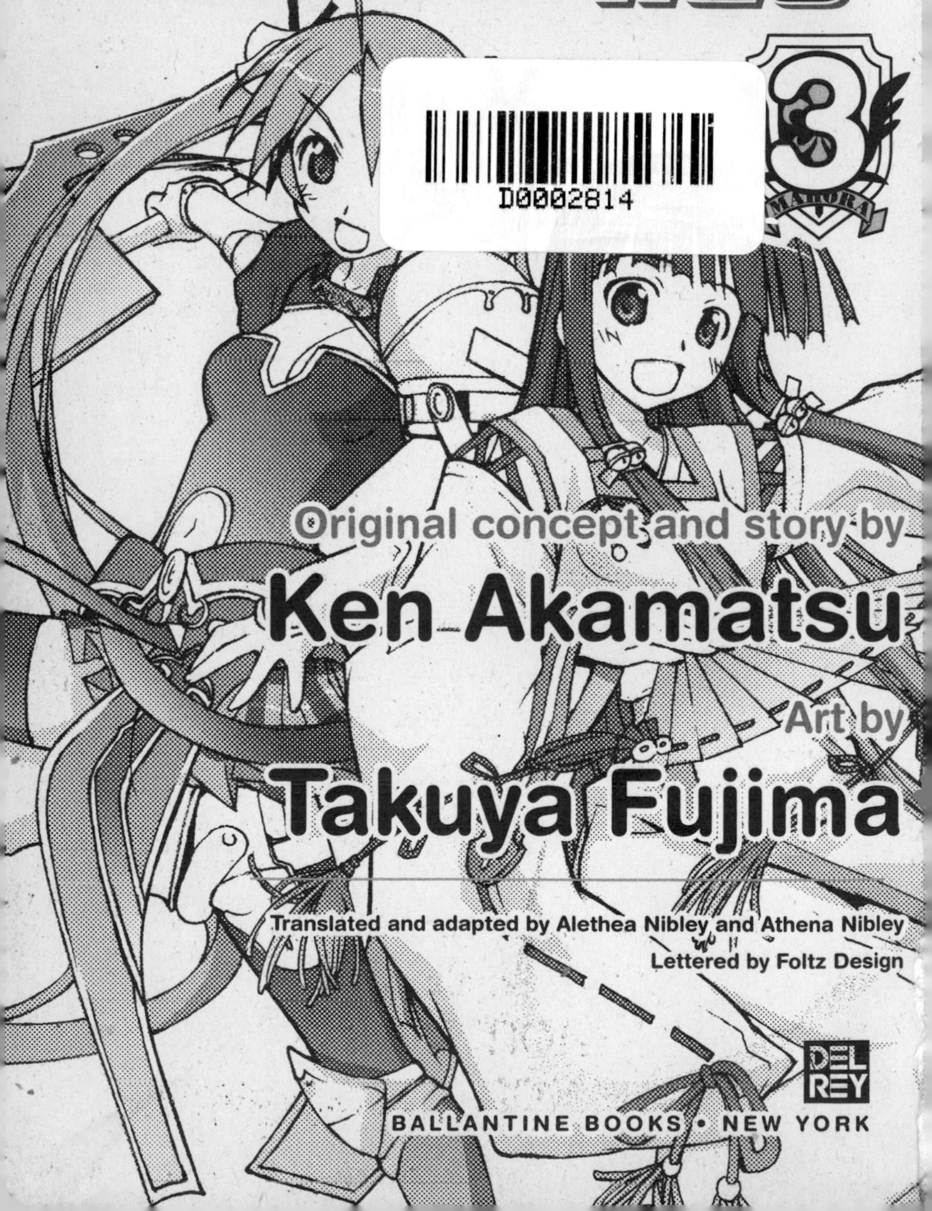
MAHORA

Original concept and story by

Ken Akamatsu

Art by

Takuya Fujima

Translated and adapted by Alethea Nibley and Athena Nibley

Lettered by Foltz Design

DEL REY

BALLANTINE BOOKS • NEW YORK

A Del Rey Manga/Kodansha Trade Paperback Original

Negima!? neo volume 3 copyright © 2007 Takuya Fujima © Ken Akamatsu © KODANSHA/
Kanto Maho Association/TV Tokyo. All rights reserved.
English translation copyright © 2009 Takuya Fujima © Ken Akamatsu
© KODANSHA/Kanto Maho Association/TV Tokyo. All rights reserved.

Published in the United States by Del Rey, an imprint of
The Random House Publishing Group, a division of Random House, Inc., New York.

DEL REY is a registered trademark and the Del Rey colophon
is a trademark of Random House, Inc.

Publication rights arranged through Kodansha Ltd.

First published in Japan in 2007 by Kodansha Ltd., Tokyo

Based on the manga *Mahoh Sensei Negima!* by Ken Akamatsu,
originally serialized in the weekly *Shonen Magazine* published by Kodansha, Ltd.

ISBN 978-0-345-51018-1

Printed in the United States of America

www.delreymanga.com

1 2 3 4 5 6 7 8 9

Translators/adapters: Alethea Nibley and Athena Nibley
Lettering: Foltz Design

CONTENTS

A Word from the Artist

It's been awhile, everyone. This is Fujima. I say it's been awhile, but volume two only came out four months ago. That's the shortest time I've ever had between comic releases. Every time, I draw one picture to cover the cover, back cover, and cover flaps. It's always really hard to make it (laugh). Please unfold it and take a look.

It's been a whole year since *Negima!? neo* started. I think some of you already know, but after its December issue, Bombom Comics magazine will stop being published.

But thanks to all of your support, *Negima!? neo* will be serialized in *Magazine Special*! I want to use this space to offer my thanks m(__)m

Now, about this volume, the star crystal arc that started in volume two will finally reach its climax. Volume three is full of big moments, and I hope you will enjoy it.

—Takuya Fujima

Honorifics Explained

Throughout the Del Rey Manga books, you will find Japanese honorifics left intact in the translations. For those not familiar with how the Japanese use honorifics and, more important, how they differ from American honorifics, we present this brief overview.

Politeness has always been a critical facet of Japanese culture. Ever since the feudal era, when Japan was a highly stratified society, use of honorifics—which can be defined as polite speech that indicates relationship or status—has played an essential role in the Japanese language. When you address someone in Japanese, an honorific usually takes the form of a suffix attached to one's name (example: "Asuna-san"), is used as a title at the end of one's name, or appears in place of the name itself (example: "Negi-sensei," or simply "Sensei!").

Honorifics can be expressions of respect or endearment. In the context of manga and anime, honorifics give insight into the nature of the relationship between characters. Many English translations leave out these important honorifics and therefore distort the feel of the original Japanese. Because Japanese honorifics contain nuances that English honorifics lack, it is our policy at Del Rey not to translate them. Here, instead, is a guide to some of the honorifics you may encounter in Del Rey Manga.

-san: This is the most common honorific and is equivalent to Mr., Miss, Ms., or Mrs. It is the all-purpose honorific and can be used in any situation where politeness is required.

-sama: This is one level higher than "-san" and is used to confer great respect.

-dono: This comes from the word "tono," which means "lord." It is an even higher level than "-sama" and confers utmost respect.

-kun: This suffix is used at the end of boys' names to express familiarity or endearment. It is also sometimes used by men among friends, or when addressing someone younger or of a lower station.

-chan: This is used to express endearment, mostly toward girls. It is also used for little boys, pets, and even among lovers. It gives a sense of childish cuteness.

Bozu: This is an informal way to refer to a boy, similar to the English terms "kid" and "squirt."

**Sempai/
Senpai:** This title suggests that the addressee is one's senior in a group or organization. It is most often used in a school setting, where underclassmen refer to their upperclassmen as "sempai." It can also be used in the workplace, such as when a newer employee addresses an employee who has seniority in the company.

Kohai: This is the opposite of "sempai" and is used toward underclassmen in school or newcomers in the workplace. It connotes that the addressee is of a lower station.

Sensei: Literally meaning "one who has come before," this title is used for teachers, doctors, or masters of any profession or art.

-[blank]: This is usually forgotten in these lists, but it is perhaps the most significant difference between Japanese and English. The lack of honorific, known as *yobisute,* means that the speaker has permission to address the person in a very intimate way. Usually, only family, spouses, or very close friends have this kind of permission. It can be gratifying when someone who has earned the intimacy starts to call one by one's name without an honorific. But when that intimacy hasn't been earned, it can be very insulting.

NEGIMA!? NEO

MAGISTER NEGI MAGI

3

MAHORA

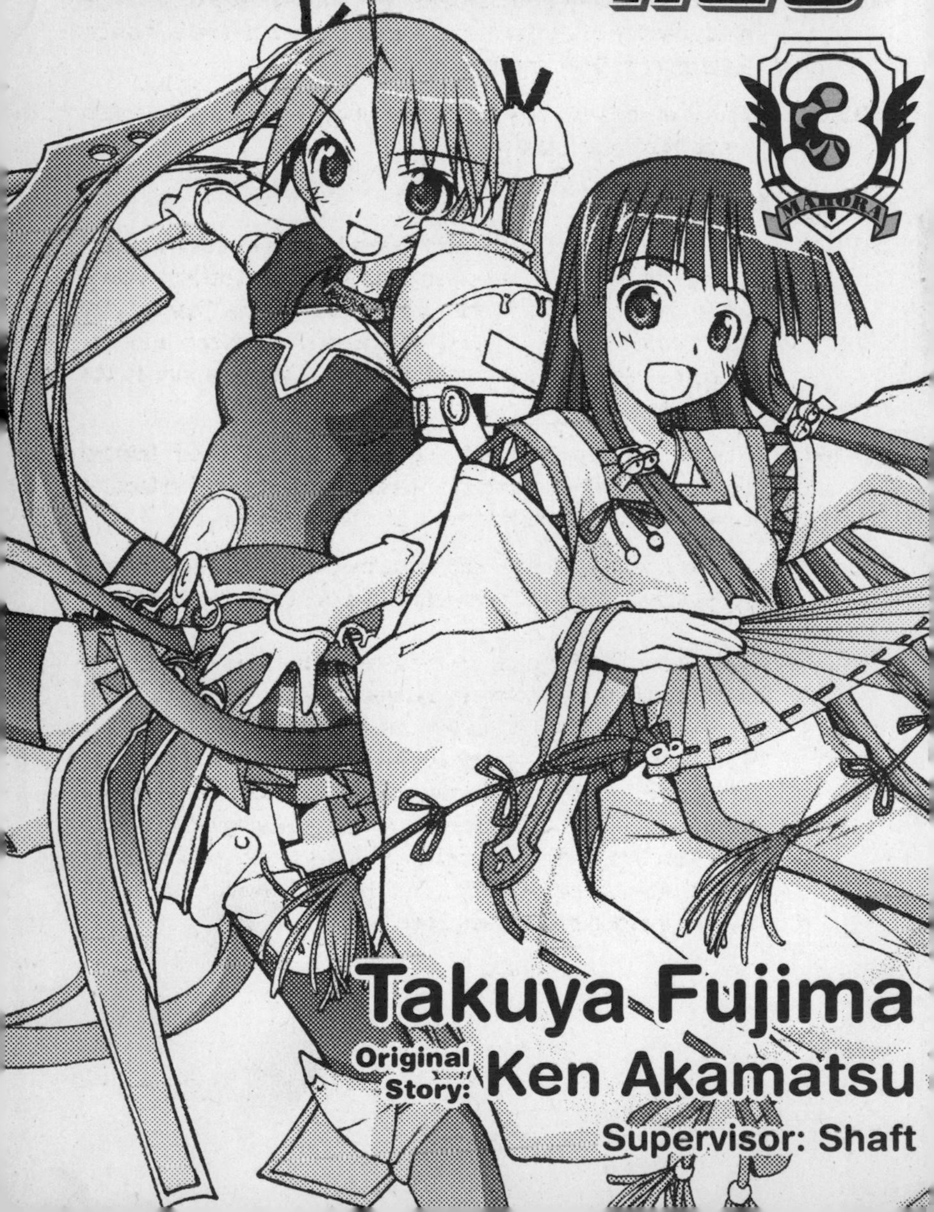

Takuya Fujima

Original Story: Ken Akamatsu

Supervisor: Shaft

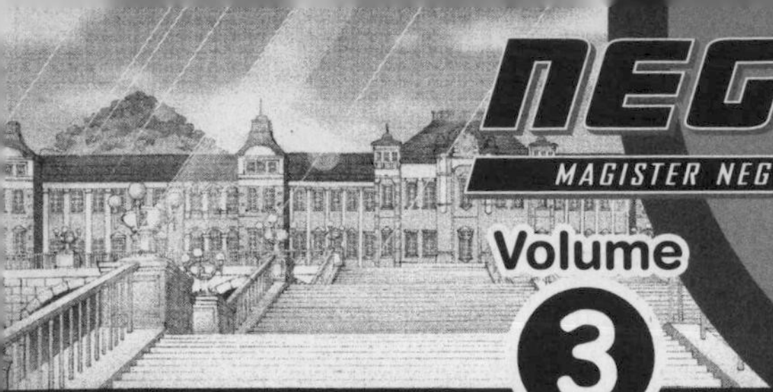

NEGIMA!? NEO

MAGISTER NEGI MAGI

Volume 3

Contents

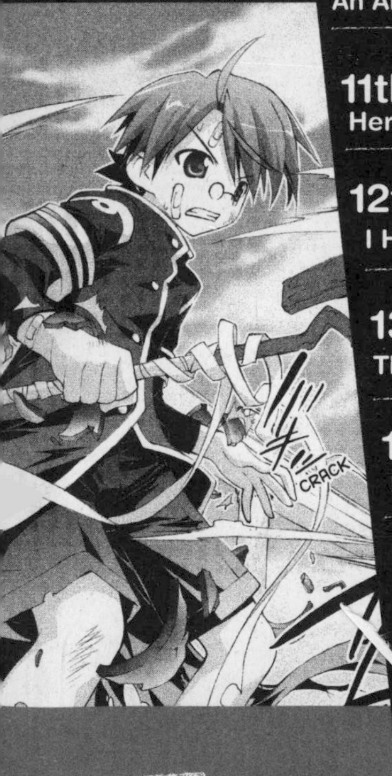
CRACK

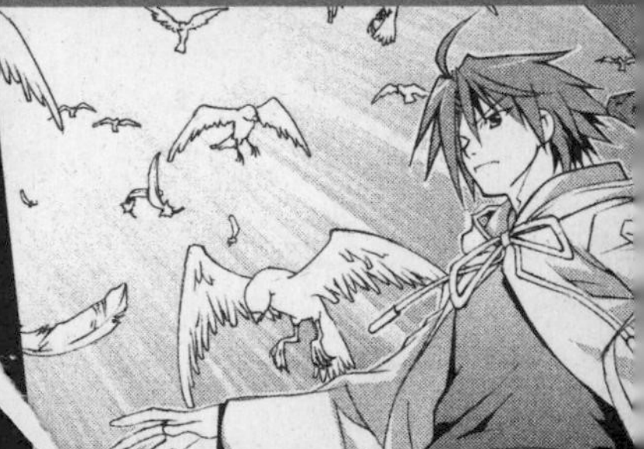

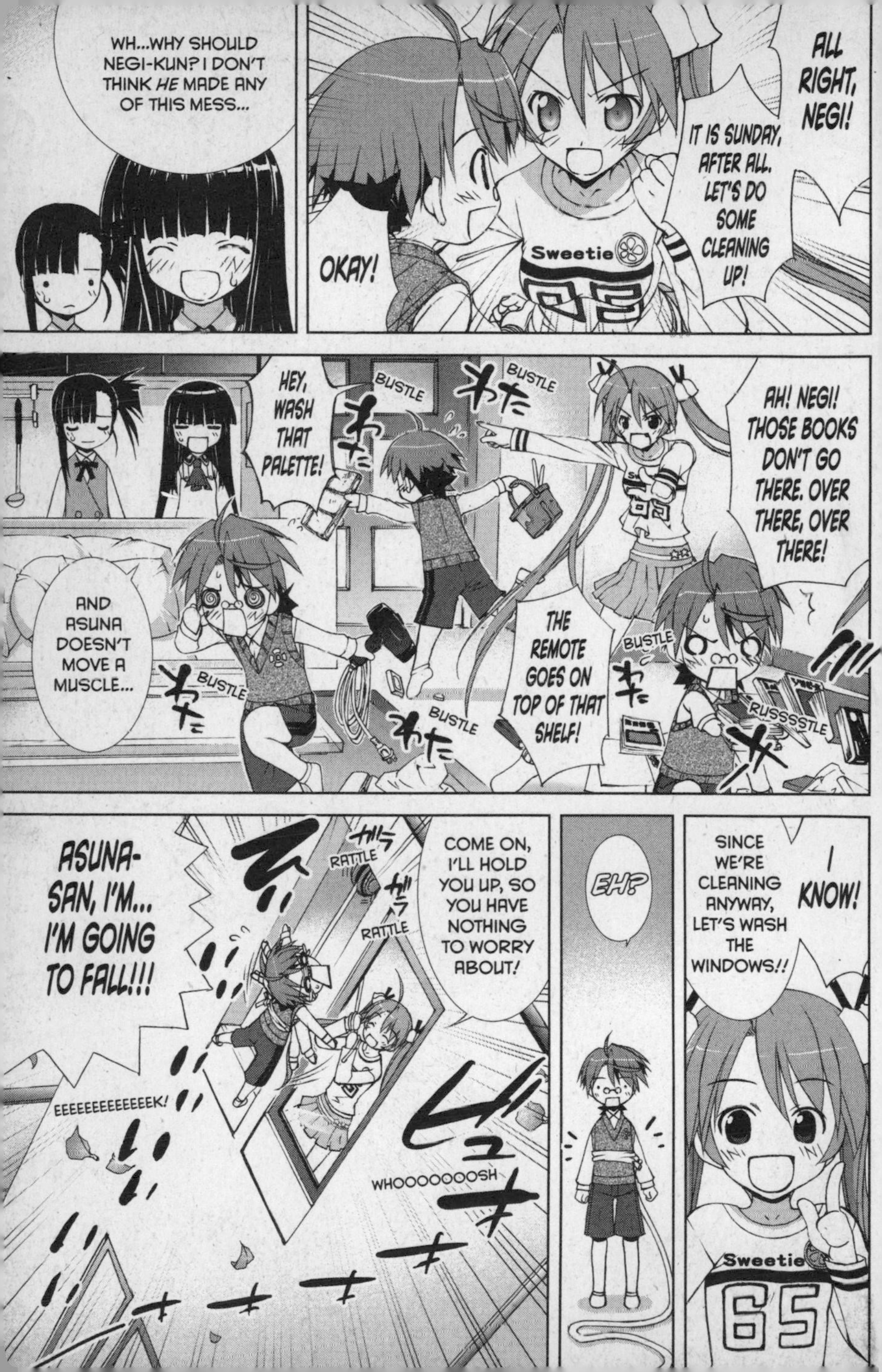
ALL RIGHT, NEGI!
IT IS SUNDAY, AFTER ALL. LET'S DO SOME CLEANING UP!
OKAY!
WH...WHY SHOULD NEGI-KUN? I DON'T THINK *HE* MADE ANY OF THIS MESS...
AH! NEGI! THOSE BOOKS DON'T GO THERE. OVER THERE, OVER THERE!
BUSTLE
RUSSSSTLE
THE REMOTE GOES ON TOP OF THAT SHELF!
BUSTLE
BUSTLE
HEY, WASH THAT PALETTE!
BUSTLE
BUSTLE
AND ASUNA DOESN'T MOVE A MUSCLE...
BUSTLE
I KNOW!
SINCE WE'RE CLEANING ANYWAY, LET'S WASH THE WINDOWS!!
EH?
COME ON, I'LL HOLD YOU UP, SO YOU HAVE NOTHING TO WORRY ABOUT!
RATTLE
RATTLE
ASUNA-SAN, I'M... I'M GOING TO FALL!!!
WHOOOOOOOOSH
EEEEEEEEEEEEK!

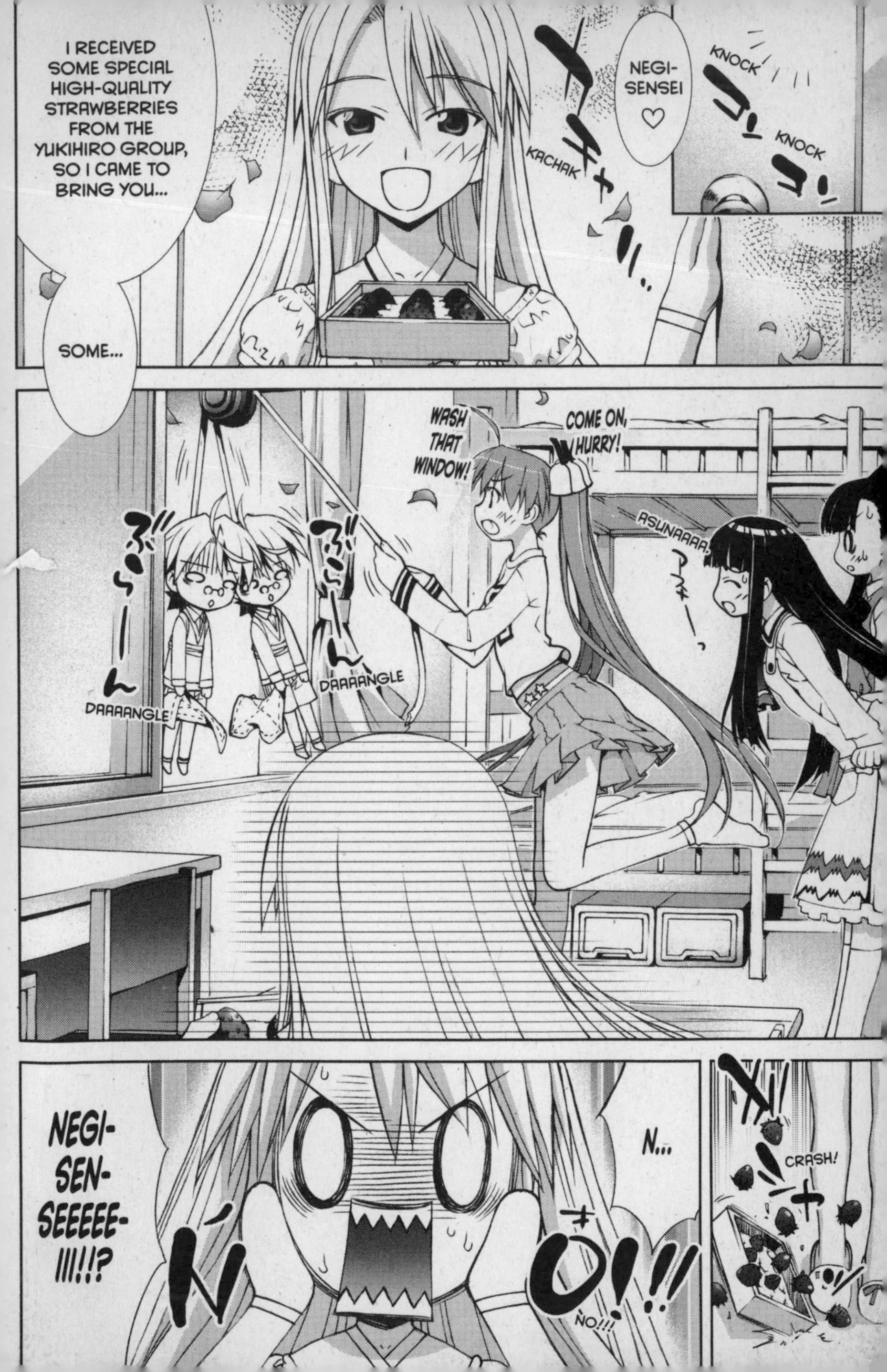
KNOCK
KNOCK
NEGI-SENSEI ♡
KACHAK
I RECEIVED SOME SPECIAL HIGH-QUALITY STRAWBERRIES FROM THE YUKIHIRO GROUP, SO I CAME TO BRING YOU...
SOME...
COME ON, HURRY!
WASH THAT WINDOW!
ASUNAAAA.
DAAAANGLE
DAAAANGLE!
CRASH!
N...
NO!!!
NEGI-SEN-SEEEEEE-IIII!!!?

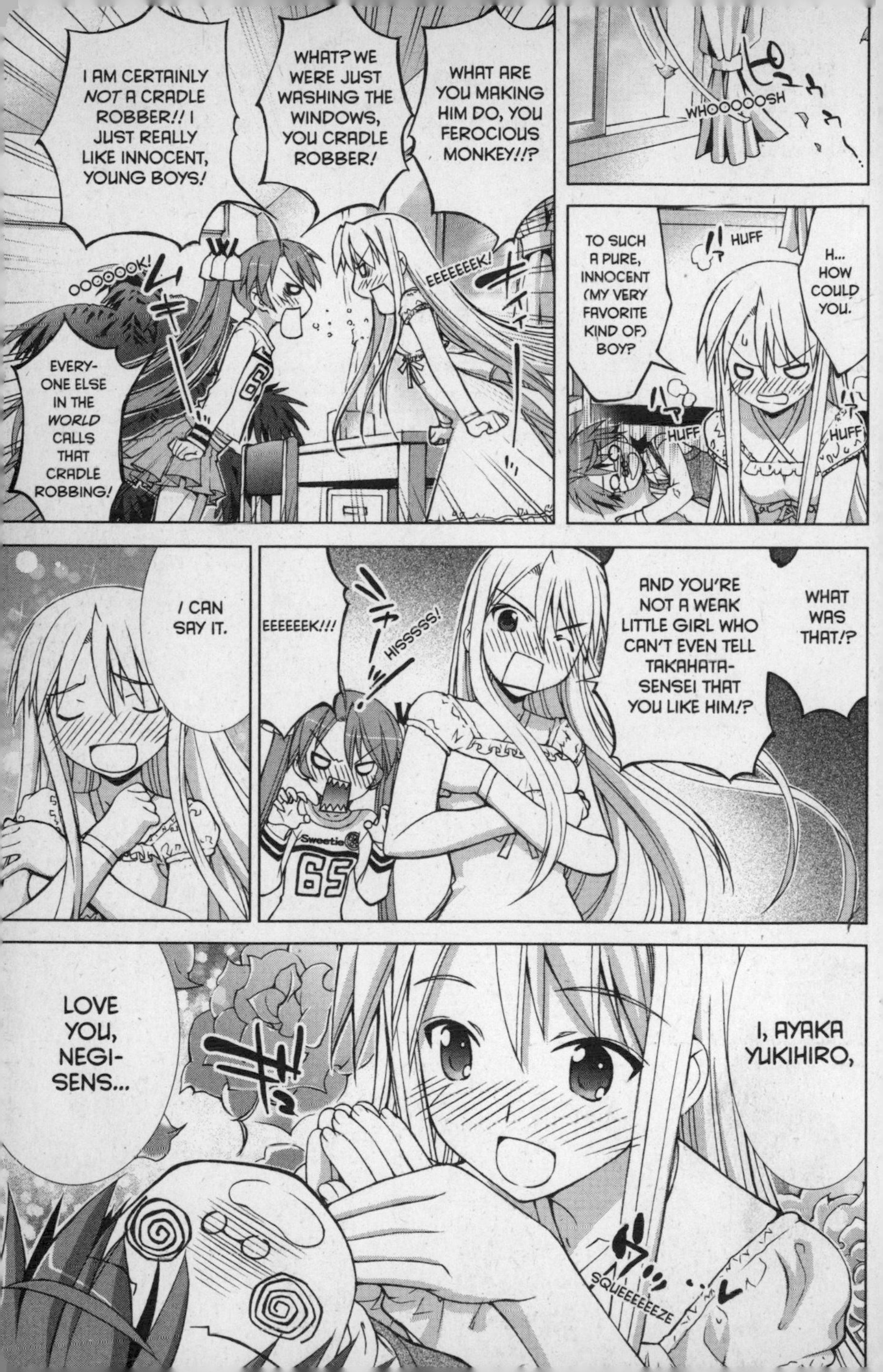

WHOOOOOOSH
H... HOW COULD YOU.
TO SUCH A PURE, INNOCENT (MY VERY FAVORITE KIND OF) BOY?
HUFF
HUFF
HUFF
WHAT ARE YOU MAKING HIM DO, YOU FEROCIOUS MONKEY!!?
WHAT? WE WERE JUST WASHING THE WINDOWS, YOU CRADLE ROBBER!
I AM CERTAINLY *NOT* A CRADLE ROBBER!! I JUST REALLY LIKE INNOCENT, YOUNG BOYS!
EEEEEEEK!
OOOOOOOK!
EVERY-ONE ELSE IN THE *WORLD* CALLS THAT CRADLE ROBBING!
WHAT WAS THAT!?
AND YOU'RE NOT A WEAK LITTLE GIRL WHO CAN'T EVEN TELL TAKAHATA-SENSEI THAT YOU LIKE HIM!?
HISSSSS!
EEEEEEK!!!
I CAN SAY IT.
I, AYAKA YUKIHIRO,
LOVE YOU, NEGI-SENS...
SQUEEEEEEZE

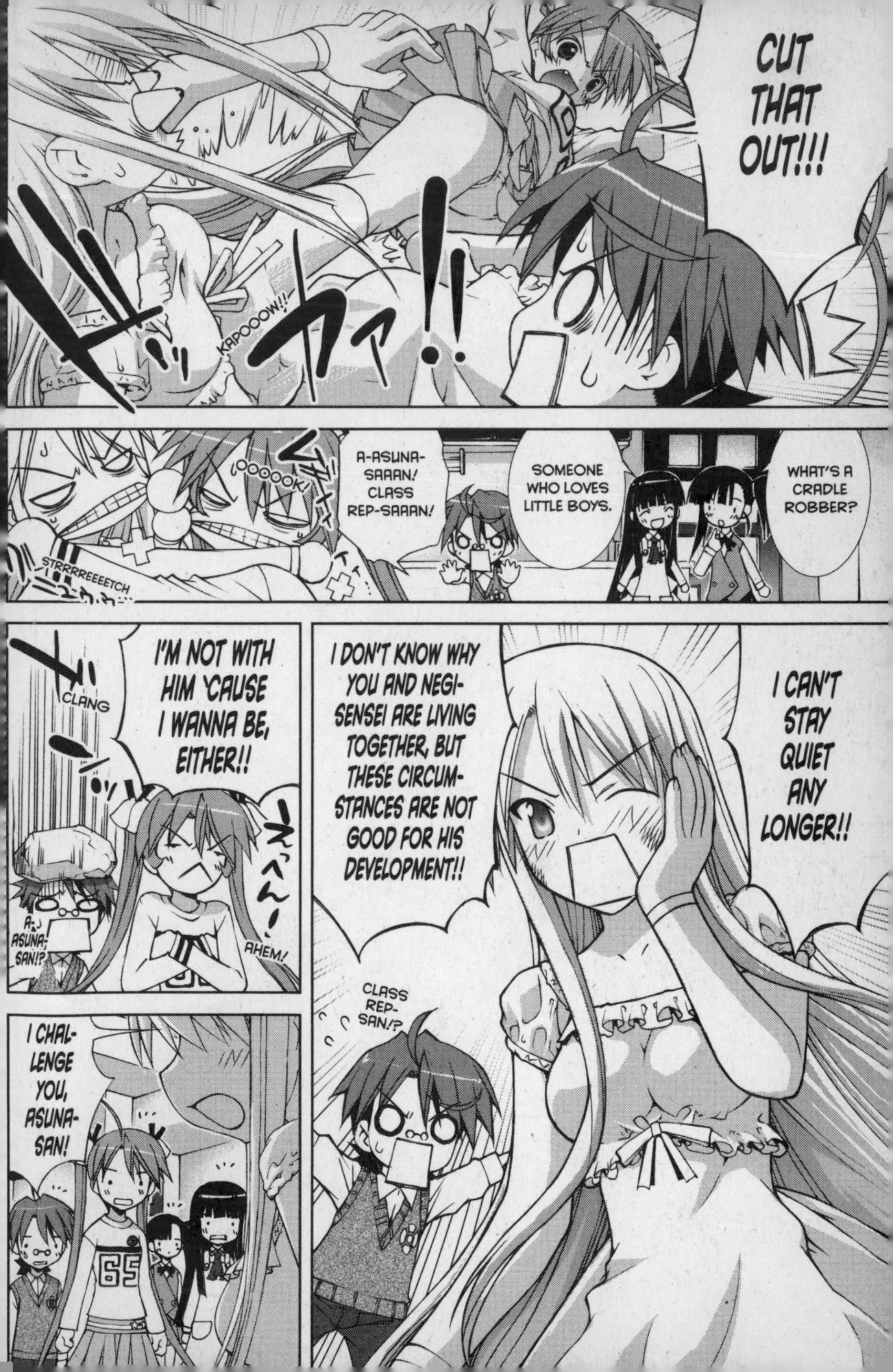
CUT THAT OUT!!!
KAPOOOW!!
WHAT'S A CRADLE ROBBER?
SOMEONE WHO LOVES LITTLE BOYS.
A-ASUNA-SAAAN! CLASS REP-SAAAN!
OOOOOK!
STRRRREEEETCH
I CAN'T STAY QUIET ANY LONGER!!
I DON'T KNOW WHY YOU AND NEGI-SENSEI ARE LIVING TOGETHER, BUT THESE CIRCUMSTANCES ARE NOT GOOD FOR HIS DEVELOPMENT!!
CLASS REP-SAN!?
I'M NOT WITH HIM 'CAUSE I WANNA BE, EITHER!!
CLANG
AHEM!
A-ASUNA-SAN!?
I CHAL-LENGE YOU, ASUNA-SAN!

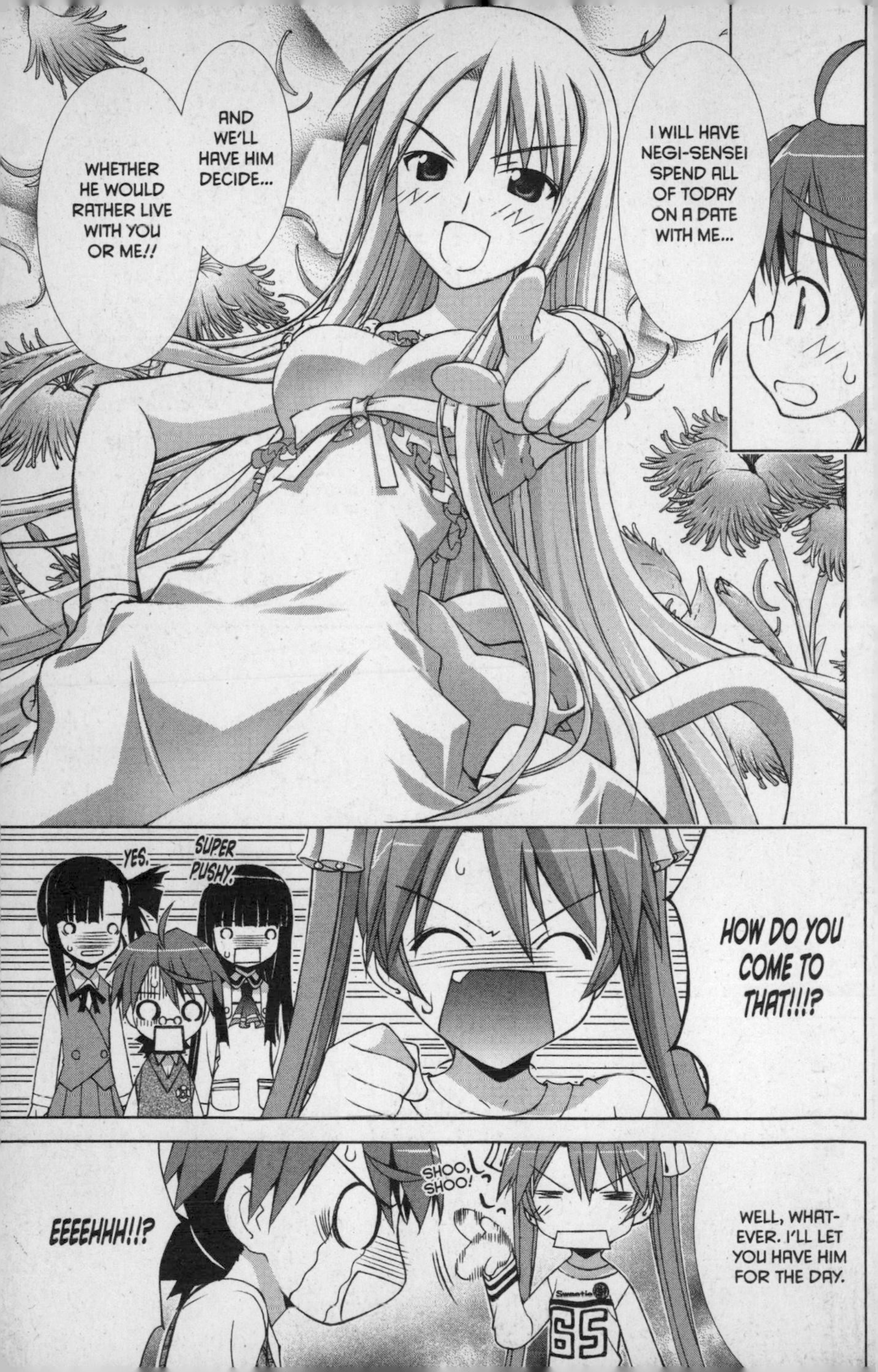
I WILL HAVE NEGI-SENSEI SPEND ALL OF TODAY ON A DATE WITH ME...
AND WE'LL HAVE HIM DECIDE...
WHETHER HE WOULD RATHER LIVE WITH YOU OR ME!!
HOW DO YOU COME TO THAT!!!?
SUPER PUSHY.
YES.
WELL, WHAT-EVER. I'LL LET YOU HAVE HIM FOR THE DAY.
SHOO, SHOO!
EEEEHHH!!?

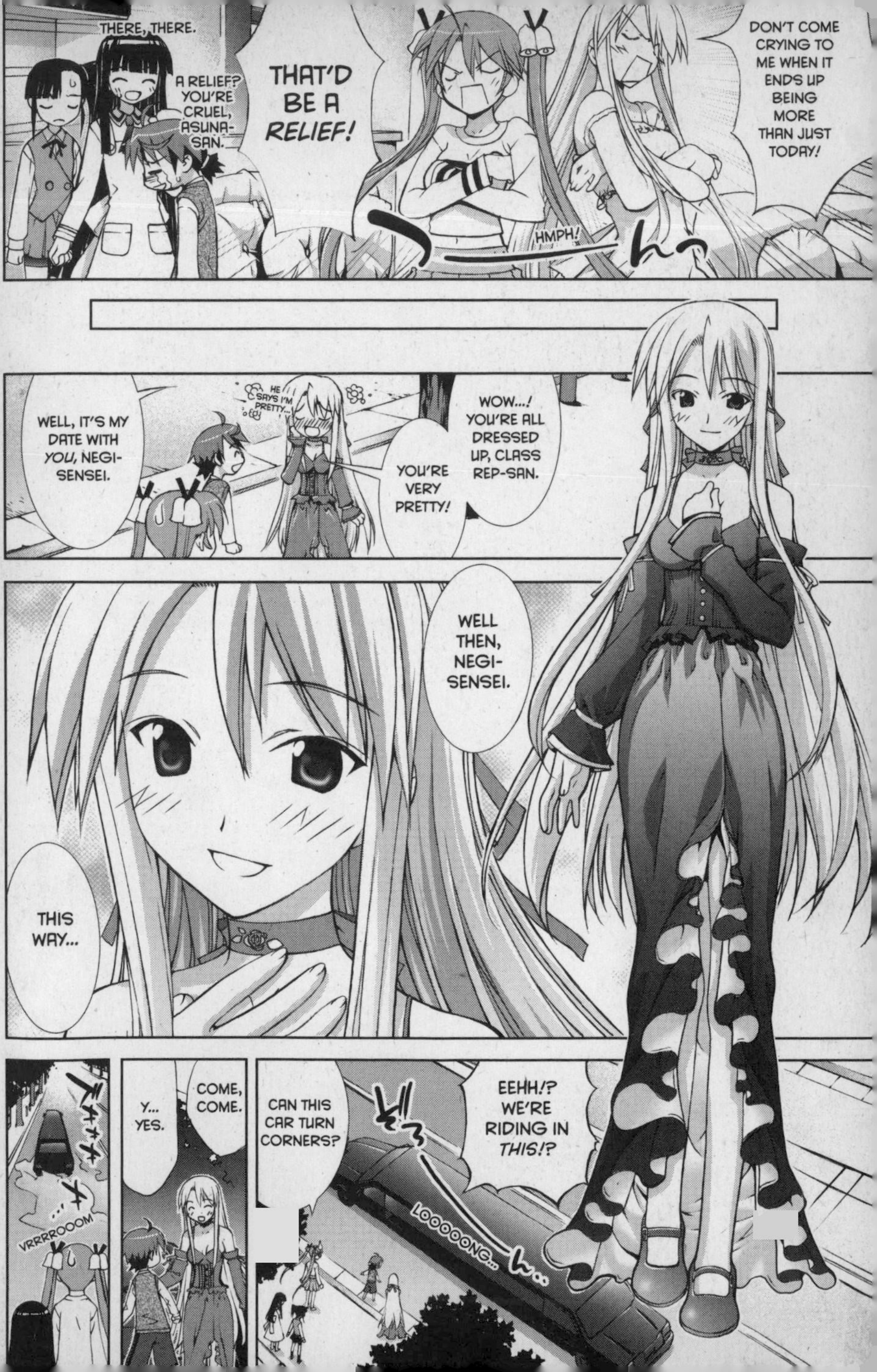
DON'T COME CRYING TO ME WHEN IT ENDS UP BEING MORE THAN JUST TODAY!
HMPH!
THAT'D BE A RELIEF!
A RELIEF? YOU'RE CRUEL, ASUNA-SAN.
THERE, THERE.
WOW...! YOU'RE ALL DRESSED UP, CLASS REP-SAN.
YOU'RE VERY PRETTY!
HE SAYS I'M PRETTY...
WELL, IT'S MY DATE WITH YOU, NEGI-SENSEI.
WELL THEN, NEGI-SENSEI.
THIS WAY...
EEHH!? WE'RE RIDING IN THIS!?
LOOOOONG...
CAN THIS CAR TURN CORNERS?
COME, COME.
Y... YES.
VRRRROOOM

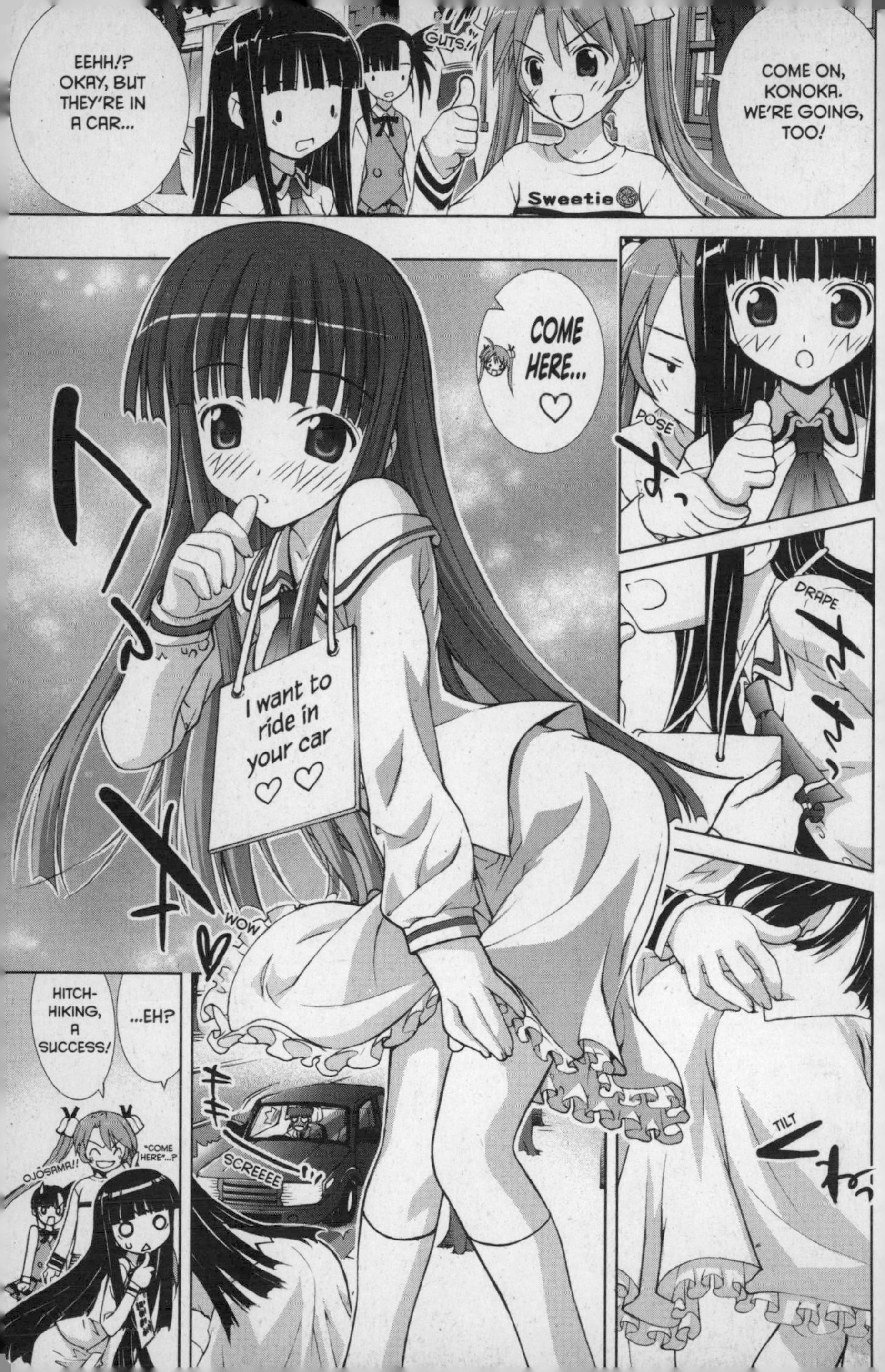
COME ON, KONOKA. WE'RE GOING, TOO!
GUTS!
Sweetie
EEHH!? OKAY, BUT THEY'RE IN A CAR...
POSE
DRAPE
TILT
COME HERE... ♡
I want to ride in your car ♡ ♡
WOW
...EH?
HITCH-HIKING, A SUCCESS!
SCREEEE
"COME HERE"...?
OJŌSAMA!!

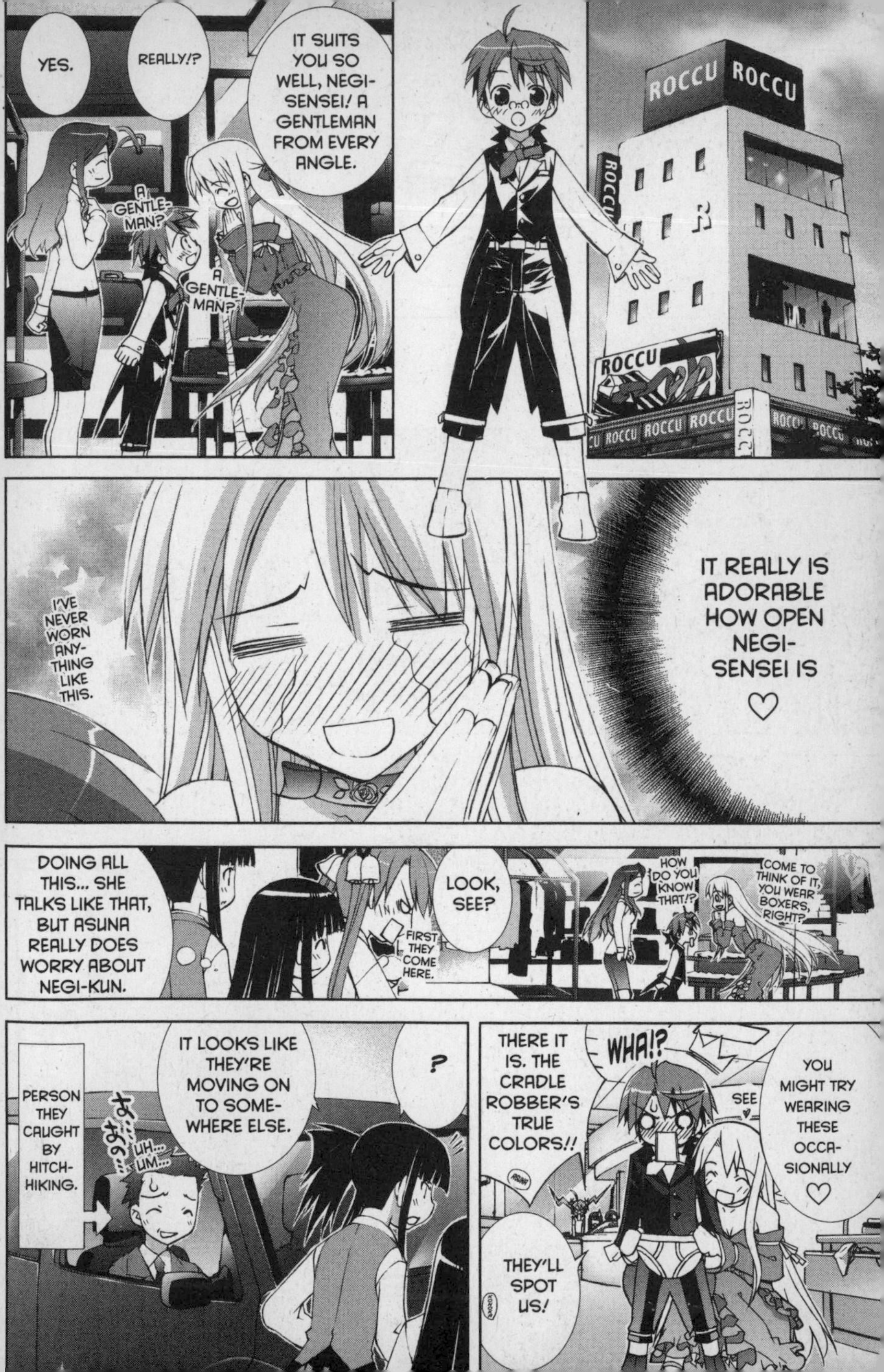
ROCCU
IT SUITS YOU SO WELL, NEGI-SENSEI! A GENTLEMAN FROM EVERY ANGLE.
REALLY!?
YES.
A GENTLE-MAN?
A GENTLE-MAN?
IT REALLY IS ADORABLE HOW OPEN NEGI-SENSEI IS ♡
I'VE NEVER WORN ANY-THING LIKE THIS.
COME TO THINK OF IT, YOU WEAR BOXERS, RIGHT?
HOW DO YOU KNOW THAT!?
LOOK, SEE?
FIRST THEY COME HERE.
DOING ALL THIS... SHE TALKS LIKE THAT, BUT ASUNA REALLY DOES WORRY ABOUT NEGI-KUN.
YOU MIGHT TRY WEARING THESE OCCA-SIONALLY ♡
SEE ♡
WHA!?
THERE IT IS. THE CRADLE ROBBER'S TRUE COLORS!!
THEY'LL SPOT US!
?
IT LOOKS LIKE THEY'RE MOVING ON TO SOME-WHERE ELSE.
あ…あの…
UH... UM...
PERSON THEY CAUGHT BY HITCH-HIKING.

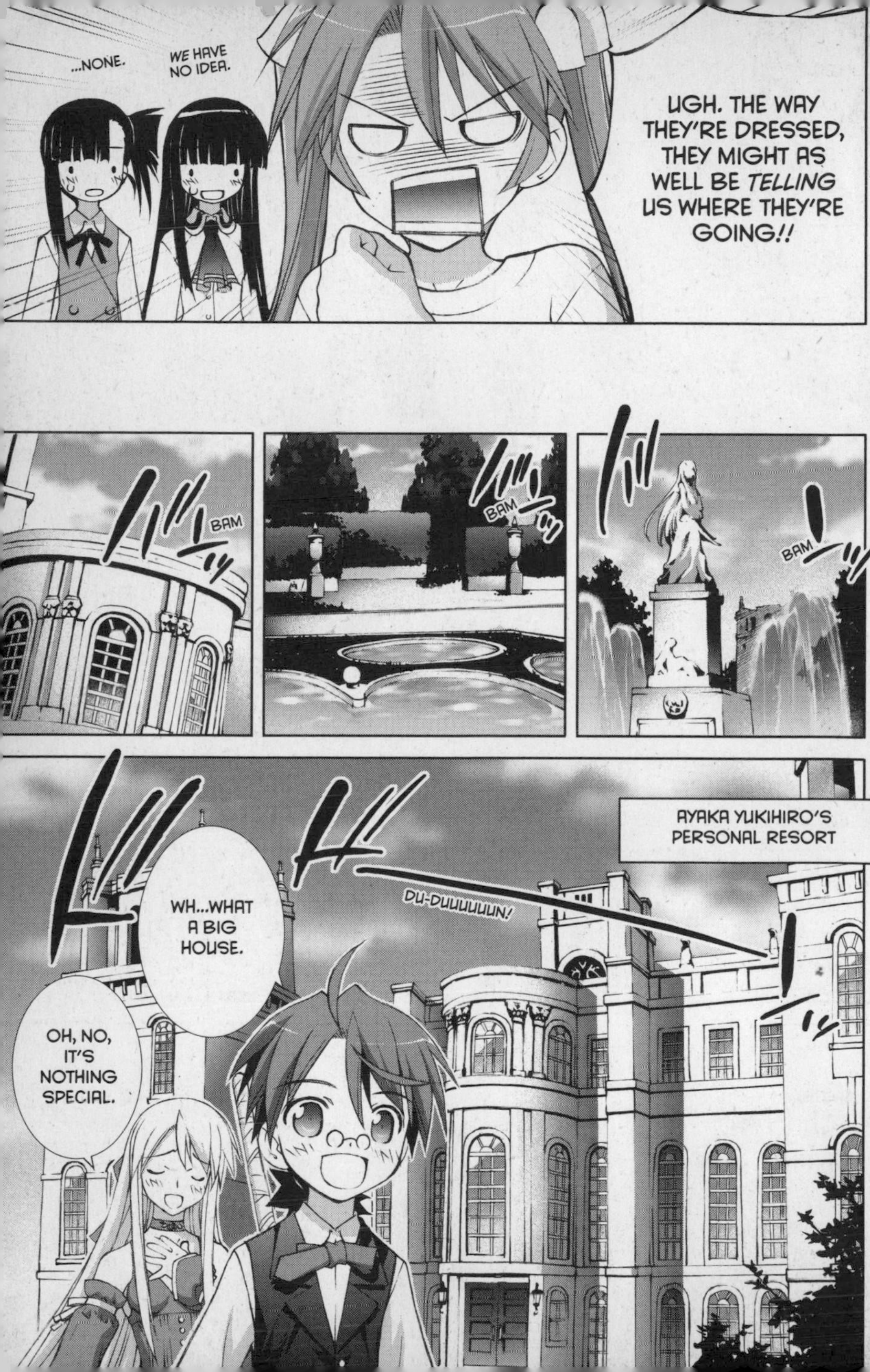
UGH. THE WAY THEY'RE DRESSED, THEY MIGHT AS WELL BE *TELLING* US WHERE THEY'RE GOING!!
WE HAVE NO IDEA.
...NONE.
BAM
BAM
BAM
AYAKA YUKIHIRO'S PERSONAL RESORT
DU-DUUUUUUN!
WH...WHAT A BIG HOUSE.
OH, NO, IT'S NOTHING SPECIAL.

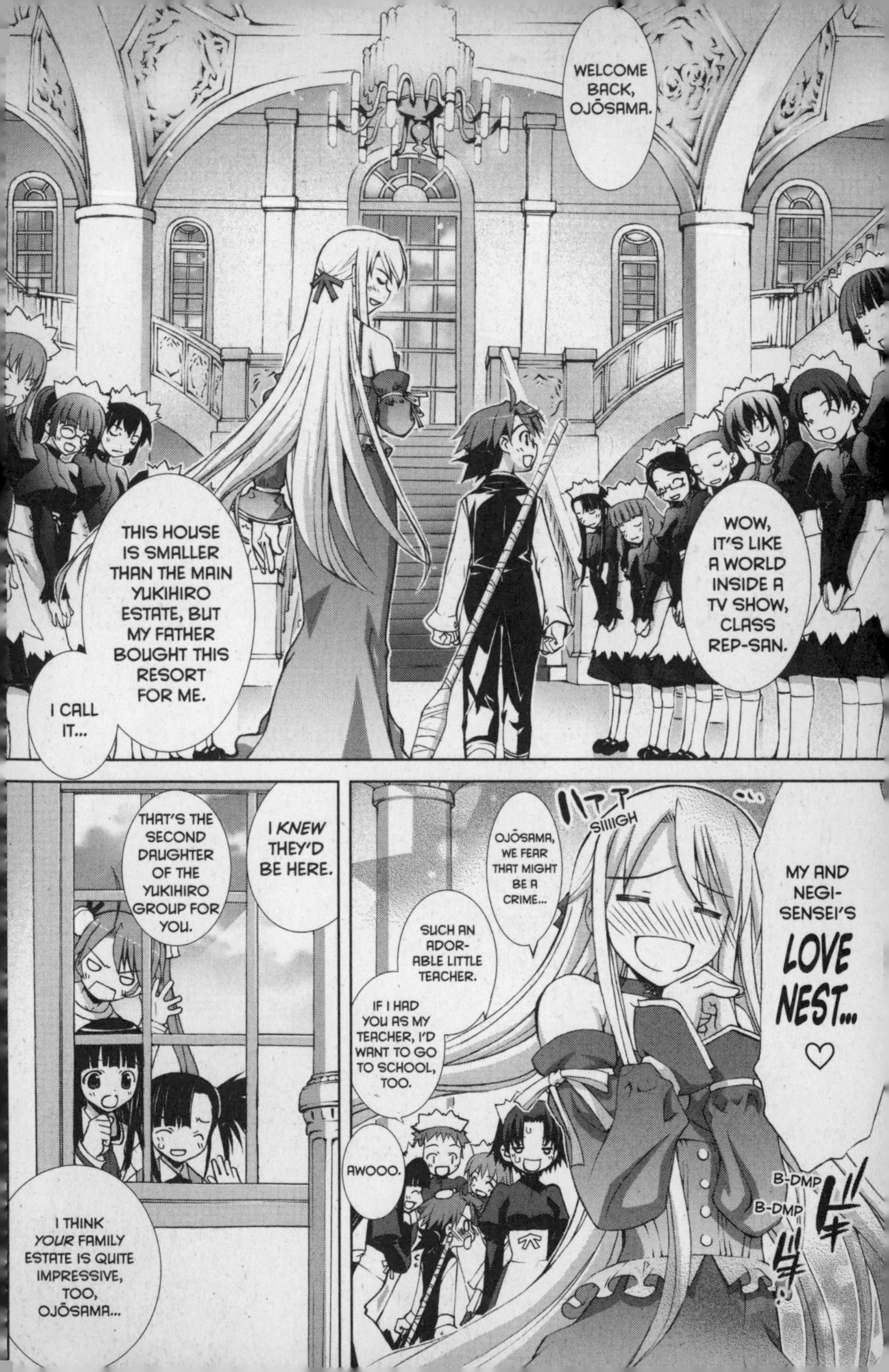
WELCOME BACK, OJŌSAMA.
WOW, IT'S LIKE A WORLD INSIDE A TV SHOW, CLASS REP-SAN.
THIS HOUSE IS SMALLER THAN THE MAIN YUKIHIRO ESTATE, BUT MY FATHER BOUGHT THIS RESORT FOR ME.
I CALL IT...
MY AND NEGI-SENSEI'S LOVE NEST... ♡
SIIIIGH
OJŌSAMA, WE FEAR THAT MIGHT BE A CRIME...
SUCH AN ADORABLE LITTLE TEACHER.
IF I HAD YOU AS MY TEACHER, I'D WANT TO GO TO SCHOOL, TOO.
AWOOO.
B-DMP
B-DMP
I *KNEW* THEY'D BE HERE.
THAT'S THE SECOND DAUGHTER OF THE YUKIHIRO GROUP FOR YOU.
I THINK *YOUR* FAMILY ESTATE IS QUITE IMPRESSIVE, TOO, OJŌSAMA...

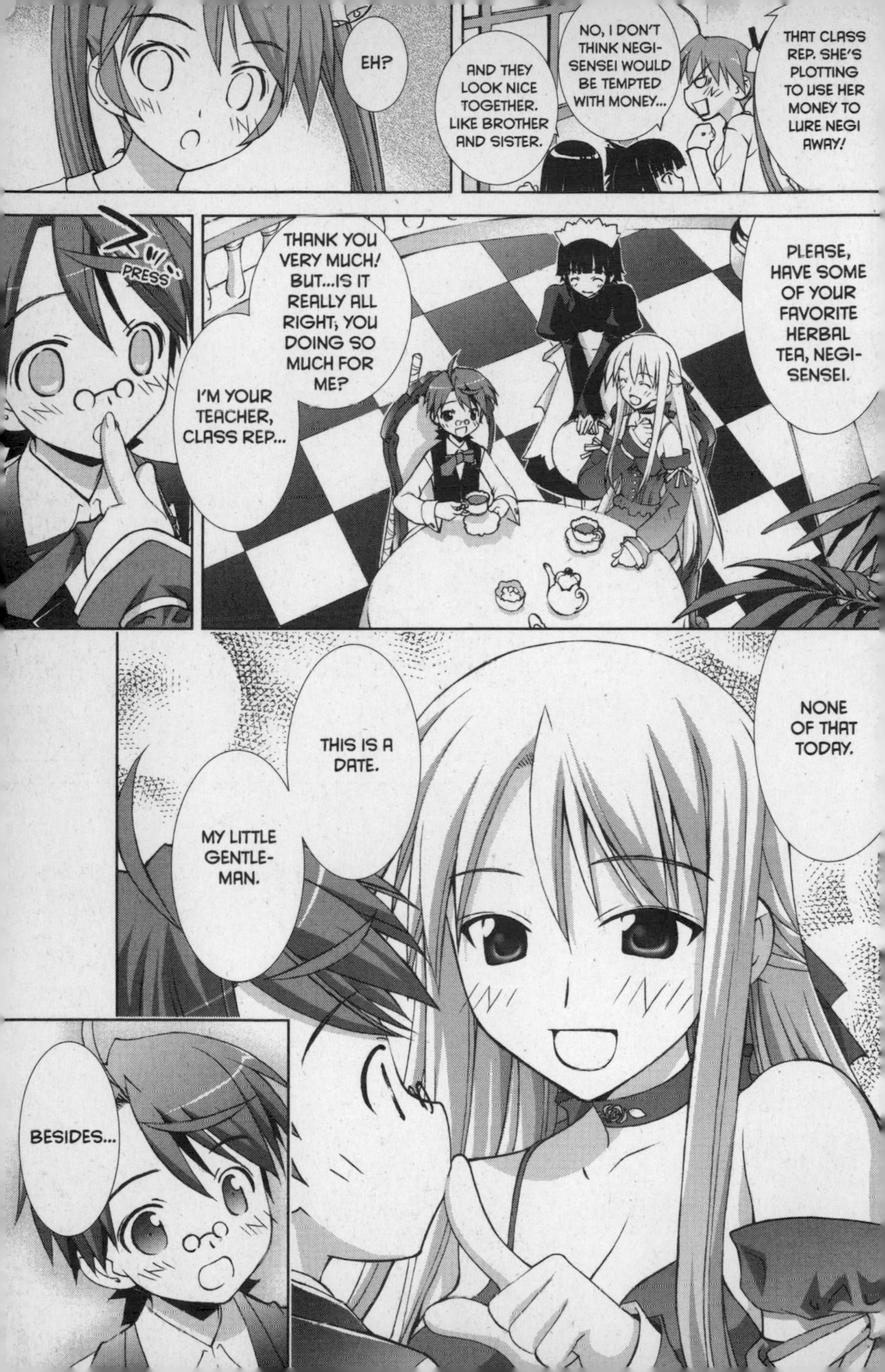
THAT CLASS REP. SHE'S PLOTTING TO USE HER MONEY TO LURE NEGI AWAY!
NO, I DON'T THINK NEGI-SENSEI WOULD BE TEMPTED WITH MONEY...
AND THEY LOOK NICE TOGETHER. LIKE BROTHER AND SISTER.
EH?
PLEASE, HAVE SOME OF YOUR FAVORITE HERBAL TEA, NEGI-SENSEI.
THANK YOU VERY MUCH! BUT...IS IT REALLY ALL RIGHT, YOU DOING SO MUCH FOR ME?
PRESS
I'M YOUR TEACHER, CLASS REP...
NONE OF THAT TODAY.
THIS IS A DATE.
MY LITTLE GENTLEMAN.
BESIDES...

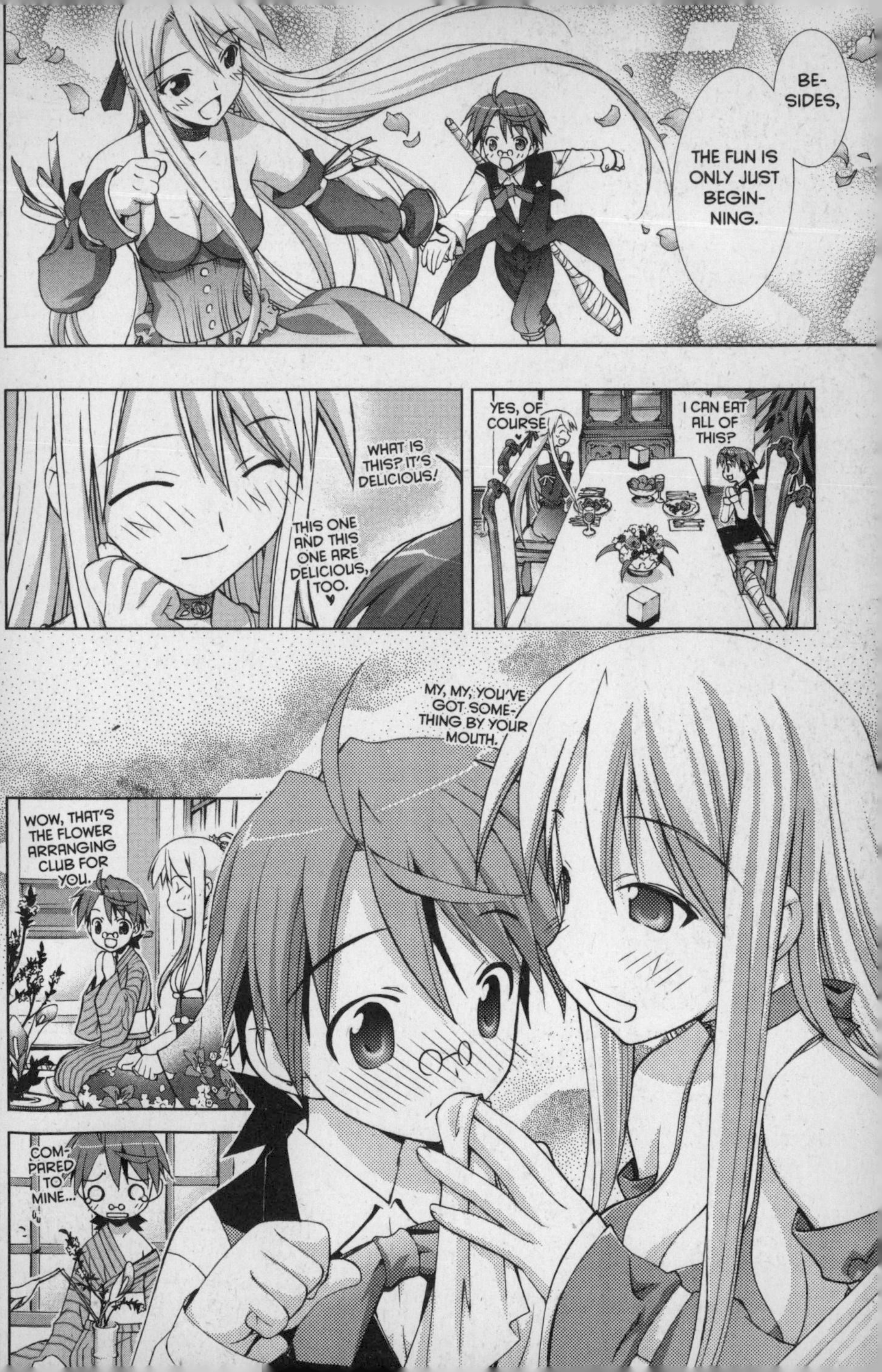
BE-SIDES,
THE FUN IS ONLY JUST BEGIN-NING.
I CAN EAT ALL OF THIS?
YES, OF COURSE
WHAT IS THIS? IT'S DELICIOUS!
THIS ONE AND THIS ONE ARE DELICIOUS, TOO.
MY, MY, YOU'VE GOT SOME-THING BY YOUR MOUTH.
WOW, THAT'S THE FLOWER ARRANGING CLUB FOR YOU.
COM-PARED TO MINE...

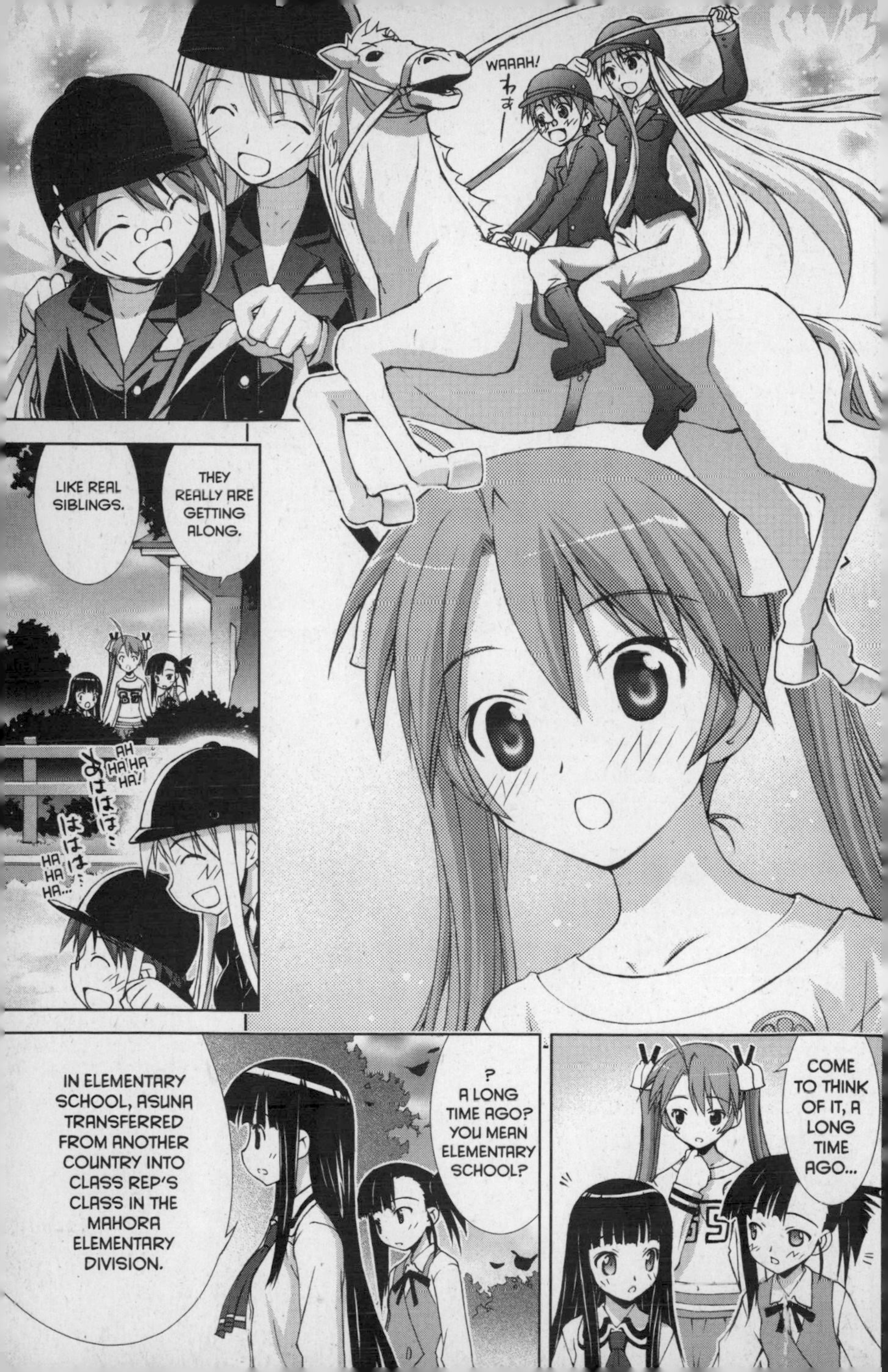
WAAAH!
わぁー
THEY REALLY ARE GETTING ALONG.
LIKE REAL SIBLINGS.
AH HA HA HA!
あははは
ははは…
HA HA HA...
COME TO THINK OF IT, A LONG TIME AGO...
? A LONG TIME AGO? YOU MEAN ELEMENTARY SCHOOL?
IN ELEMENTARY SCHOOL, ASUNA TRANSFERRED FROM ANOTHER COUNTRY INTO CLASS REP'S CLASS IN THE MAHORA ELEMENTARY DIVISION.

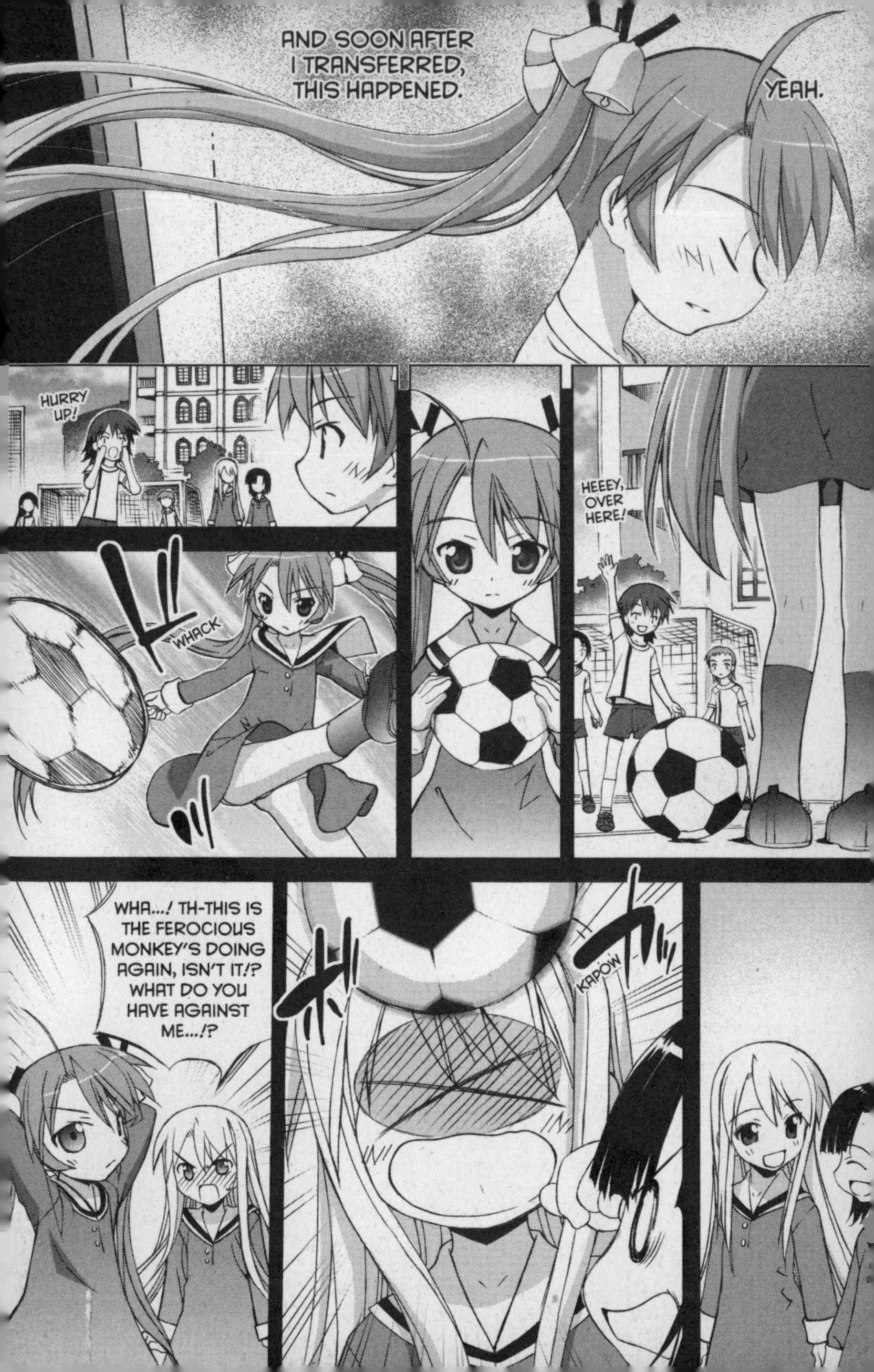
YEAH.
AND SOON AFTER I TRANSFERRED, THIS HAPPENED.
HEEEY, OVER HERE!
HURRY UP!
WHACK
KAPOW
WHA...! TH-THIS IS THE FEROCIOUS MONKEY'S DOING AGAIN, ISN'T IT!? WHAT DO YOU HAVE AGAINST ME...!?

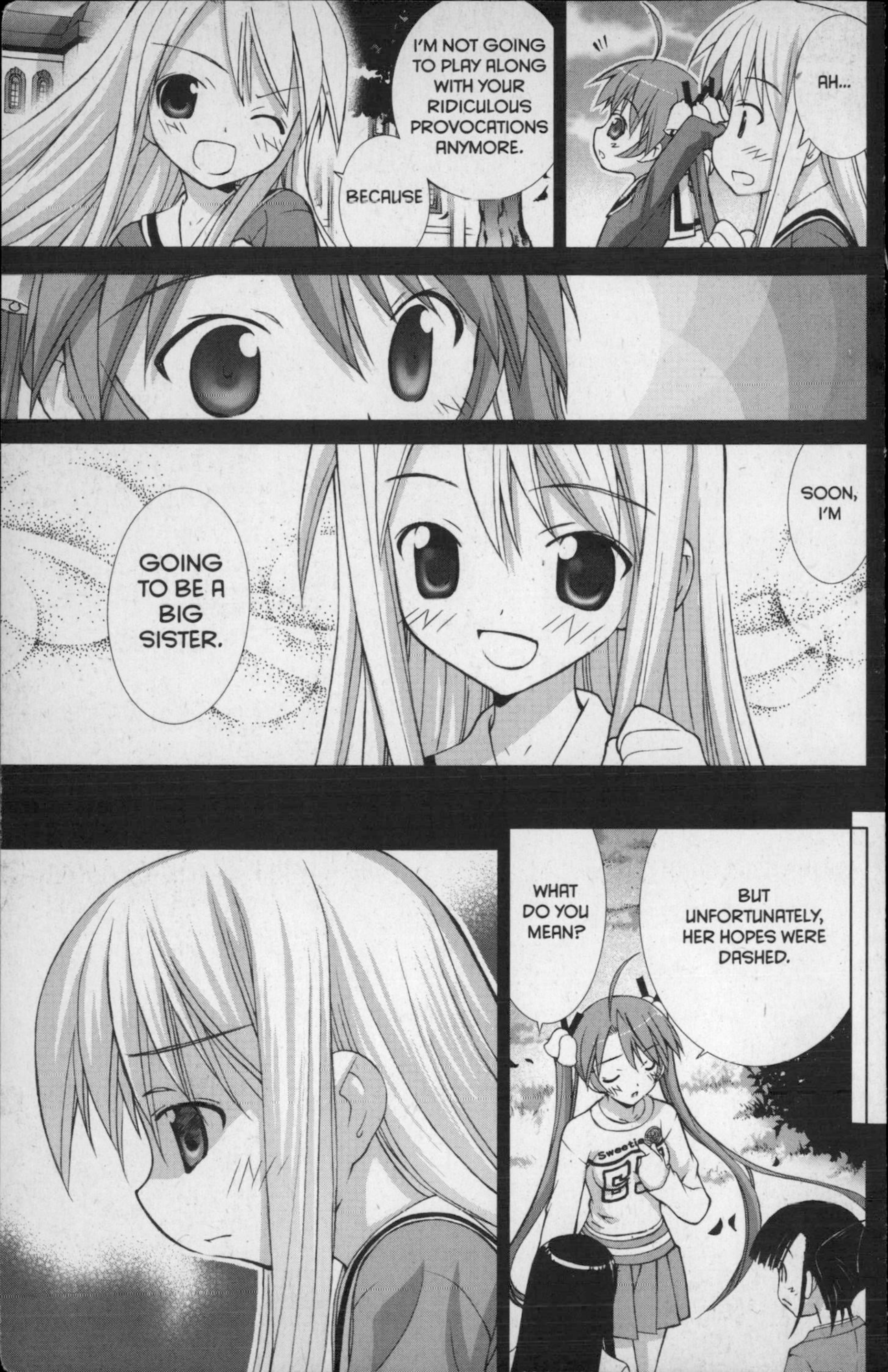
AH...
I'M NOT GOING TO PLAY ALONG WITH YOUR RIDICULOUS PROVOCATIONS ANYMORE.
BECAUSE
SOON, I'M
GOING TO BE A BIG SISTER.
BUT UNFORTUNATELY, HER HOPES WERE DASHED.
WHAT DO YOU MEAN?

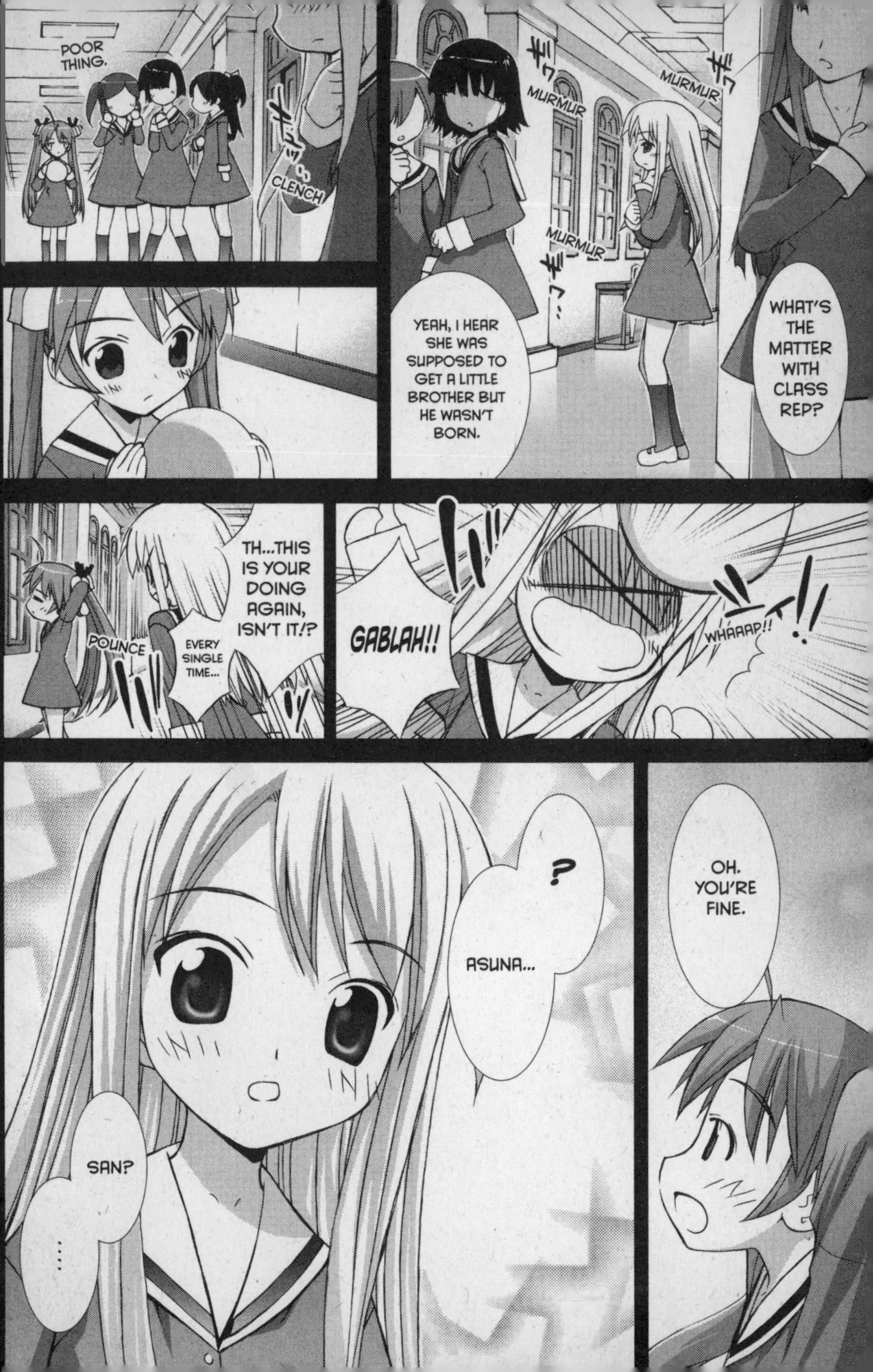

MURMUR
MURMUR
WHAT'S THE MATTER WITH CLASS REP?
MURMUR
YEAH, I HEAR SHE WAS SUPPOSED TO GET A LITTLE BROTHER BUT HE WASN'T BORN.
POOR THING.
CLENCH
WHAAAP!!
GABLAH!!
TH...THIS IS YOUR DOING AGAIN, ISN'T IT!?
EVERY SINGLE TIME...
POUNCE
OH. YOU'RE FINE.
?
ASUNA...
SAN?
.....

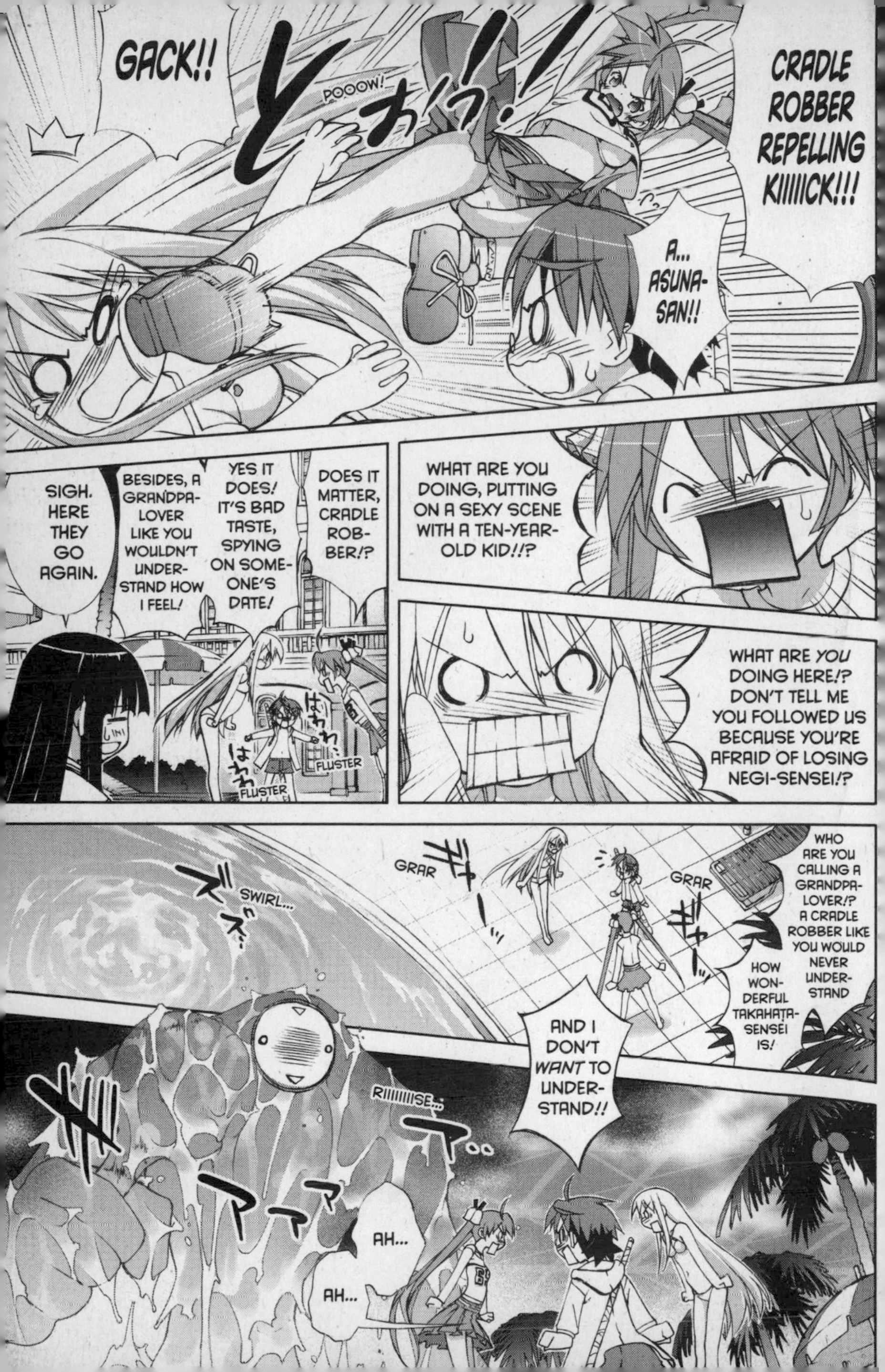
CRADLE ROBBER REPELLING KIIIIICK!!!
A... ASUNA-SAN!!
POOOW!
GACK!!
WHAT ARE YOU DOING, PUTTING ON A SEXY SCENE WITH A TEN-YEAR-OLD KID!!?
WHAT ARE *YOU* DOING HERE!? DON'T TELL ME YOU FOLLOWED US BECAUSE YOU'RE AFRAID OF LOSING NEGI-SENSEI!?
DOES IT MATTER, CRADLE ROBBER!?
YES IT DOES! IT'S BAD TASTE, SPYING ON SOMEONE'S DATE!
BESIDES, A GRANDPA-LOVER LIKE YOU WOULDN'T UNDERSTAND HOW I FEEL!
SIGH. HERE THEY GO AGAIN.
FLUSTER
FLUSTER
WHO ARE YOU CALLING A GRANDPA-LOVER!? A CRADLE ROBBER LIKE YOU WOULD NEVER UNDERSTAND
HOW WONDERFUL TAKAHATA-SENSEI IS!
GRAR
GRAR
AND I DON'T *WANT* TO UNDERSTAND!!
SWIRL...
RIIIIIIISE...
AH...
AH...

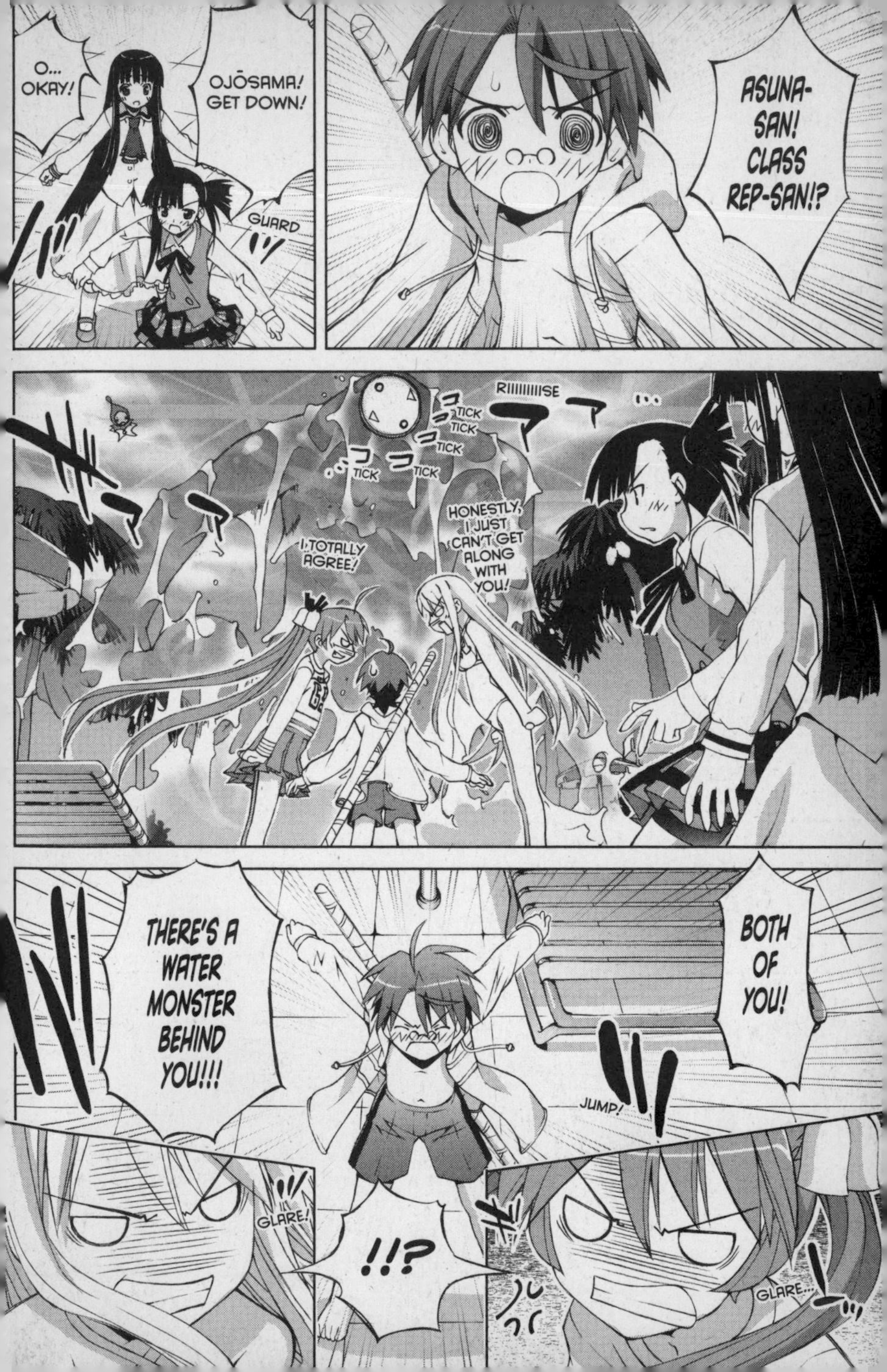
ASUNA-SAN! CLASS REP-SAN!?
OJŌSAMA! GET DOWN!
O... OKAY!
GUARD
RIIIIIIIISE
TICK
TICK
TICK
TICK
TICK
HONESTLY, I JUST CAN'T GET ALONG WITH YOU!
I TOTALLY AGREE!
BOTH OF YOU!
THERE'S A WATER MONSTER BEHIND YOU!!!
JUMP!
GLARE...
!!?
GLARE!

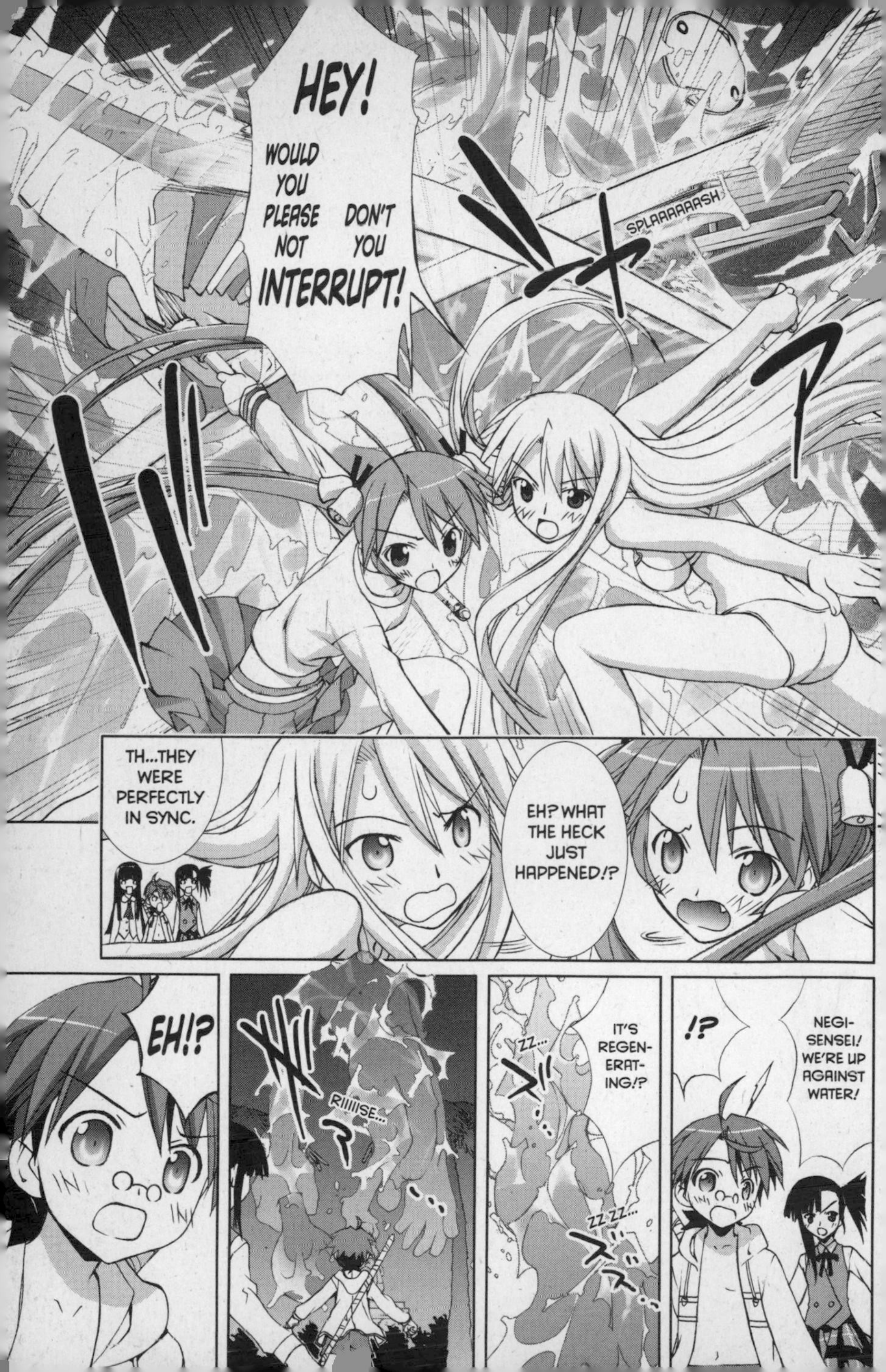
HEY!
WOULD YOU PLEASE NOT
DON'T YOU
INTERRUPT!
SPLAAAAAAASH
EH? WHAT THE HECK JUST HAPPENED!?
TH...THEY WERE PERFECTLY IN SYNC.
NEGI-SENSEI! WE'RE UP AGAINST WATER!
!?
IT'S REGEN-ERATING!?
ZZ...
ZZ ZZ...
RIIIIISE...
EH!?

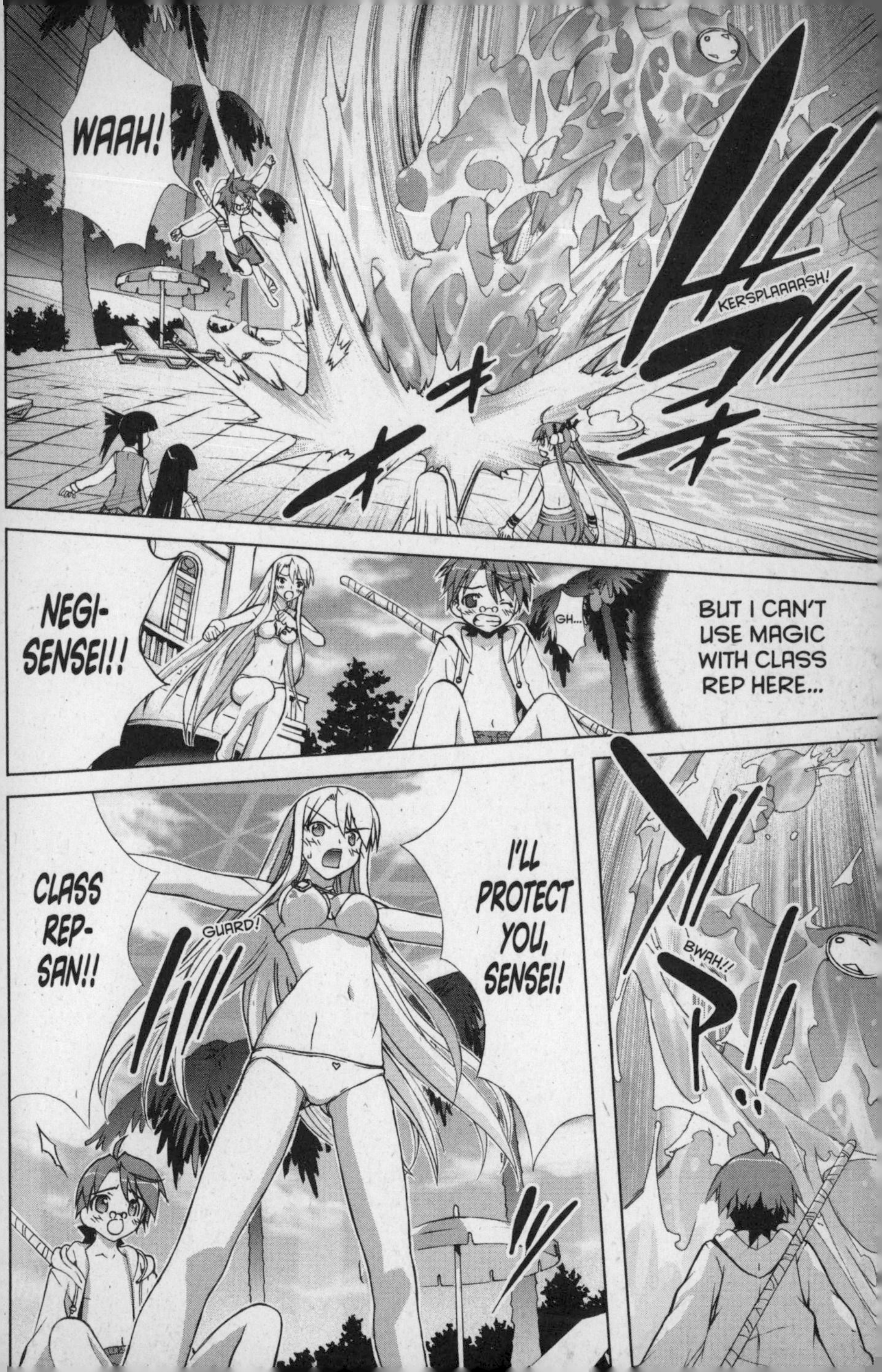
WAAH!
KERSPLAAAASH!
BUT I CAN'T USE MAGIC WITH CLASS REP HERE...
GH...
NEGI-SENSEI!!
BWAH!!
I'LL PROTECT YOU, SENSEI!
GUARD!
CLASS REP-SAN!!

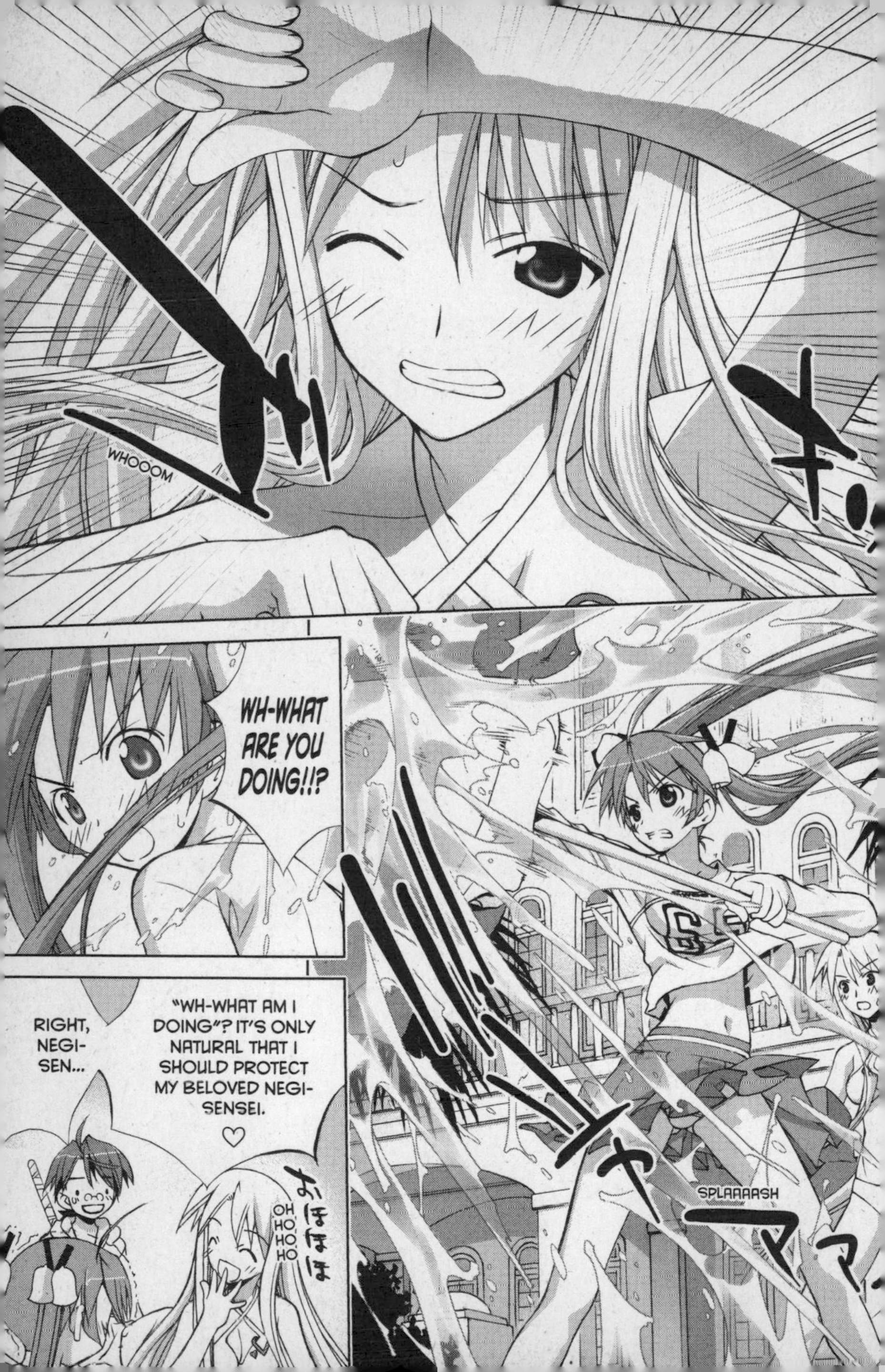
WHOOOM
SPLAAAASH
WH-WHAT ARE YOU DOING!!?
"WH-WHAT AM I DOING"? IT'S ONLY NATURAL THAT I SHOULD PROTECT MY BELOVED NEGI-SENSEI. ♡
RIGHT, NEGI-SEN...
OH HO HO HO

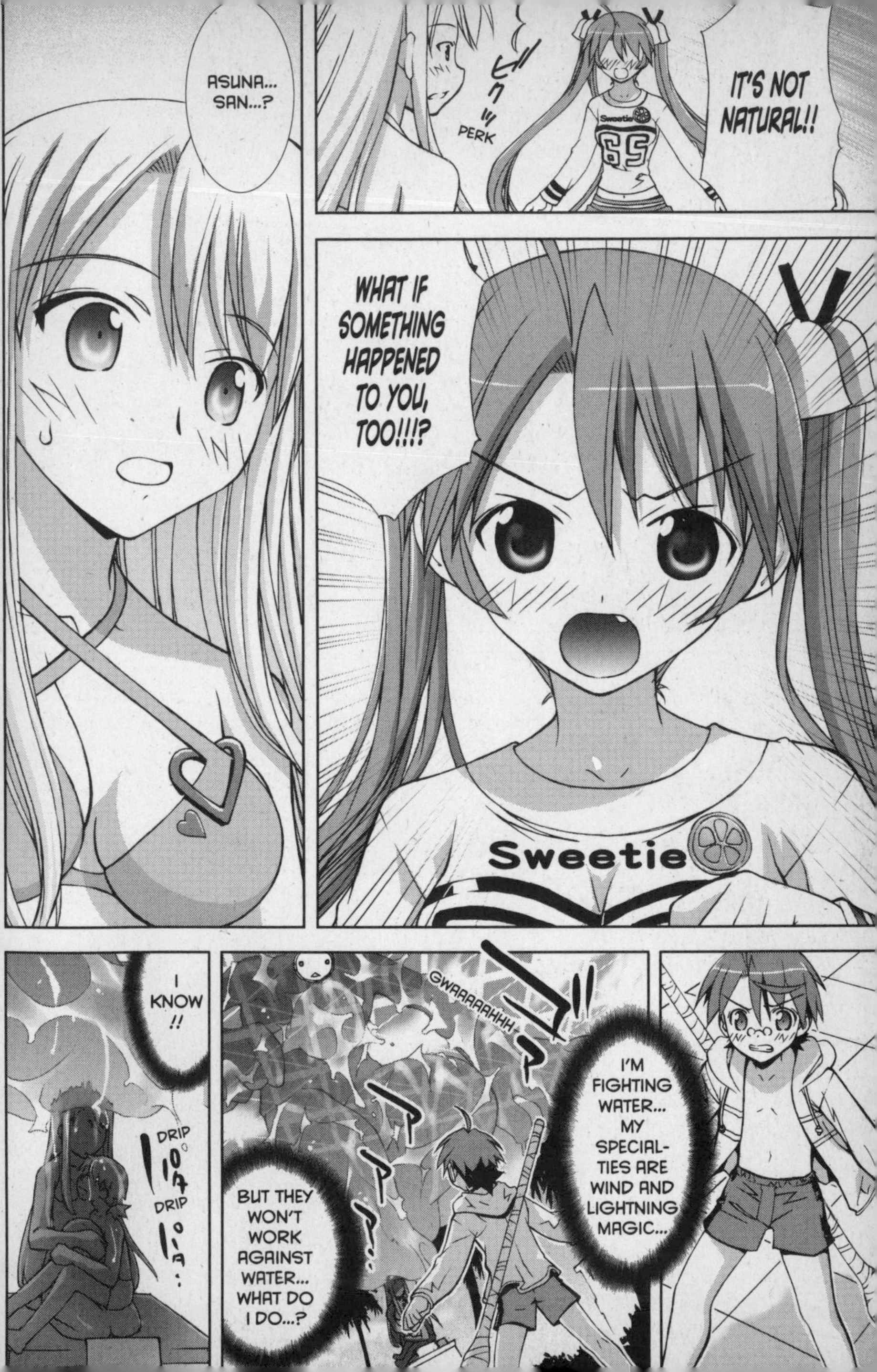
IT'S NOT NATURAL!!
PERK
WHAT IF SOMETHING HAPPENED TO YOU, TOO!!!?
ASUNA... SAN...?
I'M FIGHTING WATER... MY SPECIAL-TIES ARE WIND AND LIGHTNING MAGIC...
GWAAAAAHHH
BUT THEY WON'T WORK AGAINST WATER... WHAT DO I DO...?
I KNOW!!
DRIP
DRIP

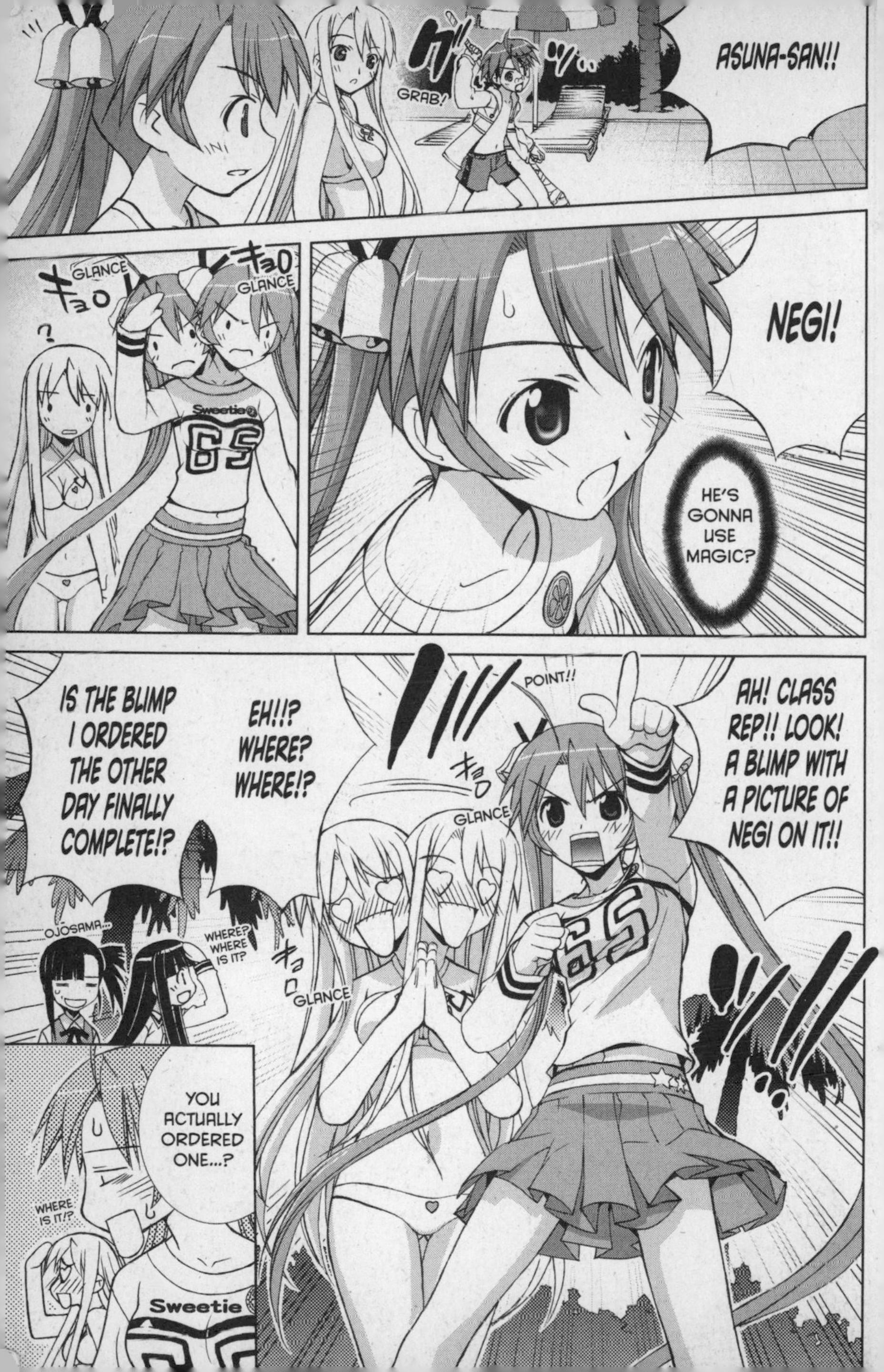
ASUNA-SAN!!
GRAB!
NEGI!
HE'S GONNA USE MAGIC?
GLANCE
GLANCE
AH! CLASS REP!! LOOK! A BLIMP WITH A PICTURE OF NEGI ON IT!!
POINT!!
GLANCE
EH!!? WHERE? WHERE!?
IS THE BLIMP I ORDERED THE OTHER DAY FINALLY COMPLETE!?
GLANCE
WHERE? WHERE IS IT?
OJOSAMA...
YOU ACTUALLY ORDERED ONE...?
WHERE IS IT!?

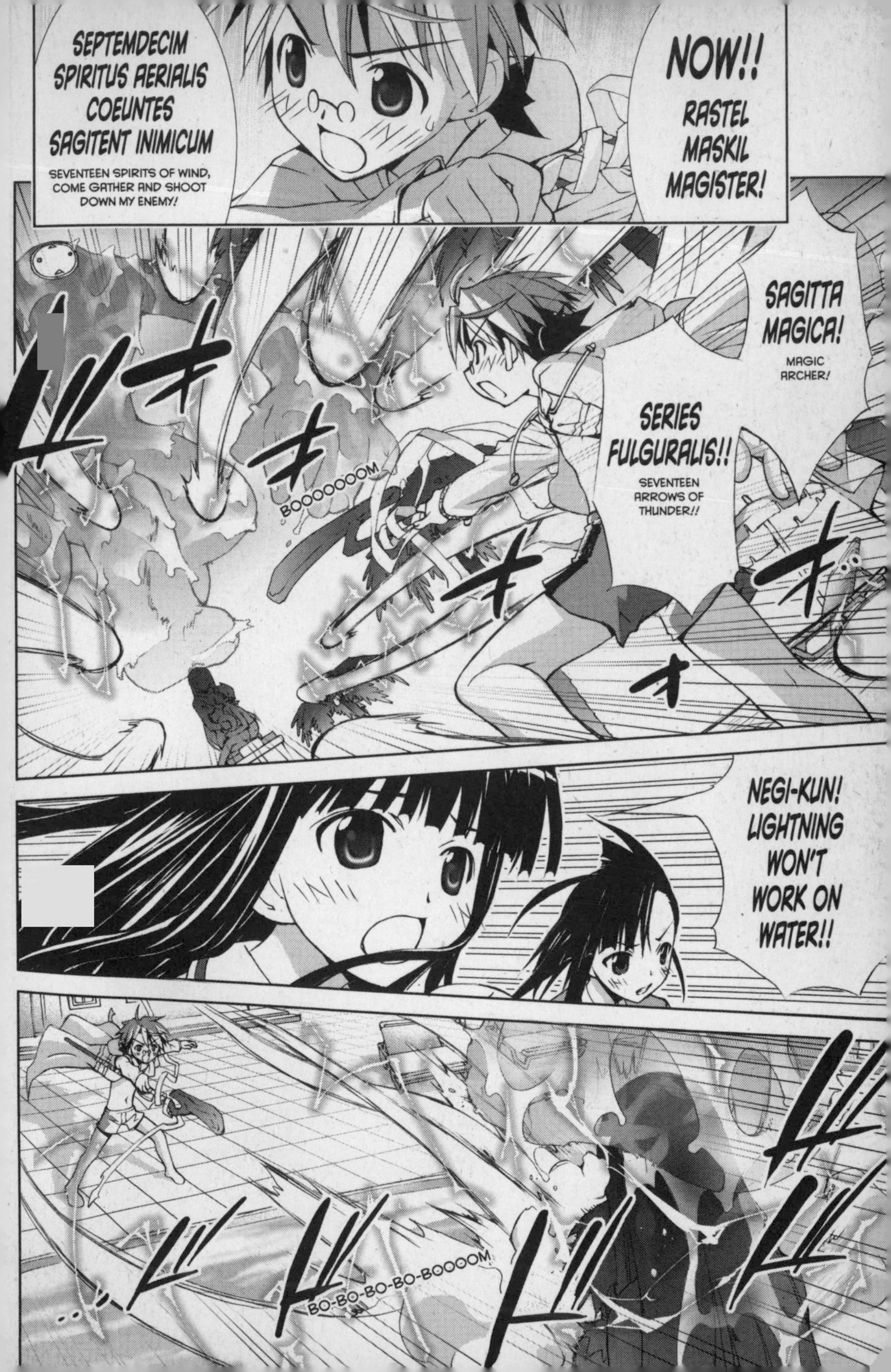
NOW!!
RASTEL MASKIL MAGISTER!
SEPTEMDECIM SPIRITUS AERIALIS COEUNTES SAGITENT INIMICUM
SEVENTEEN SPIRITS OF WIND, COME GATHER AND SHOOT DOWN MY ENEMY!
SAGITTA MAGICA!
MAGIC ARCHER!
SERIES FULGURALIS!!
SEVENTEEN ARROWS OF THUNDER!!
BOOOOOOOM
NEGI-KUN! LIGHTNING WON'T WORK ON WATER!!
BO-BO-BO-BO-BOOOOM

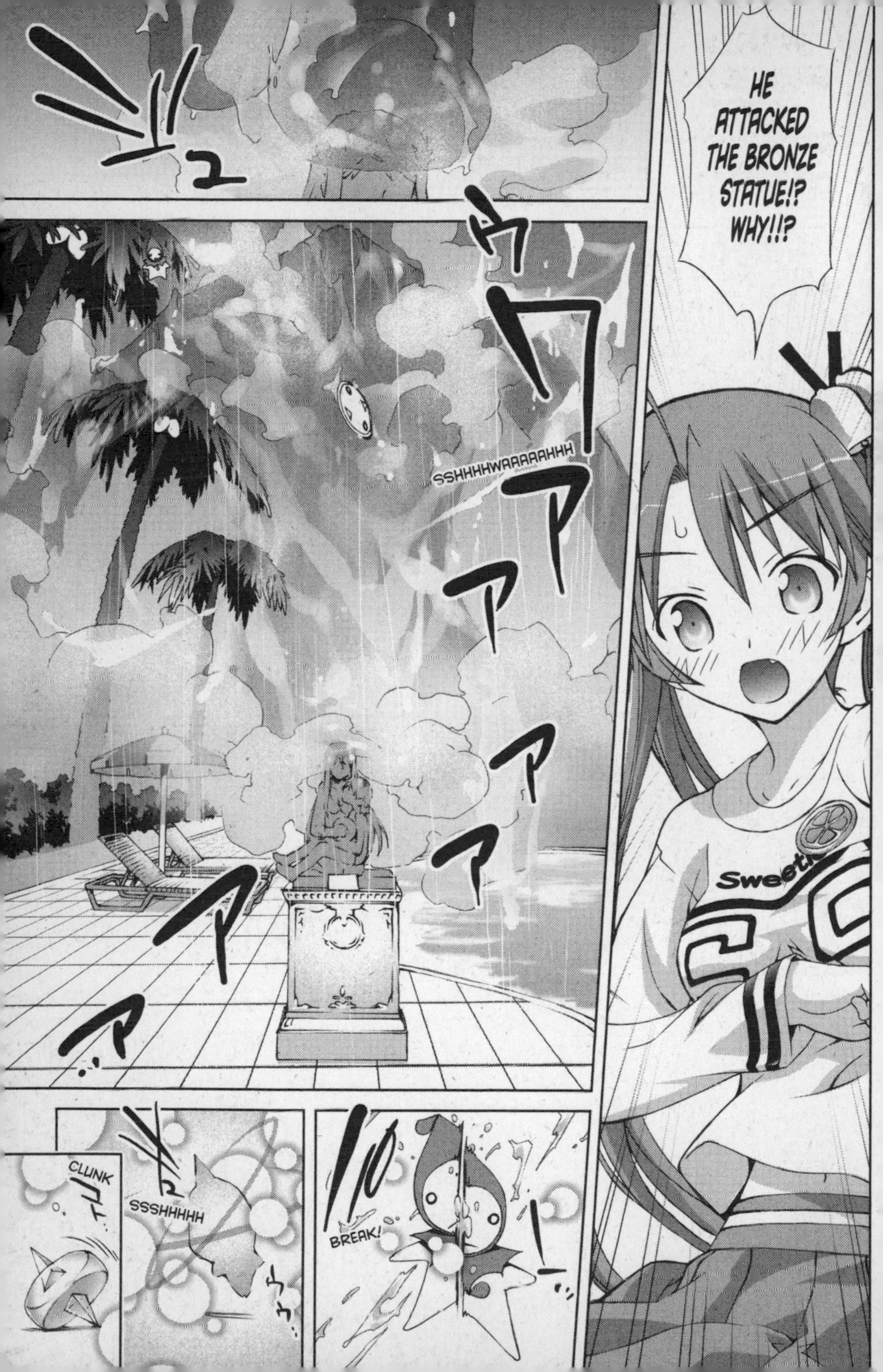
HE ATTACKED THE BRONZE STATUE!? WHY!!?
SSHHHHWAAAAAHHH
BREAK!
SSSHHHHH
CLUNK

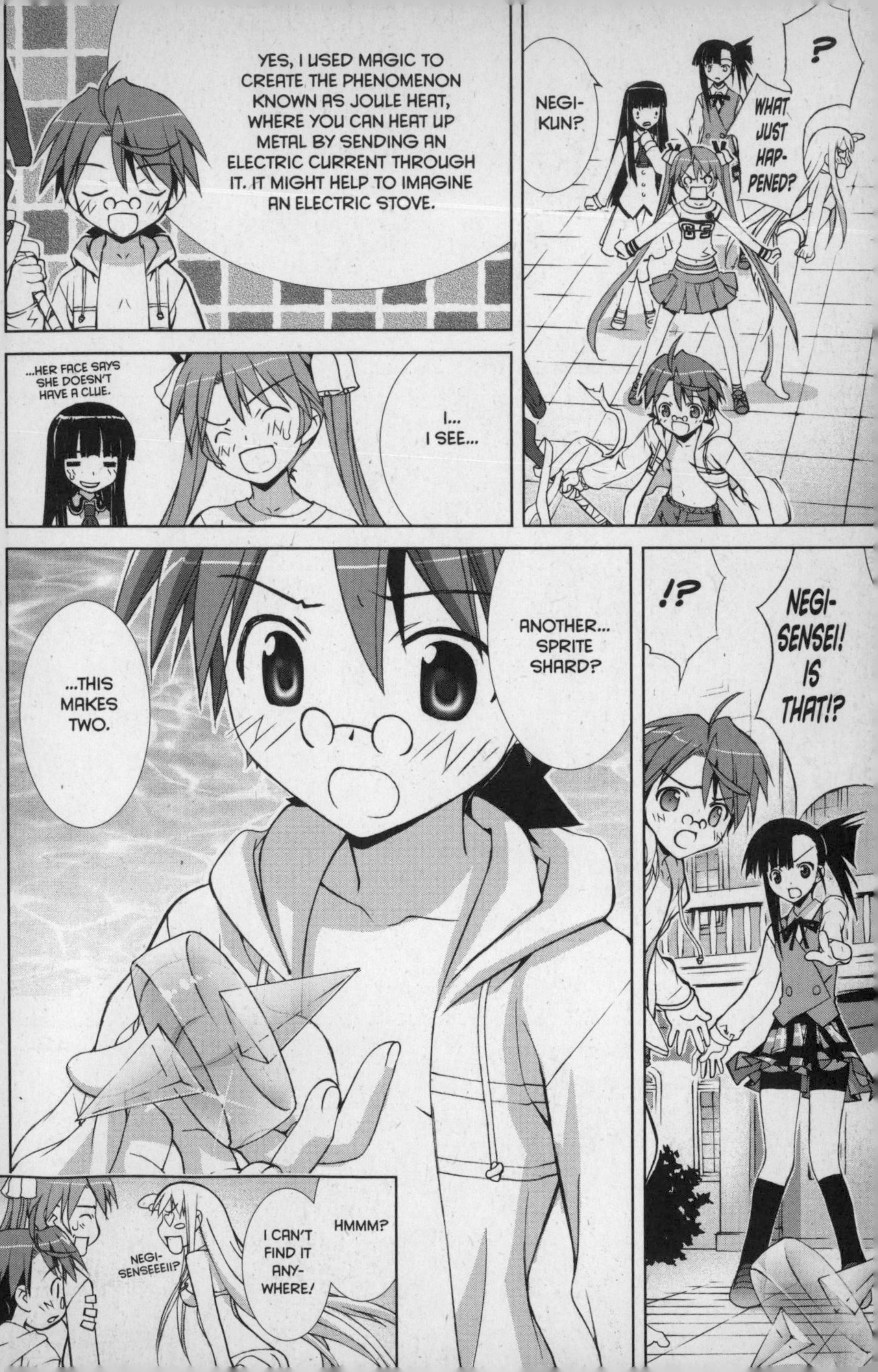
?
WHAT JUST HAP-PENED?
NEGI-KUN?
YES, I USED MAGIC TO CREATE THE PHENOMENON KNOWN AS JOULE HEAT, WHERE YOU CAN HEAT UP METAL BY SENDING AN ELECTRIC CURRENT THROUGH IT. IT MIGHT HELP TO IMAGINE AN ELECTRIC STOVE.
I... I SEE...
...HER FACE SAYS SHE DOESN'T HAVE A CLUE.
!?
NEGI-SENSEI! IS THAT!?
ANOTHER... SPRITE SHARD?
...THIS MAKES TWO.
HMMM?
I CAN'T FIND IT ANY-WHERE!
NEGI-SENSEEEI!?

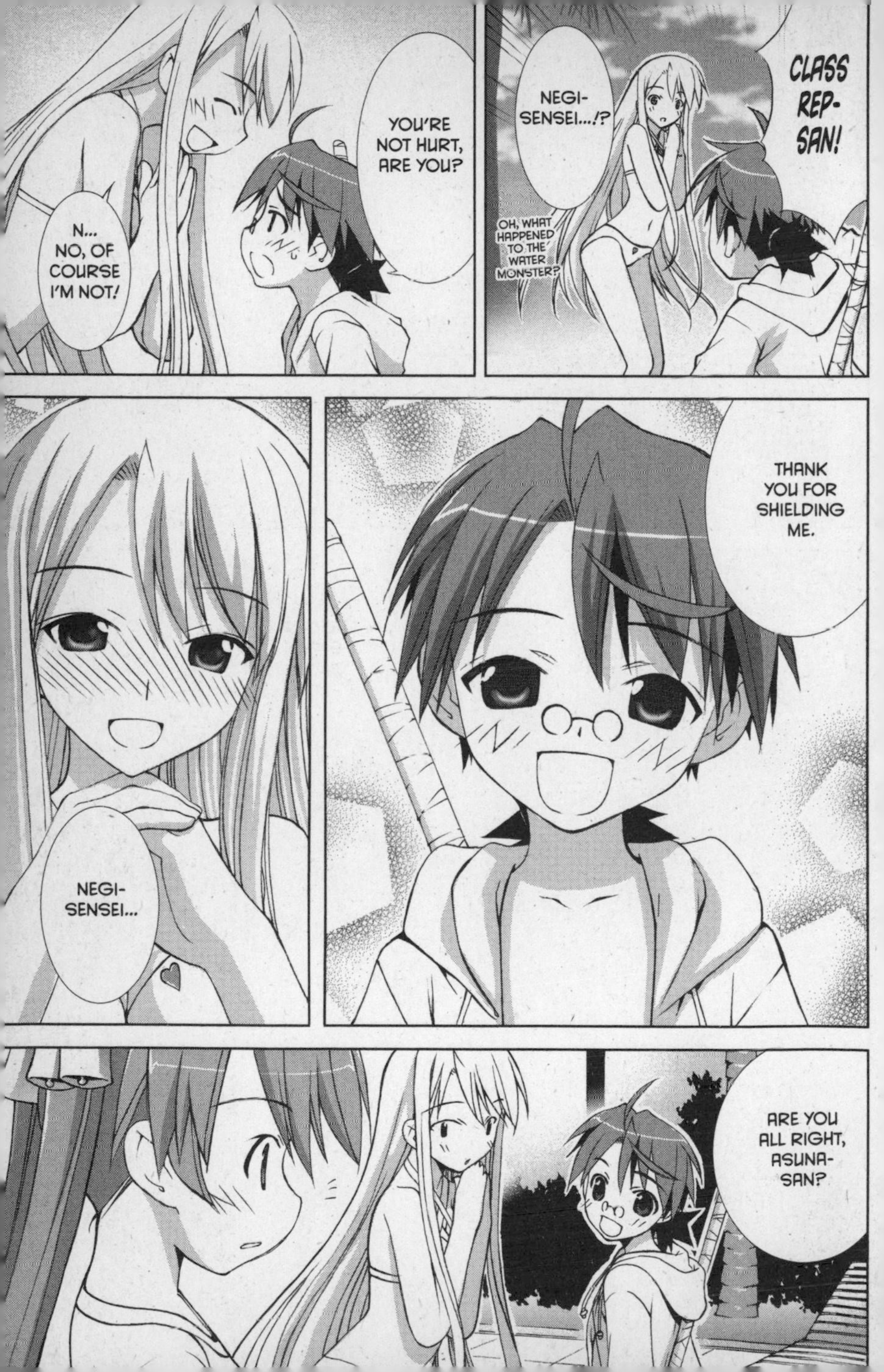
CLASS REP-SAN!
NEGI-SENSEI...!?
OH, WHAT HAPPENED TO THE WATER MONSTER?
YOU'RE NOT HURT, ARE YOU?
N... NO, OF COURSE I'M NOT!
THANK YOU FOR SHIELDING ME.
NEGI-SENSEI...
ARE YOU ALL RIGHT, ASUNA-SAN?

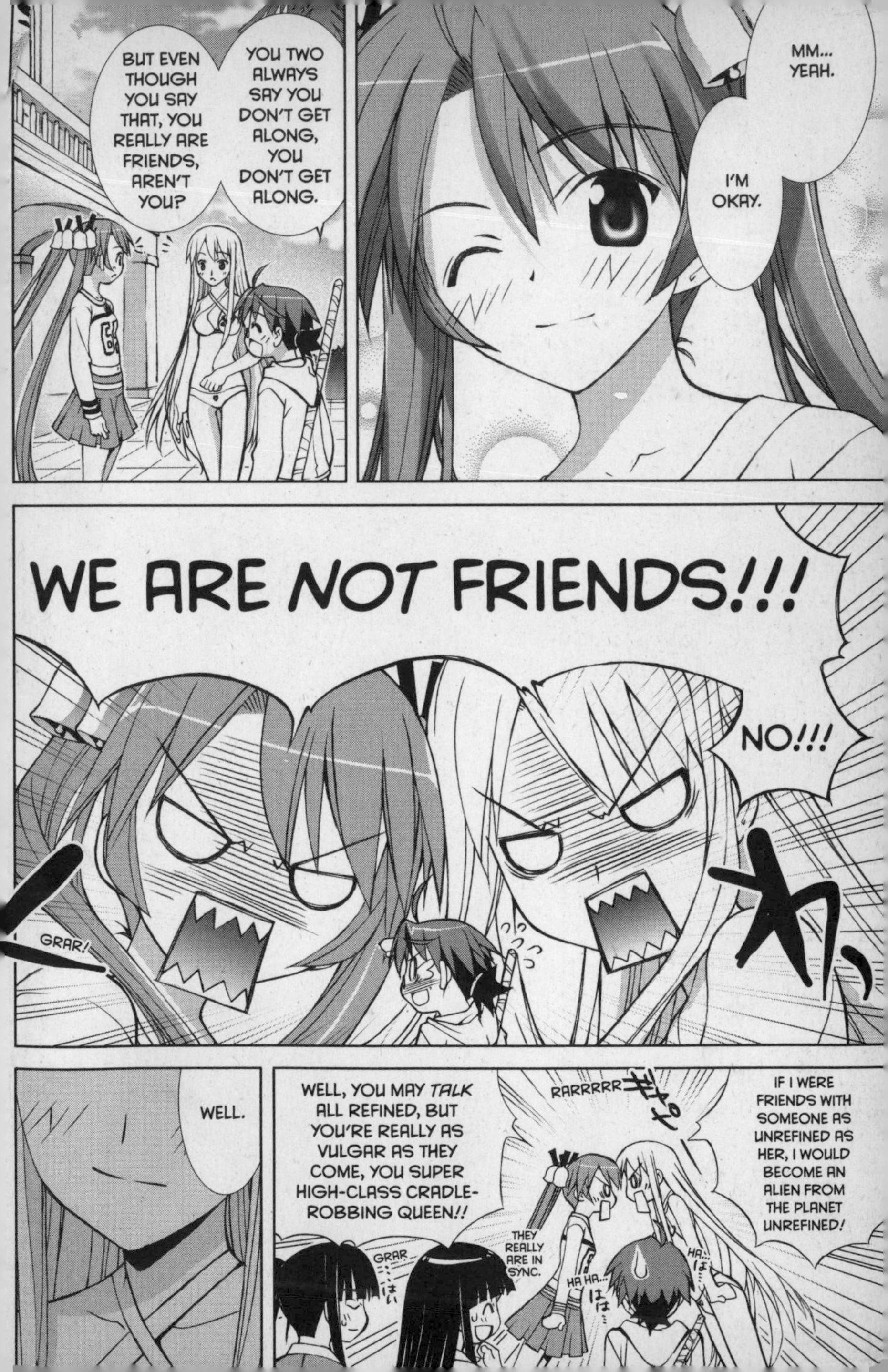
MM... YEAH.
I'M OKAY.
YOU TWO ALWAYS SAY YOU DON'T GET ALONG, YOU DON'T GET ALONG.
BUT EVEN THOUGH YOU SAY THAT, YOU REALLY ARE FRIENDS, AREN'T YOU?
WE ARE NOT FRIENDS!!!
NO!!!
GRAR!
IF I WERE FRIENDS WITH SOMEONE AS UNREFINED AS HER, I WOULD BECOME AN ALIEN FROM THE PLANET UNREFINED!
RARRRRR
HA...
HA HA...
THEY REALLY ARE IN SYNC.
WELL, YOU MAY TALK ALL REFINED, BUT YOU'RE REALLY AS VULGAR AS THEY COME, YOU SUPER HIGH-CLASS CRADLE-ROBBING QUEEN!!
GRAR
WELL.

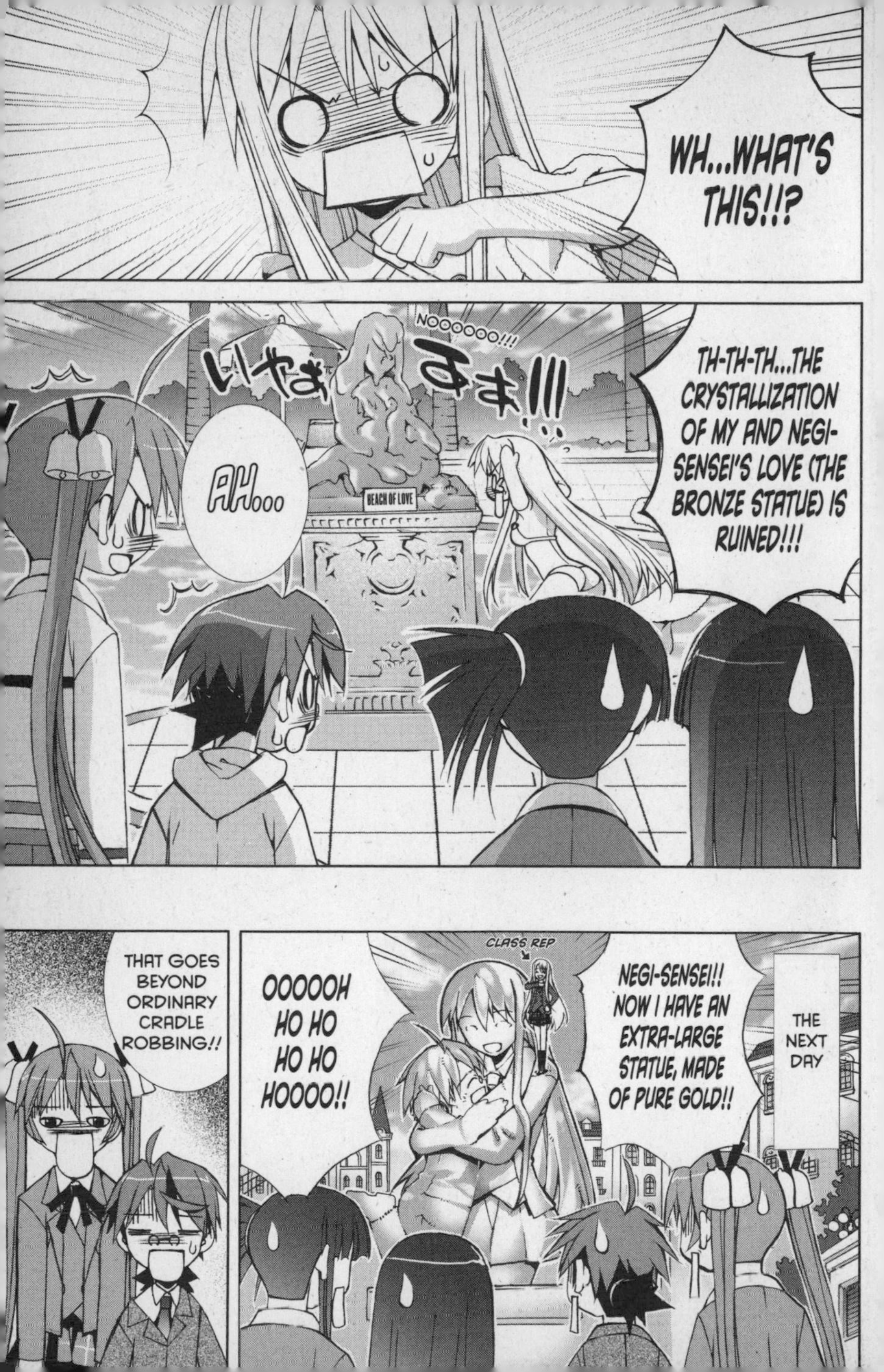
WH...WHAT'S THIS!!?
TH-TH-TH...THE CRYSTALLIZATION OF MY AND NEGI-SENSEI'S LOVE (THE BRONZE STATUE) IS RUINED!!!
NOOOOOOO!!!
BEACH OF LOVE
AH...
THE NEXT DAY
NEGI-SENSEI!! NOW I HAVE AN EXTRA-LARGE STATUE, MADE OF PURE GOLD!!
CLASS REP
OOOOOH HO HO HO HO HOOOO!!
THAT GOES BEYOND ORDINARY CRADLE ROBBING!!

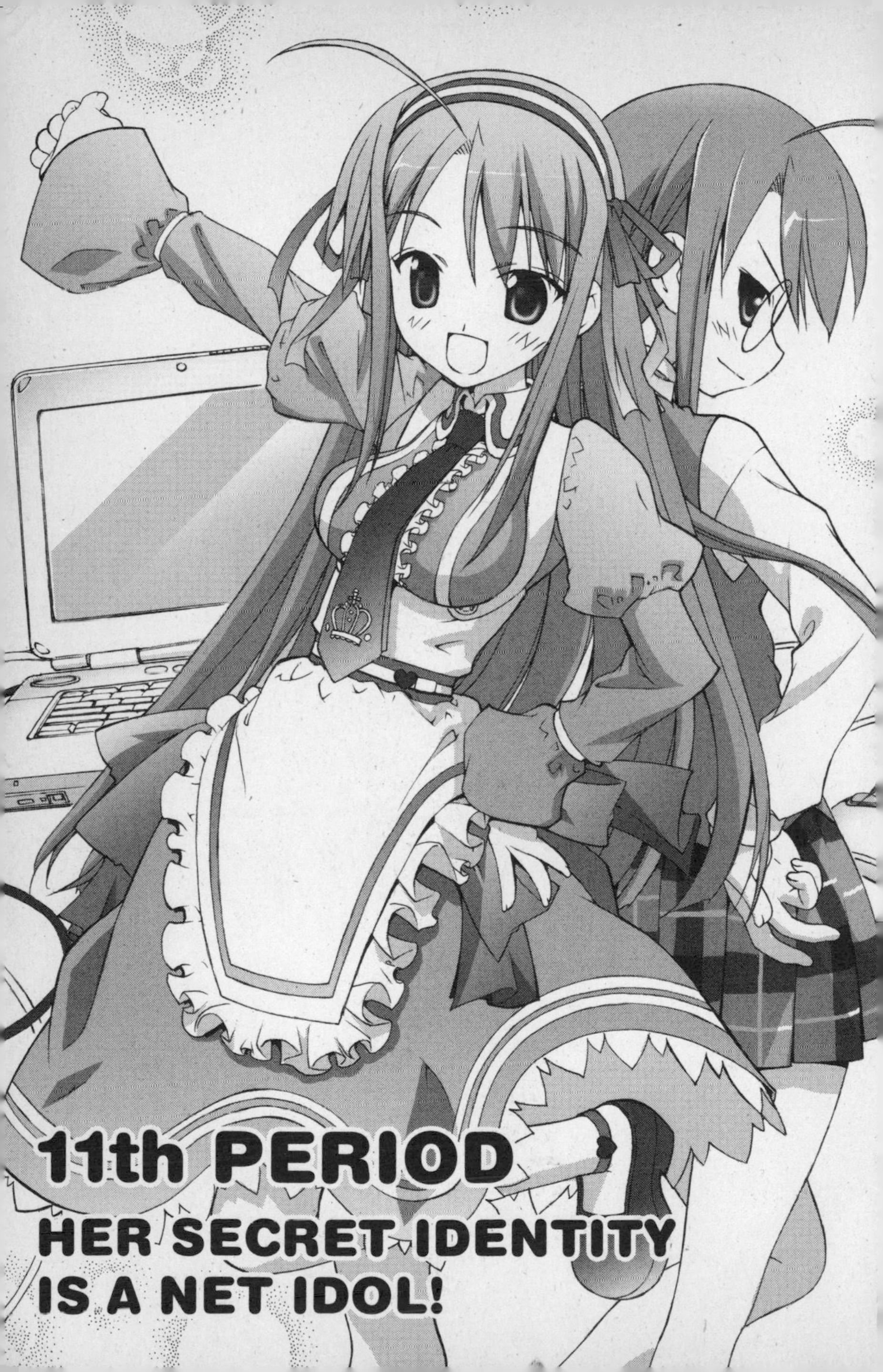

11th PERIOD
HER SECRET IDENTITY IS A NET IDOL!

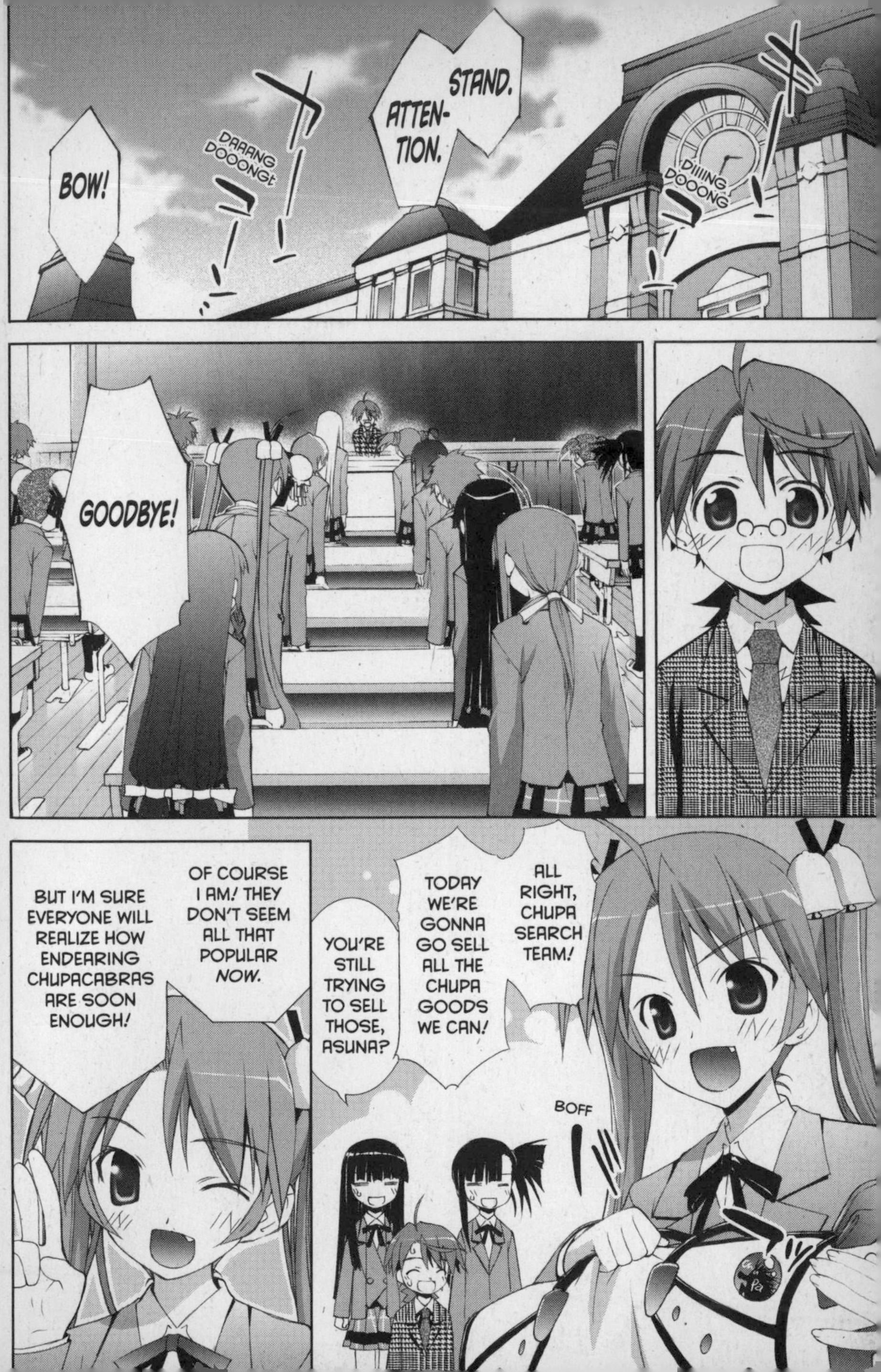
DIIING DOOONG
STAND. ATTEN-TION.
DAAANG DOOONG
BOW!
GOODBYE!
ALL RIGHT, CHUPA SEARCH TEAM!
TODAY WE'RE GONNA GO SELL ALL THE CHUPA GOODS WE CAN!
BOFF
YOU'RE STILL TRYING TO SELL THOSE, ASUNA?
OF COURSE I AM! THEY DON'T SEEM ALL THAT POPULAR *NOW*.
BUT I'M SURE EVERYONE WILL REALIZE HOW ENDEARING CHUPACABRAS ARE SOON ENOUGH!

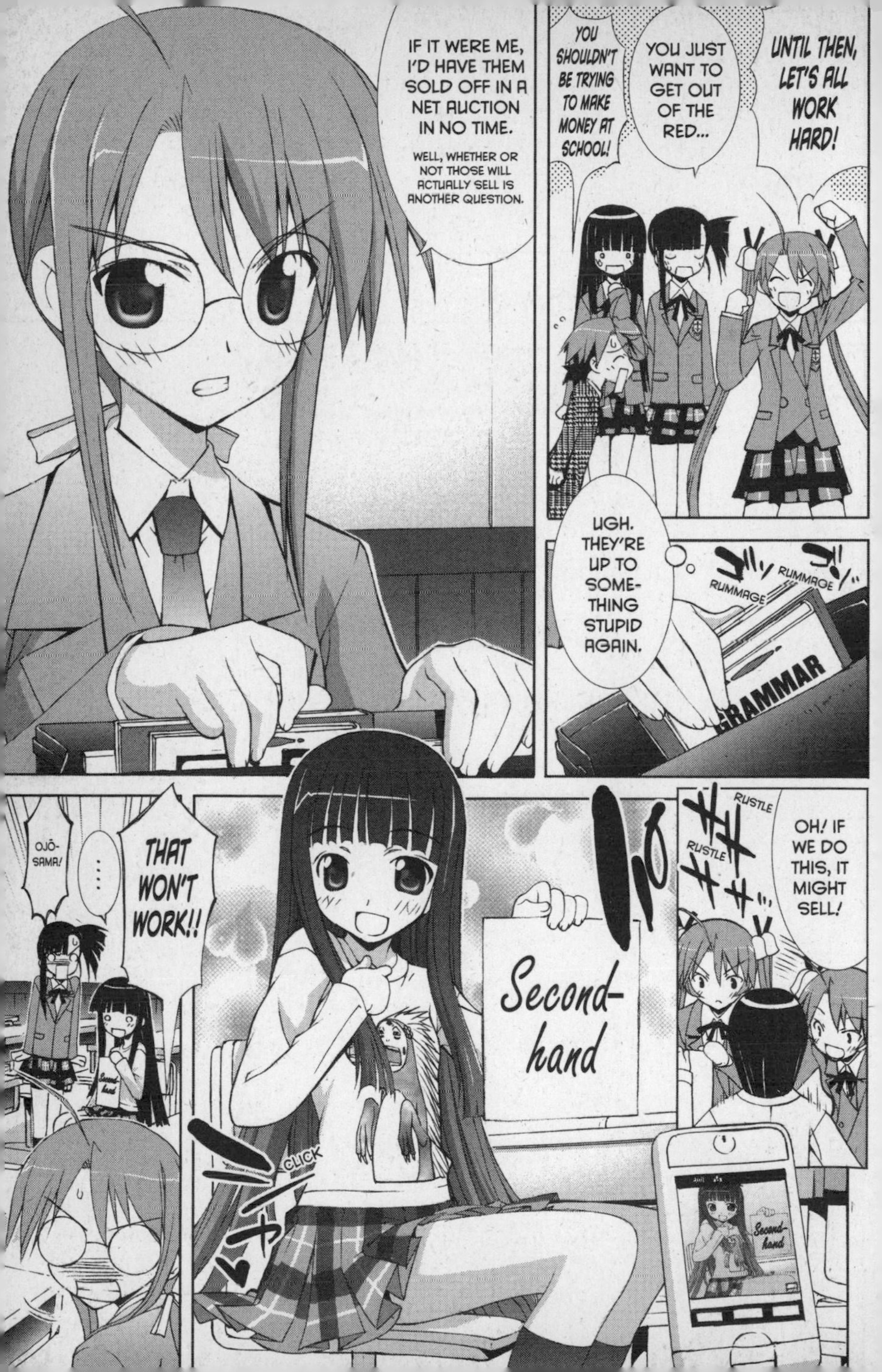
UNTIL THEN, LET'S ALL WORK HARD!
YOU JUST WANT TO GET OUT OF THE RED...
YOU SHOULDN'T BE TRYING TO MAKE MONEY AT SCHOOL!
RUMMAGE
RUMMAGE
UGH. THEY'RE UP TO SOMETHING STUPID AGAIN.
GRAMMAR
IF IT WERE ME, I'D HAVE THEM SOLD OFF IN A NET AUCTION IN NO TIME.
WELL, WHETHER OR NOT THOSE WILL ACTUALLY SELL IS ANOTHER QUESTION.
RUSTLE
RUSTLE
OH! IF WE DO THIS, IT MIGHT SELL!
Second-hand
CLICK
Second-hand
THAT WON'T WORK!!
....
OJŌ-SAMA!

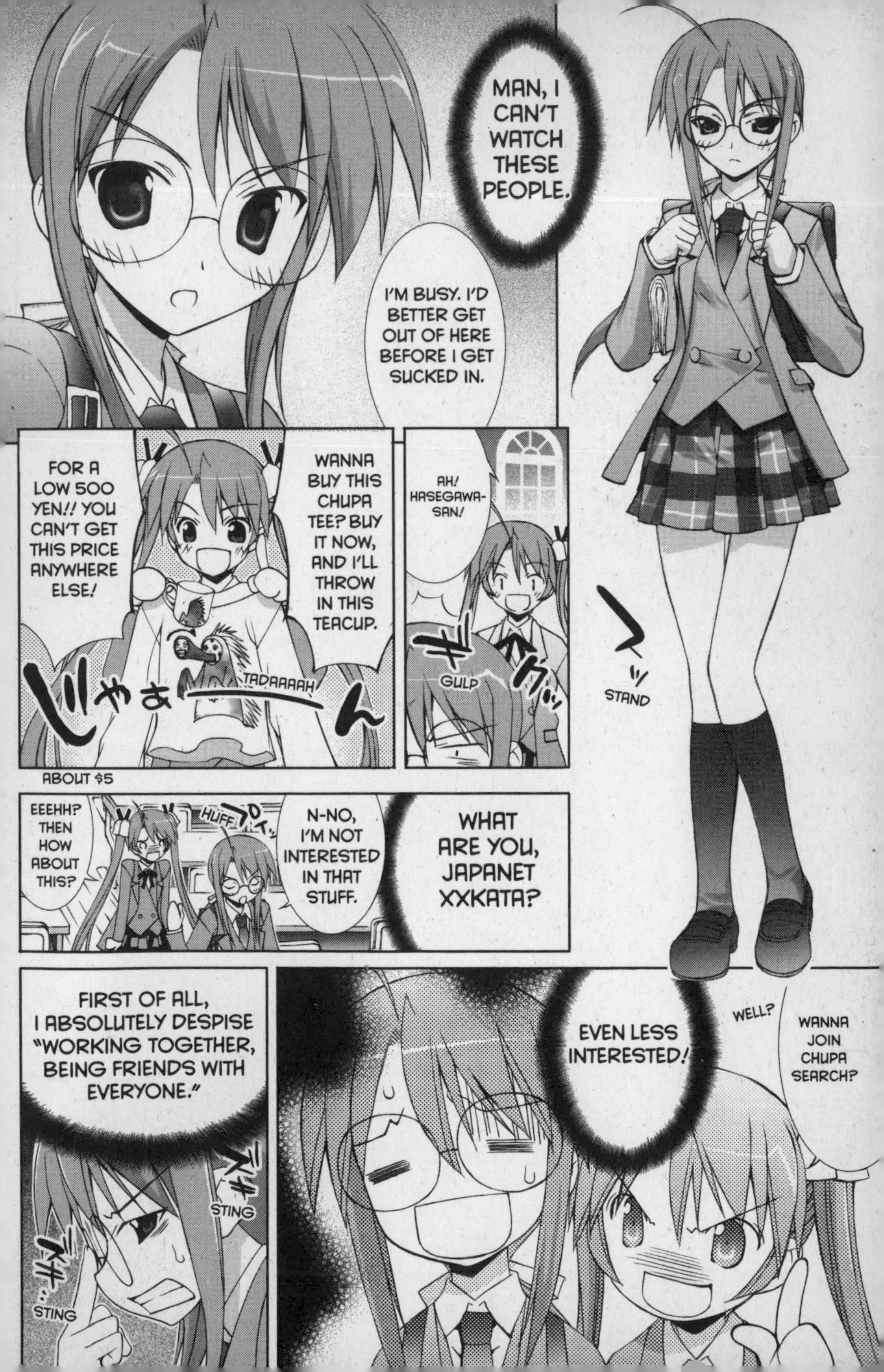
STAND
MAN, I CAN'T WATCH THESE PEOPLE.
I'M BUSY. I'D BETTER GET OUT OF HERE BEFORE I GET SUCKED IN.
AH! HASEGAWA-SAN!
GULP
WANNA BUY THIS CHUPA TEE? BUY IT NOW, AND I'LL THROW IN THIS TEACUP.
FOR A LOW 500 YEN!! YOU CAN'T GET THIS PRICE ANYWHERE ELSE!
TADAAAAH
ABOUT $5
WHAT ARE YOU, JAPANET XXKATA?
N-NO, I'M NOT INTERESTED IN THAT STUFF.
HUFF
EEEHH? THEN HOW ABOUT THIS?
WANNA JOIN CHUPA SEARCH?
WELL?
EVEN LESS INTERESTED!
FIRST OF ALL, I ABSOLUTELY DESPISE "WORKING TOGETHER, BEING FRIENDS WITH EVERYONE."
STING
STING

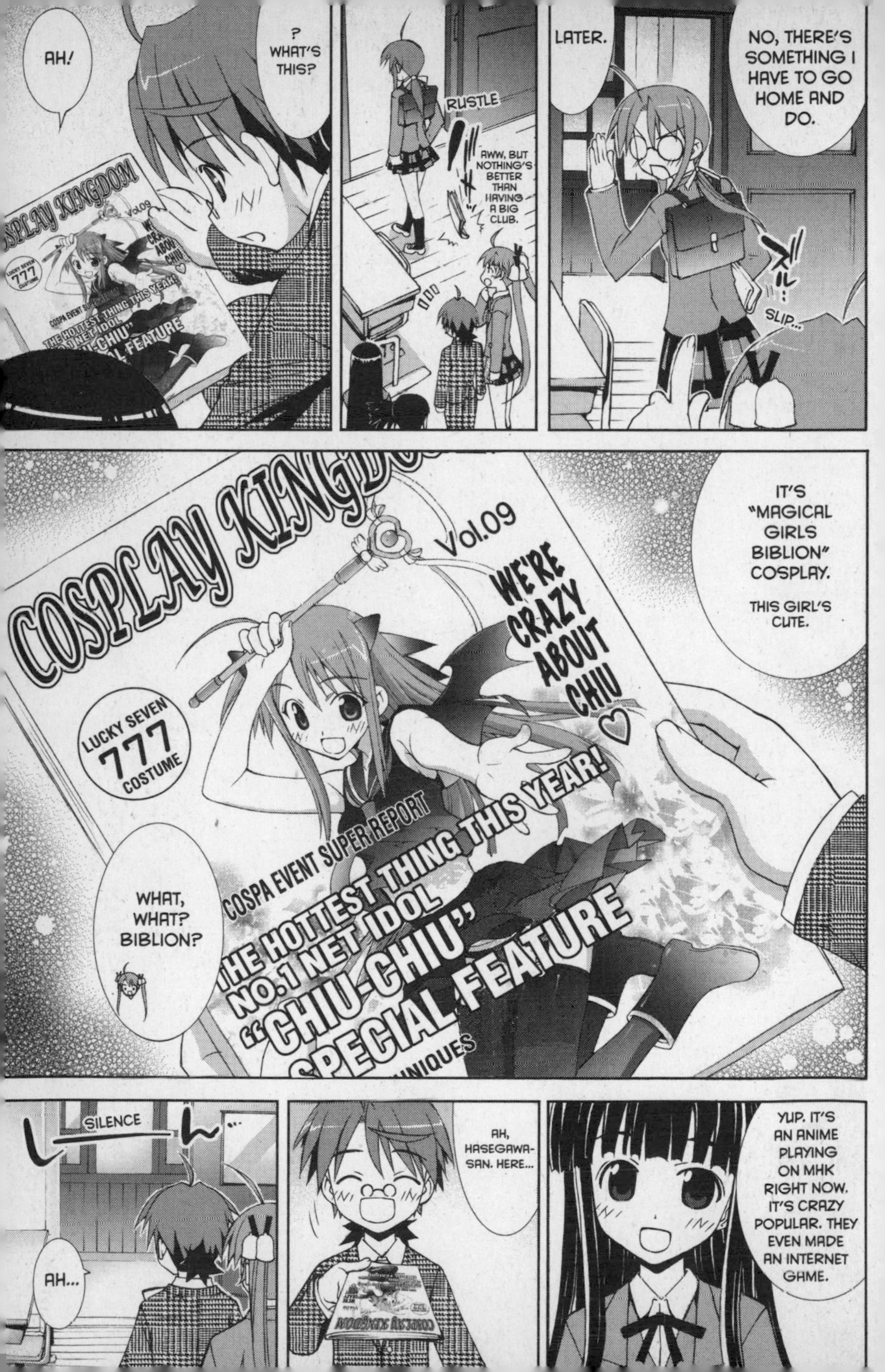
NO, THERE'S SOMETHING I HAVE TO GO HOME AND DO.
SLIP...
LATER.
RUSTLE
AWW, BUT NOTHING'S BETTER THAN HAVING A BIG CLUB.
? WHAT'S THIS?
AH!
IT'S "MAGICAL GIRLS BIBLION" COSPLAY.
THIS GIRL'S CUTE.
COSPLAY KINGDOM
Vol.09
WE'RE CRAZY ABOUT CHIU ♥
LUCKY SEVEN 777 COSTUME
COSPA EVENT SUPER REPORT
THE HOTTEST THING THIS YEAR!
NO.1 NET IDOL
"CHIU-CHIU" SPECIAL FEATURE
WHAT, WHAT? BIBLION?
YUP. IT'S AN ANIME PLAYING ON MHK RIGHT NOW. IT'S CRAZY POPULAR. THEY EVEN MADE AN INTERNET GAME.
AH, HASEGAWA-SAN. HERE...
SILENCE
AH...

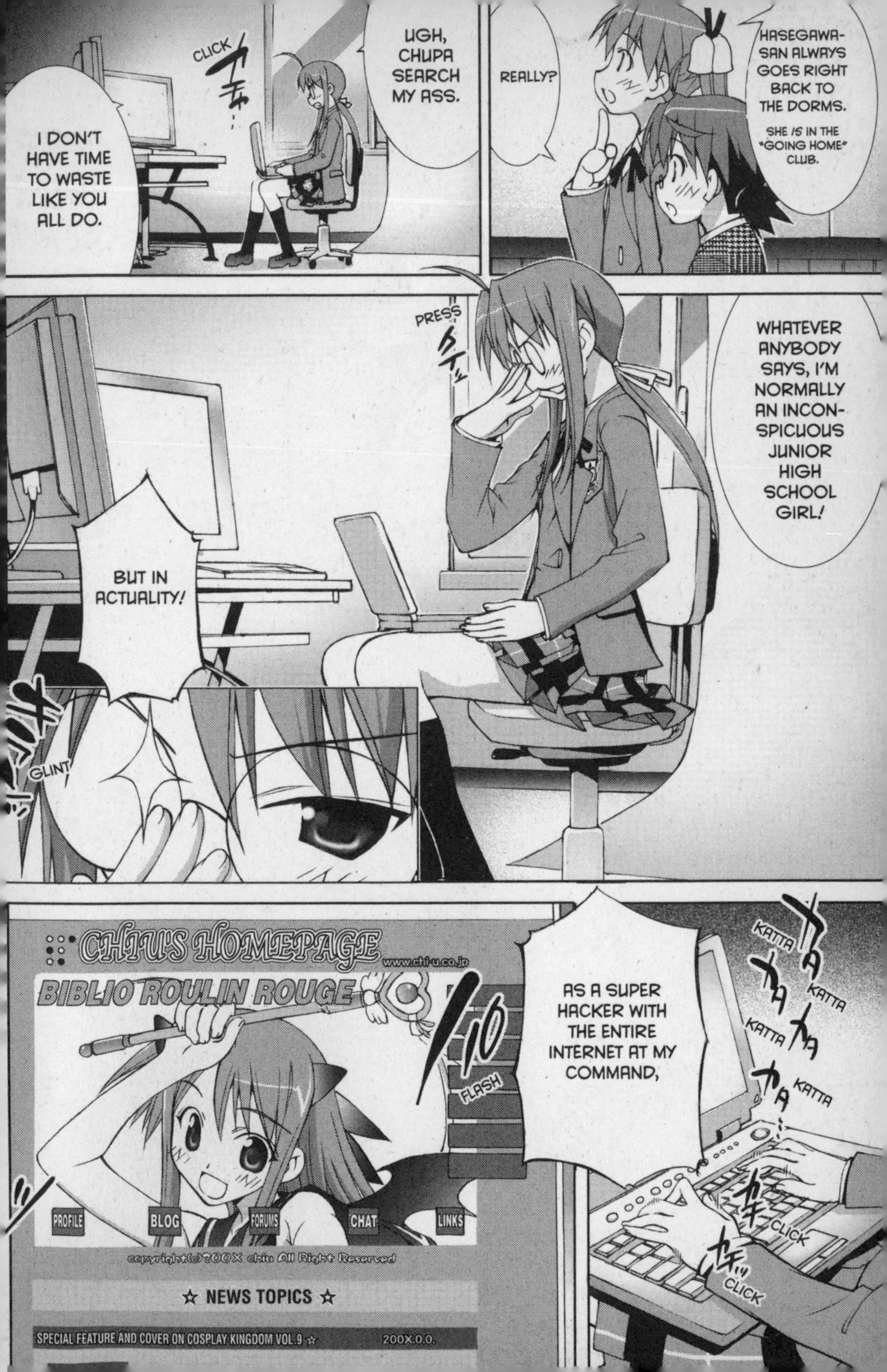
HASEGAWA-SAN ALWAYS GOES RIGHT BACK TO THE DORMS.
SHE IS IN THE "GOING HOME" CLUB.
REALLY?
UGH, CHUPA SEARCH MY ASS.
CLICK
I DON'T HAVE TIME TO WASTE LIKE YOU ALL DO.
WHATEVER ANYBODY SAYS, I'M NORMALLY AN INCON-SPICUOUS JUNIOR HIGH SCHOOL GIRL!
PRESS
BUT IN ACTUALITY!
GLINT
KATTA
KATTA
KATTA
KATTA
AS A SUPER HACKER WITH THE ENTIRE INTERNET AT MY COMMAND,
CLICK
CLICK
FLASH
CHIU'S HOMEPAGE
www.chi-u.co.jp
BIBLIO ROULIN ROUGE
PROFILE
BLOG
FORUMS
CHAT
LINKS
copyright(c)200X chiu All Right Reserved
☆ NEWS TOPICS ☆
SPECIAL FEATURE AND COVER ON COSPLAY KINGDOM VOL.9 ☆
200X.0.0.

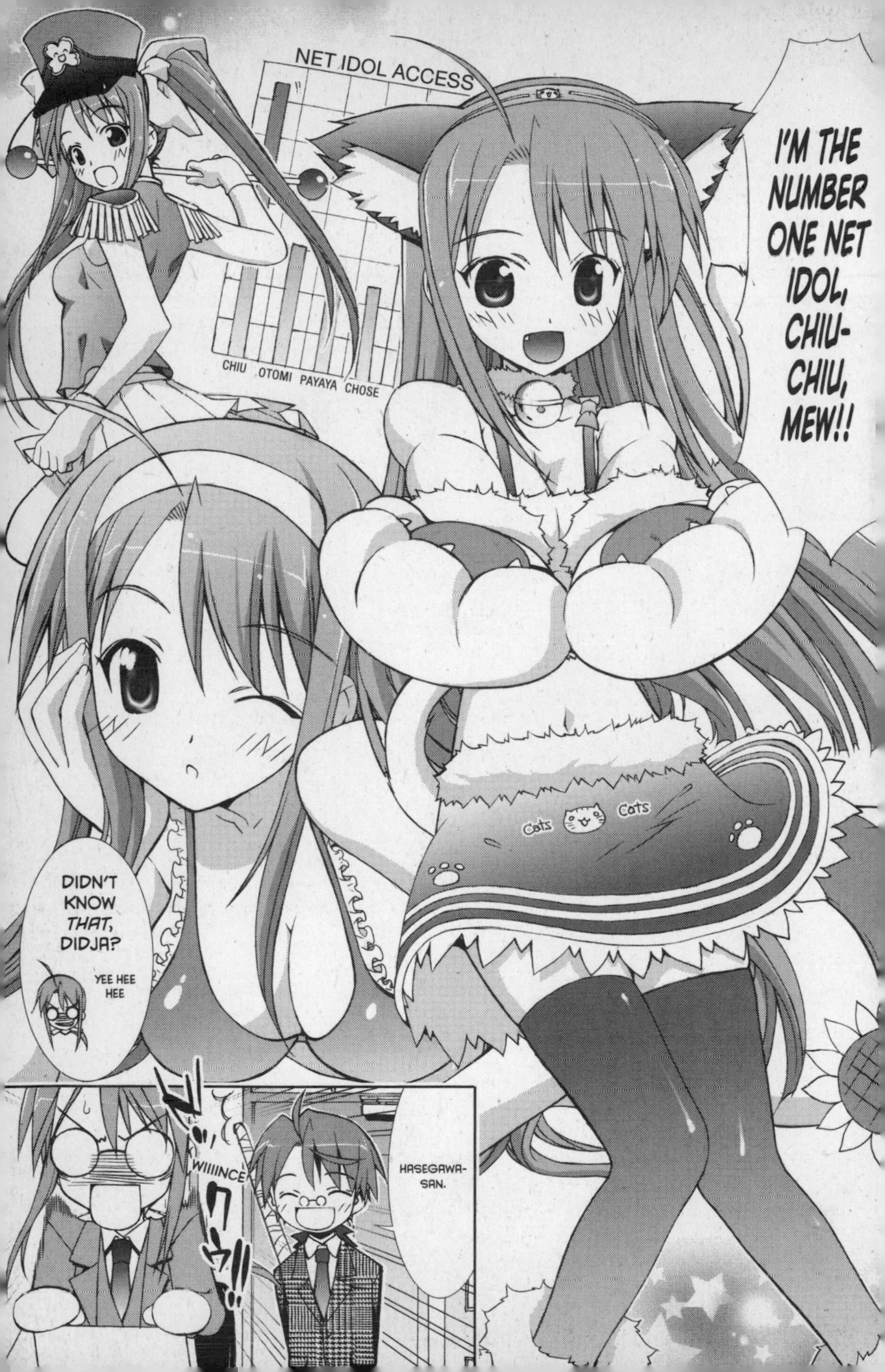
I'M THE NUMBER ONE NET IDOL, CHIU-CHIU, MEW!!
NET IDOL ACCESS
CHIU
OTOMI
PAYAYA
CHOSE
Cats
Cats
DIDN'T KNOW *THAT,* DIDJA?
YEE HEE HEE
HASEGAWA-SAN.
WIIIINCE

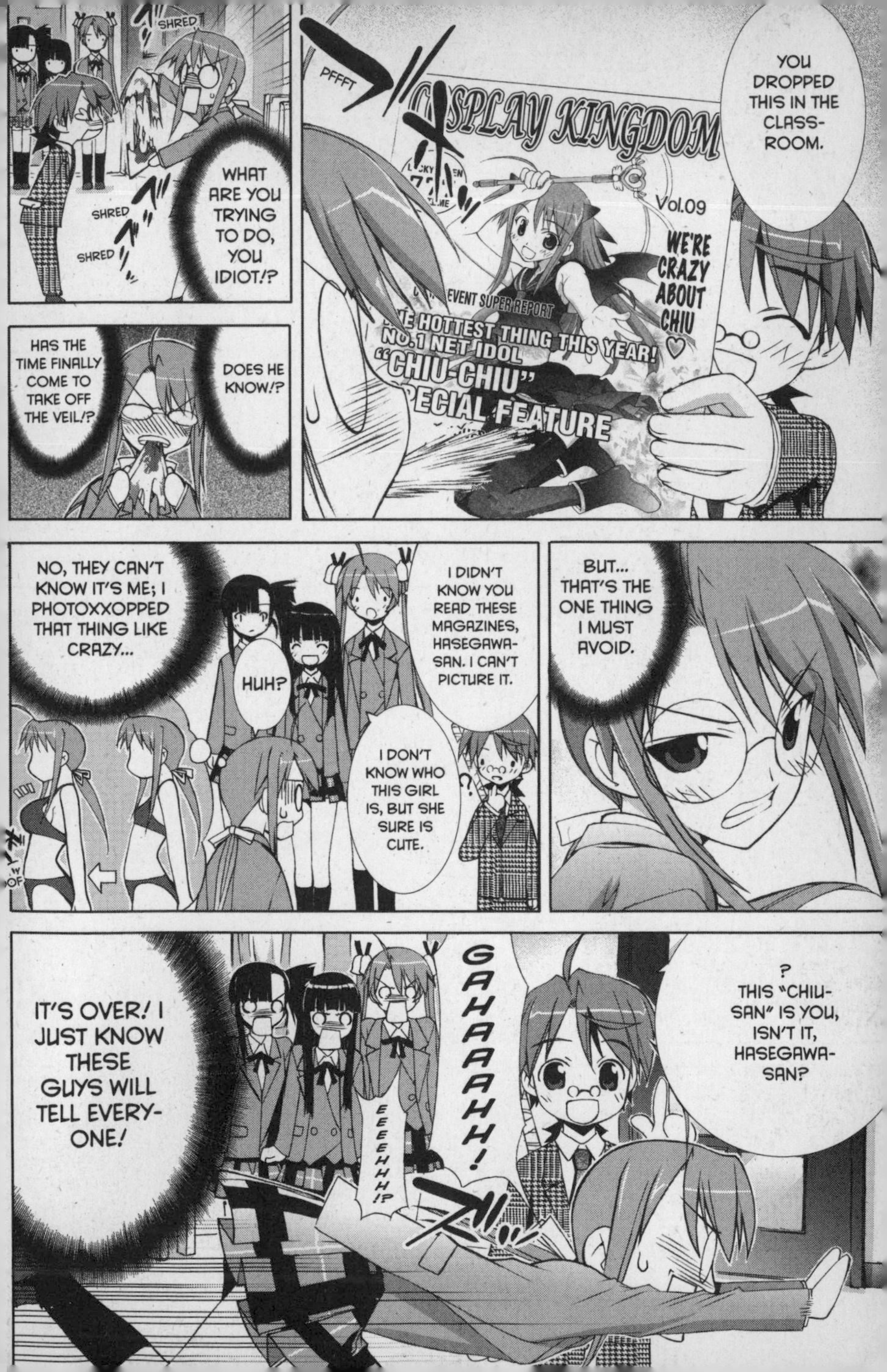
YOU DROPPED THIS IN THE CLASS-ROOM.
PFFFT
SPLAY KINGDOM
Vol.09
WE'RE CRAZY ABOUT CHIU ♥
EVENT SUPER REPORT
E HOTTEST THING THIS YEAR! NO.1 NET IDOL
“CHIU-CHIU”
PECIAL FEATURE
SHRED
WHAT ARE YOU TRYING TO DO, YOU IDIOT!?
SHRED
SHRED
DOES HE KNOW!?
HAS THE TIME FINALLY COME TO TAKE OFF THE VEIL!?
BUT... THAT'S THE ONE THING I MUST AVOID.
I DIDN'T KNOW YOU READ THESE MAGAZINES, HASEGAWA-SAN. I CAN'T PICTURE IT.
I DON'T KNOW WHO THIS GIRL IS, BUT SHE SURE IS CUTE.
HUH?
NO, THEY CAN'T KNOW IT'S ME; I PHOTOXXOPPED THAT THING LIKE CRAZY...
? THIS "CHIU-SAN" IS YOU, ISN'T IT, HASEGAWA-SAN?
GAHAAAAHH!
EEEEHHH!?
IT'S OVER! I JUST KNOW THESE GUYS WILL TELL EVERY-ONE!

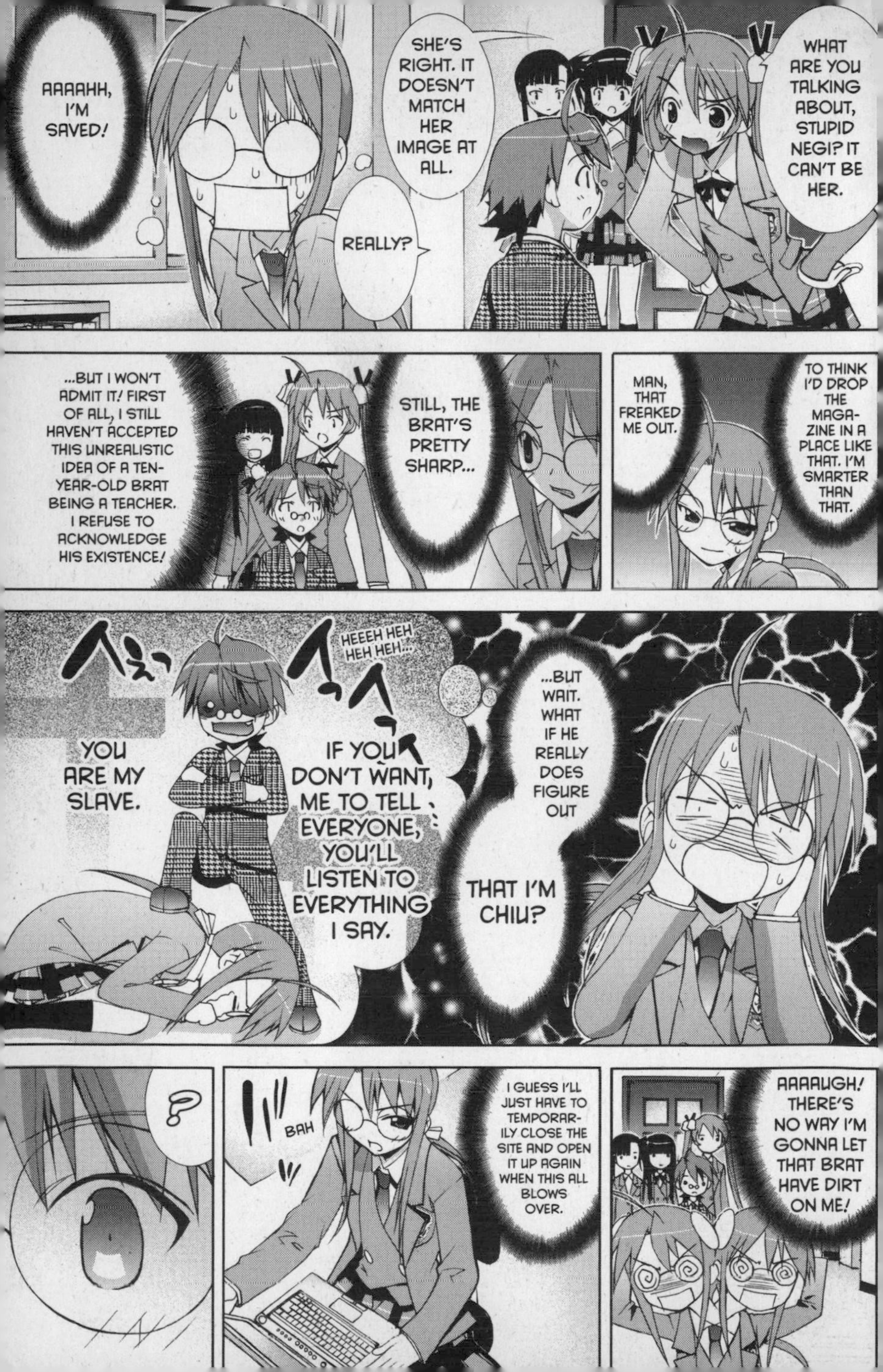
WHAT ARE YOU TALKING ABOUT, STUPID NEGI? IT CAN'T BE HER.
SHE'S RIGHT. IT DOESN'T MATCH HER IMAGE AT ALL.
REALLY?
AAAAHH, I'M SAVED!
TO THINK I'D DROP THE MAGA-ZINE IN A PLACE LIKE THAT. I'M SMARTER THAN THAT.
MAN, THAT FREAKED ME OUT.
STILL, THE BRAT'S PRETTY SHARP...
...BUT I WON'T ADMIT IT! FIRST OF ALL, I STILL HAVEN'T ACCEPTED THIS UNREALISTIC IDEA OF A TEN-YEAR-OLD BRAT BEING A TEACHER. I REFUSE TO ACKNOWLEDGE HIS EXISTENCE!
...BUT WAIT. WHAT IF HE REALLY DOES FIGURE OUT
THAT I'M CHIU?
HEEEH HEH HEH HEH...
IF YOU DON'T WANT ME TO TELL EVERYONE, YOU'LL LISTEN TO EVERYTHING I SAY.
YOU ARE MY SLAVE.
AAAAUGH! THERE'S NO WAY I'M GONNA LET THAT BRAT HAVE DIRT ON ME!
I GUESS I'LL JUST HAVE TO TEMPORAR-ILY CLOSE THE SITE AND OPEN IT UP AGAIN WHEN THIS ALL BLOWS OVER.
BAH
?

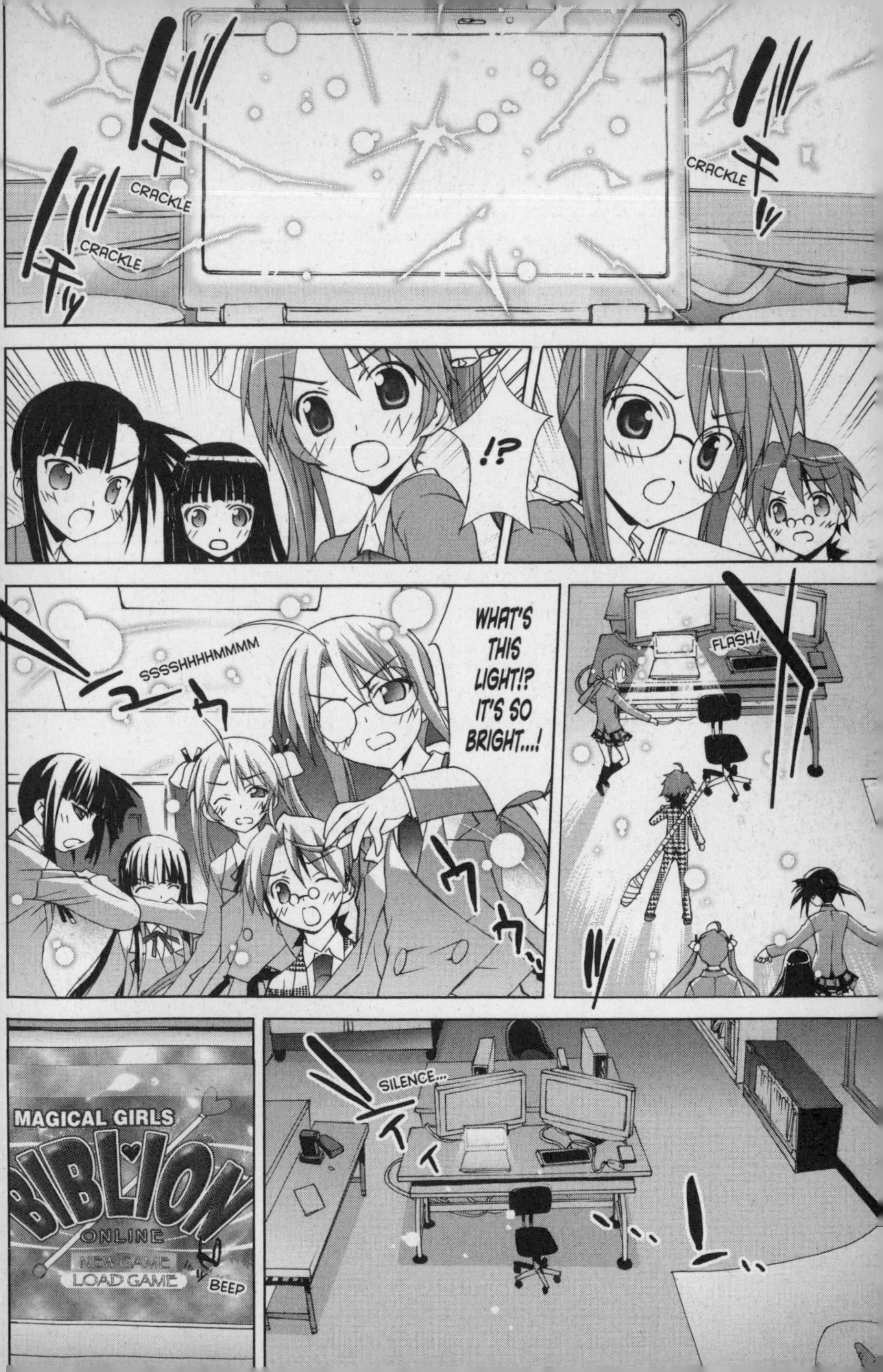
CRACKLE
CRACKLE
CRACKLE
!?
FLASH!
WHAT'S THIS LIGHT!? IT'S SO BRIGHT...!
SSSSHHHHMMMM
SILENCE...
MAGICAL GIRLS
BIBLION
ONLINE
NEW GAME
LOAD GAME
BEEP

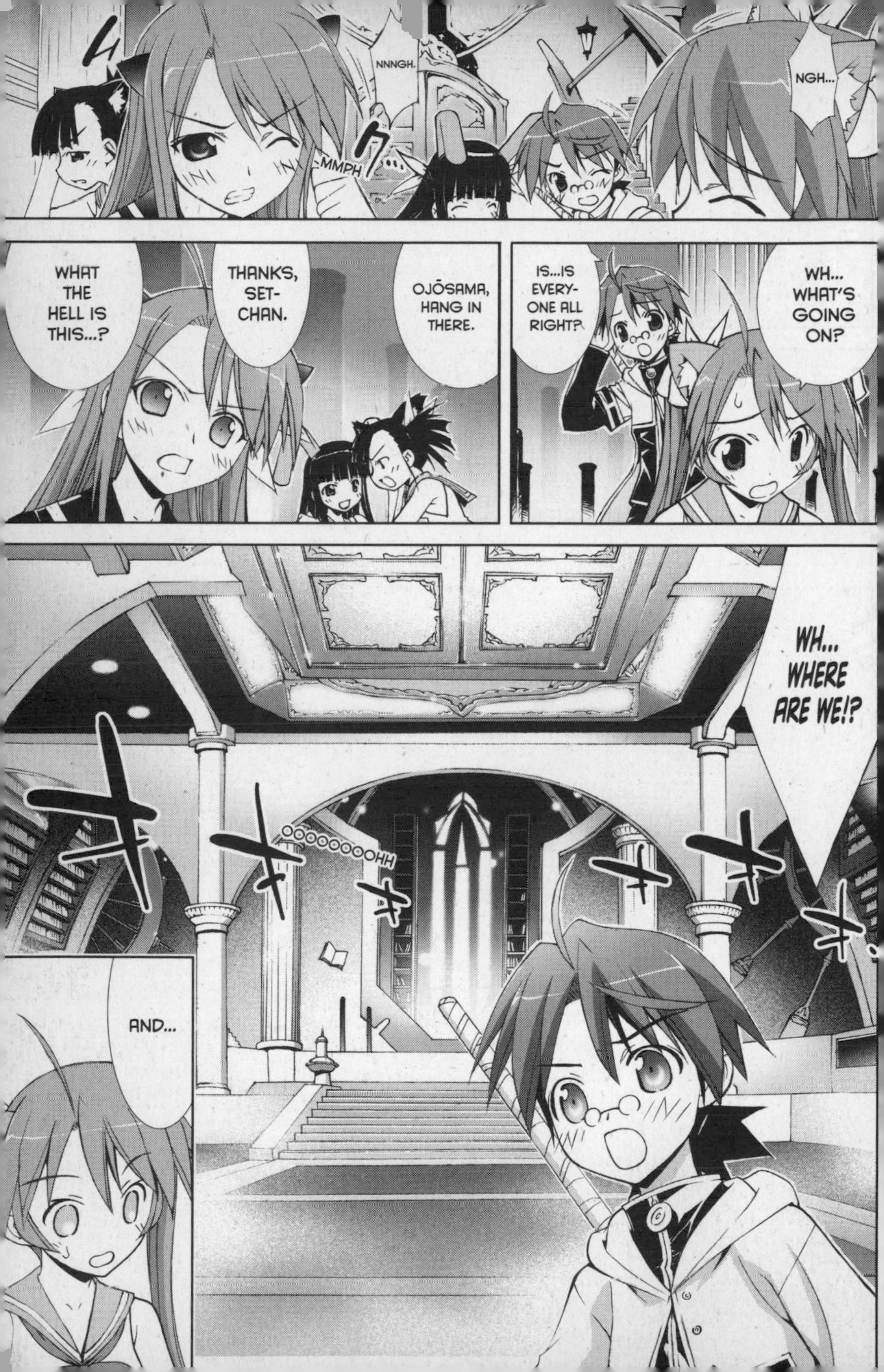
NGH...
NNNGH.
MMPH
WH... WHAT'S GOING ON?
IS...IS EVERY-ONE ALL RIGHT?
OJŌSAMA, HANG IN THERE.
THANKS, SET-CHAN.
WHAT THE HELL IS THIS...?
WH... WHERE ARE WE!?
OOOOOOOOOHH
AND...

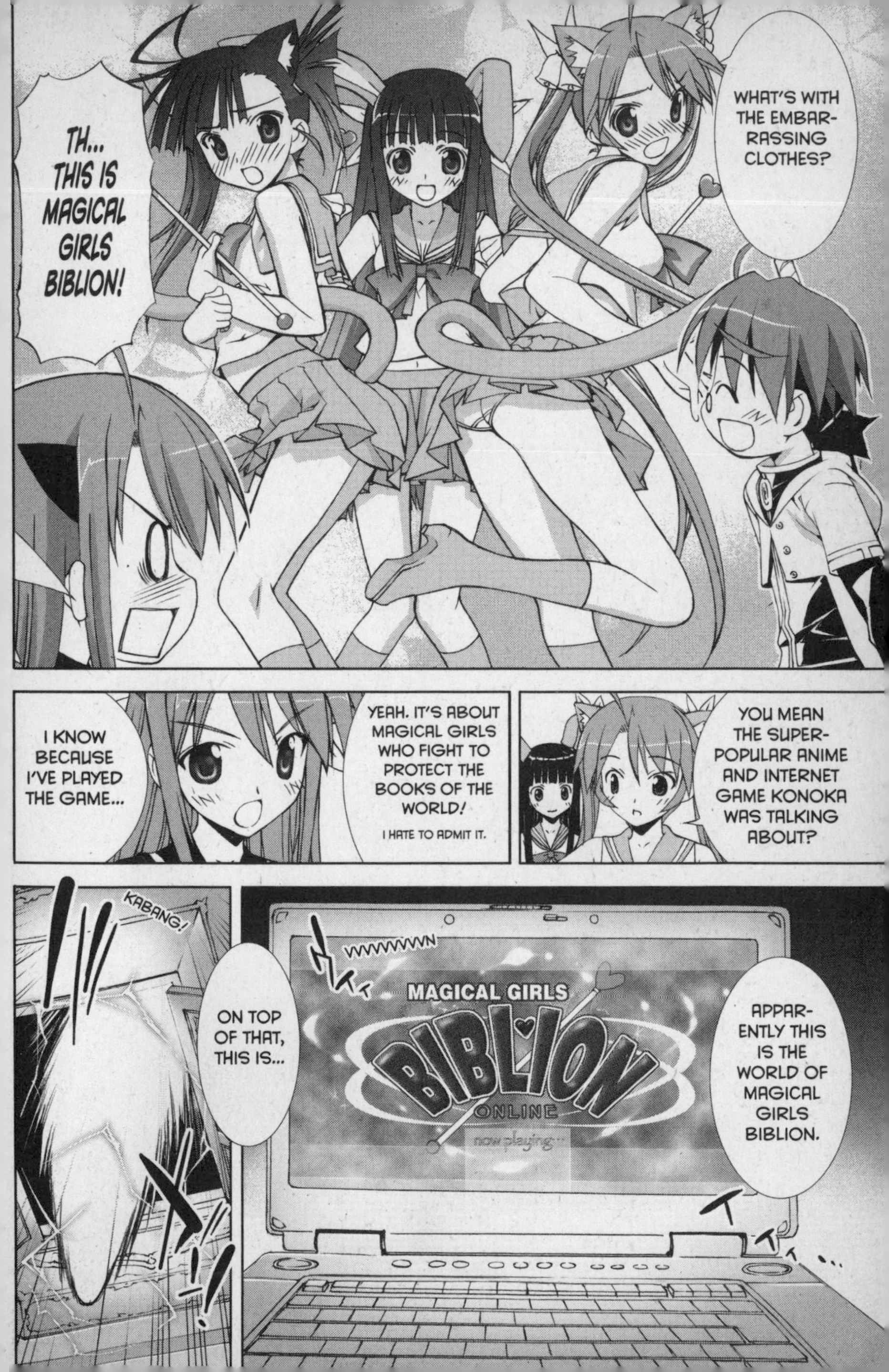
WHAT'S WITH THE EMBAR-RASSING CLOTHES?
TH... THIS IS MAGICAL GIRLS BIBLION!
YOU MEAN THE SUPER-POPULAR ANIME AND INTERNET GAME KONOKA WAS TALKING ABOUT?
YEAH. IT'S ABOUT MAGICAL GIRLS WHO FIGHT TO PROTECT THE BOOKS OF THE WORLD!
I HATE TO ADMIT IT.
I KNOW BECAUSE I'VE PLAYED THE GAME...
APPAR-ENTLY THIS IS THE WORLD OF MAGICAL GIRLS BIBLION.
MAGICAL GIRLS
BIBLION
ONLINE
now playing...
VVVVVVVVN
ON TOP OF THAT, THIS IS...
KABANG!

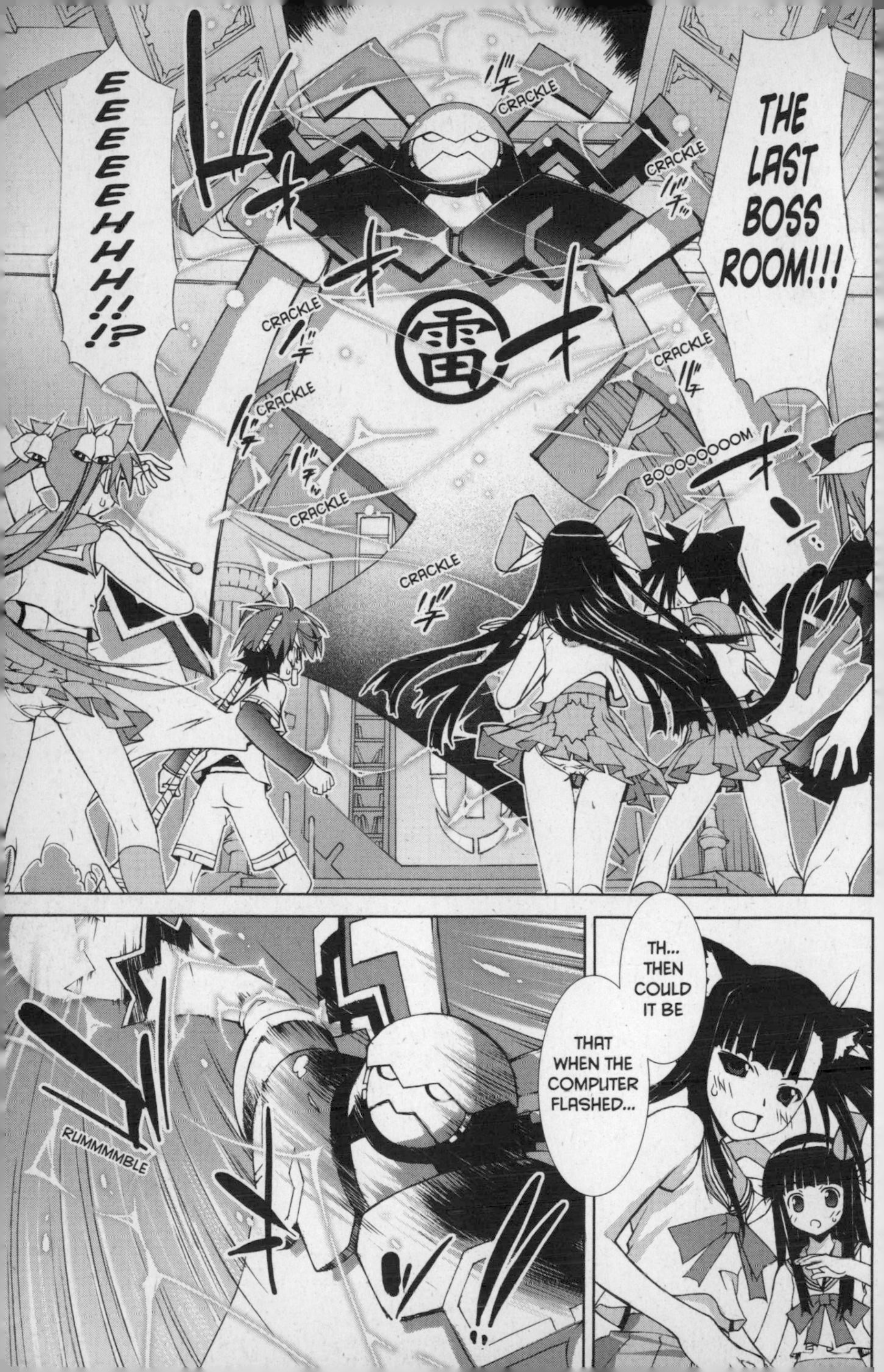
THE LAST BOSS ROOM!!!
CRACKLE
CRACKLE
EEEEEEHHHHH!!!?
CRACKLE
CRACKLE
CRACKLE
CRACKLE
BOOOOOOOOM
CRACKLE
TH... THEN COULD IT BE
THAT WHEN THE COMPUTER FLASHED...
RUMMMMBLE

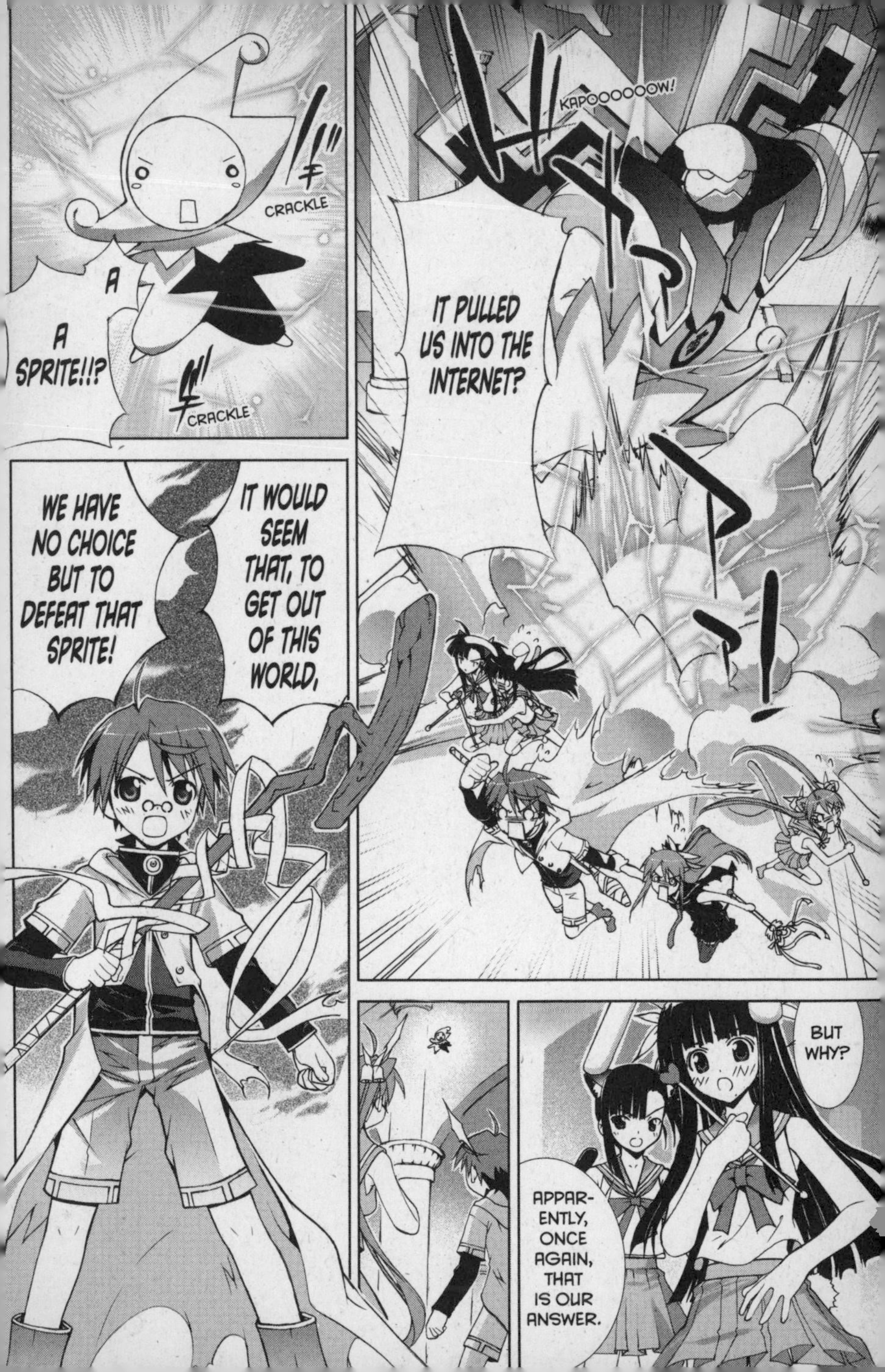

CRACKLE
A
A SPRITE!!?
CRACKLE
KAPOOOOOOW!
IT PULLED US INTO THE INTERNET?
IT WOULD SEEM THAT, TO GET OUT OF THIS WORLD,
WE HAVE NO CHOICE BUT TO DEFEAT THAT SPRITE!
BUT WHY?
APPARENTLY, ONCE AGAIN, THAT IS OUR ANSWER.

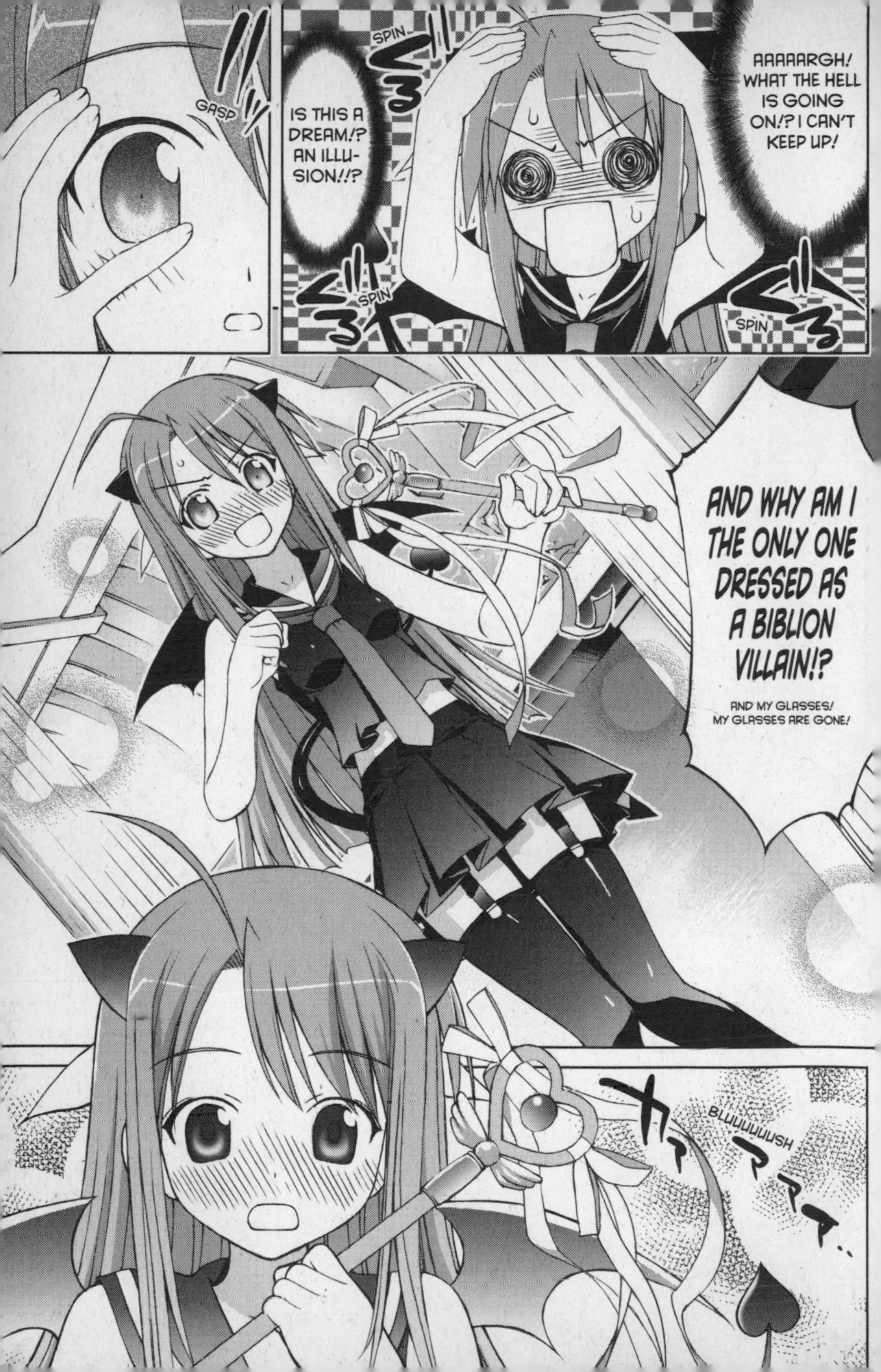

AAAAARGH! WHAT THE HELL IS GOING ON!? I CAN'T KEEP UP!
SPIN
IS THIS A DREAM!? AN ILLUSION!!?
SPIN
SPIN
GASP
AND WHY AM I THE ONLY ONE DRESSED AS A BIBLION VILLAIN!?
AND MY GLASSES! MY GLASSES ARE GONE!
BLUUUUUUSH

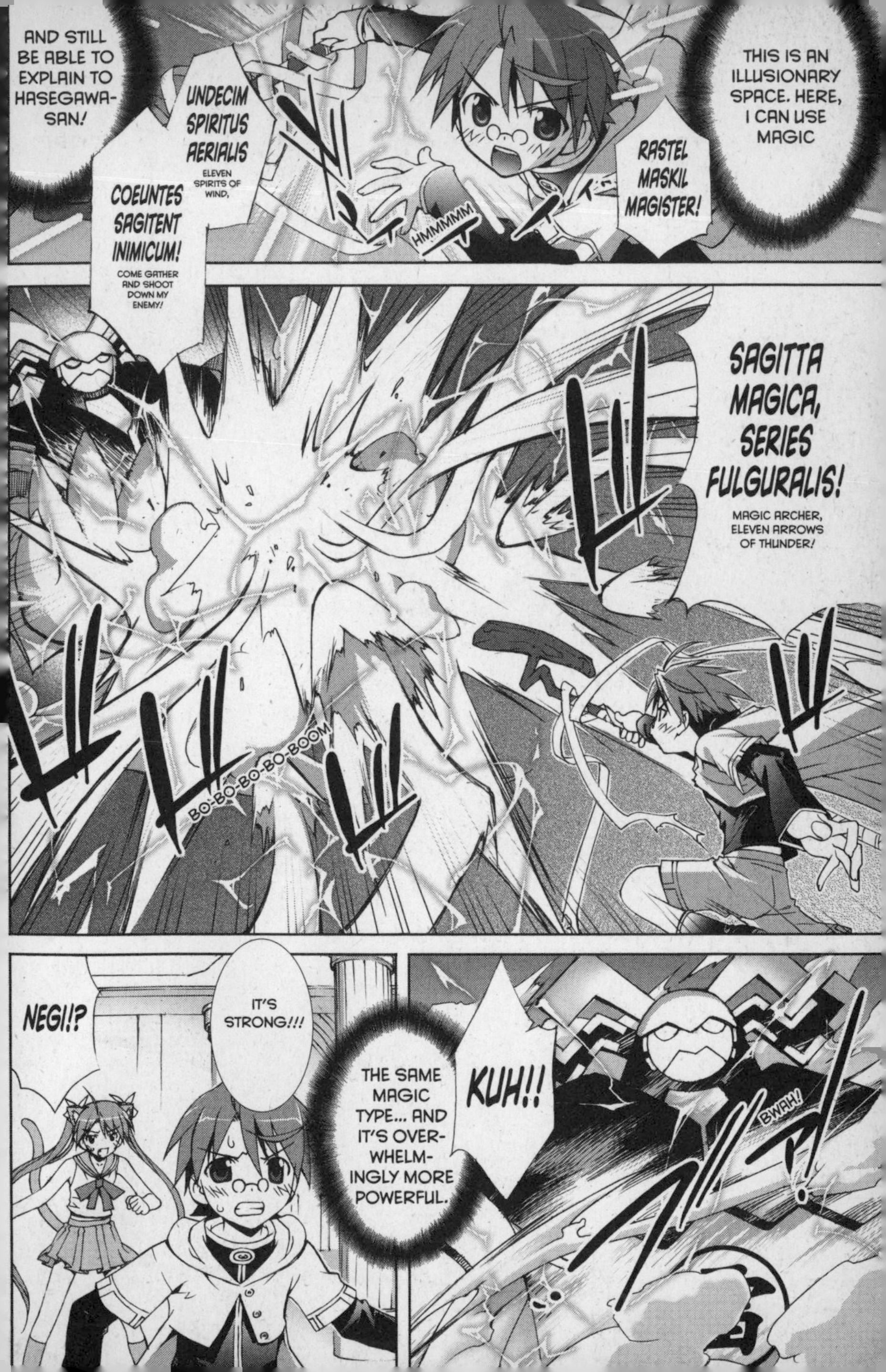
THIS IS AN ILLUSIONARY SPACE. HERE, I CAN USE MAGIC
RASTEL MASKIL MAGISTER!
HMMMMM
UNDECIM SPIRITUS AERIALIS
ELEVEN SPIRITS OF WIND,
AND STILL BE ABLE TO EXPLAIN TO HASEGAWA-SAN!
COEUNTES SAGITENT INIMICUM!
COME GATHER AND SHOOT DOWN MY ENEMY!
SAGITTA MAGICA, SERIES FULGURALIS!
MAGIC ARCHER, ELEVEN ARROWS OF THUNDER!
BO-BO-BO-BO-BOOM
BWAH!
KUH!!
THE SAME MAGIC TYPE... AND IT'S OVER-WHELM-INGLY MORE POWERFUL.
IT'S STRONG!!!
NEGI!?

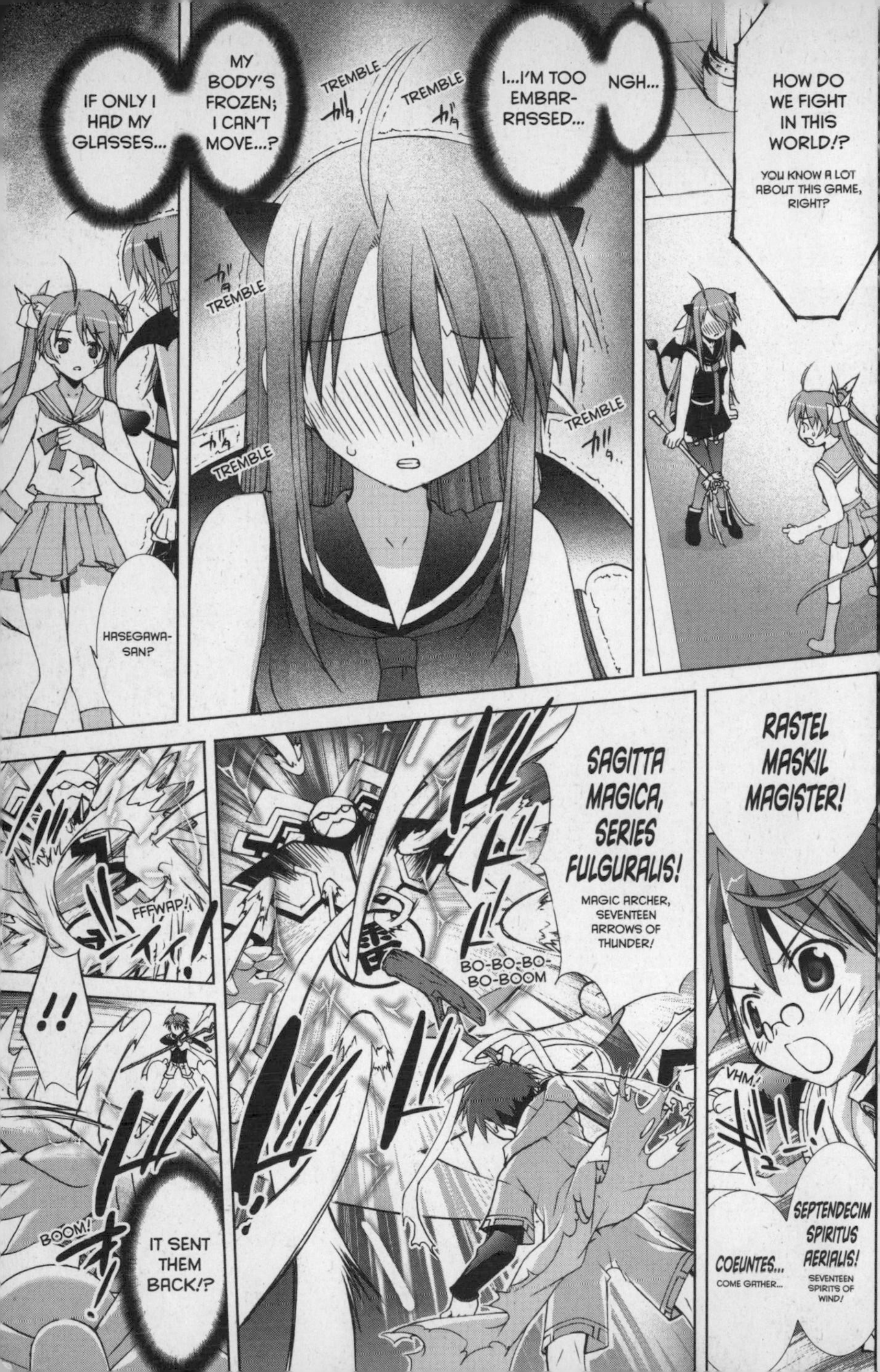
HOW DO WE FIGHT IN THIS WORLD!?
YOU KNOW A LOT ABOUT THIS GAME, RIGHT?
NGH...
I...I'M TOO EMBARRASSED...
TREMBLE
TREMBLE
TREMBLE
TREMBLE
TREMBLE
MY BODY'S FROZEN; I CAN'T MOVE...?
IF ONLY I HAD MY GLASSES...
HASEGAWA-SAN?
RASTEL MASKIL MAGISTER!
VHM!
SEPTENDECIM SPIRITUS AERIALIS!
SEVENTEEN SPIRITS OF WIND!
COEUNTES...
COME GATHER...
SAGITTA MAGICA, SERIES FULGURALIS!
MAGIC ARCHER, SEVENTEEN ARROWS OF THUNDER!
BO-BO-BO-BO-BOOM
FFFWAP!
!!
BOOM!
IT SENT THEM BACK!?

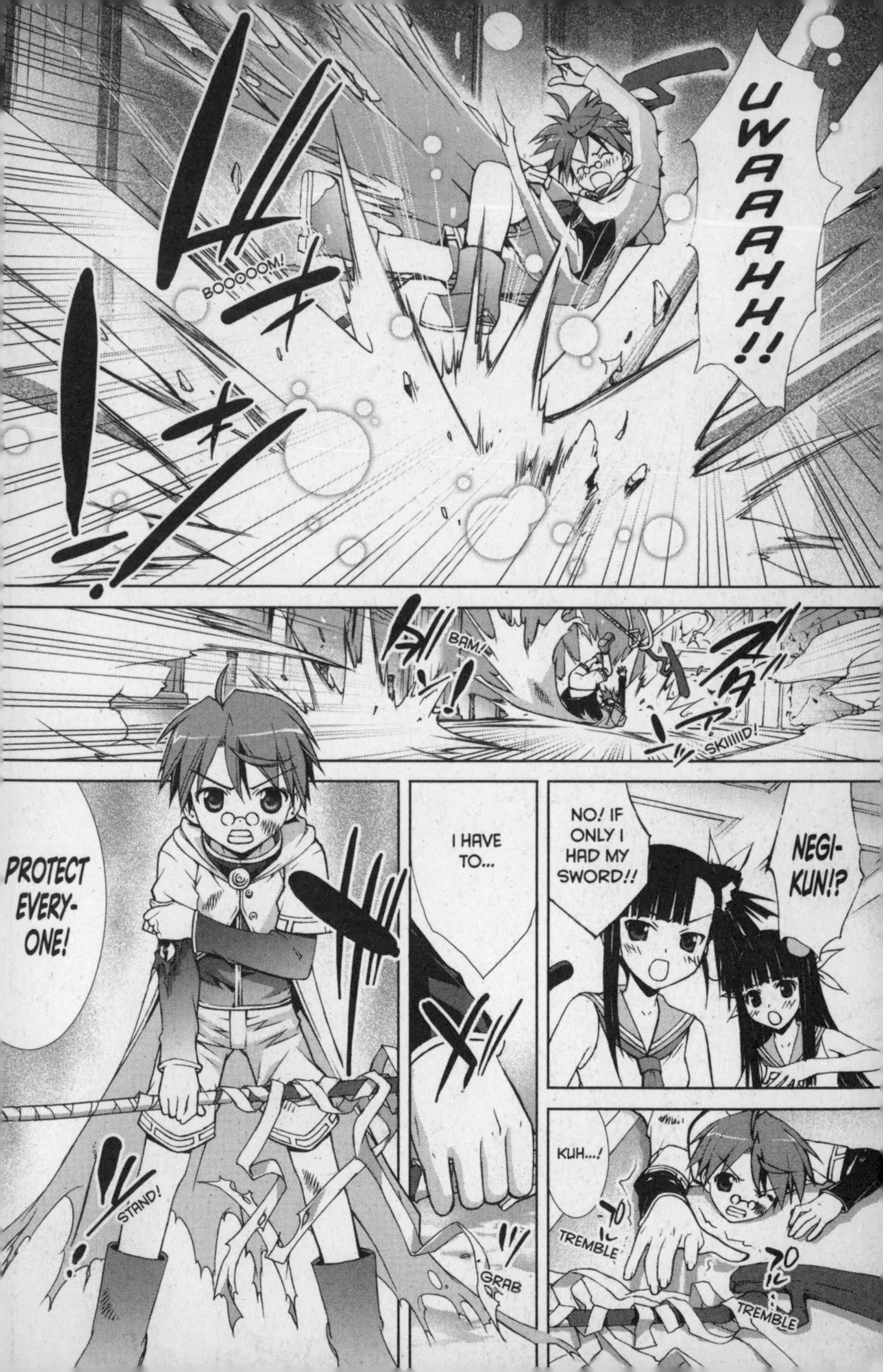
UWAAAAHH!!
BOOOOOOM!
BAM!
SKIIIIID!
NEGI-KUN!?
NO! IF ONLY I HAD MY SWORD!!
KUH...!
TREMBLE
TREMBLE
I HAVE TO...
GRAB
PROTECT EVERY-ONE!
STAND!

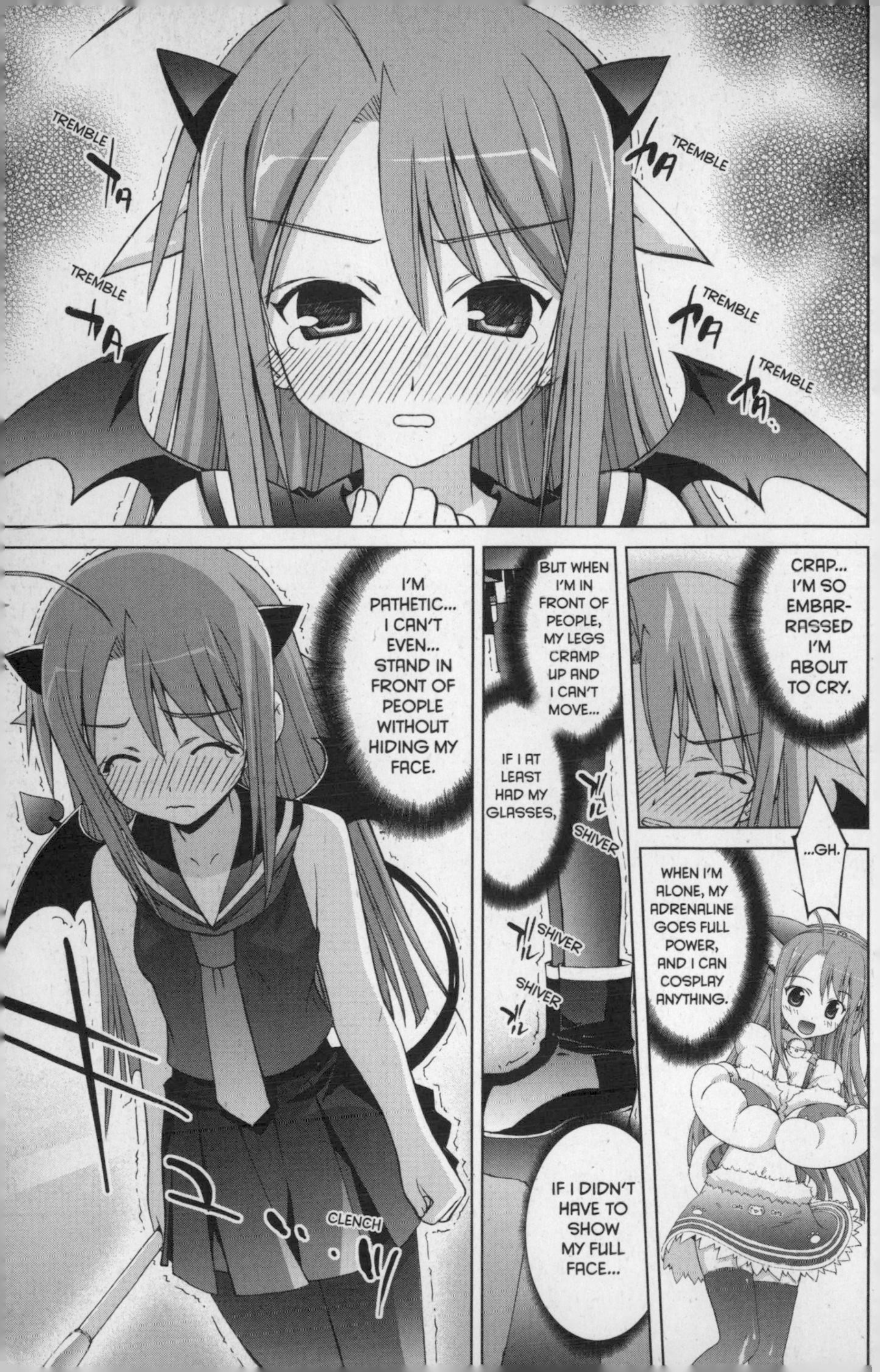
TREMBLE
HA
TREMBLE
HA
TREMBLE
HA
TREMBLE
HA
TREMBLE
HA..
CRAP... I'M SO EMBARRASSED I'M ABOUT TO CRY.
...GH.
WHEN I'M ALONE, MY ADRENALINE GOES FULL POWER, AND I CAN COSPLAY ANYTHING.
BUT WHEN I'M IN FRONT OF PEOPLE, MY LEGS CRAMP UP AND I CAN'T MOVE...
IF I AT LEAST HAD MY GLASSES,
SHIVER
SHIVER
SHIVER
IF I DIDN'T HAVE TO SHOW MY FULL FACE...
I'M PATHETIC... I CAN'T EVEN... STAND IN FRONT OF PEOPLE WITHOUT HIDING MY FACE.
CLENCH

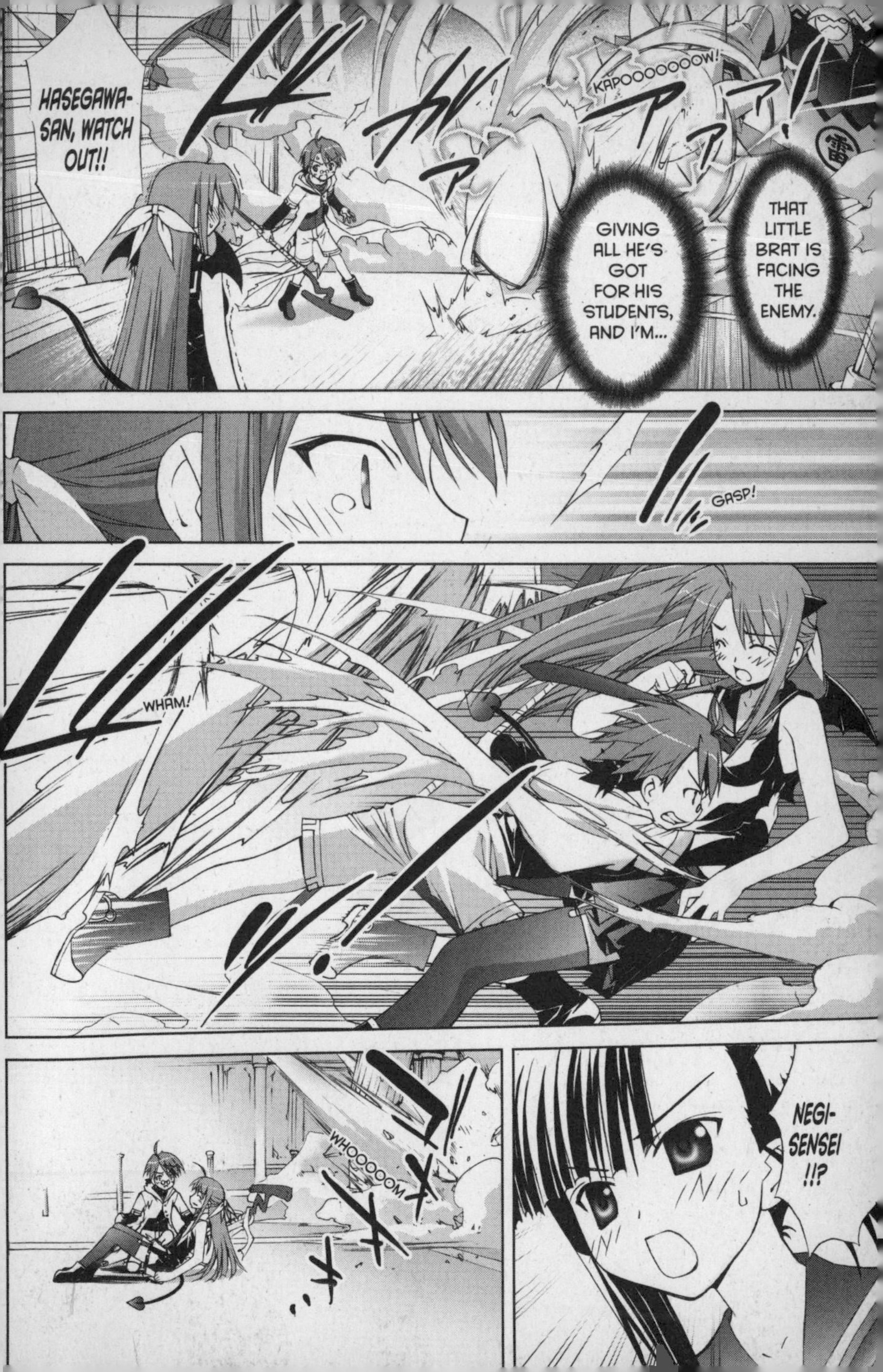

KAPOOOOOOOW!
雷
THAT LITTLE BRAT IS FACING THE ENEMY.
GIVING ALL HE'S GOT FOR HIS STUDENTS, AND I'M...
HASEGAWA-SAN, WATCH OUT!!
GASP!
WHAM!
NEGI-SENSEI !!?
WHOOOOOOM

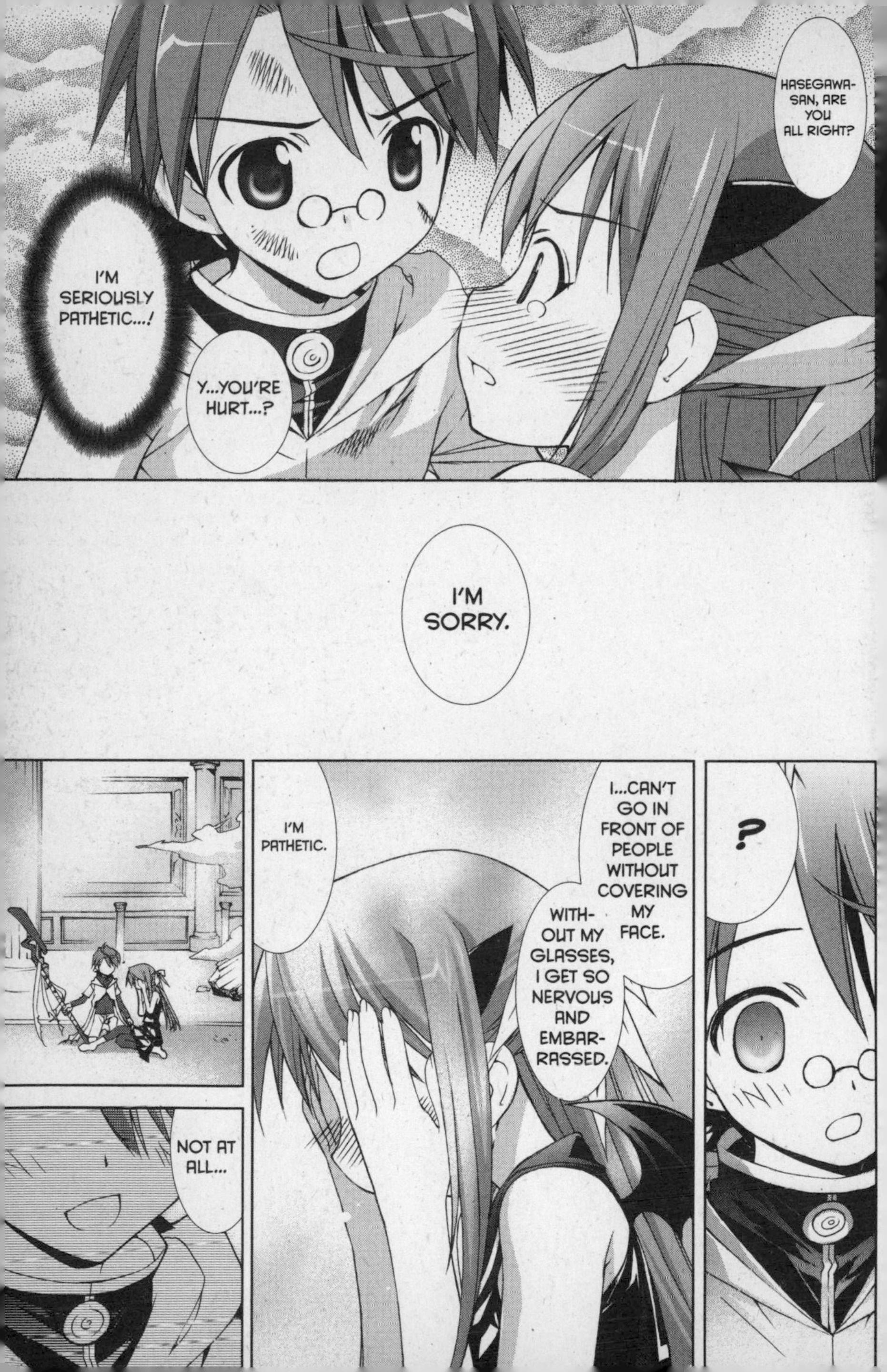
HASEGAWA-SAN, ARE YOU ALL RIGHT?
Y...YOU'RE HURT...?
I'M SERIOUSLY PATHETIC...!
I'M SORRY.
?
I...CAN'T GO IN FRONT OF PEOPLE WITHOUT COVERING MY FACE.
WITH-OUT MY GLASSES, I GET SO NERVOUS AND EMBAR-RASSED.
I'M PATHETIC.
NOT AT ALL...

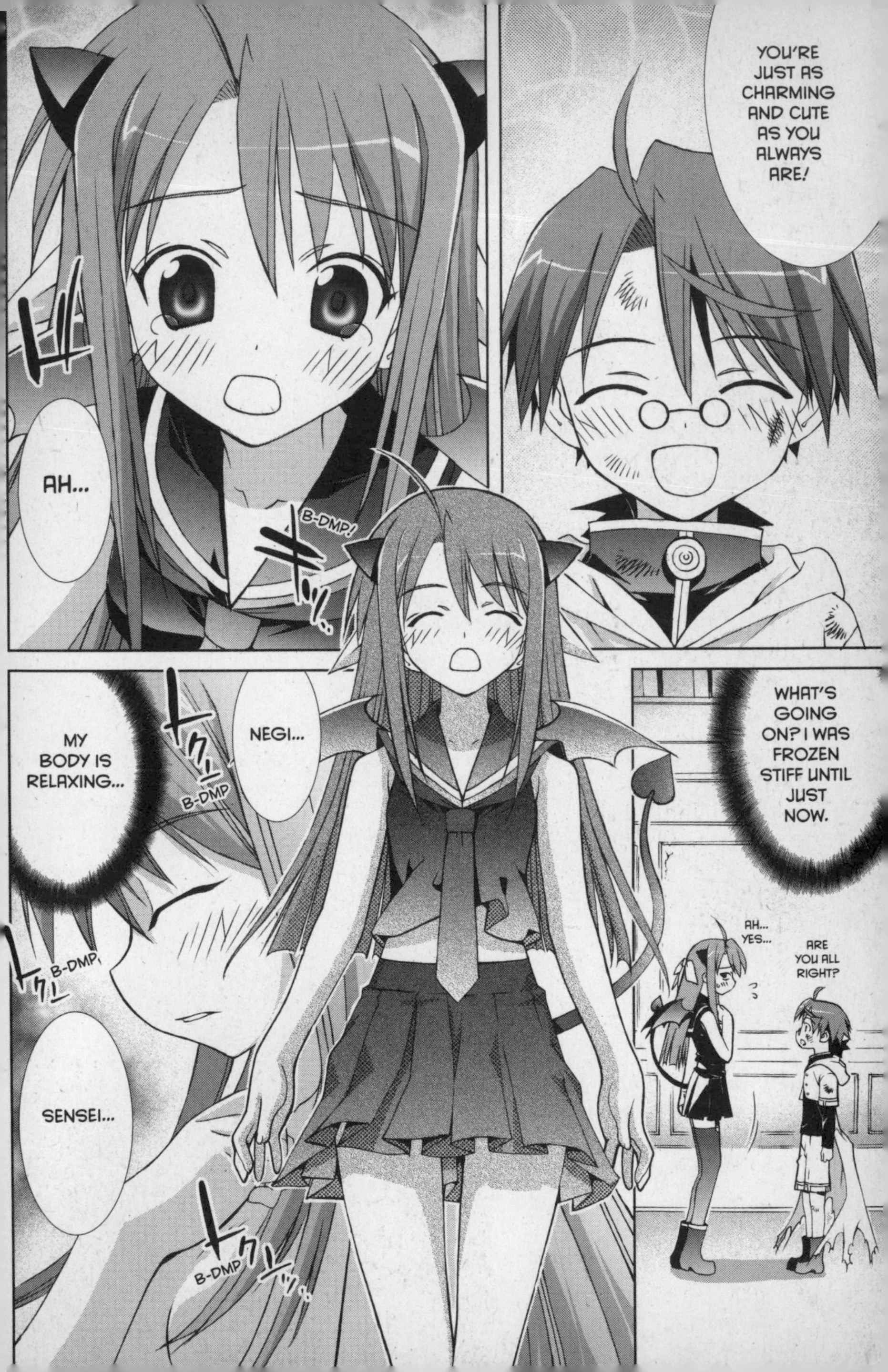
YOU'RE JUST AS CHARMING AND CUTE AS YOU ALWAYS ARE!
AH...
B-DMP!
WHAT'S GOING ON? I WAS FROZEN STIFF UNTIL JUST NOW.
ARE YOU ALL RIGHT?
AH... YES...
NEGI...
MY BODY IS RELAXING...
B-DMP
B-DMP
SENSEI...
B-DMP

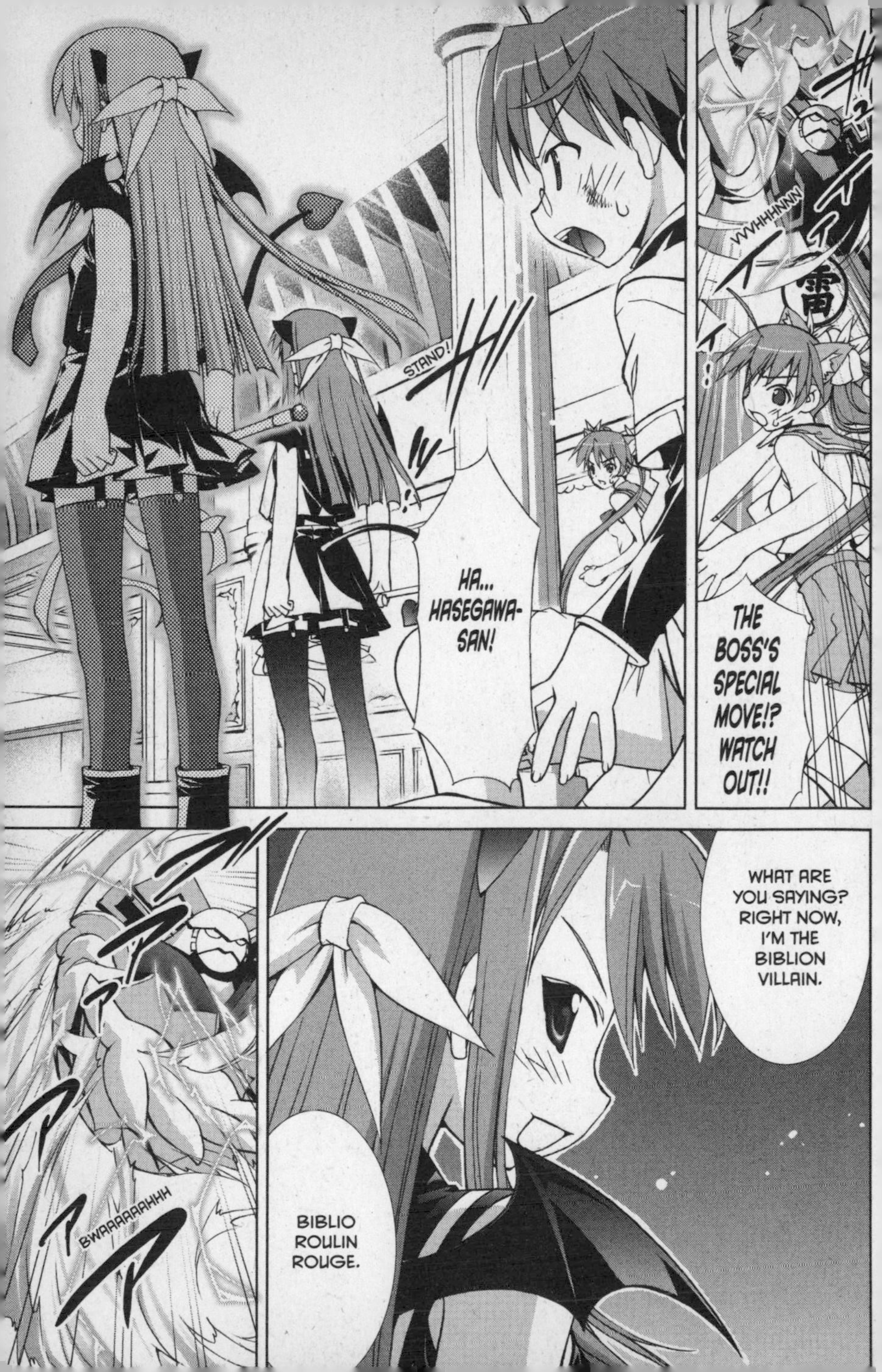
VVVHHHNNN
雷
THE BOSS'S SPECIAL MOVE!? WATCH OUT!!
STAND!
HA... HASEGAWA-SAN!
WHAT ARE YOU SAYING? RIGHT NOW, I'M THE BIBLION VILLAIN.
BIBLIO ROULIN ROUGE.
BWAAAAAAAHHH

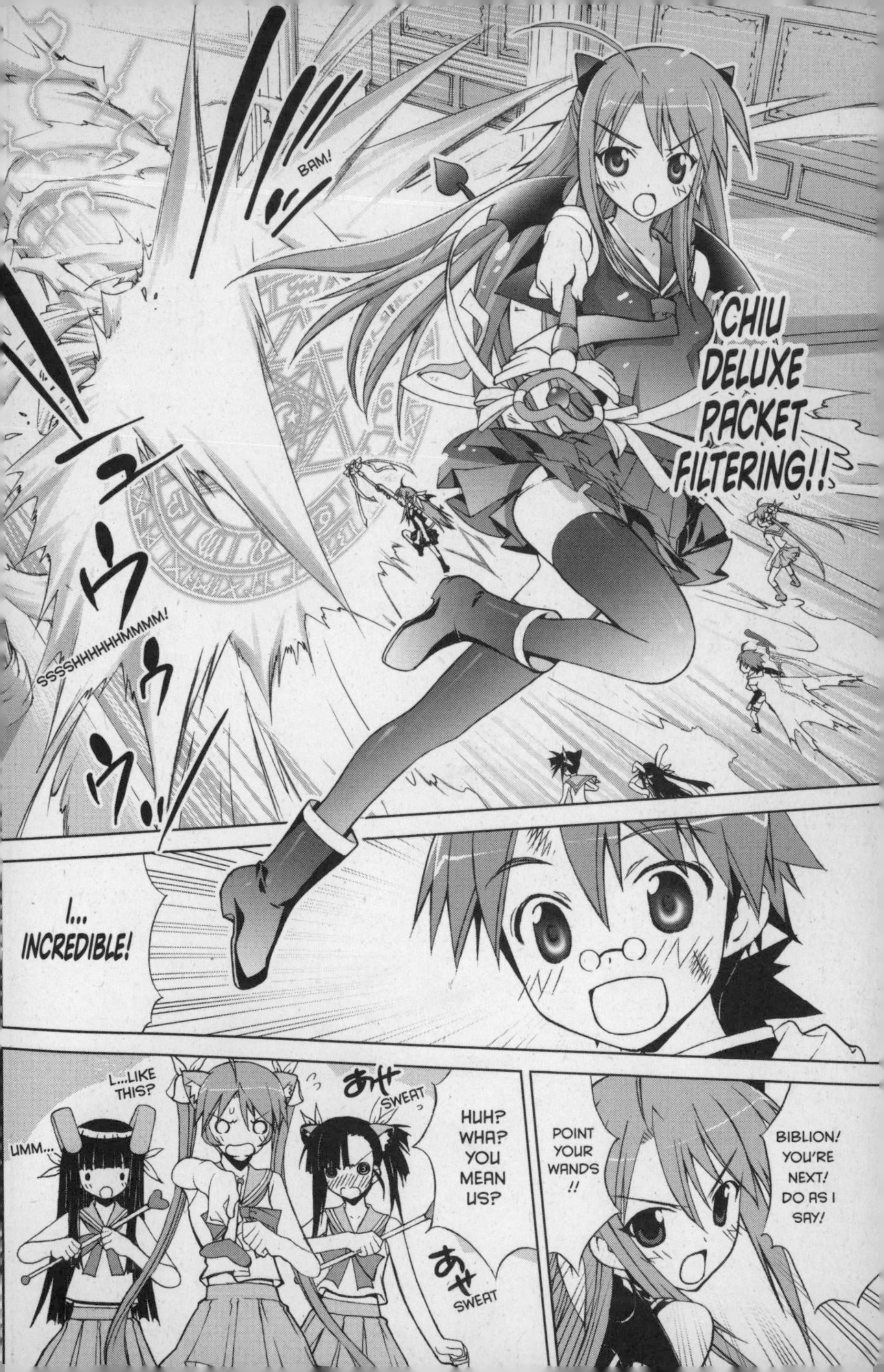

CHIU DELUXE PACKET FILTERING!!
BAM!
SSSSHHHHHHMMMM!
I... INCREDIBLE!
BIBLION! YOU'RE NEXT! DO AS I SAY!
POINT YOUR WANDS !!
HUH? WHA? YOU MEAN US?
SWEAT
L...LIKE THIS?
UMM...
SWEAT

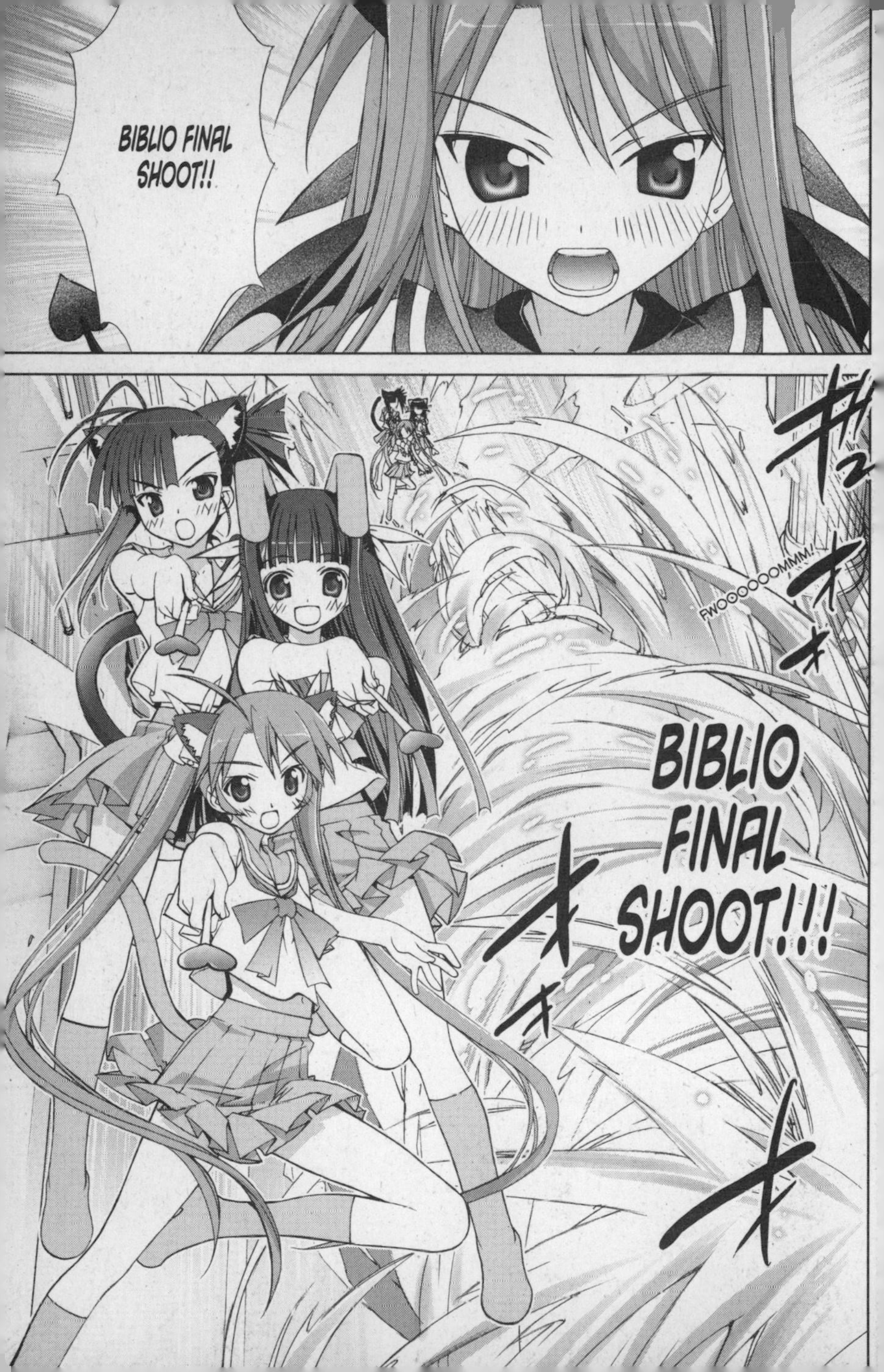
BIBLIO FINAL SHOOT!!
FWOOOOOOMMM!
BIBLIO FINAL SHOOT!!!

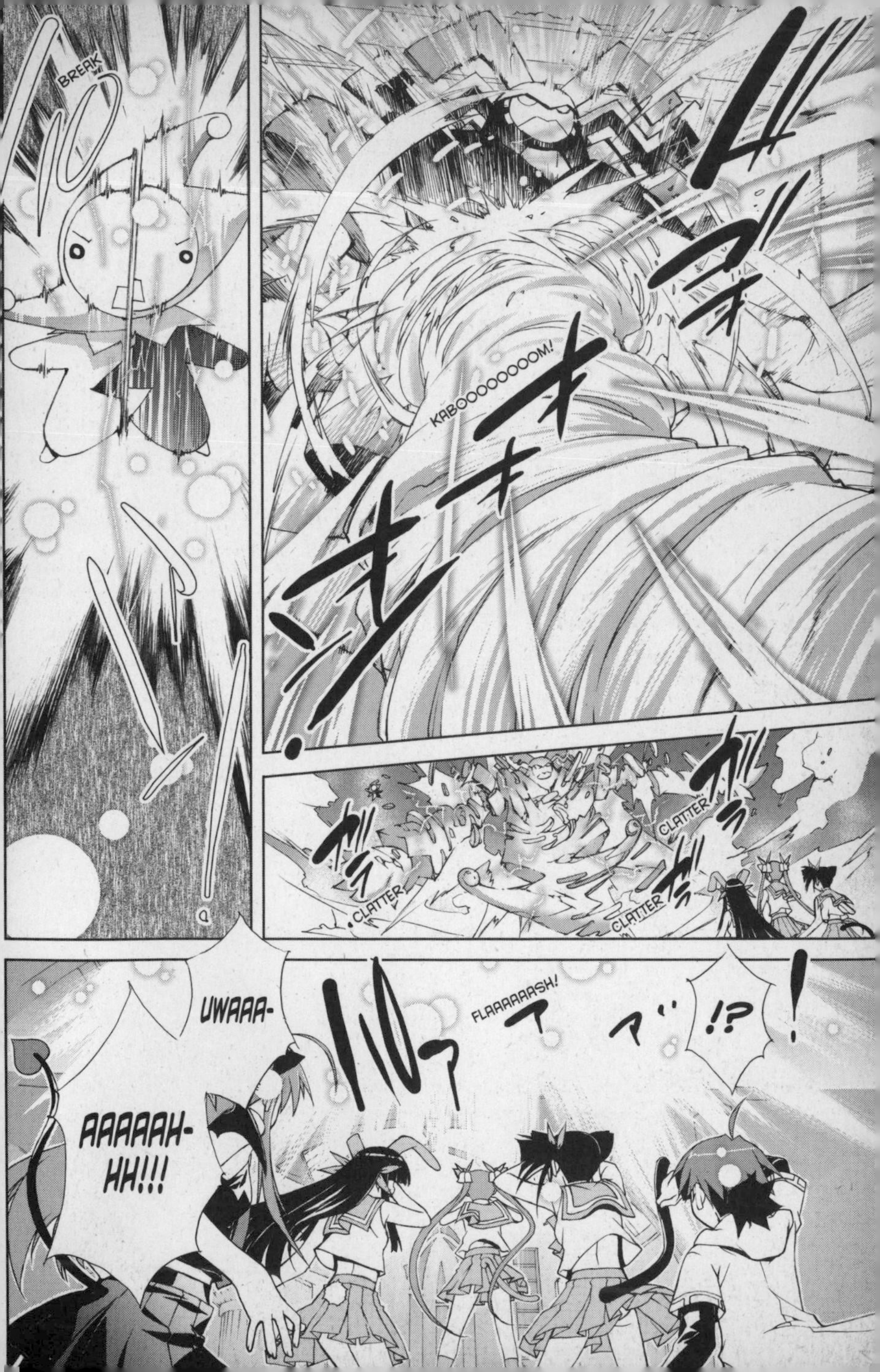
KABOOOOOOOOOOM!
CLATTER
CLATTER
CLATTER
BREAK
!
!?
FLAAAAAAASH!
UWAAA-
AAAAAH-
HH!!!

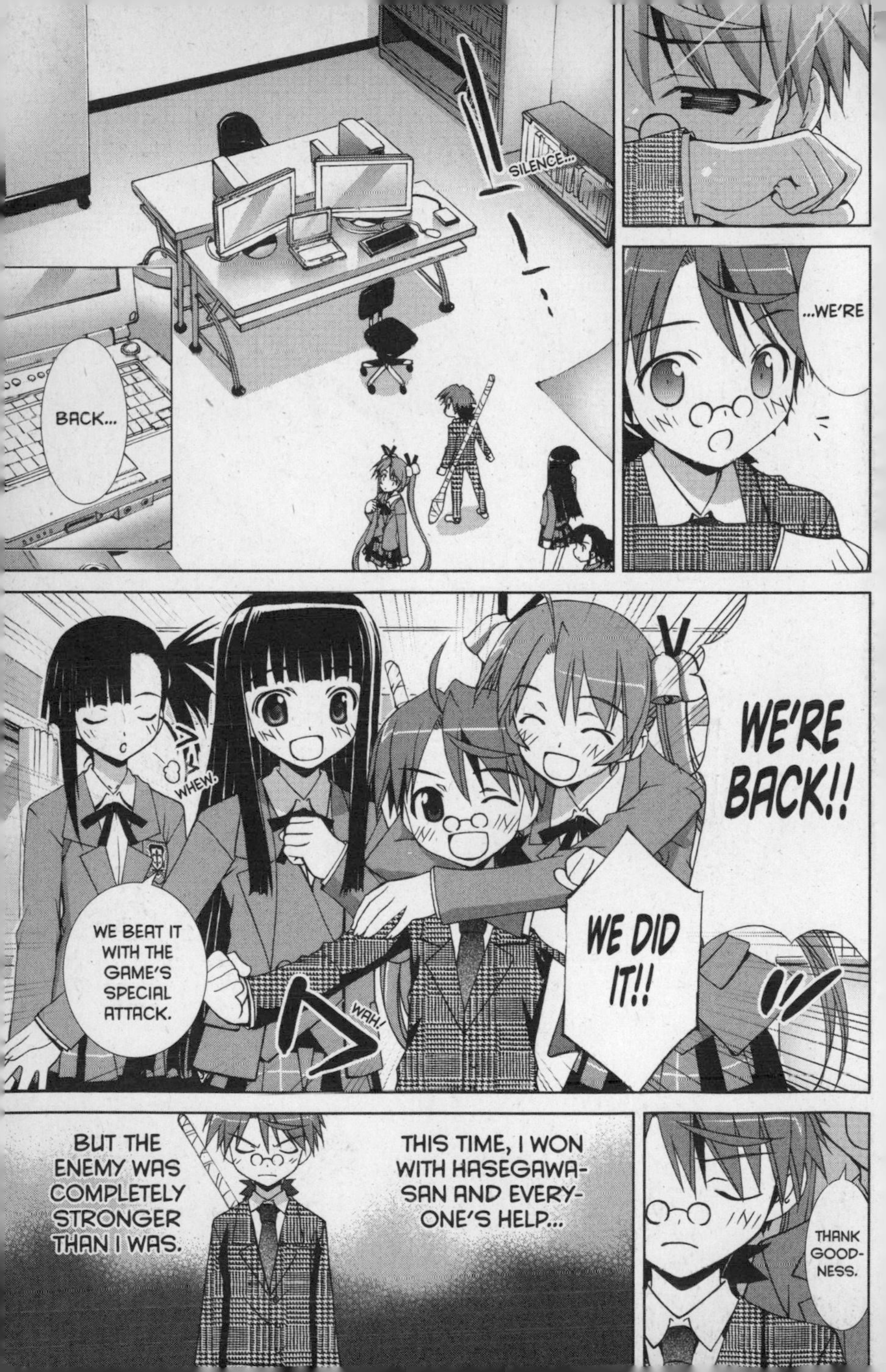
...WE'RE
SILENCE...
BACK...
WE'RE BACK!!
WE DID IT!!
WAH!
WHEW.
WE BEAT IT WITH THE GAME'S SPECIAL ATTACK.
THANK GOOD-NESS.
THIS TIME, I WON WITH HASEGAWA-SAN AND EVERY-ONE'S HELP...
BUT THE ENEMY WAS COMPLETELY STRONGER THAN I WAS.

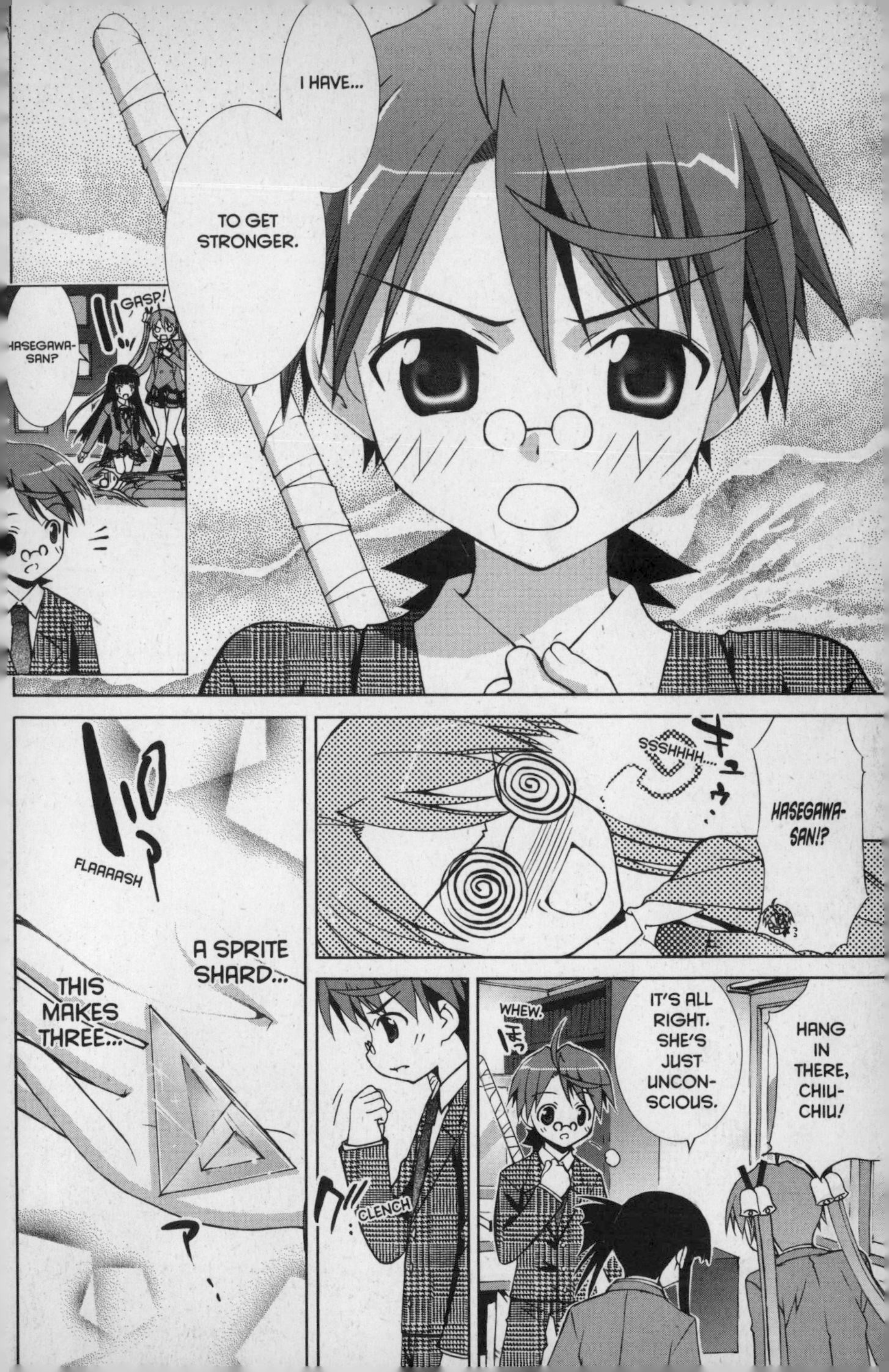
I HAVE...
TO GET STRONGER.
GASP!
HASEGAWA-SAN?
SSSHHHH...
HASEGAWA-SAN!?
HANG IN THERE, CHIU-CHIU!
IT'S ALL RIGHT. SHE'S JUST UNCONSCIOUS.
WHEW.
CLENCH
FLAAAASH
A SPRITE SHARD...
THIS MAKES THREE...

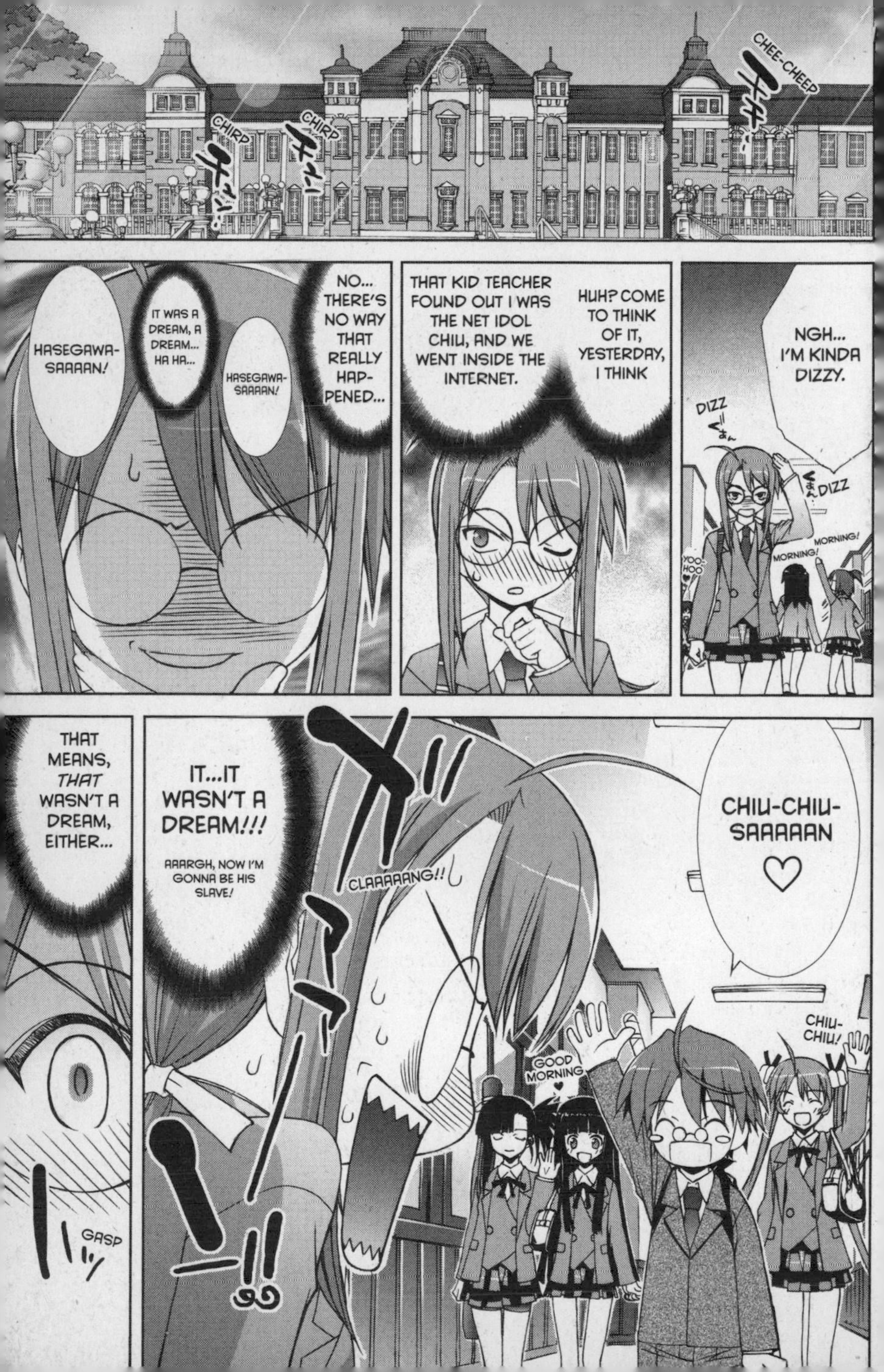
CHEE-CHEEP
CHIRP
CHIRP
NGH... I'M KINDA DIZZY.
DIZZ
DIZZ
MORNING!
MORNING!
YOO-HOO ♥
HUH? COME TO THINK OF IT, YESTERDAY, I THINK
THAT KID TEACHER FOUND OUT I WAS THE NET IDOL CHIU, AND WE WENT INSIDE THE INTERNET.
NO... THERE'S NO WAY THAT REALLY HAP-PENED...
HASEGAWA-SAAAAN!
IT WAS A DREAM, A DREAM... HA HA...
HASEGAWA-SAAAAN!
CHIU-CHIU-SAAAAAN ♥
CHIU-CHIU!
GOOD MORNING ♥
IT...IT WASN'T A DREAM!!!
AAARGH, NOW I'M GONNA BE HIS SLAVE!
CLAAAAANG!!
THAT MEANS, *THAT* WASN'T A DREAM, EITHER...
GASP

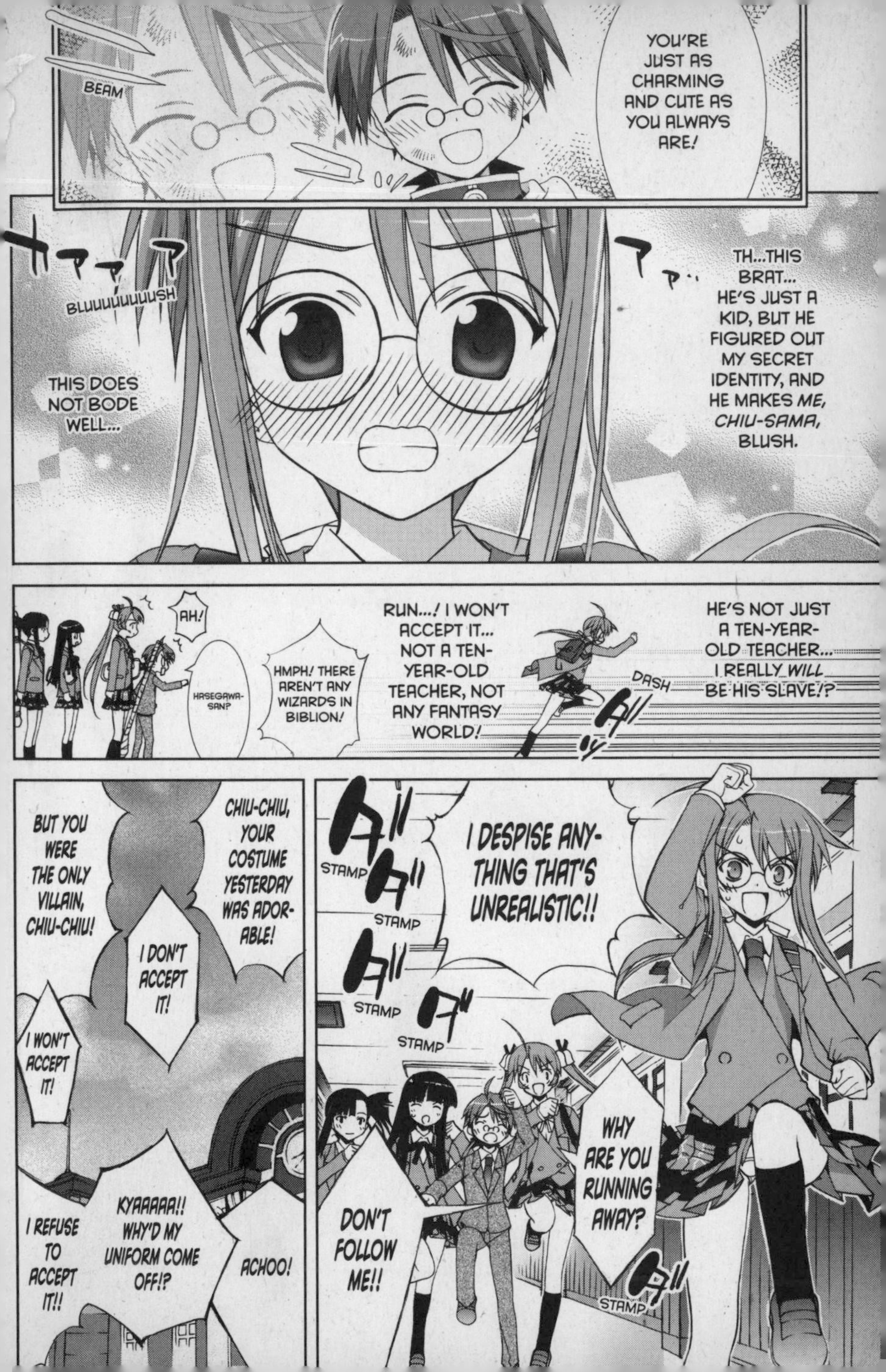
YOU'RE JUST AS CHARMING AND CUTE AS YOU ALWAYS ARE!
BEAM
TH...THIS BRAT... HE'S JUST A KID, BUT HE FIGURED OUT MY SECRET IDENTITY, AND HE MAKES *ME, CHIU-SAMA,* BLUSH.
BLUUUUUUUUSH
THIS DOES NOT BODE WELL...
HE'S NOT JUST A TEN-YEAR-OLD TEACHER... I REALLY *WILL* BE HIS SLAVE!?
DASH
RUN...! I WON'T ACCEPT IT... NOT A TEN-YEAR-OLD TEACHER, NOT ANY FANTASY WORLD!
HMPH! THERE AREN'T ANY WIZARDS IN BIBLION!
AH!
HASEGAWA-SAN?
I DESPISE ANY-THING THAT'S UNREALISTIC!!
STAMP
STAMP
STAMP
STAMP
WHY ARE YOU RUNNING AWAY?
DON'T FOLLOW ME!!
STAMP
CHIU-CHIU, YOUR COSTUME YESTERDAY WAS ADOR-ABLE!
BUT YOU WERE THE ONLY VILLAIN, CHIU-CHIU!
I DON'T ACCEPT IT!
I WON'T ACCEPT IT!
ACHOO!
KYAAAAA!! WHY'D MY UNIFORM COME OFF!?
I REFUSE TO ACCEPT IT!!

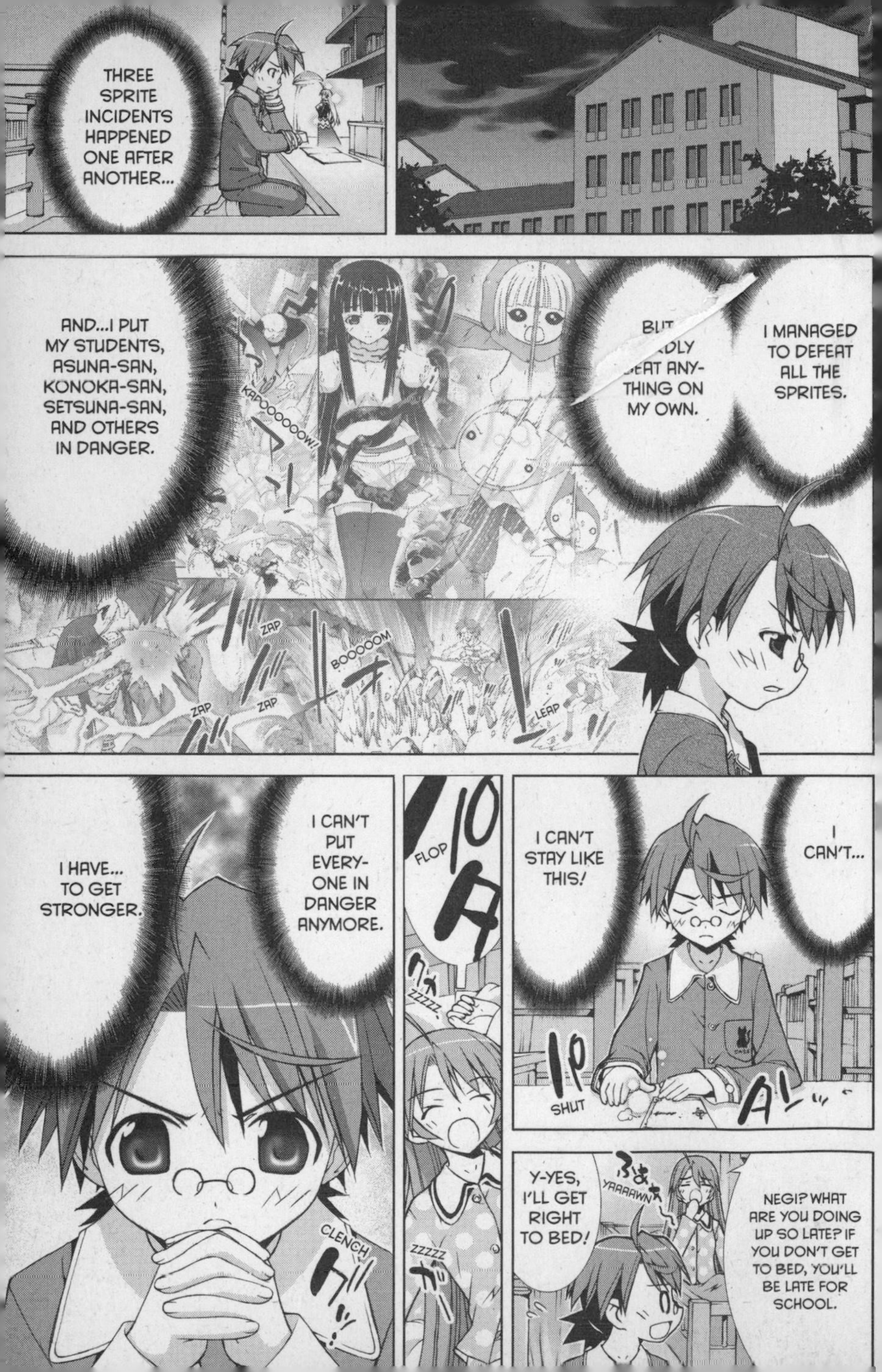
THREE SPRITE INCIDENTS HAPPENED ONE AFTER ANOTHER...
I MANAGED TO DEFEAT ALL THE SPRITES.
BUT ... RDLY ... EAT ANYTHING ON MY OWN.
AND...I PUT MY STUDENTS, ASUNA-SAN, KONOKA-SAN, SETSUNA-SAN, AND OTHERS IN DANGER.
KAPOOOOOOOW!
ZAP
BOOOOOM
ZAP
ZAP
LEAP
I CAN'T...
I CAN'T STAY LIKE THIS!
SHUT
NEGI? WHAT ARE YOU DOING UP SO LATE? IF YOU DON'T GET TO BED, YOU'LL BE LATE FOR SCHOOL.
YAAAAWN
Y-YES, I'LL GET RIGHT TO BED!
FLOP
ZZZZZ
ZZZZZ
I CAN'T PUT EVERYONE IN DANGER ANYMORE.
I HAVE... TO GET STRONGER.
CLENCH

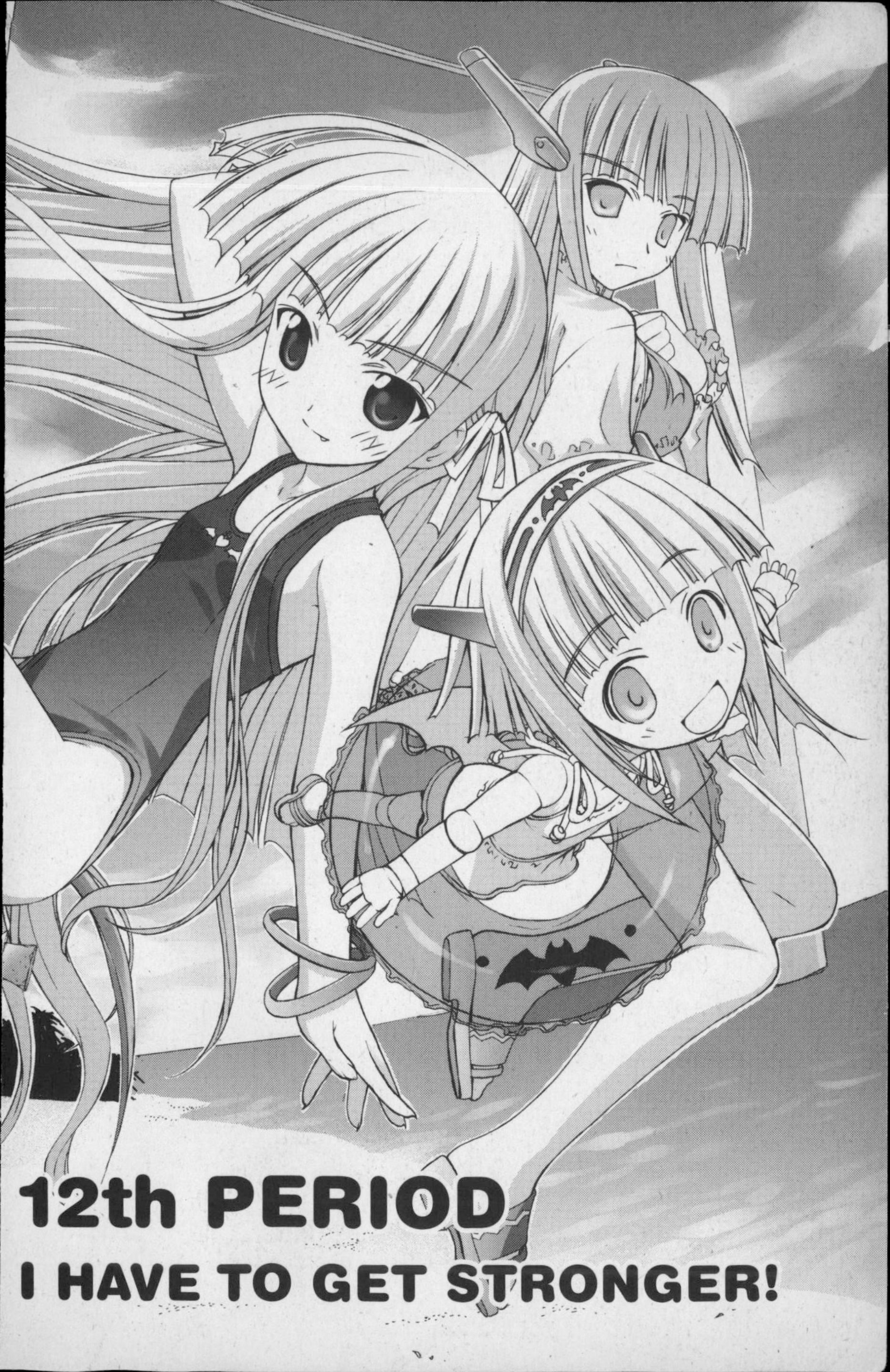

12th PERIOD

I HAVE TO GET STRONGER!

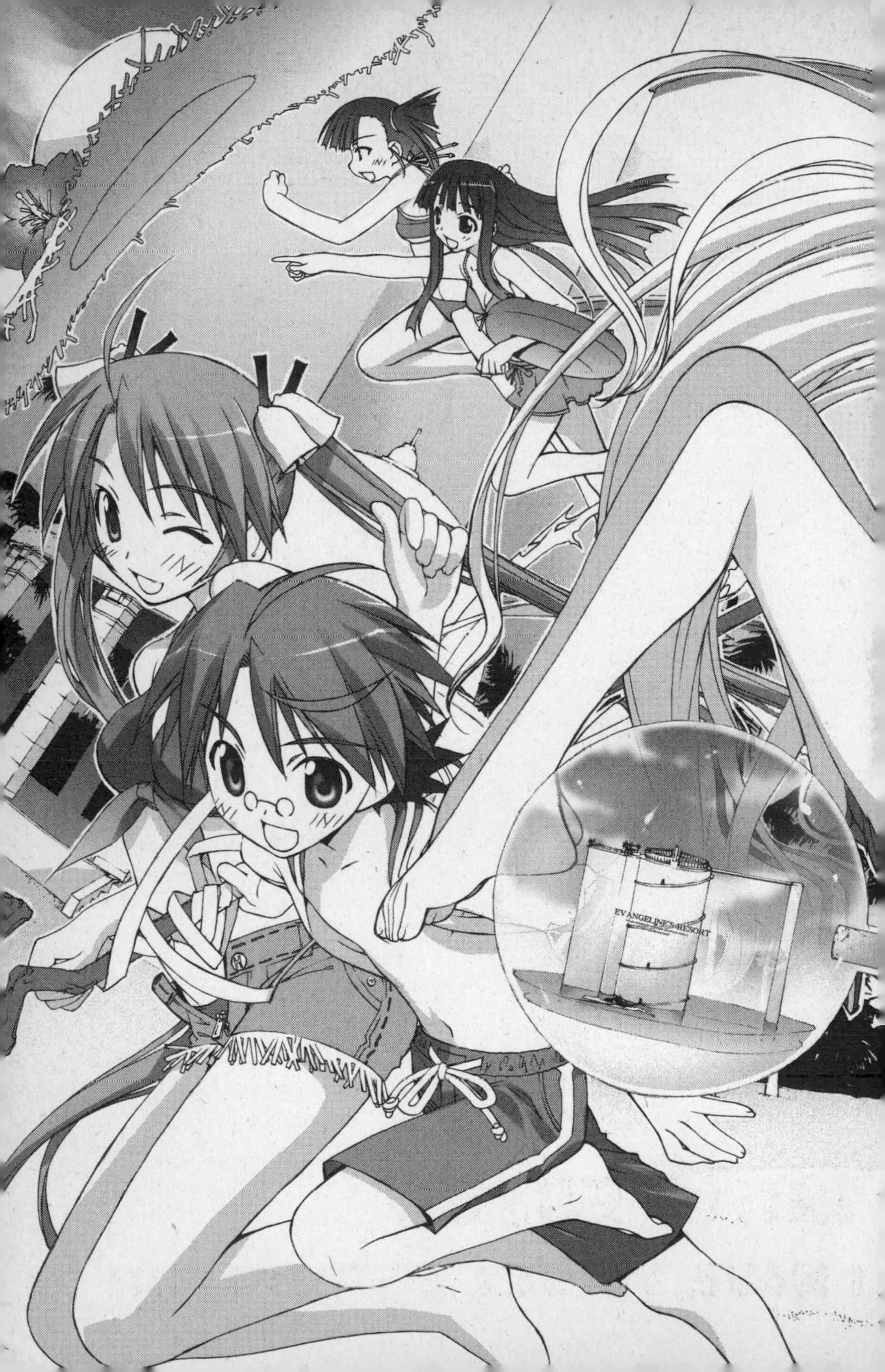
EVANGELINE'S RESORT

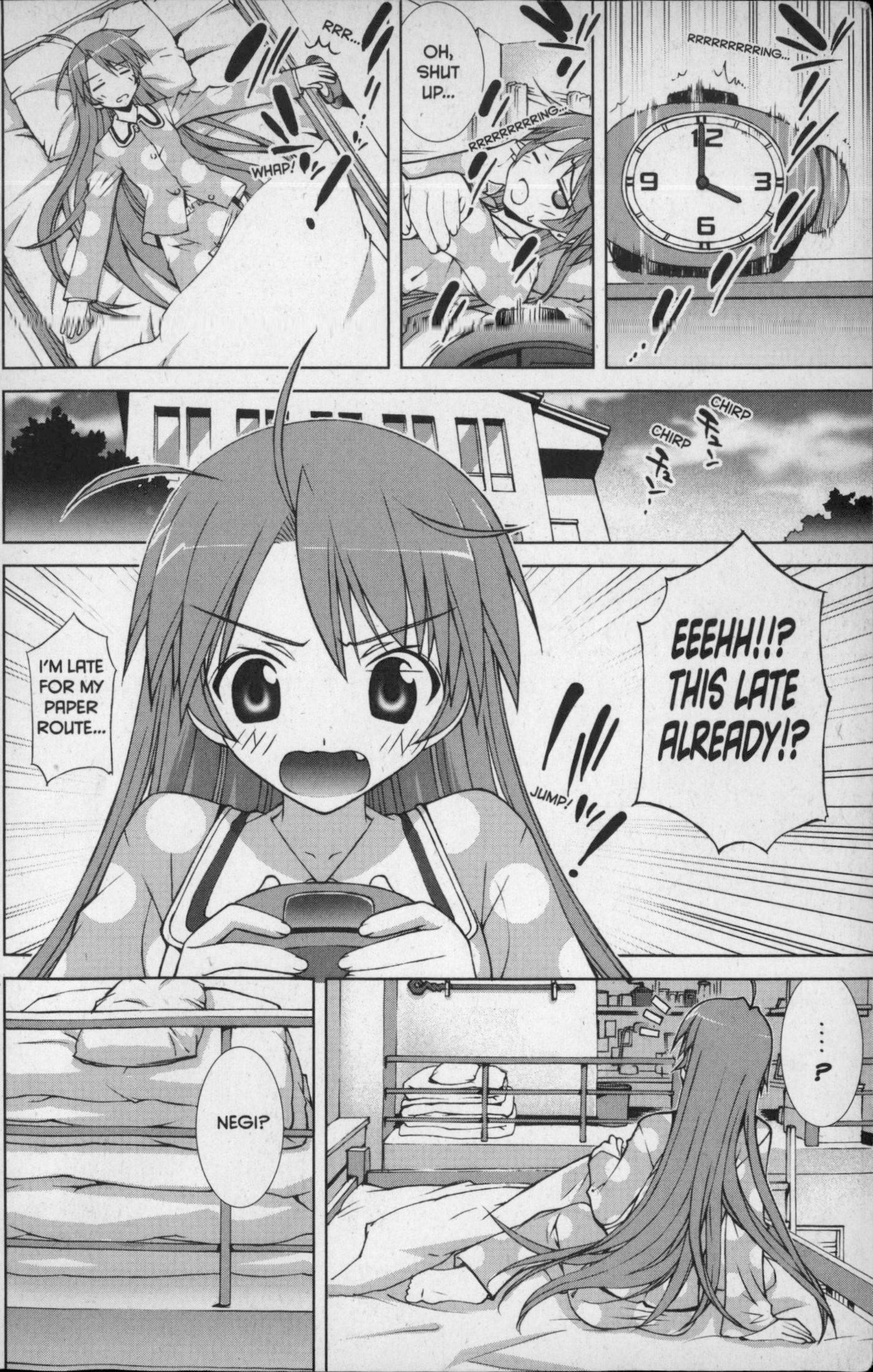
RRRRRRRRRING...
OH, SHUT UP...
RRRRRRRRRING...
RRR...
WHAP!
CHIRP
CHIRP
EEEHH!!? THIS LATE ALREADY!?
JUMP!
I'M LATE FOR MY PAPER ROUTE...
...?
NEGI?

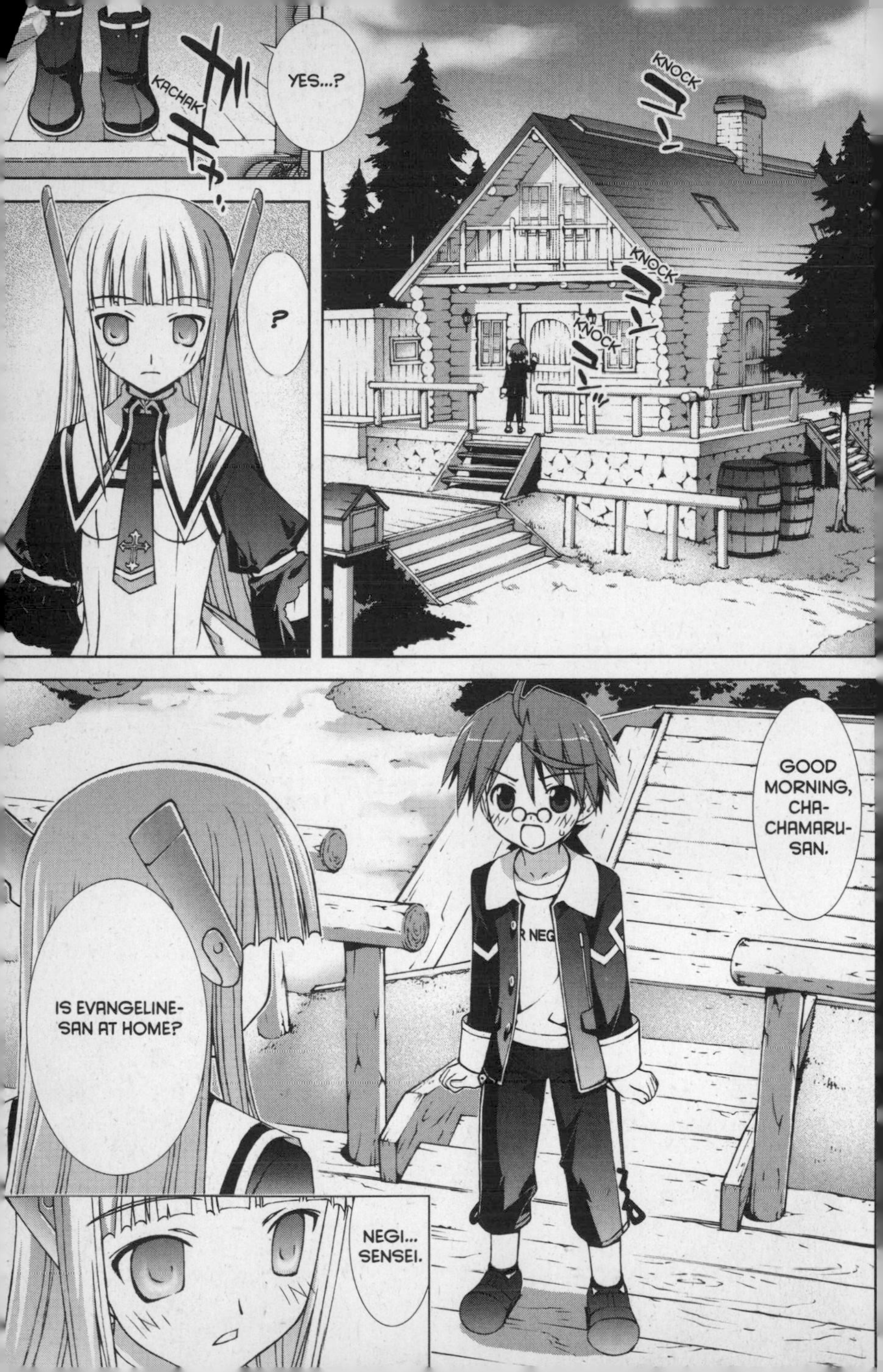
KNOCK
KNOCK
KNOCK
KACHAK
YES...?
?
GOOD MORNING, CHA-CHAMARU-SAN.
IS EVANGELINE-SAN AT HOME?
NEGI... SENSEI.

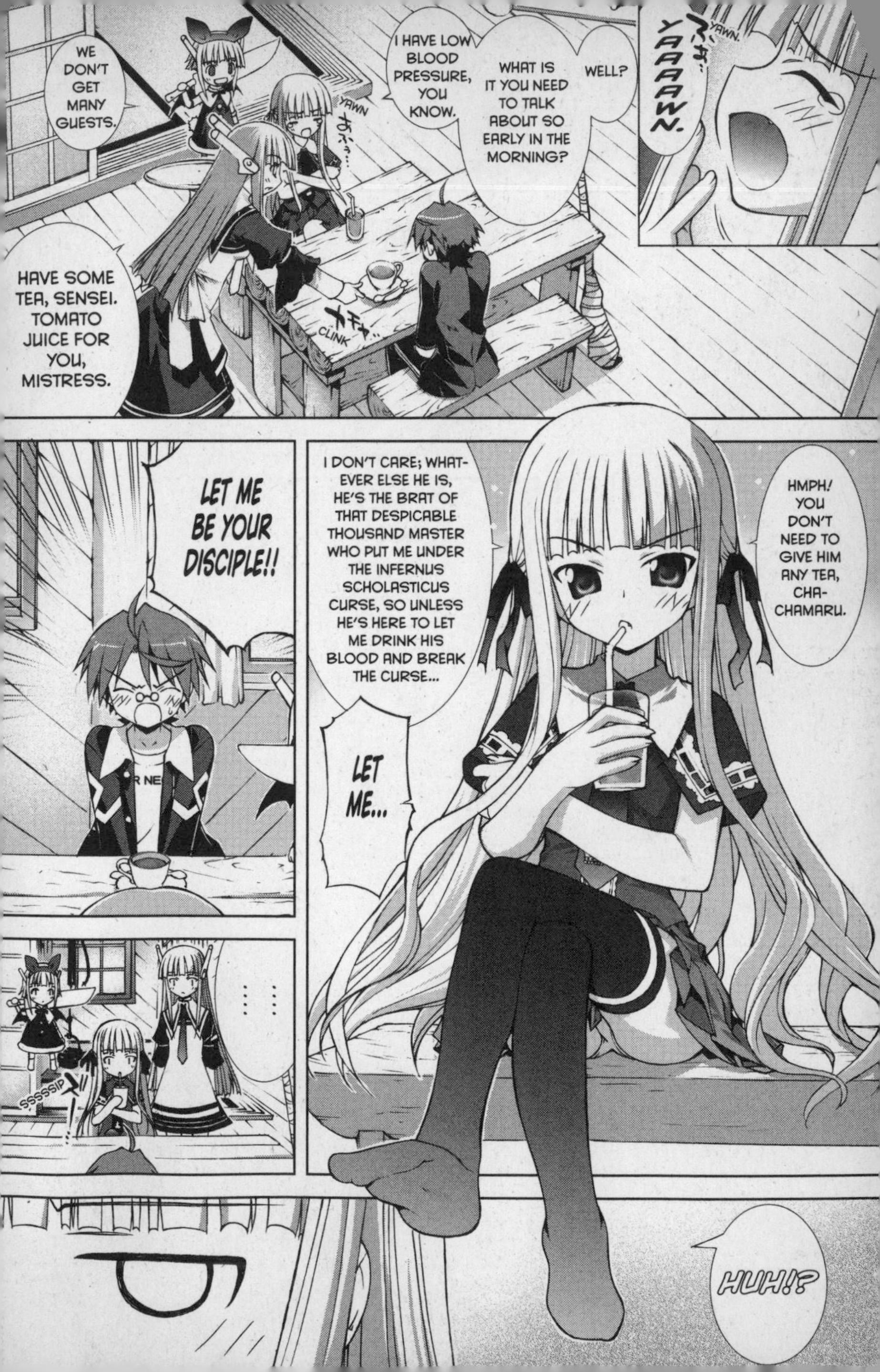

YAWN.
YAAAAAWN.
WELL?
WHAT IS IT YOU NEED TO TALK ABOUT SO EARLY IN THE MORNING?
I HAVE LOW BLOOD PRESSURE, YOU KNOW.
YAWN
WE DON'T GET MANY GUESTS.
CLINK
HAVE SOME TEA, SENSEI. TOMATO JUICE FOR YOU, MISTRESS.
HMPH! YOU DON'T NEED TO GIVE HIM ANY TEA, CHA-CHAMARU.
I DON'T CARE; WHAT-EVER ELSE HE IS, HE'S THE BRAT OF THAT DESPICABLE THOUSAND MASTER WHO PUT ME UNDER THE INFERNUS SCHOLASTICUS CURSE, SO UNLESS HE'S HERE TO LET ME DRINK HIS BLOOD AND BREAK THE CURSE...
LET ME...
LET ME BE YOUR DISCIPLE!!
......
SSSSSIP
HUH!?

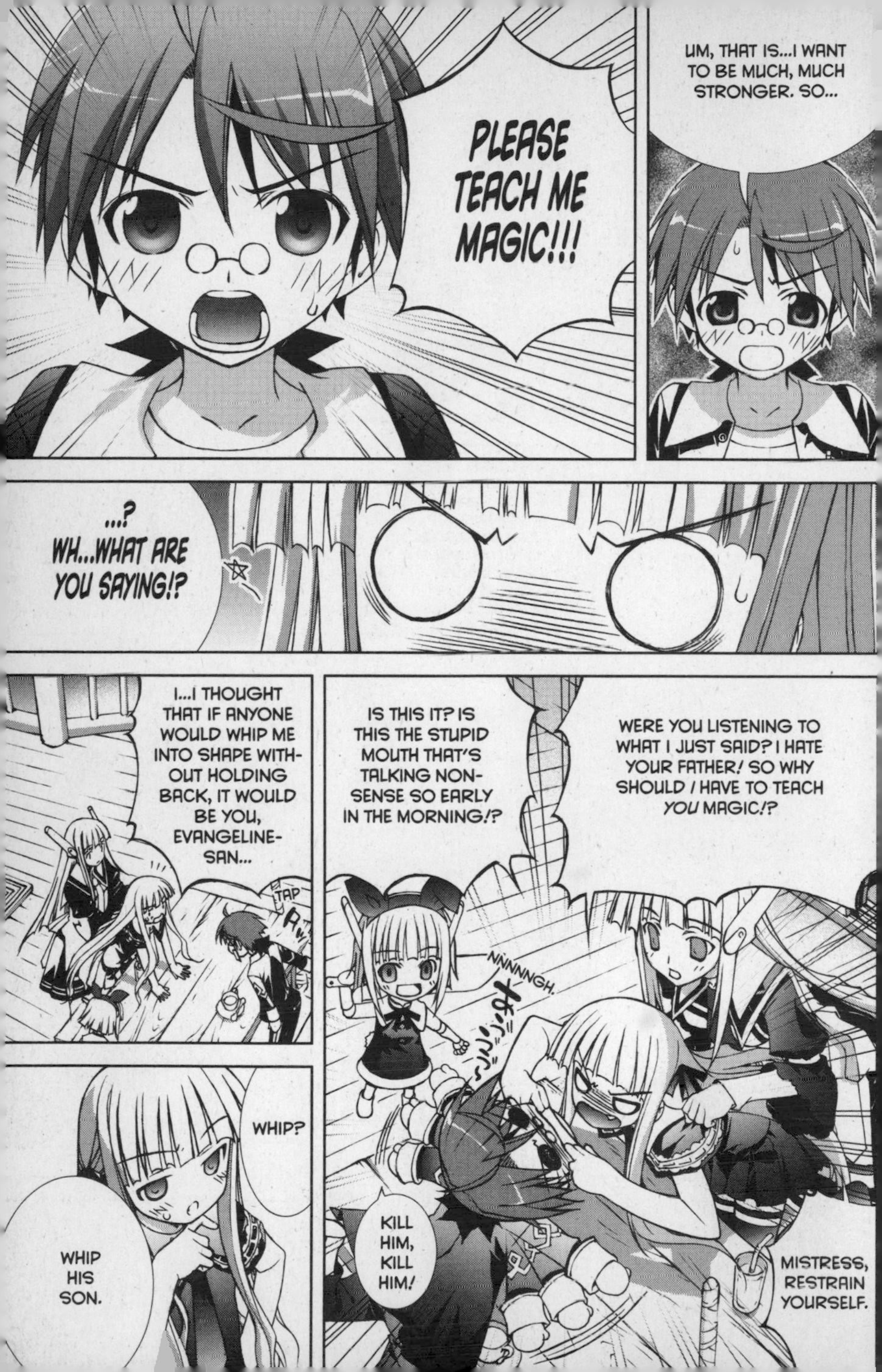
UM, THAT IS...I WANT TO BE MUCH, MUCH STRONGER. SO...
PLEASE TEACH ME MAGIC!!!
...? WH...WHAT ARE YOU SAYING!?
WERE YOU LISTENING TO WHAT I JUST SAID? I HATE YOUR FATHER! SO WHY SHOULD I HAVE TO TEACH YOU MAGIC!?
IS THIS IT? IS THIS THE STUPID MOUTH THAT'S TALKING NON-SENSE SO EARLY IN THE MORNING!?
NNNNNGH.
MISTRESS, RESTRAIN YOURSELF.
KILL HIM, KILL HIM!
I...I THOUGHT THAT IF ANYONE WOULD WHIP ME INTO SHAPE WITH-OUT HOLDING BACK, IT WOULD BE YOU, EVANGELINE-SAN...
TAP
WHIP?
WHIP HIS SON.

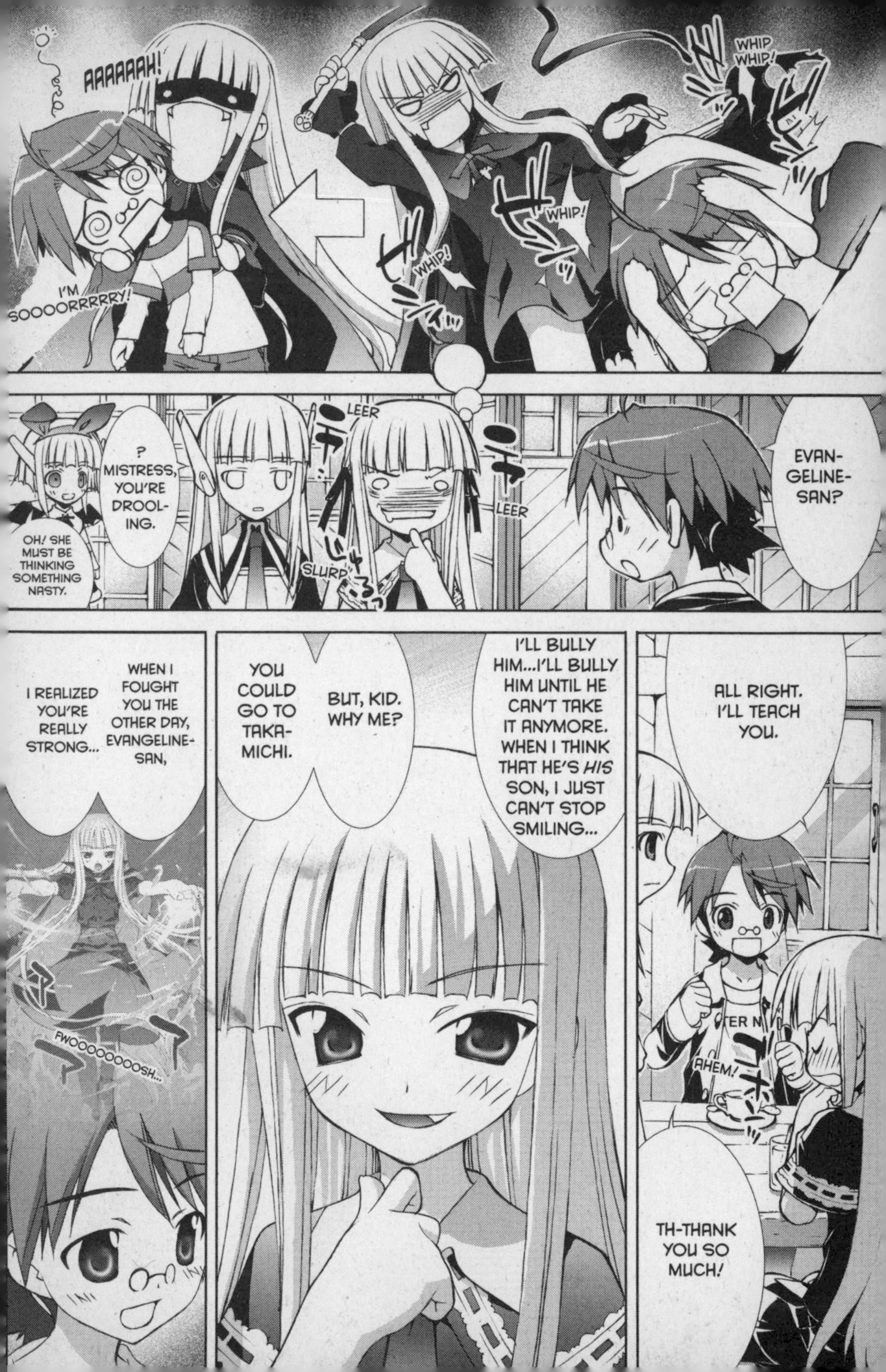
WHIP WHIP!
WHIP!
WHIP!
AAAAAAH!
I'M SOOOORRRRRY!
EVAN-GELINE-SAN?
LEER
LEER
SLURP
? MISTRESS, YOU'RE DROOL-ING.
OH! SHE MUST BE THINKING SOMETHING NASTY.
ALL RIGHT. I'LL TEACH YOU.
AHEM!
TH-THANK YOU SO MUCH!
I'LL BULLY HIM...I'LL BULLY HIM UNTIL HE CAN'T TAKE IT ANYMORE. WHEN I THINK THAT HE'S *HIS* SON, I JUST CAN'T STOP SMILING...
BUT, KID. WHY ME?
YOU COULD GO TO TAKA-MICHI.
WHEN I FOUGHT YOU THE OTHER DAY, EVANGELINE-SAN,
I REALIZED YOU'RE REALLY STRONG...
FWOOOOOOOOSH...

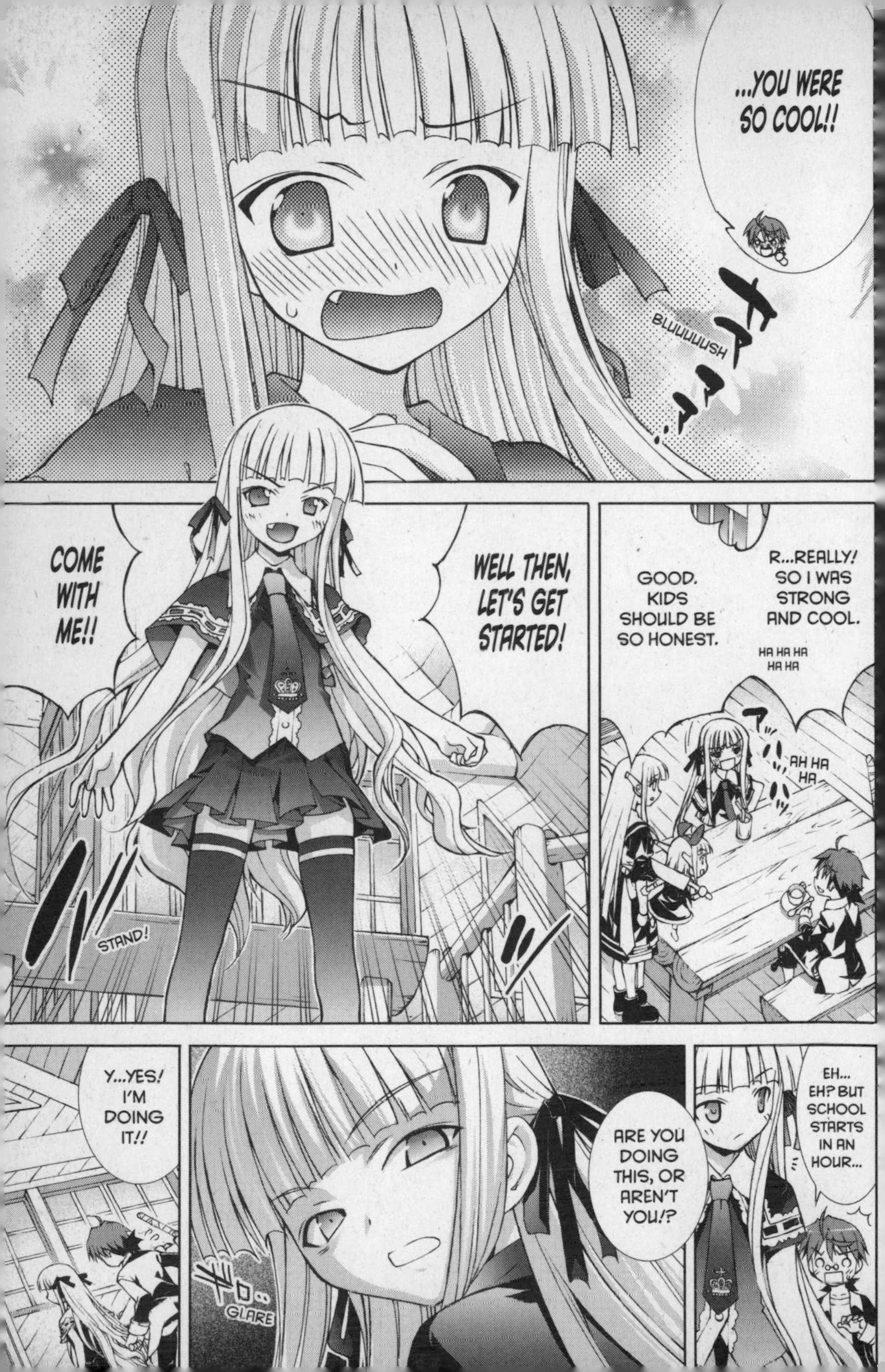
...YOU WERE SO COOL!!
BLUUUUUSH
R...REALLY! SO I WAS STRONG AND COOL.
HA HA HA HA HA
GOOD. KIDS SHOULD BE SO HONEST.
AH HA HA
WELL THEN, LET'S GET STARTED!
COME WITH ME!!
STAND!
EH... EH? BUT SCHOOL STARTS IN AN HOUR...
ARE YOU DOING THIS, OR AREN'T YOU!?
GLARE
Y...YES! I'M DOING IT!!

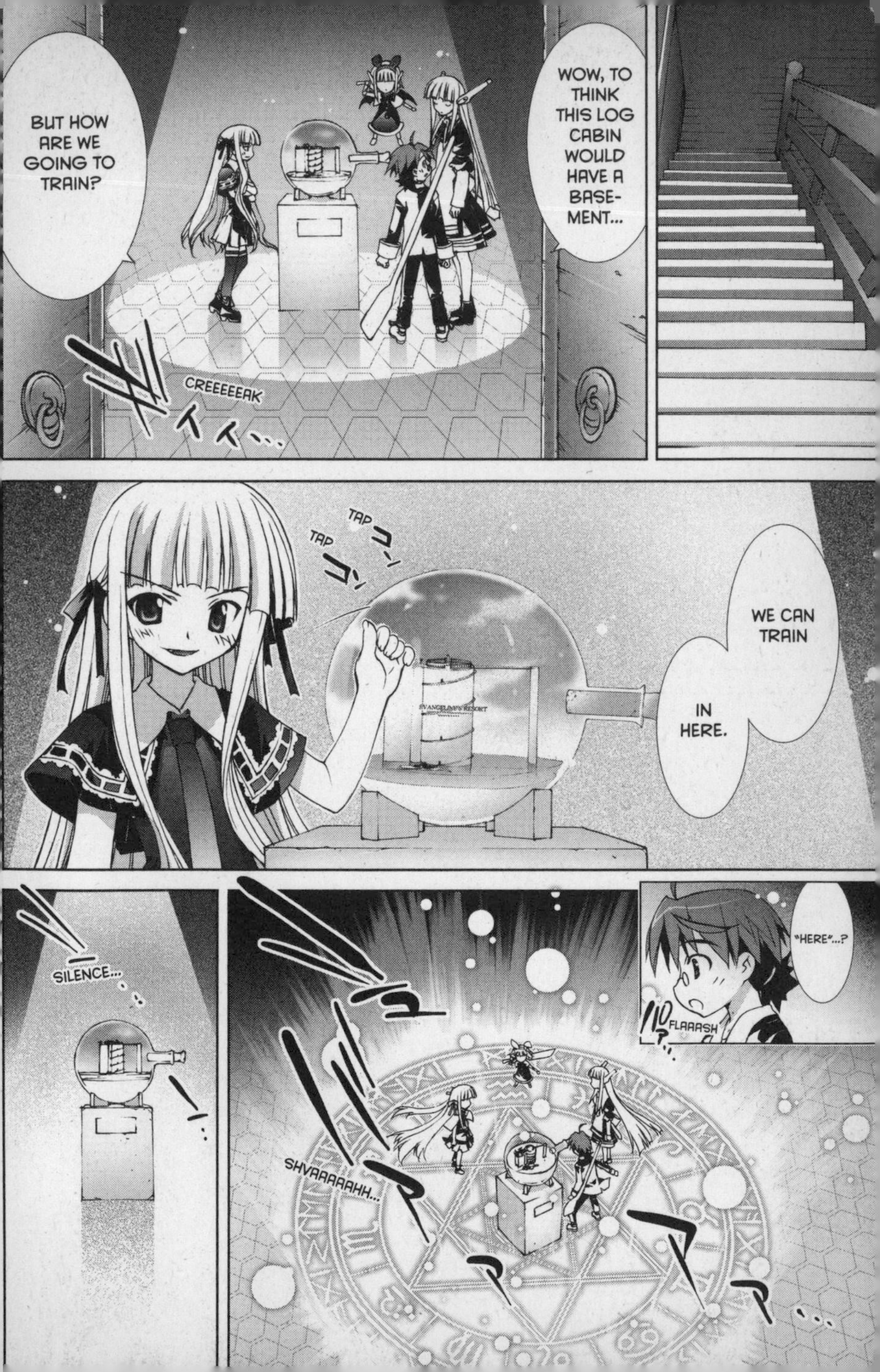

WOW, TO THINK THIS LOG CABIN WOULD HAVE A BASE-MENT...
BUT HOW ARE WE GOING TO TRAIN?
CREEEEEAK
TAP
TAP
WE CAN TRAIN
IN HERE.
"HERE"...?
FLAAASH
SHVAAAAAHH...
SILENCE...

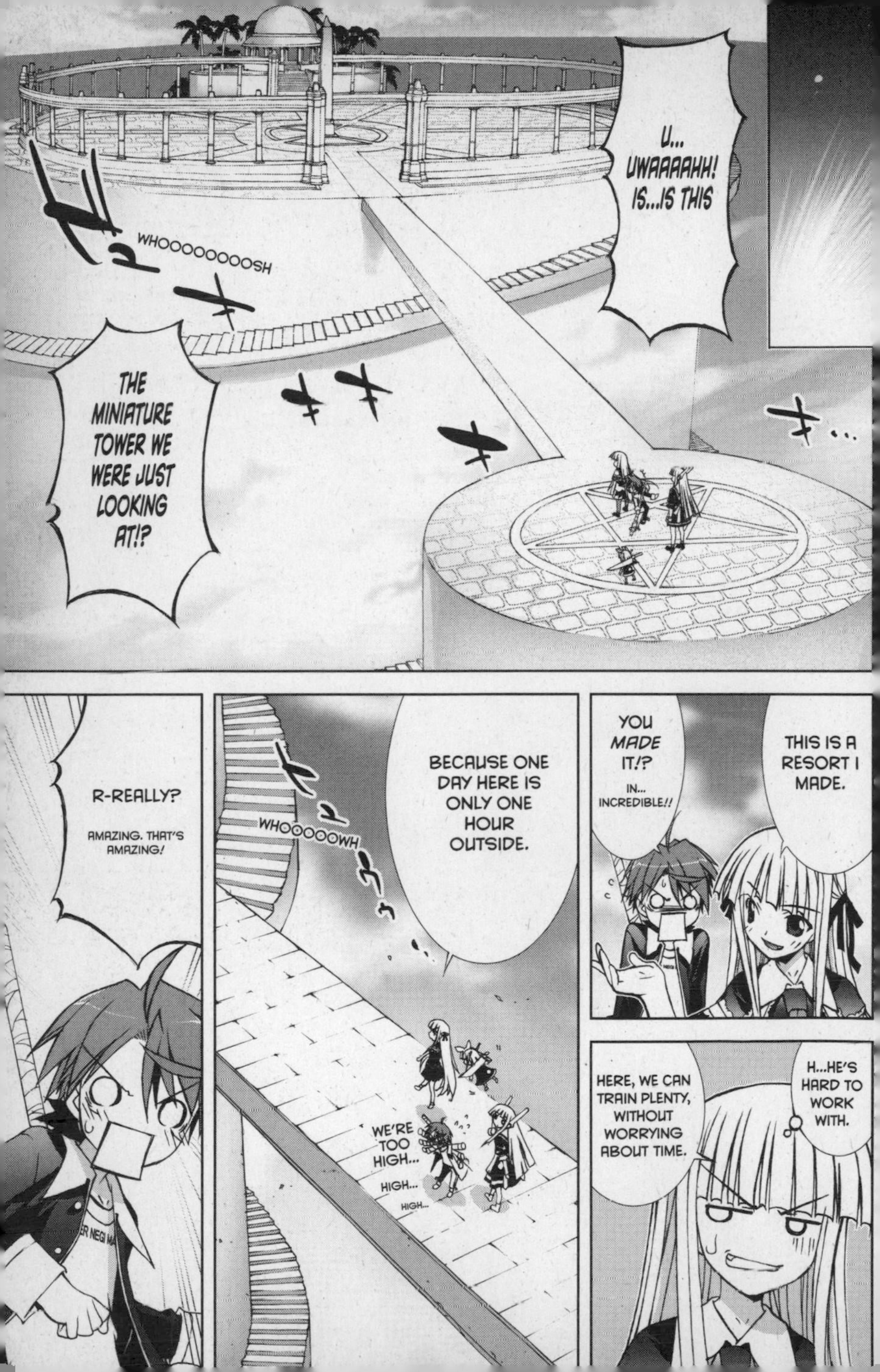
U... UWAAAAHH! IS...IS THIS
WHOOOOOOOOSH
THE MINIATURE TOWER WE WERE JUST LOOKING AT!?
THIS IS A RESORT I MADE.
YOU MADE IT!?
IN... INCREDIBLE!!
H...HE'S HARD TO WORK WITH.
HERE, WE CAN TRAIN PLENTY, WITHOUT WORRYING ABOUT TIME.
BECAUSE ONE DAY HERE IS ONLY ONE HOUR OUTSIDE.
WHOOOOOWH
WE'RE TOO HIGH...
HIGH...
HIGH...
R-REALLY?
AMAZING. THAT'S AMAZING!

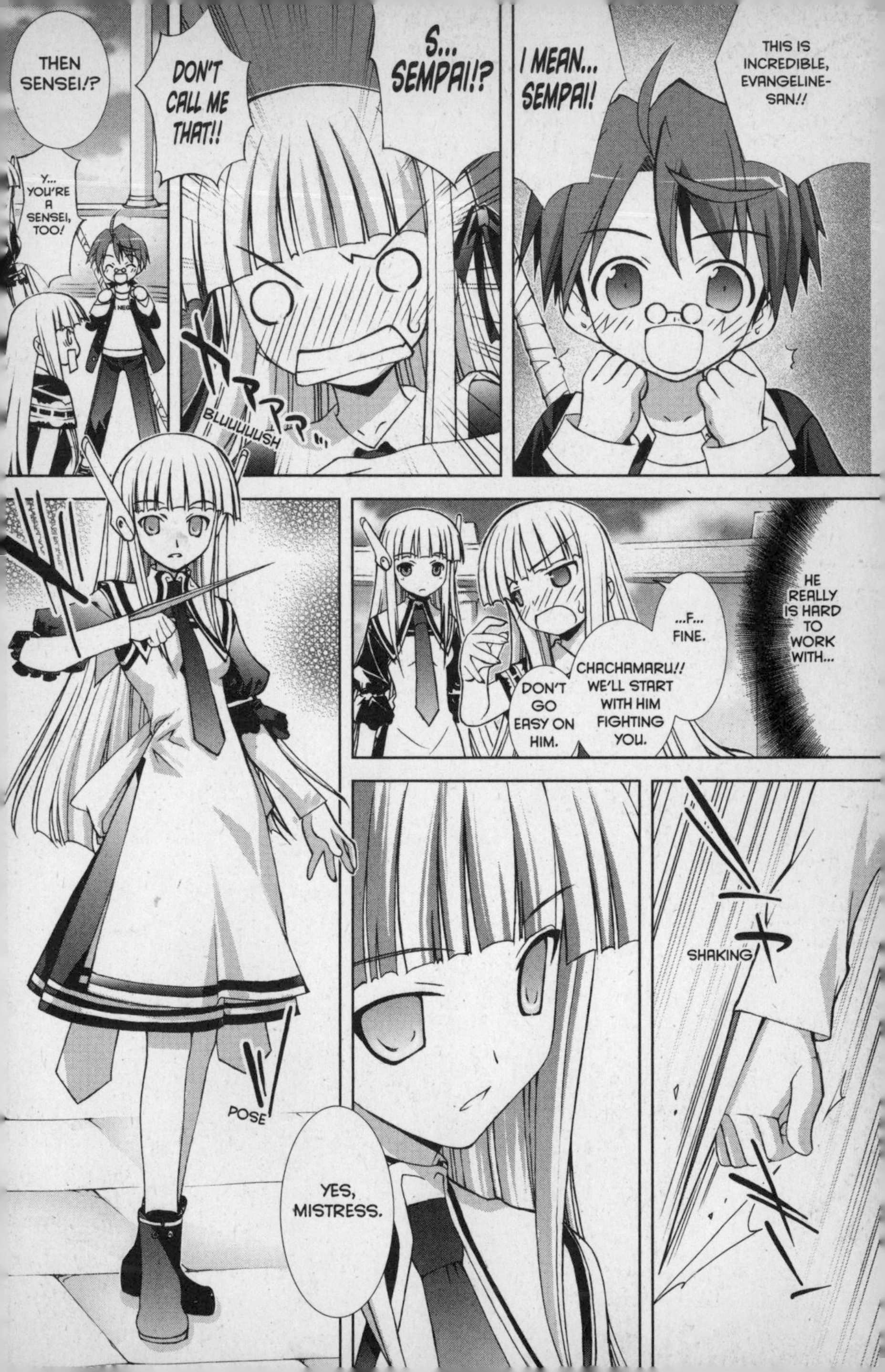
THIS IS INCREDIBLE, EVANGELINE-SAN!!
I MEAN... SEMPAI!
S... SEMPAI!?
DON'T CALL ME THAT!!
BLUUUUUSH
THEN SENSEI!?
Y... YOU'RE A SENSEI, TOO!
HE REALLY IS HARD TO WORK WITH...
...F... FINE.
CHACHAMARU!! WE'LL START WITH HIM FIGHTING YOU.
DON'T GO EASY ON HIM.
SHAKING
YES, MISTRESS.
POSE

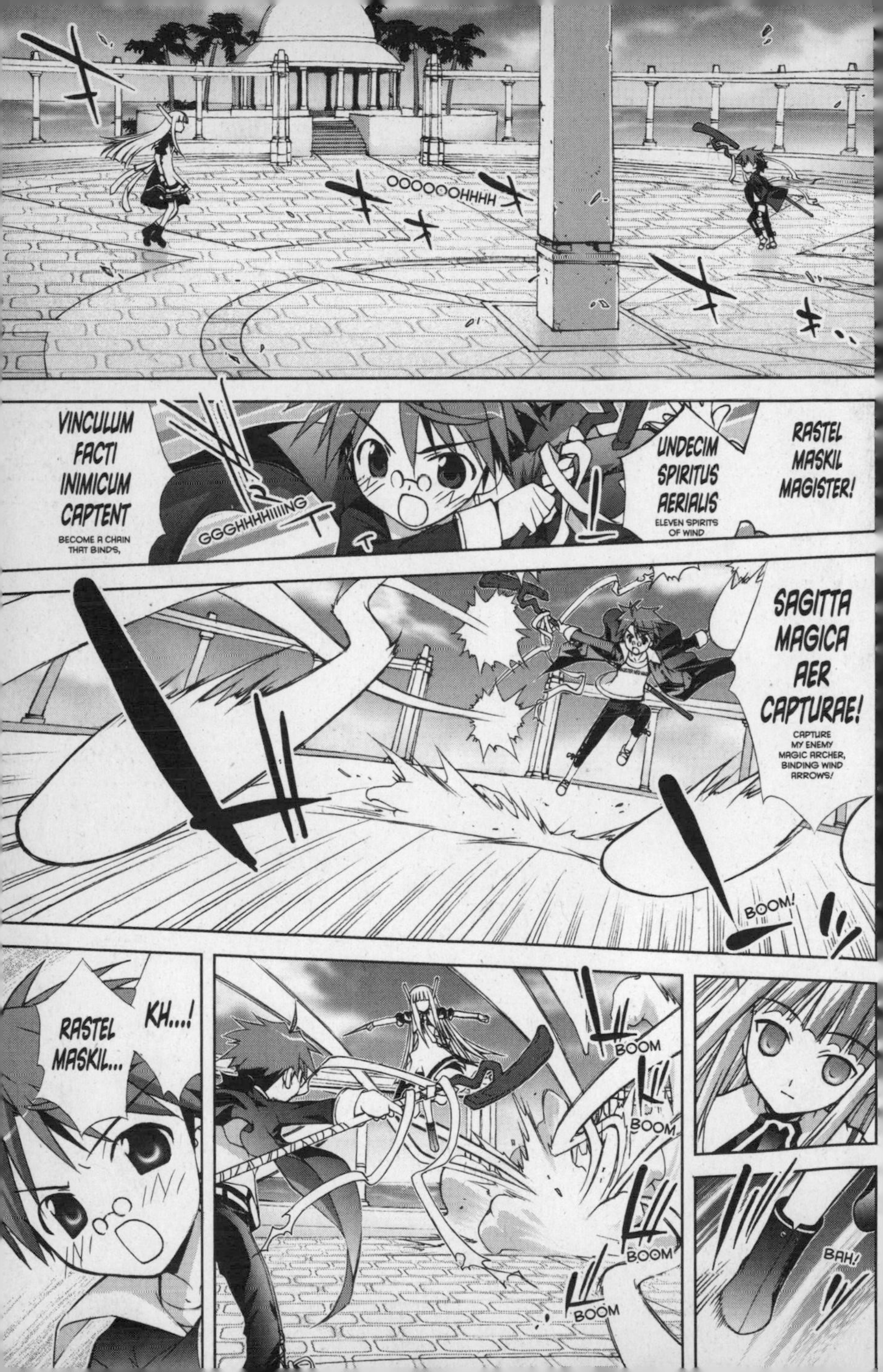
OOOOOOOHHHH
RASTEL MASKIL MAGISTER!
UNDECIM SPIRITUS AERIALIS
ELEVEN SPIRITS OF WIND
GGGHHHHIIIING
VINCULUM FACTI INIMICUM CAPTENT
BECOME A CHAIN THAT BINDS,
SAGITTA MAGICA AER CAPTURAE!
CAPTURE MY ENEMY MAGIC ARCHER, BINDING WIND ARROWS!
BOOM!
BAH!
BOOM
BOOM
BOOM
BOOM
KH...!
RASTEL MASKIL...

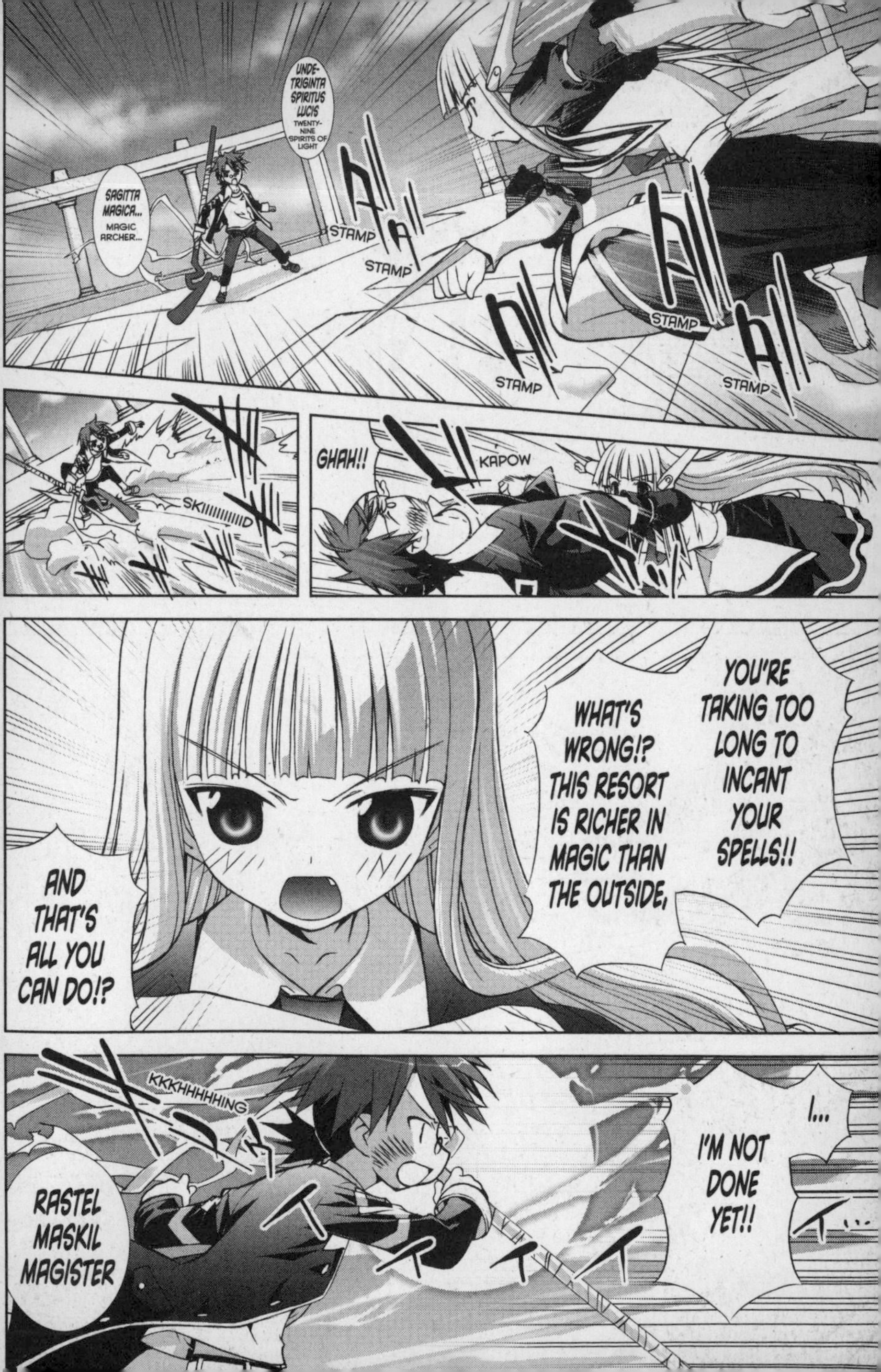
STAMP
STAMP
STAMP
STAMP
STAMP
STAMP
UNDE-TRIGINTA SPIRITUS LUCIS
TWENTY-NINE SPIRITS OF LIGHT
SAGITTA MAGICA...
MAGIC ARCHER...
KAPOW
GHAH!!
SKIIIIIIIIIID
YOU'RE TAKING TOO LONG TO INCANT YOUR SPELLS!!
WHAT'S WRONG!? THIS RESORT IS RICHER IN MAGIC THAN THE OUTSIDE,
AND THAT'S ALL YOU CAN DO!?
I...
I'M NOT DONE YET!!
KKKHHHHHHING
RASTEL MASKIL MAGISTER

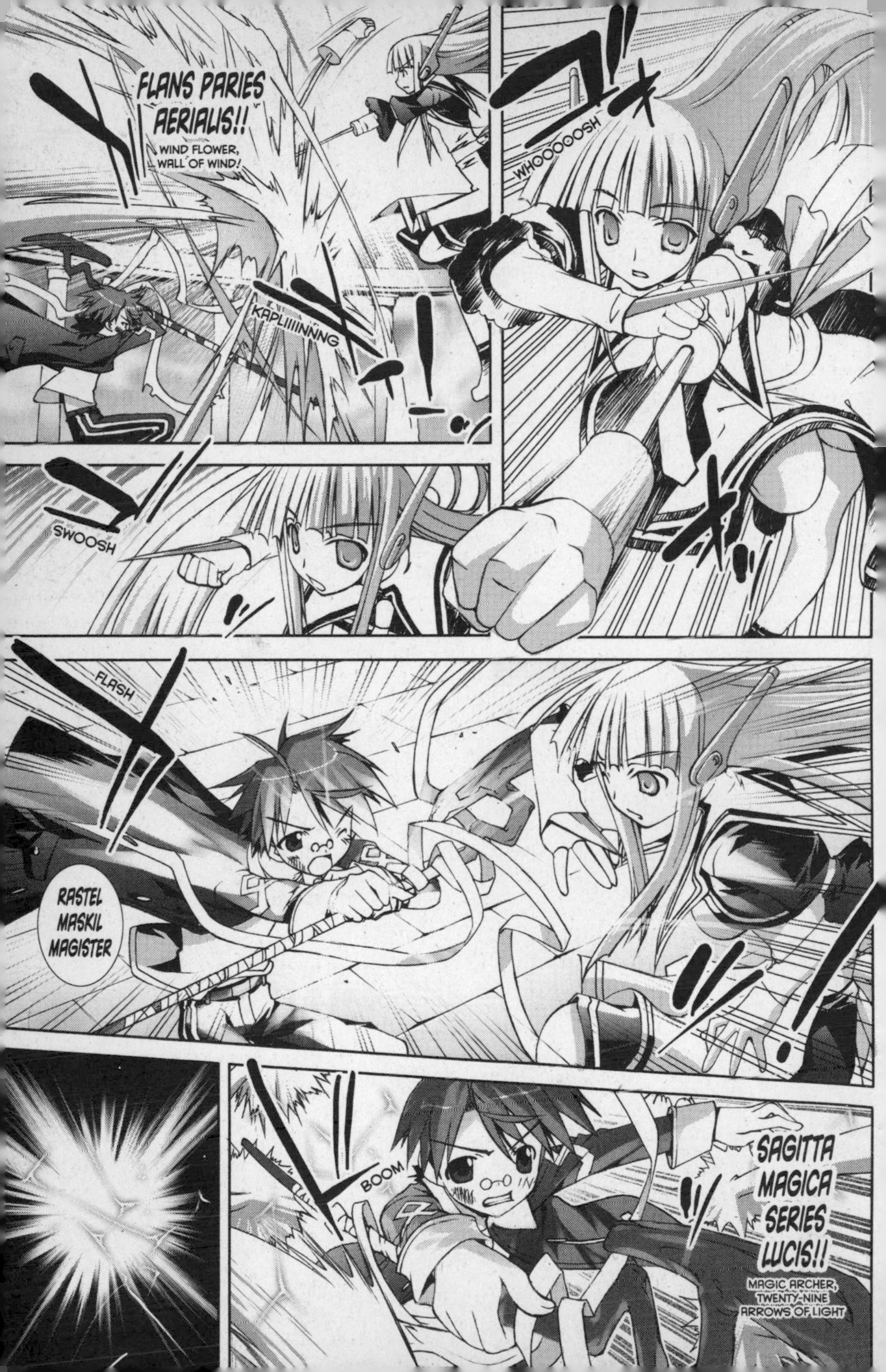
WHOOOOOOSH
FLANS PARIES AERIALIS!!
WIND FLOWER, WALL OF WIND!
KAPLIIIINNNG
SWOOSH
FLASH
RASTEL MASKIL MAGISTER
SAGITTA MAGICA SERIES LUCIS!!
MAGIC ARCHER, TWENTY-NINE ARROWS OF LIGHT
BOOM

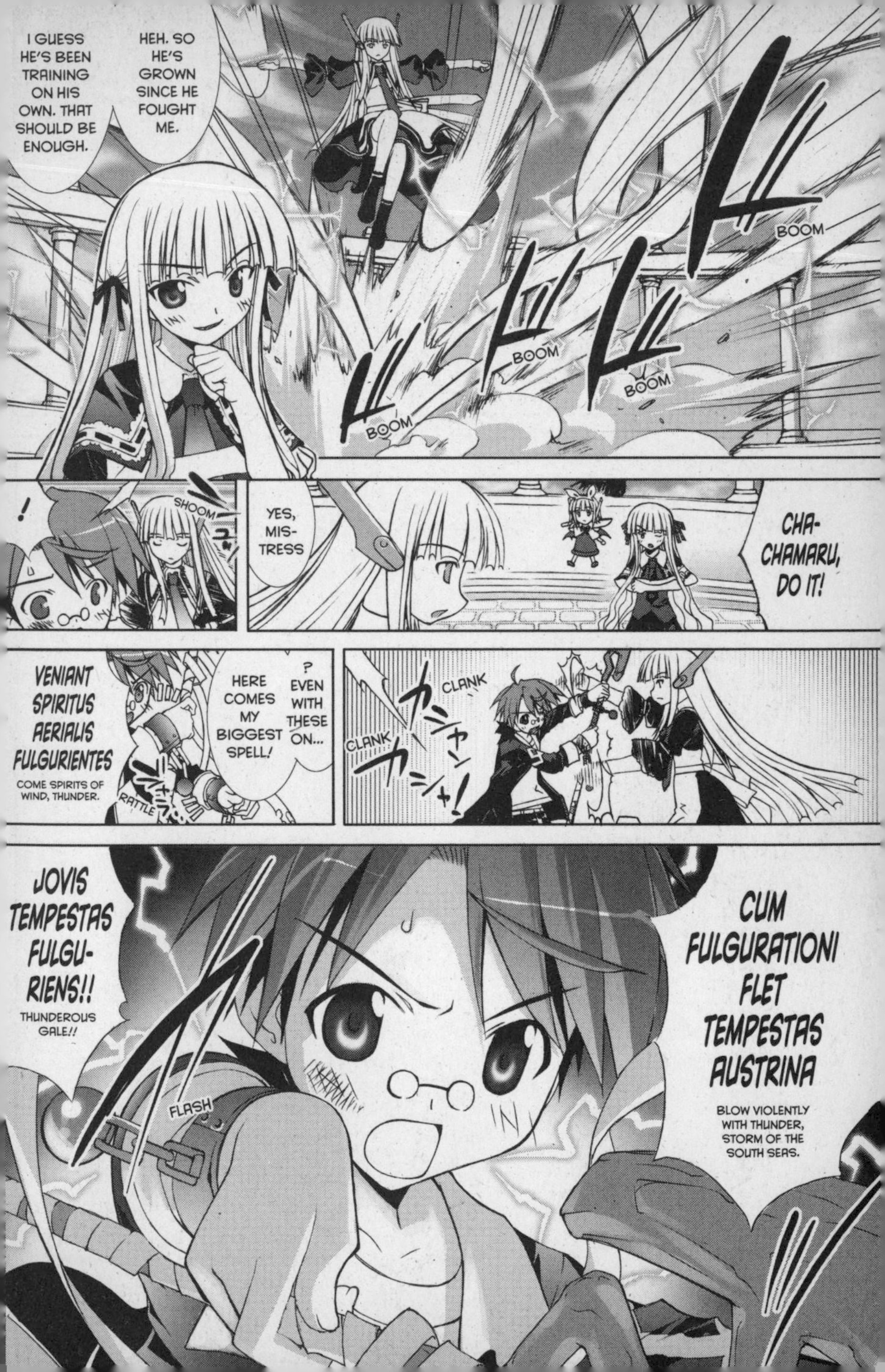
HEH. SO HE'S GROWN SINCE HE FOUGHT ME.
I GUESS HE'S BEEN TRAINING ON HIS OWN. THAT SHOULD BE ENOUGH.
BOOM
BOOM
BOOM
BOOM
CHA-CHAMARU, DO IT!
YES, MISTRESS
SHOOM
!
CLANK
CLANK
? EVEN WITH THESE ON...
HERE COMES MY BIGGEST SPELL!
VENIANT SPIRITUS AERIALIS FULGURIENTES
COME SPIRITS OF WIND, THUNDER.
RATTLE
CUM FULGURATIONI FLET TEMPESTAS AUSTRINA
BLOW VIOLENTLY WITH THUNDER, STORM OF THE SOUTH SEAS.
JOVIS TEMPESTAS FULGU-RIENS!!
THUNDEROUS GALE!!
FLASH

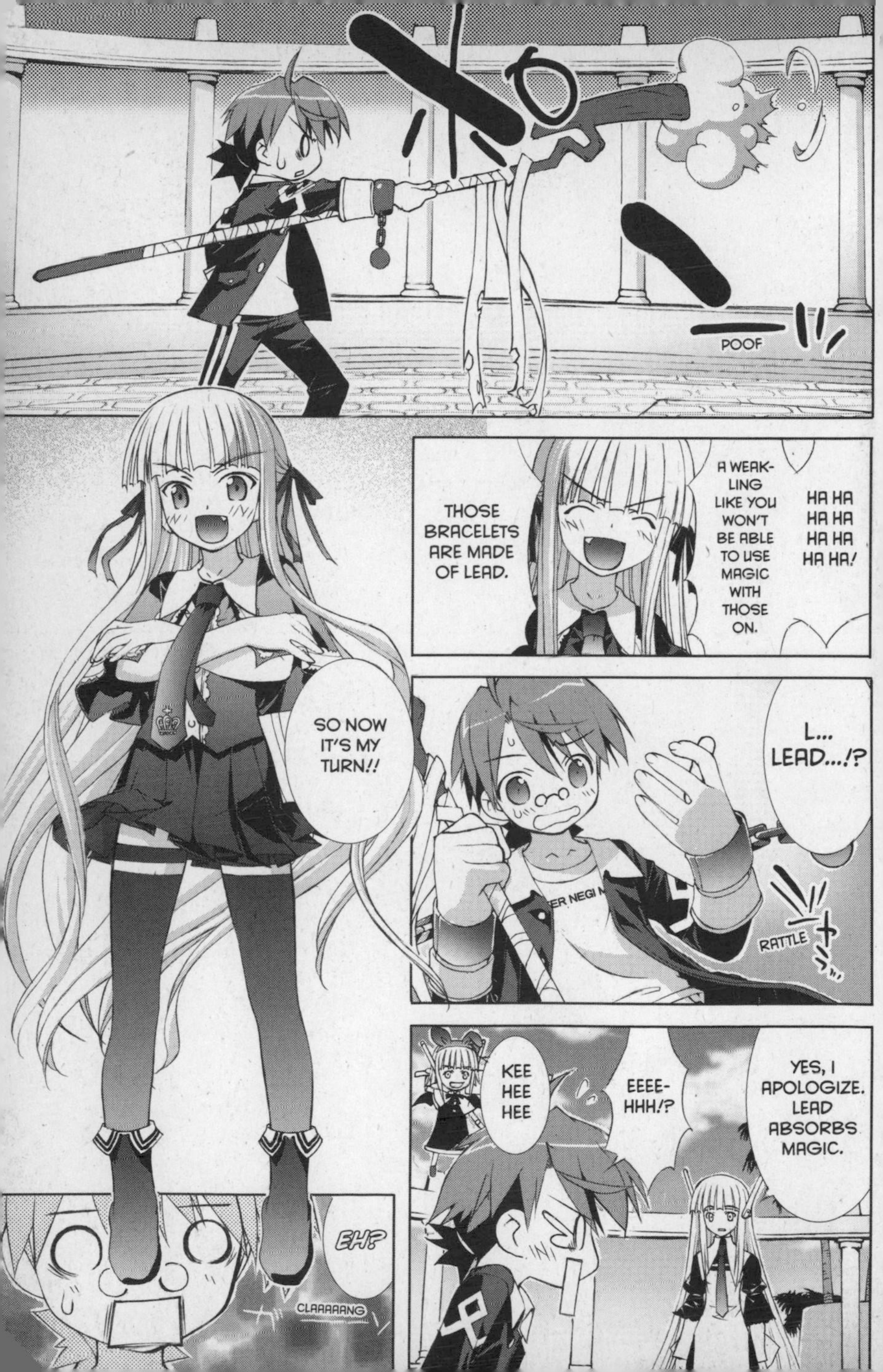
POOF
THOSE BRACELETS ARE MADE OF LEAD.
A WEAKLING LIKE YOU WON'T BE ABLE TO USE MAGIC WITH THOSE ON.
HA HA HA HA HA HA HA HA!
L... LEAD...!?
RATTLE
YES, I APOLOGIZE. LEAD ABSORBS MAGIC.
EEEE-HHH!?
KEE HEE HEE
SO NOW IT'S MY TURN!!
EH?
CLAAAAANG

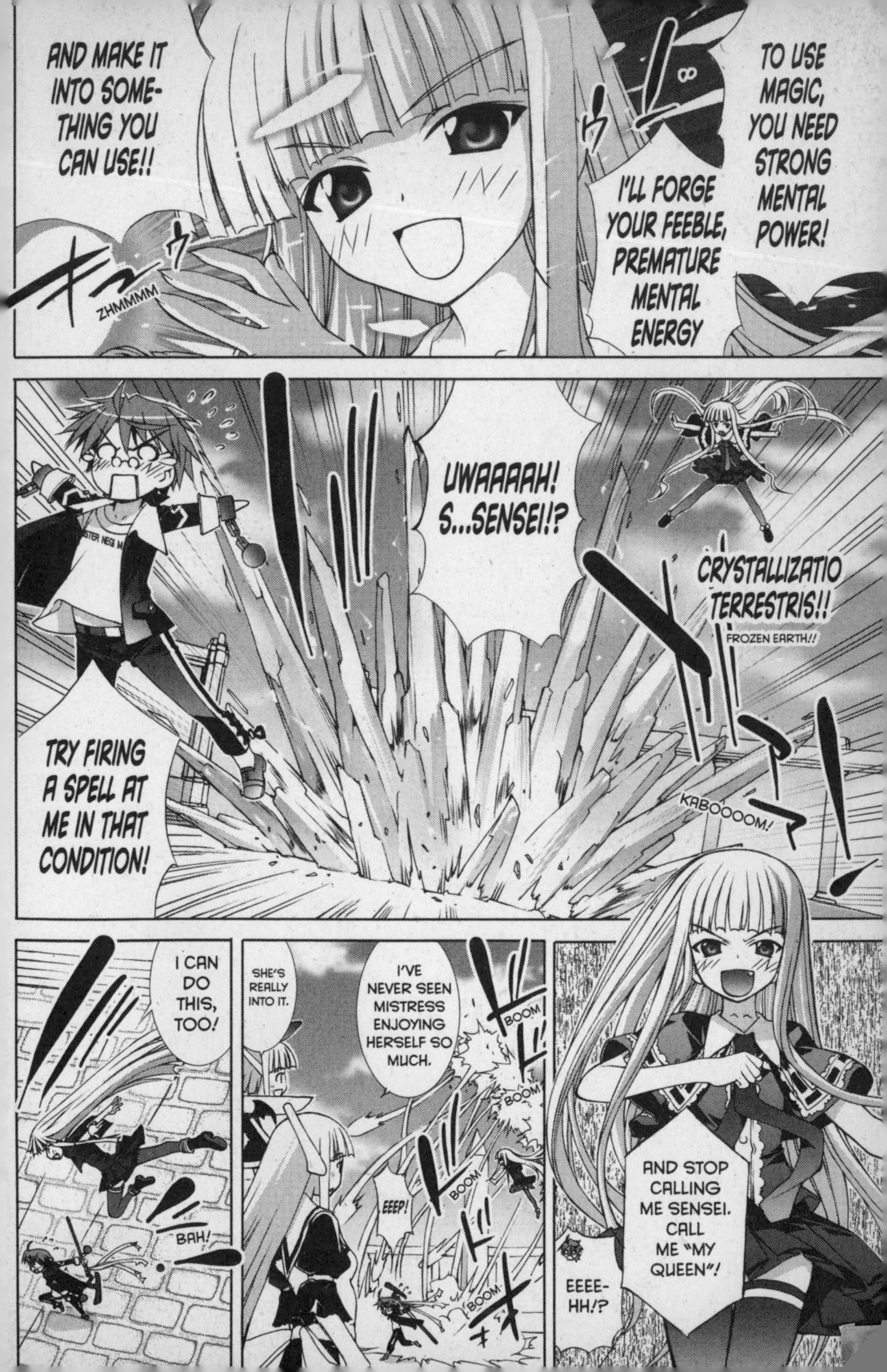
TO USE MAGIC, YOU NEED STRONG MENTAL POWER!
I'LL FORGE YOUR FEEBLE, PREMATURE MENTAL ENERGY
AND MAKE IT INTO SOME-THING YOU CAN USE!!
ZHMMMM
CRYSTALLIZATIO TERRESTRIS!!
FROZEN EARTH!!
KABOOOOM!
UWAAAAH! S...SENSEI!?
TRY FIRING A SPELL AT ME IN THAT CONDITION!
AND STOP CALLING ME SENSEI. CALL ME "MY QUEEN"!
EEEE-HH!?
I'VE NEVER SEEN MISTRESS ENJOYING HERSELF SO MUCH.
SHE'S REALLY INTO IT.
BOOM
BOOM
BOOM
EEEP!
BOOM
I CAN DO THIS, TOO!
BAH!

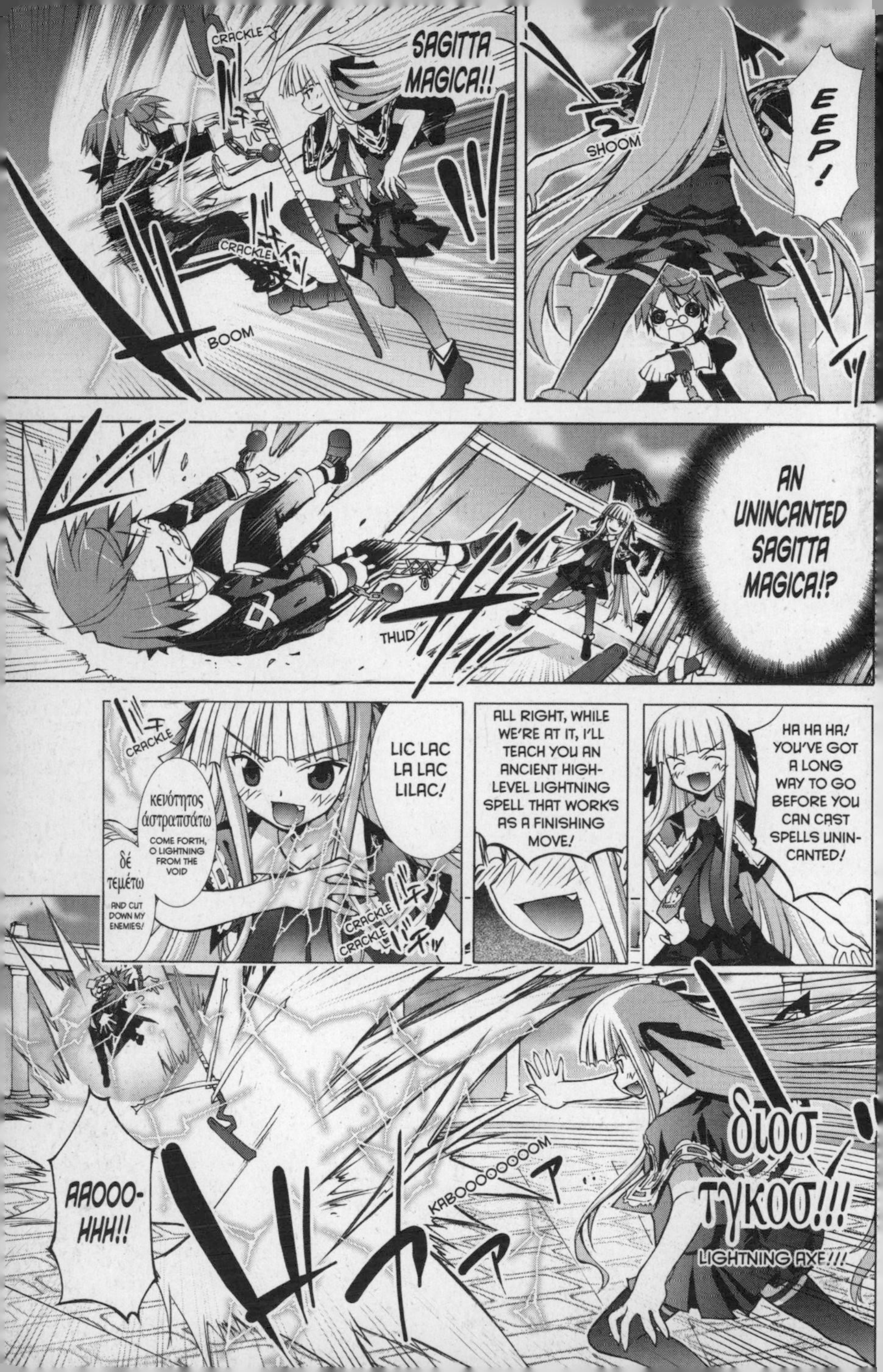
EEP!
SHOOM
SAGITTA MAGICA!!
CRACKLE
CRACKLE
BOOM
AN UNINCANTED SAGITTA MAGICA!?
THUD
HA HA HA! YOU'VE GOT A LONG WAY TO GO BEFORE YOU CAN CAST SPELLS UNIN-CANTED!
ALL RIGHT, WHILE WE'RE AT IT, I'LL TEACH YOU AN ANCIENT HIGH-LEVEL LIGHTNING SPELL THAT WORKS AS A FINISHING MOVE!
LIC LAC LA LAC LILAC!
CRACKLE
κενότητος ἀστραπσάτω
COME FORTH, O LIGHTNING FROM THE VOID
δέ τεμέτω
AND CUT DOWN MY ENEMIES!
CRACKLE CRACKLE
διοσ τγκοσ!!!
LIGHTNING AXE!!!
KABOOOOOOOOOM
AAOOOO-HHH!!

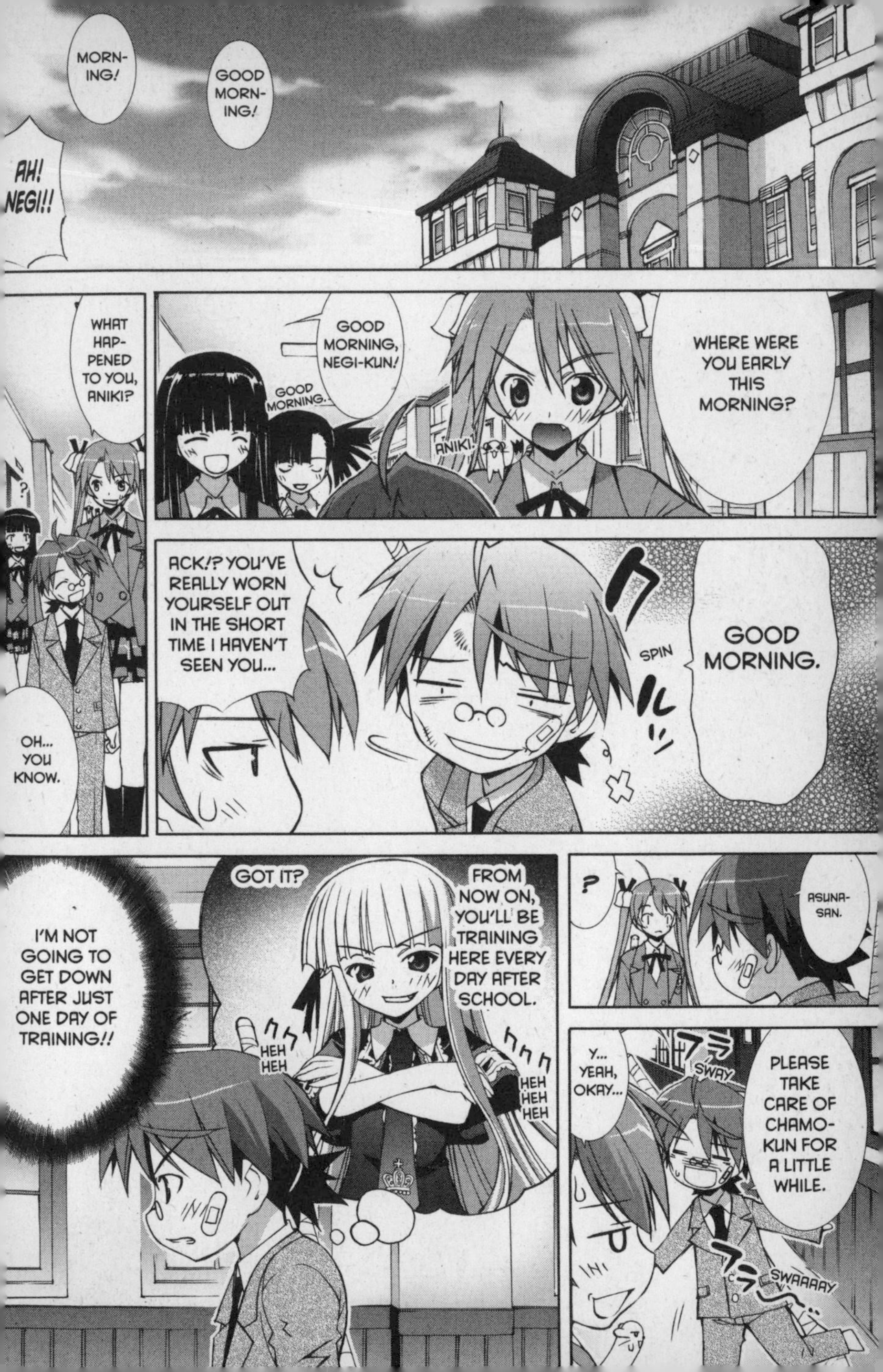

GOOD MORNING!
MORNING!
AH! NEGI!!
WHERE WERE YOU EARLY THIS MORNING?
ANIKI.
GOOD MORNING, NEGI-KUN!
GOOD MORNING...
GOOD MORNING.
SPIN
ACK!? YOU'VE REALLY WORN YOURSELF OUT IN THE SHORT TIME I HAVEN'T SEEN YOU...
WHAT HAPPENED TO YOU, ANIKI?
?
OH... YOU KNOW.
ASUNA-SAN.
?
PLEASE TAKE CARE OF CHAMO-KUN FOR A LITTLE WHILE.
SWAY
Y... YEAH, OKAY...
SWAAAAY
FROM NOW ON, YOU'LL BE TRAINING HERE EVERY DAY AFTER SCHOOL.
GOT IT?
HEH HEH HEH
HEH HEH
I'M NOT GOING TO GET DOWN AFTER JUST ONE DAY OF TRAINING!!

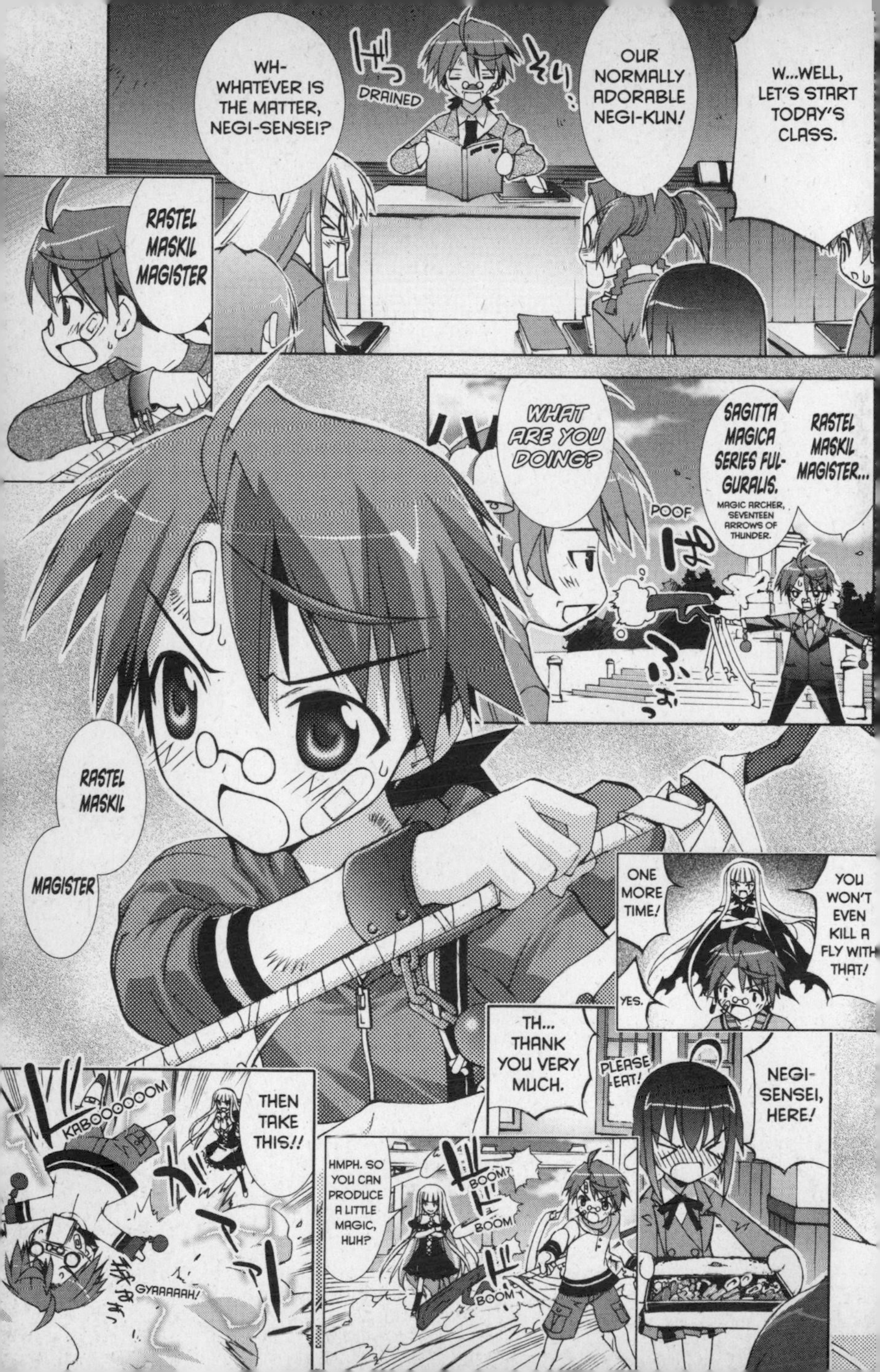
W...WELL, LET'S START TODAY'S CLASS.
OUR NORMALLY ADORABLE NEGI-KUN!
DRAINED
WH- WHATEVER IS THE MATTER, NEGI-SENSEI?
RASTEL MASKIL MAGISTER
RASTEL MASKIL MAGISTER...
SAGITTA MAGICA SERIES FUL-GURALIS.
MAGIC ARCHER, SEVENTEEN ARROWS OF THUNDER.
POOF
WHAT ARE YOU DOING?
RASTEL MASKIL
MAGISTER
YOU WON'T EVEN KILL A FLY WITH THAT!
ONE MORE TIME!
YES.
NEGI-SENSEI, HERE!
PLEASE EAT!
TH... THANK YOU VERY MUCH.
HMPH. SO YOU CAN PRODUCE A LITTLE MAGIC, HUH?
BOOM
BOOM
BOOM
THEN TAKE THIS!!
KABOOOOOOM
GYAAAAAH!

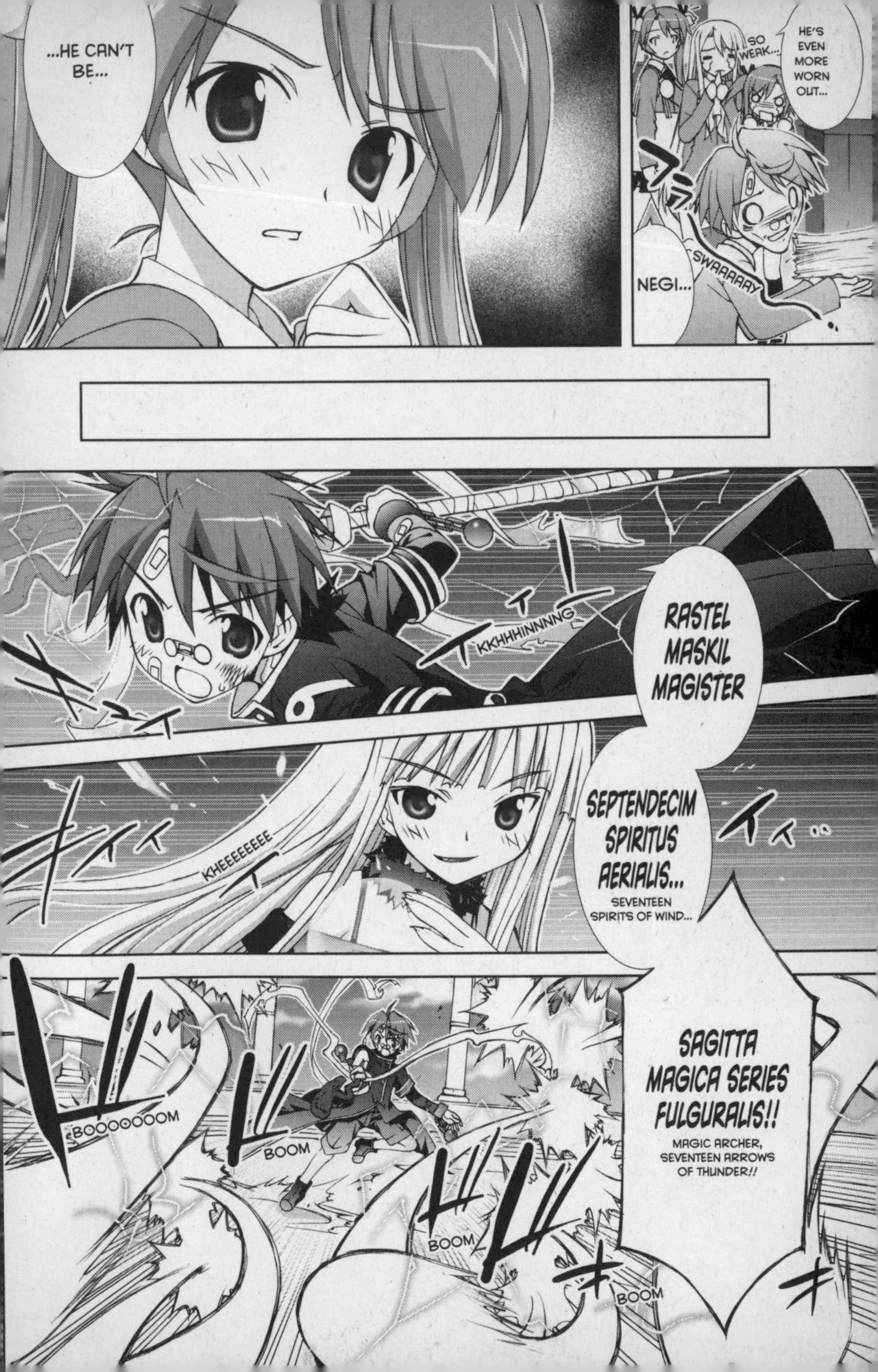

HE'S EVEN MORE WORN OUT...
SO WEAK...
SWAAAAAY
NEGI...
...HE CAN'T BE...
RASTEL MASKIL MAGISTER
KKHHHINNNNG
SEPTENDECIM SPIRITUS AERIALIS...
SEVENTEEN SPIRITS OF WIND...
KHEEEEEEEE
SAGITTA MAGICA SERIES FULGURALIS!!
MAGIC ARCHER, SEVENTEEN ARROWS OF THUNDER!!
BOOOOOOOM
BOOM
BOOM
BOOM

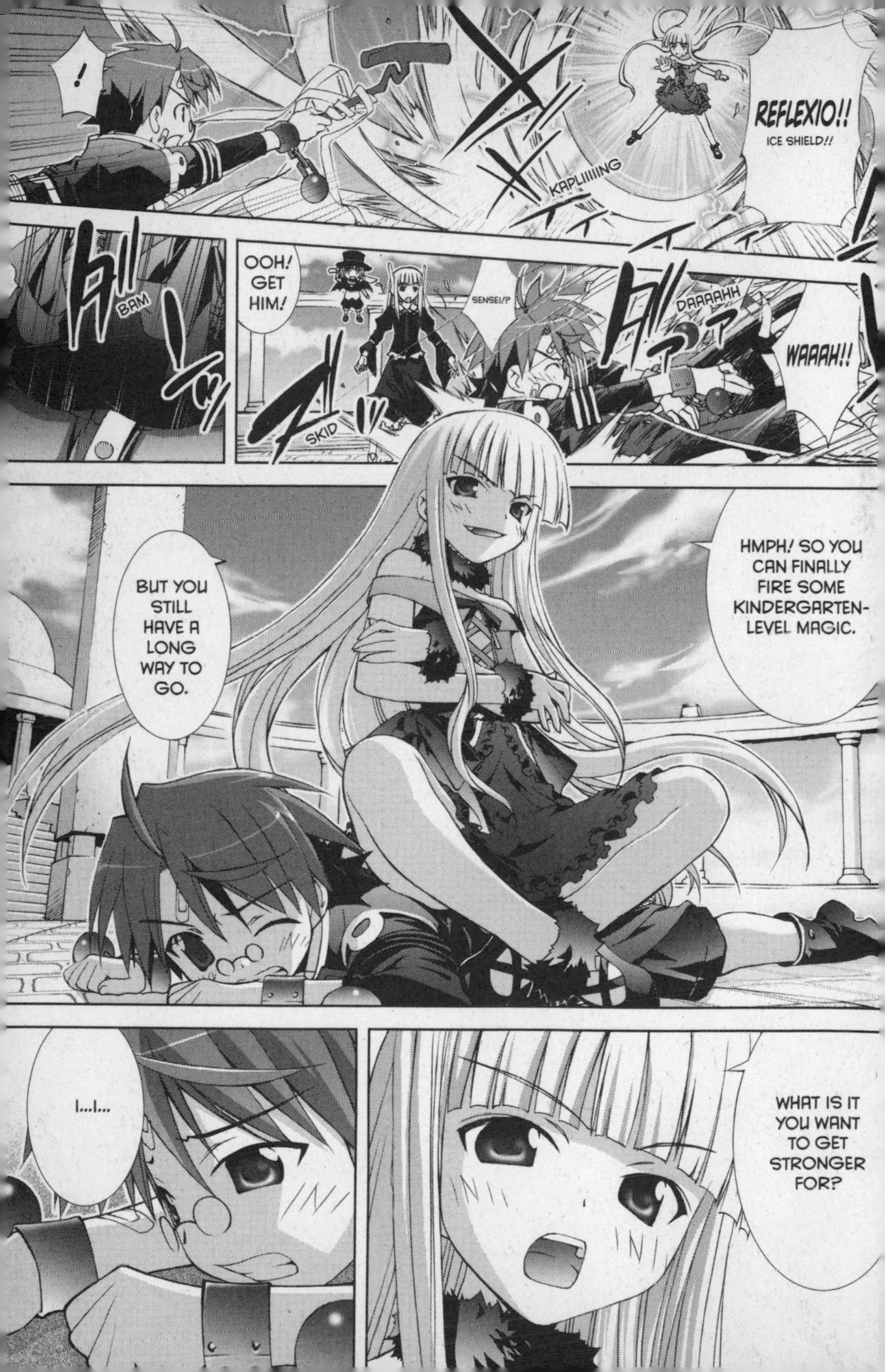
REFLEXIO!!
ICE SHIELD!!
KAPLIIIIING
!
WAAAH!!
DAAAAAHH
SENSEI!?
OOH! GET HIM!
SKID
BAM
HMPH! SO YOU CAN FINALLY FIRE SOME KINDERGARTEN-LEVEL MAGIC.
BUT YOU STILL HAVE A LONG WAY TO GO.
WHAT IS IT YOU WANT TO GET STRONGER FOR?
I...I...

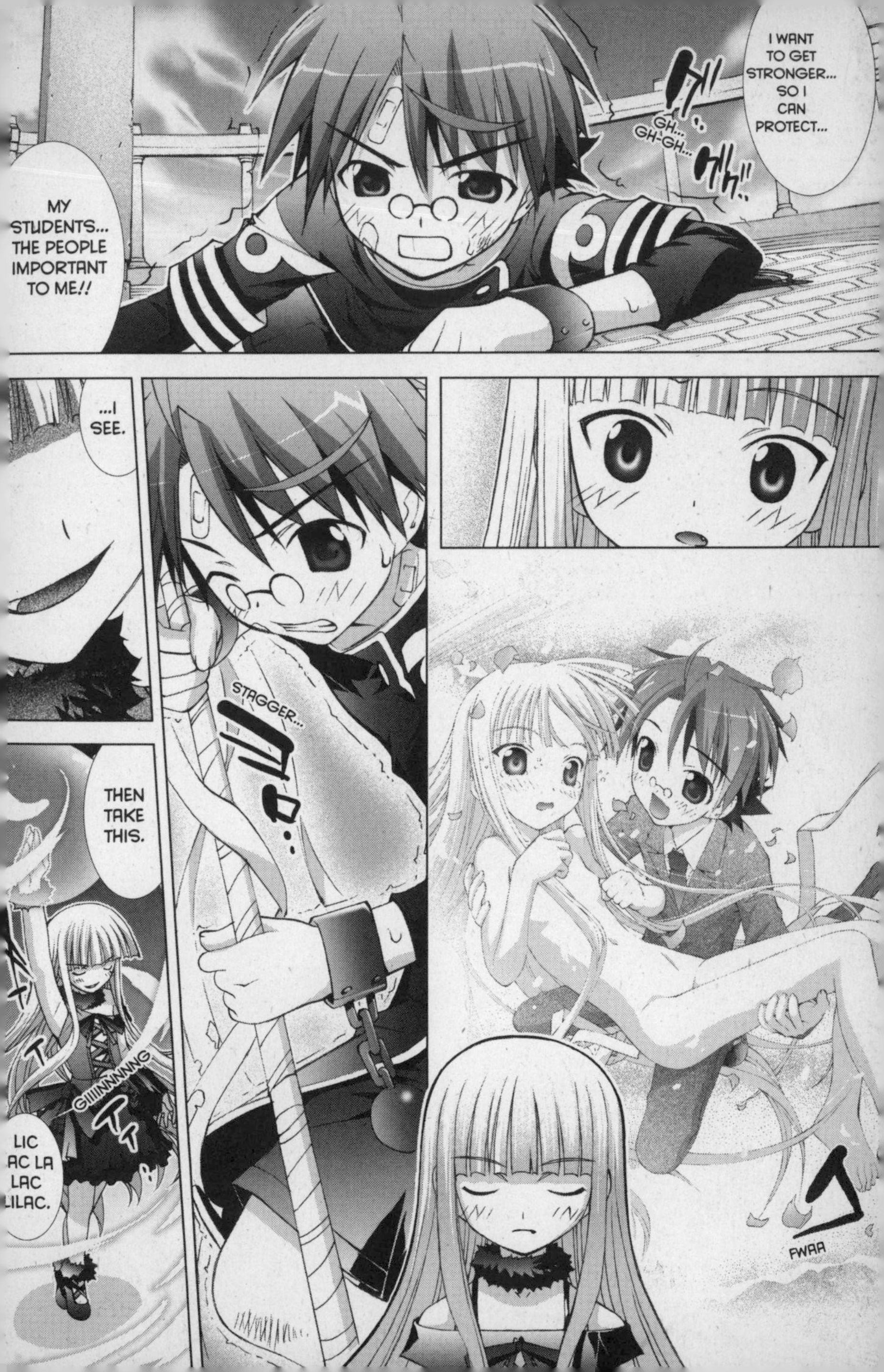
I WANT TO GET STRONGER... SO I CAN PROTECT...
GH... GH-GH...
MY STUDENTS... THE PEOPLE IMPORTANT TO ME!!
FWAA
STAGGER...
...I SEE.
THEN TAKE THIS.
GIIINNNNG
LIC LAC LA LAC LILAC.

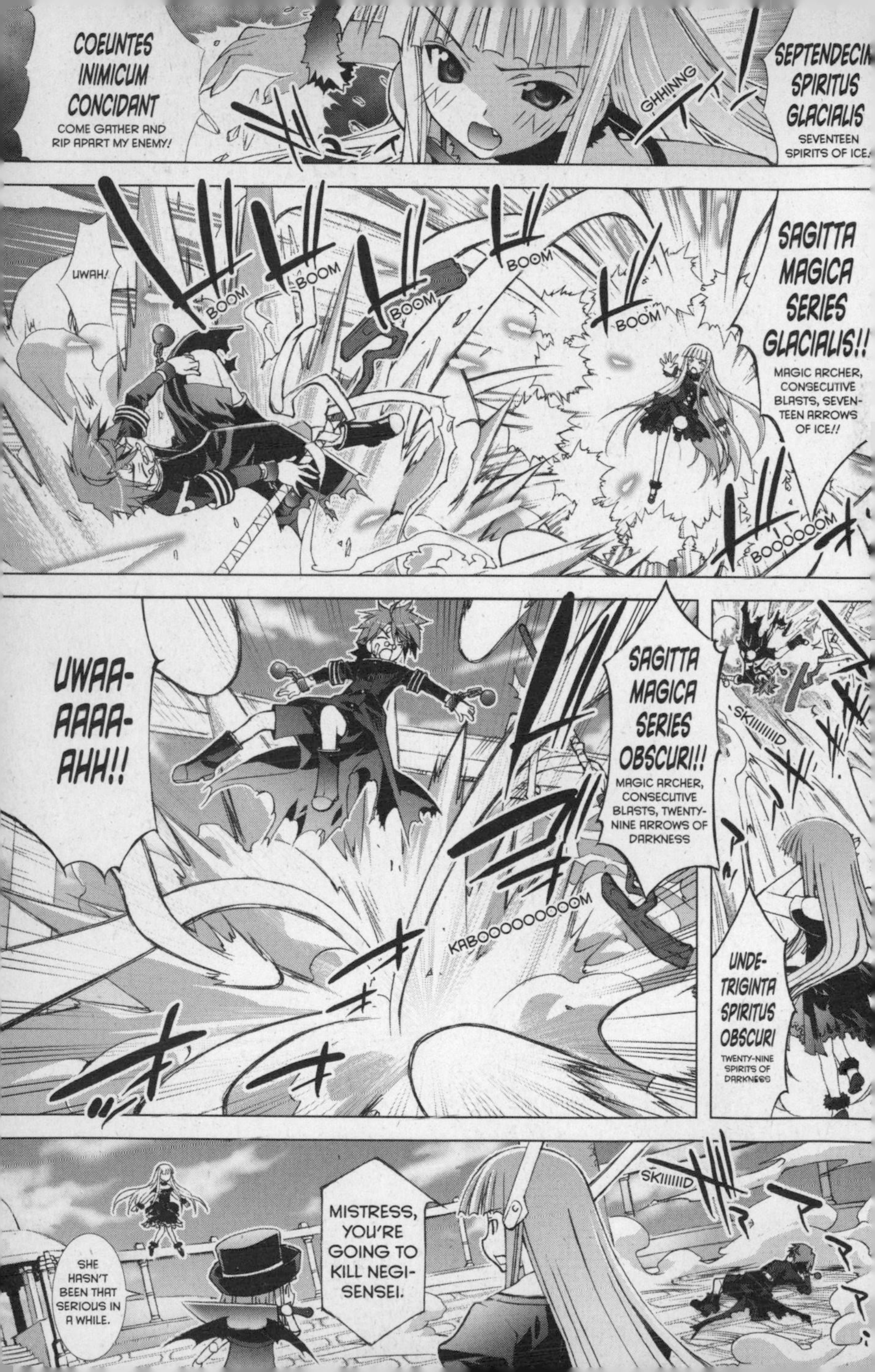
SEPTENDECIM SPIRITUS GLACIALIS
SEVENTEEN SPIRITS OF ICE.
GHHINNG
COEUNTES INIMICUM CONCIDANT
COME GATHER AND RIP APART MY ENEMY!
SAGITTA MAGICA SERIES GLACIALIS!!
MAGIC ARCHER, CONSECUTIVE BLASTS, SEVENTEEN ARROWS OF ICE!!
BOOOOOOM
BOOM
BOOM
BOOM
BOOM
BOOM
UWAH!
UNDE-TRIGINTA SPIRITUS OBSCURI
TWENTY-NINE SPIRITS OF DARKNESS
SKIIIIIID
SAGITTA MAGICA SERIES OBSCURI!!
MAGIC ARCHER, CONSECUTIVE BLASTS, TWENTY-NINE ARROWS OF DARKNESS
KABOOOOOOOOOOM
UWAA-AAAA-AHH!!
SKIIIIID
MISTRESS, YOU'RE GOING TO KILL NEGI-SENSEI.
SHE HASN'T BEEN THAT SERIOUS IN A WHILE.

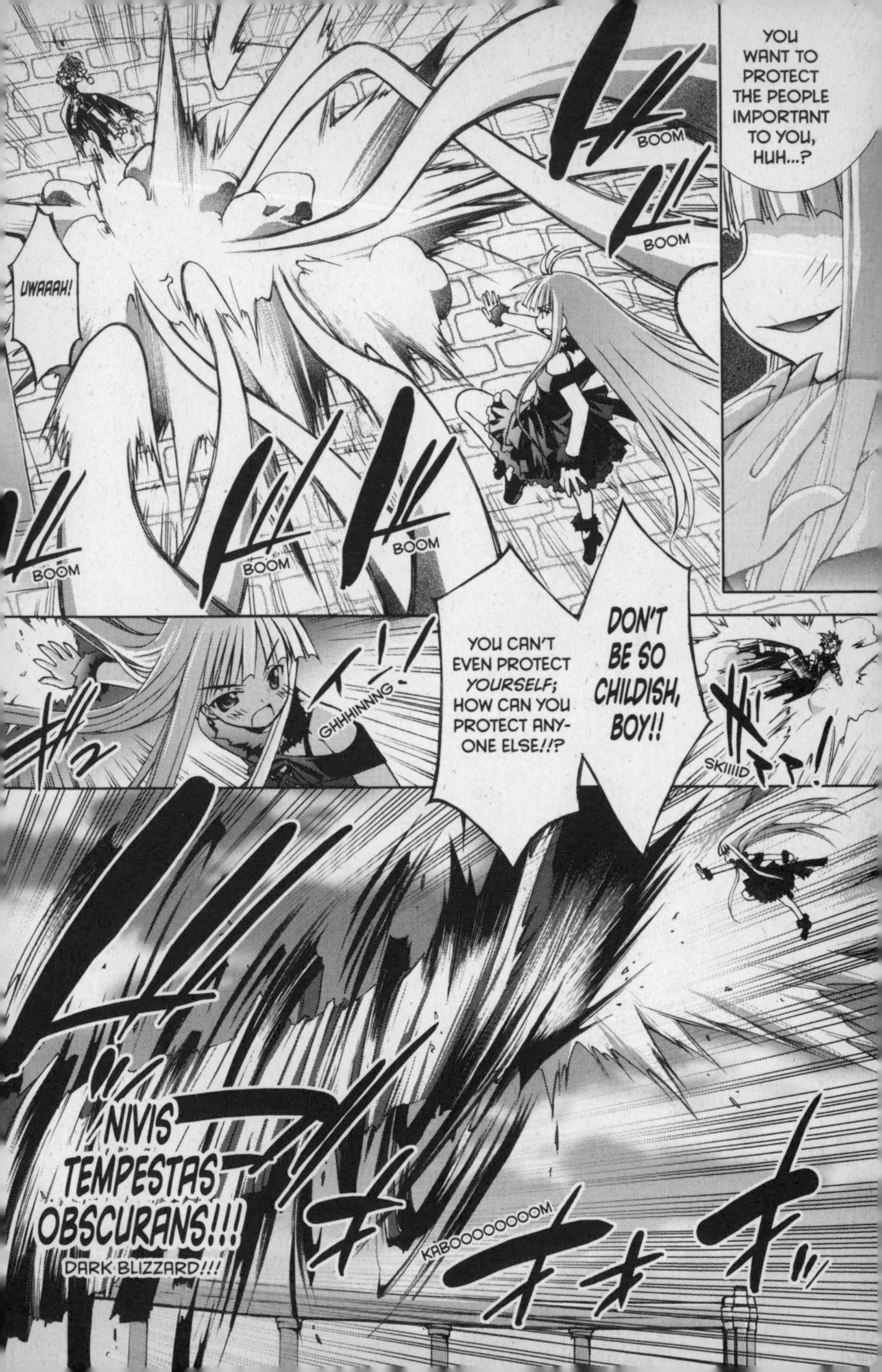
YOU WANT TO PROTECT THE PEOPLE IMPORTANT TO YOU, HUH...?
BOOM
BOOM
UWAAAH!
BOOM
BOOM
BOOM
SKIIIID
DON'T BE SO CHILDISH, BOY!!
YOU CAN'T EVEN PROTECT *YOURSELF*; HOW CAN YOU PROTECT ANYONE ELSE!!?
GHHHINNNG
NIVIS TEMPESTAS OBSCURANS!!!
DARK BLIZZARD!!!
KABOOOOOOOOOM

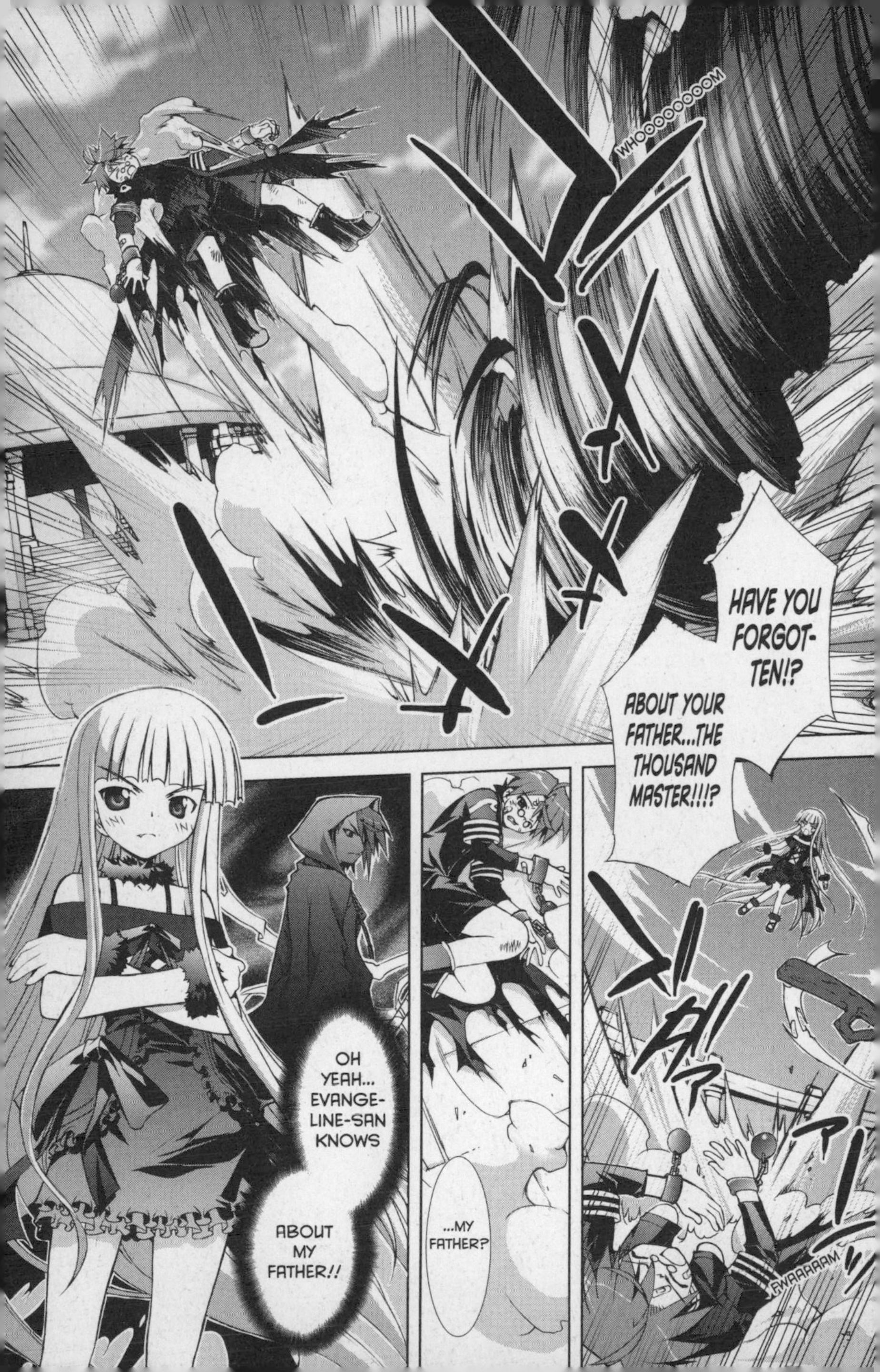
WHOOOOOOOOM
HAVE YOU FORGOT-TEN!?
ABOUT YOUR FATHER...THE THOUSAND MASTER!!!?
FWAAAAAM
...MY FATHER?
OH YEAH... EVANGE-LINE-SAN KNOWS
ABOUT MY FATHER!!

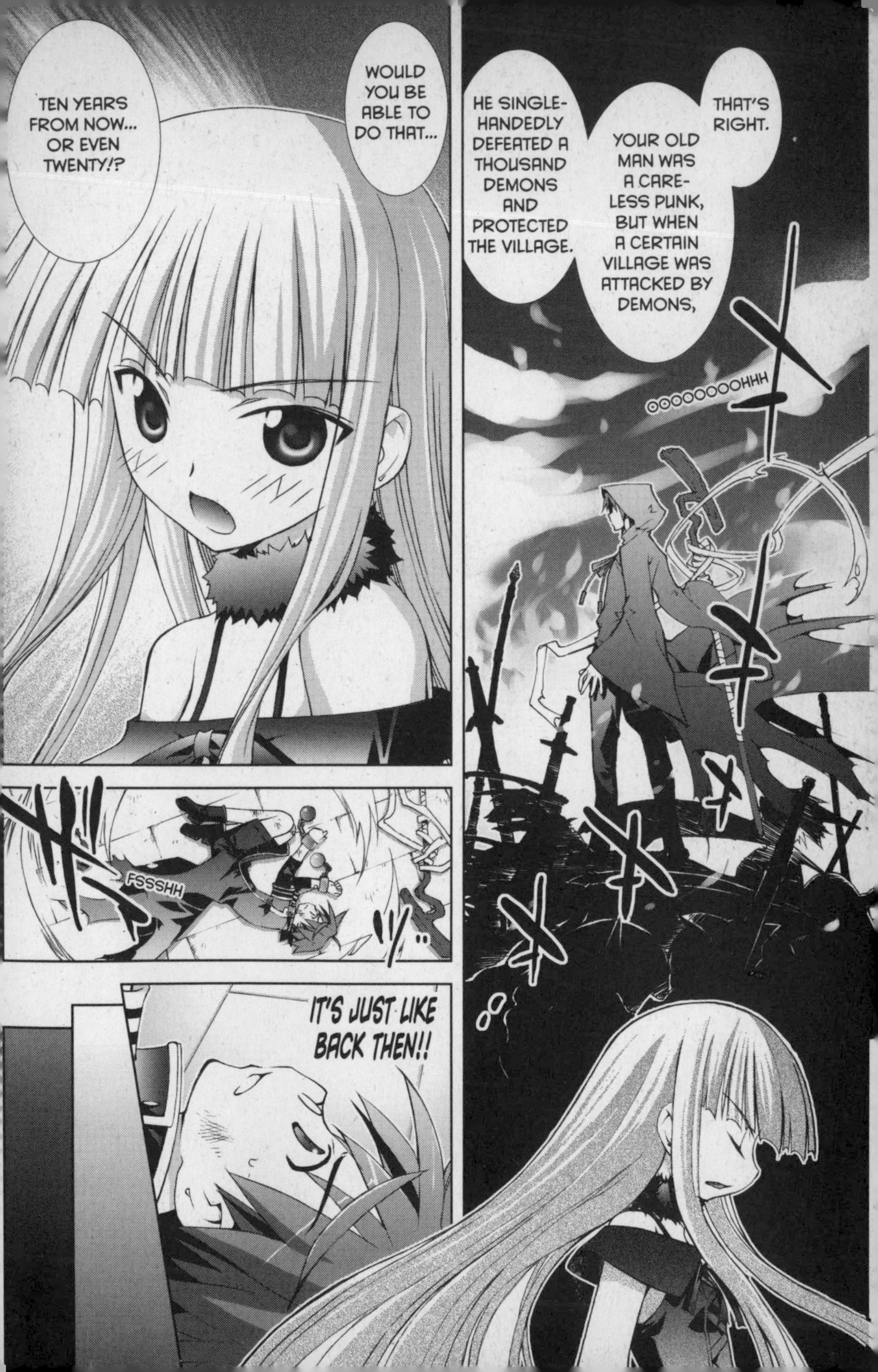
THAT'S RIGHT.
YOUR OLD MAN WAS A CARE-LESS PUNK, BUT WHEN A CERTAIN VILLAGE WAS ATTACKED BY DEMONS,
HE SINGLE-HANDEDLY DEFEATED A THOUSAND DEMONS AND PROTECTED THE VILLAGE.
OOOOOOOOHHH
WOULD YOU BE ABLE TO DO THAT...
TEN YEARS FROM NOW... OR EVEN TWENTY!?
FSSSHH
IT'S JUST LIKE BACK THEN!!

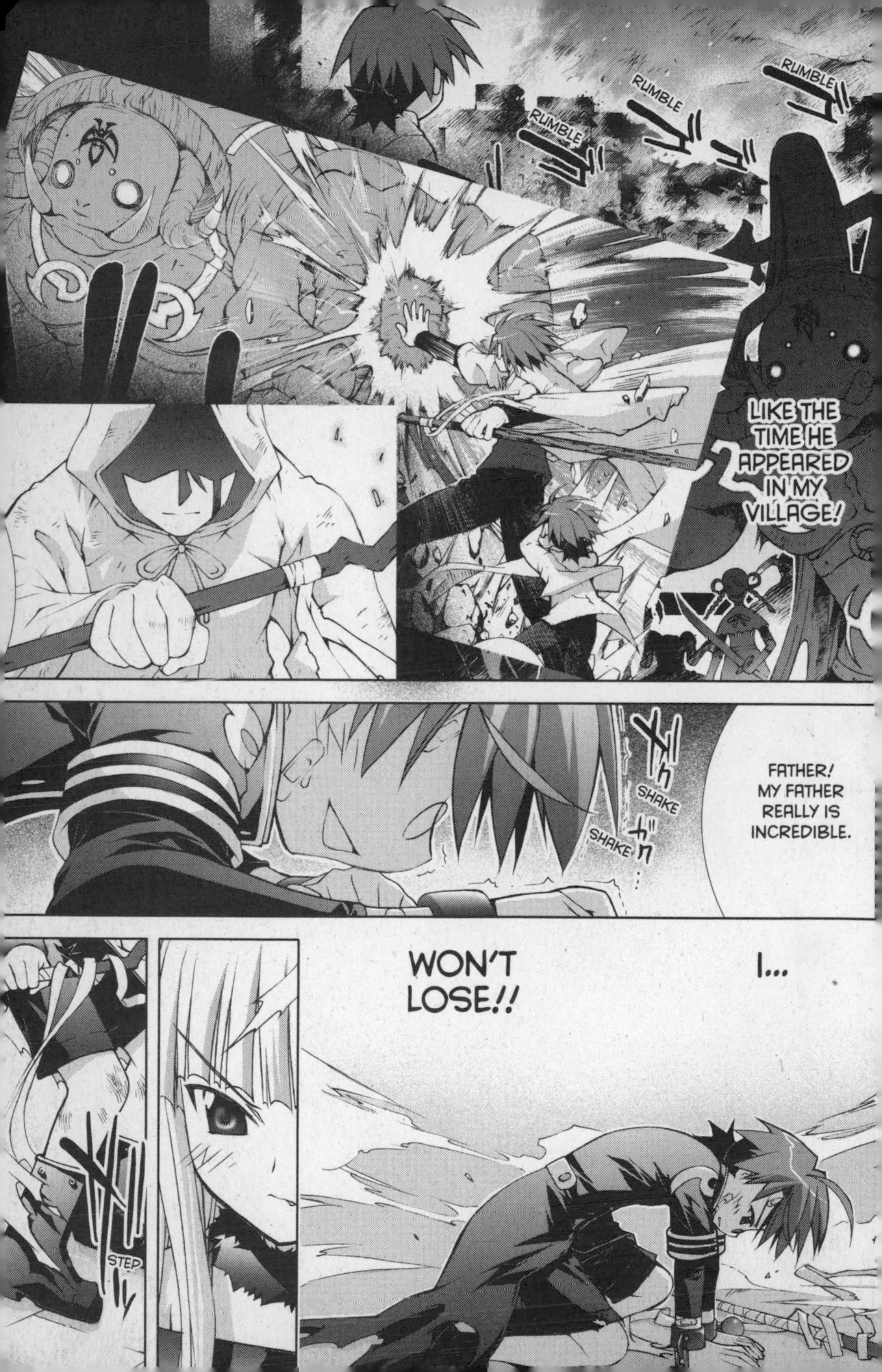
RUMBLE
RUMBLE
RUMBLE
LIKE THE TIME HE APPEARED IN MY VILLAGE!
FATHER! MY FATHER REALLY IS INCREDIBLE.
SHAKE
SHAKE
I...
WON'T LOSE!!
STEP

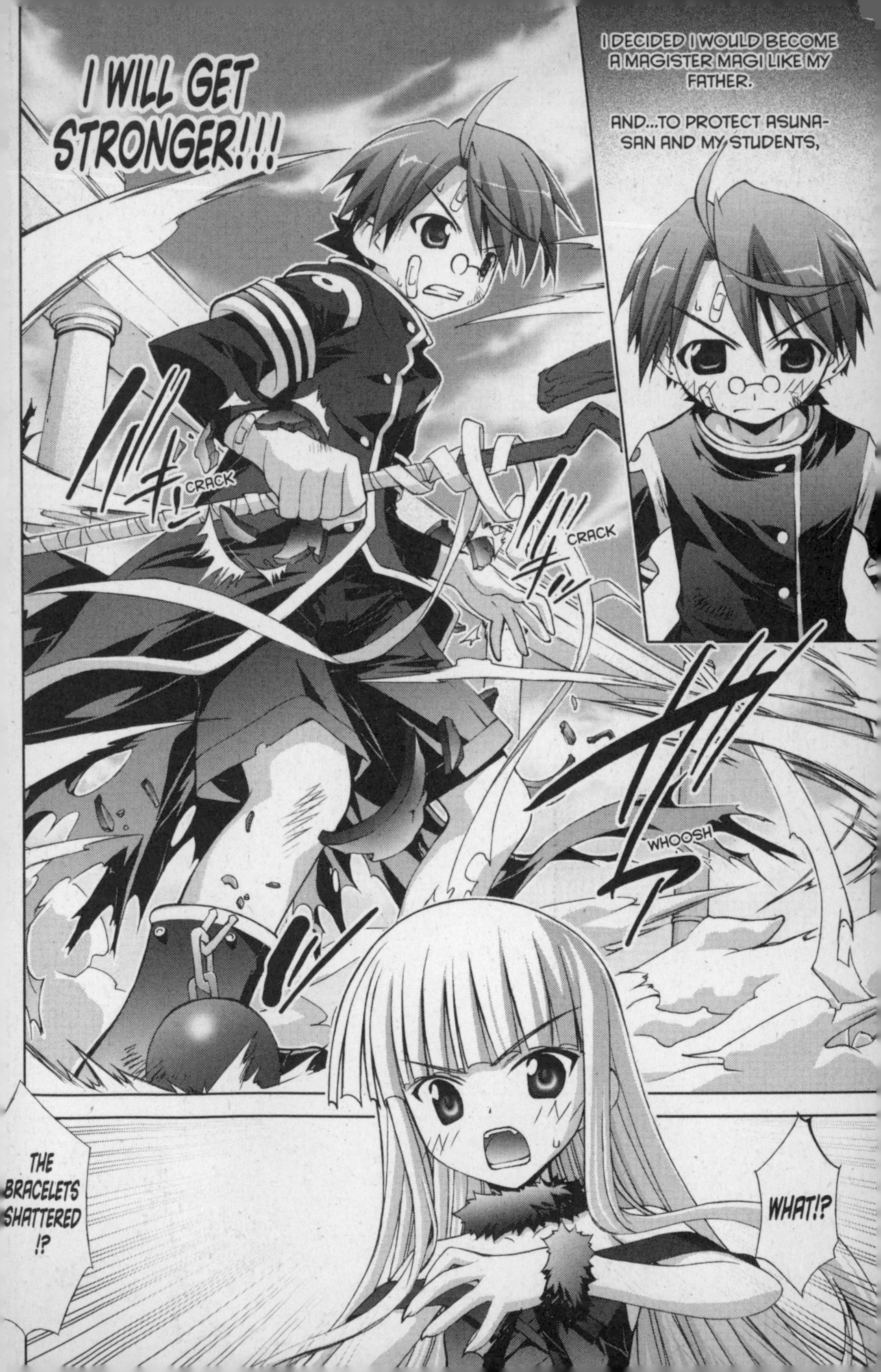
I DECIDED I WOULD BECOME A MAGISTER MAGI LIKE MY FATHER.
AND...TO PROTECT ASUNA-SAN AND MY STUDENTS,
I WILL GET STRONGER!!!
CRACK
CRACK
WHOOSH
WHAT!?
THE BRACELETS SHATTERED !?

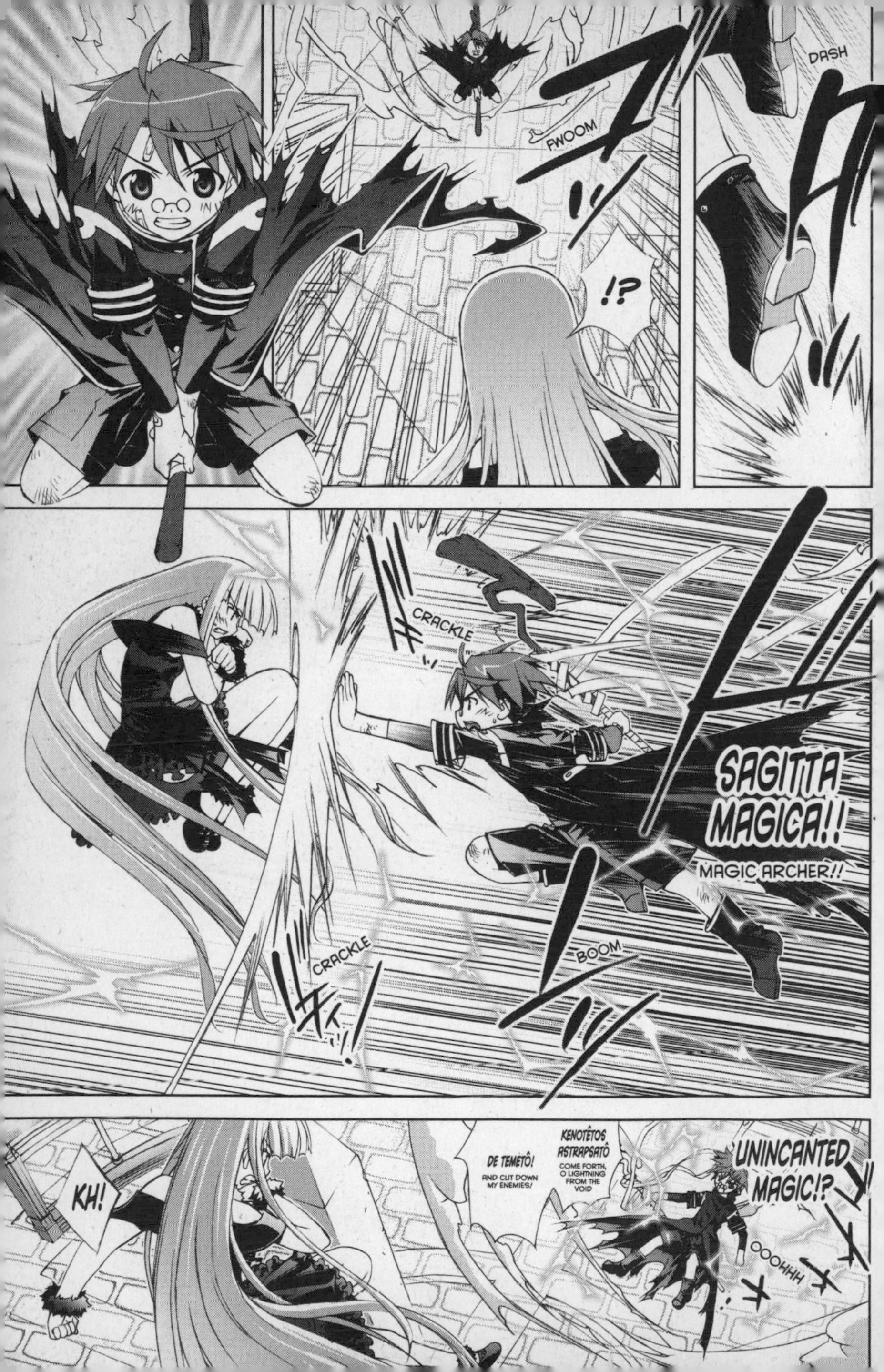
DASH
FWOOM
!?
SAGITTA MAGICA!!
MAGIC ARCHER!!
CRACKLE
BOOM
CRACKLE
UNINCANTED MAGIC!?
OOOHHH
KENOTÊTOS ASTRAPSATÔ
COME FORTH, O LIGHTNING FROM THE VOID
DE TEMETÔ!
AND CUT DOWN MY ENEMIES!
KH!

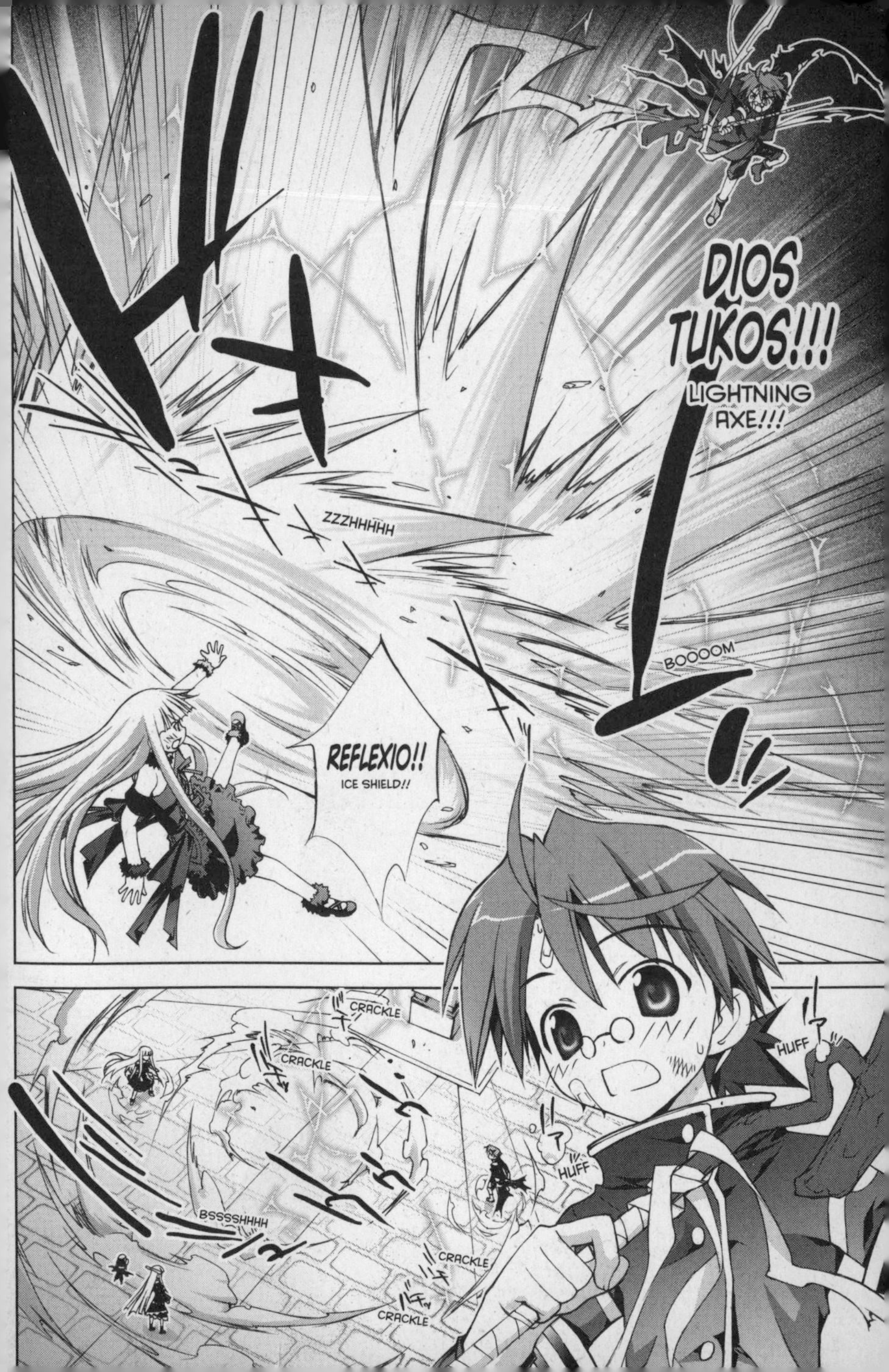
DIOS TUKOS!!!
LIGHTNING AXE!!!
ZZZHHHHH
BOOOOM
REFLEXIO!!
ICE SHIELD!!
HUFF
HUFF
CRACKLE
CRACKLE
BSSSSHHHH
CRACKLE
CRACKLE

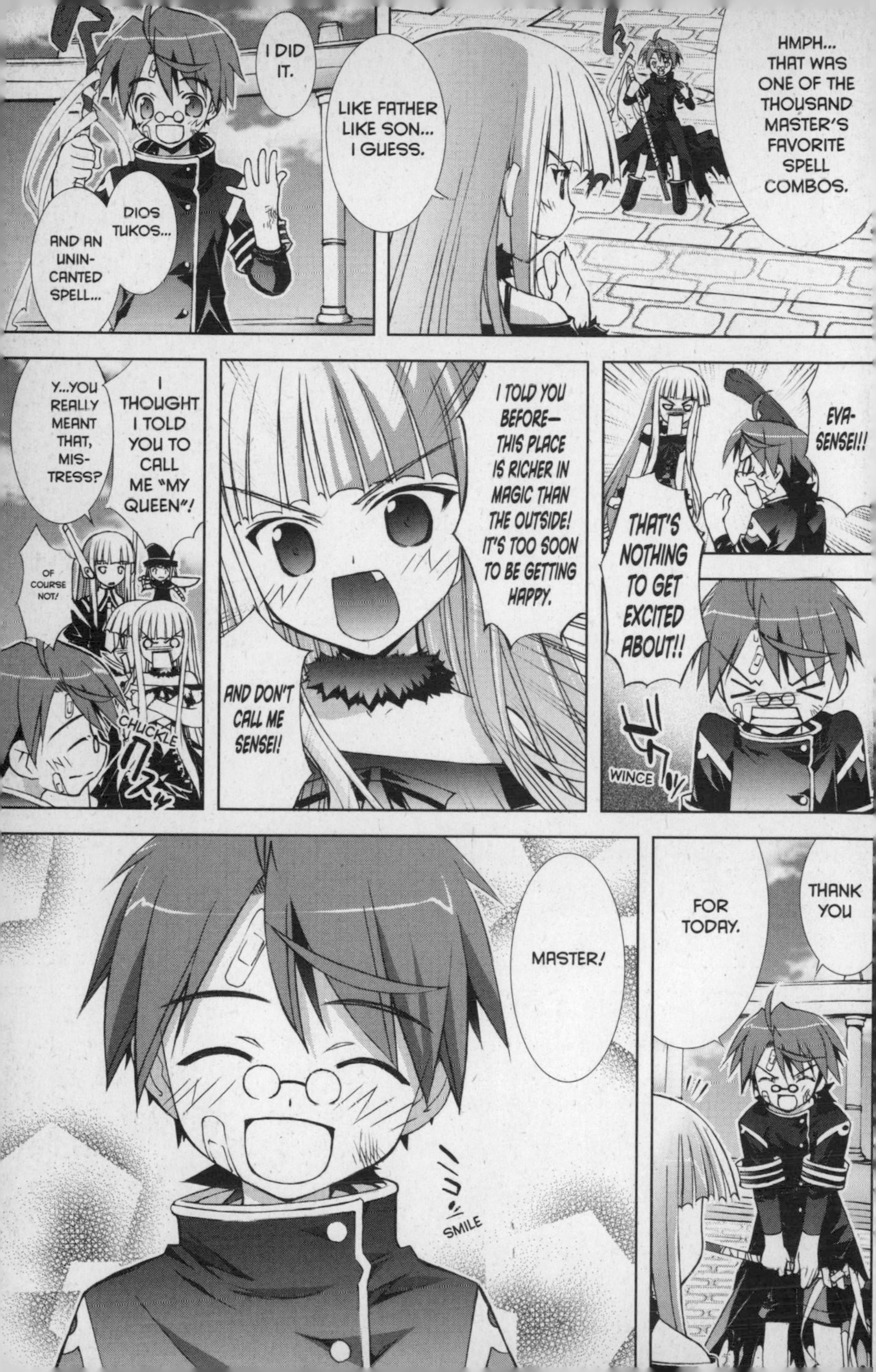
HMPH... THAT WAS ONE OF THE THOUSAND MASTER'S FAVORITE SPELL COMBOS.
LIKE FATHER LIKE SON... I GUESS.
I DID IT.
DIOS TUKOS...
AND AN UNIN-CANTED SPELL...
EVA-SENSEI!!
THAT'S NOTHING TO GET EXCITED ABOUT!!
WINCE
I TOLD YOU BEFORE—THIS PLACE IS RICHER IN MAGIC THAN THE OUTSIDE! IT'S TOO SOON TO BE GETTING HAPPY.
AND DON'T CALL ME SENSEI!
I THOUGHT I TOLD YOU TO CALL ME "MY QUEEN"!
Y...YOU REALLY MEANT THAT, MIS-TRESS?
OF COURSE NOT!
CHUCKLE
THANK YOU
FOR TODAY.
MASTER!
SMILE

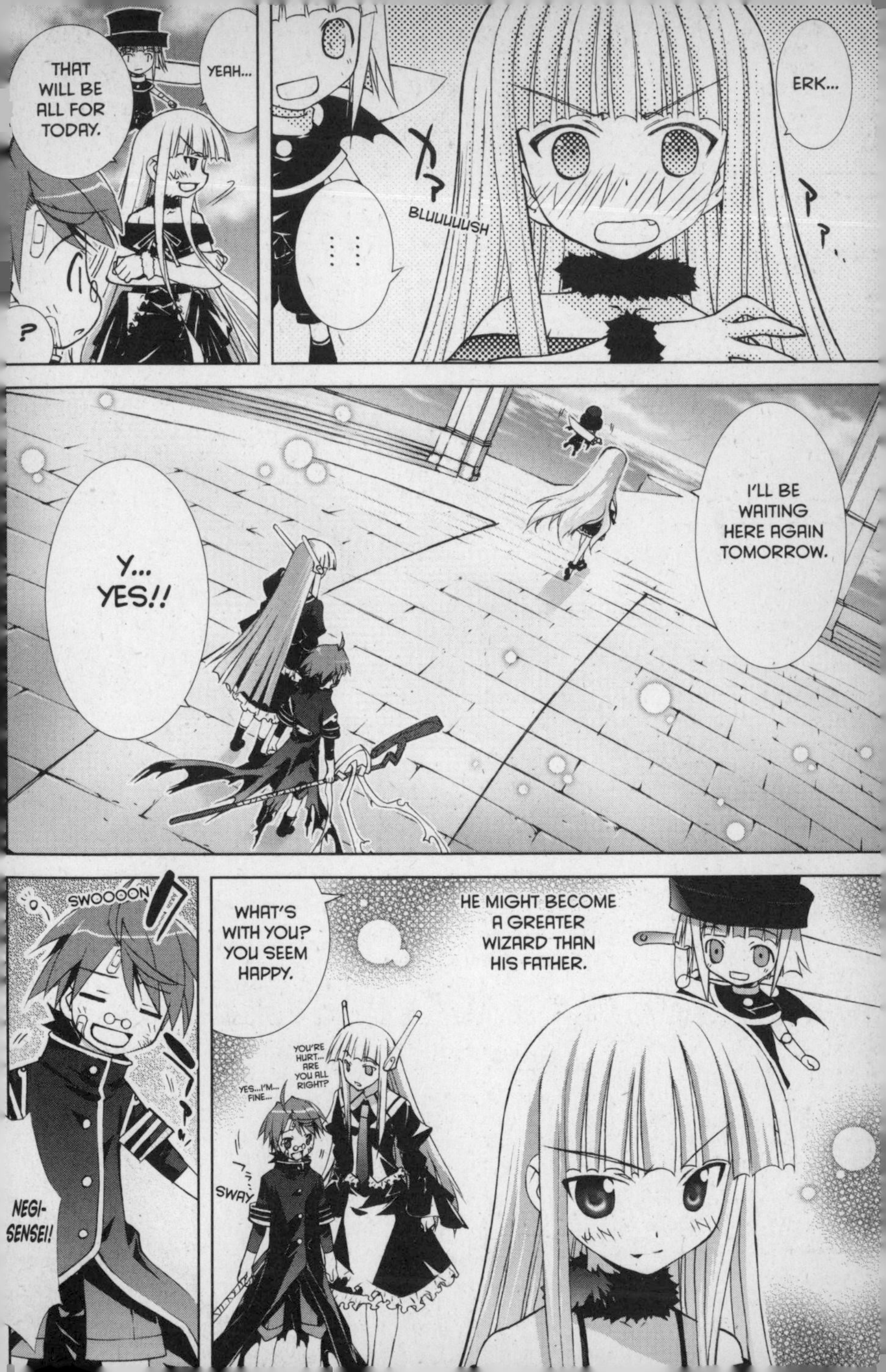
ERK...
BLUUUUUSH
......
YEAH...
THAT WILL BE ALL FOR TODAY.
?
I'LL BE WAITING HERE AGAIN TOMORROW.
Y... YES!!
HE MIGHT BECOME A GREATER WIZARD THAN HIS FATHER.
WHAT'S WITH YOU? YOU SEEM HAPPY.
YOU'RE HURT... ARE YOU ALL RIGHT?
YES...I'M... FINE...
SWAY
SWOOOON
NEGI-SENSEI!

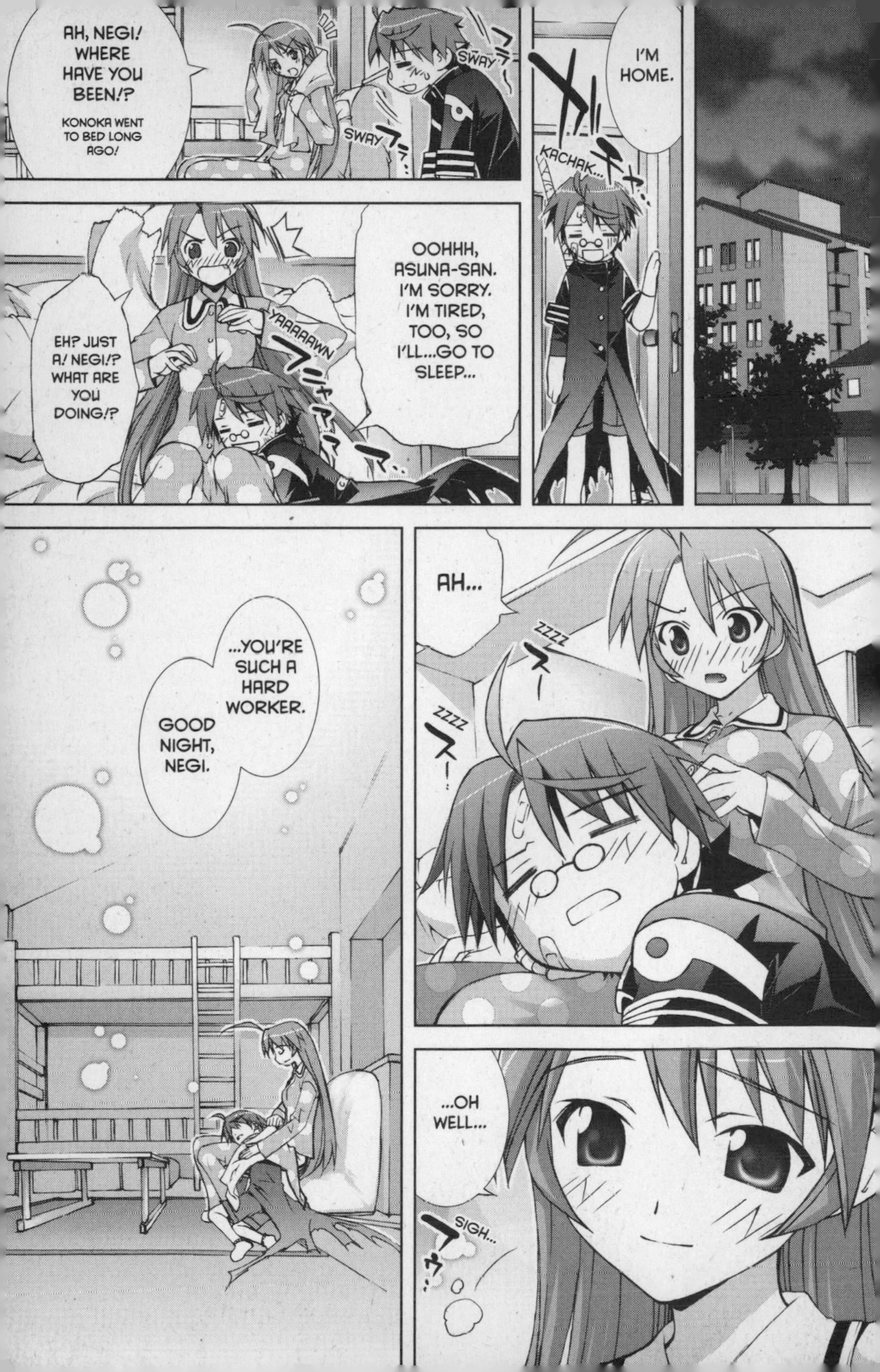
I'M HOME.
KACHAK...
SWAY
SWAY
AH, NEGI! WHERE HAVE YOU BEEN!?
KONOKA WENT TO BED LONG AGO!
OOHHH, ASUNA-SAN. I'M SORRY. I'M TIRED, TOO, SO I'LL...GO TO SLEEP...
YAAAAAWN
EH? JUST A! NEGI!? WHAT ARE YOU DOING!?
AH...
ZZZZ
ZZZZ
...OH WELL...
SIGH...
...YOU'RE SUCH A HARD WORKER.
GOOD NIGHT, NEGI.

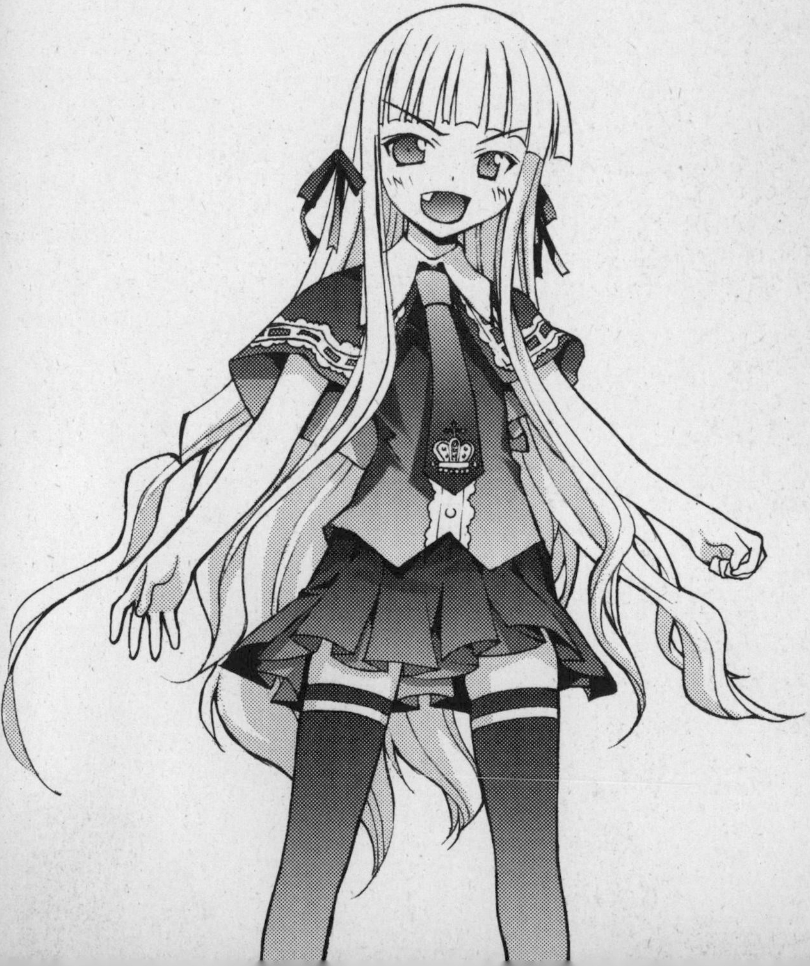

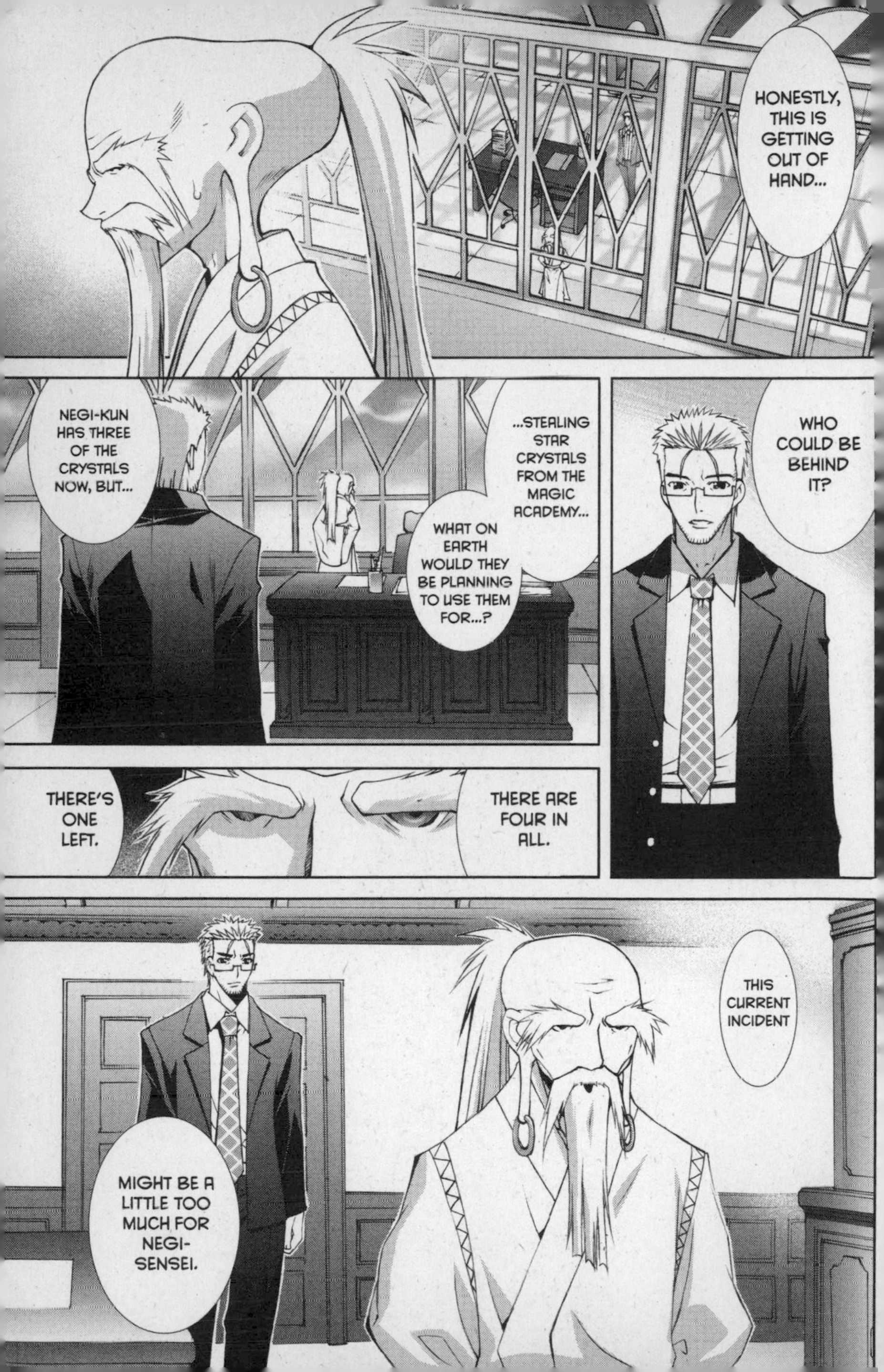
HONESTLY, THIS IS GETTING OUT OF HAND...
WHO COULD BE BEHIND IT?
...STEALING STAR CRYSTALS FROM THE MAGIC ACADEMY...
WHAT ON EARTH WOULD THEY BE PLANNING TO USE THEM FOR...?
NEGI-KUN HAS THREE OF THE CRYSTALS NOW, BUT...
THERE ARE FOUR IN ALL.
THERE'S ONE LEFT.
THIS CURRENT INCIDENT
MIGHT BE A LITTLE TOO MUCH FOR NEGI-SENSEI.

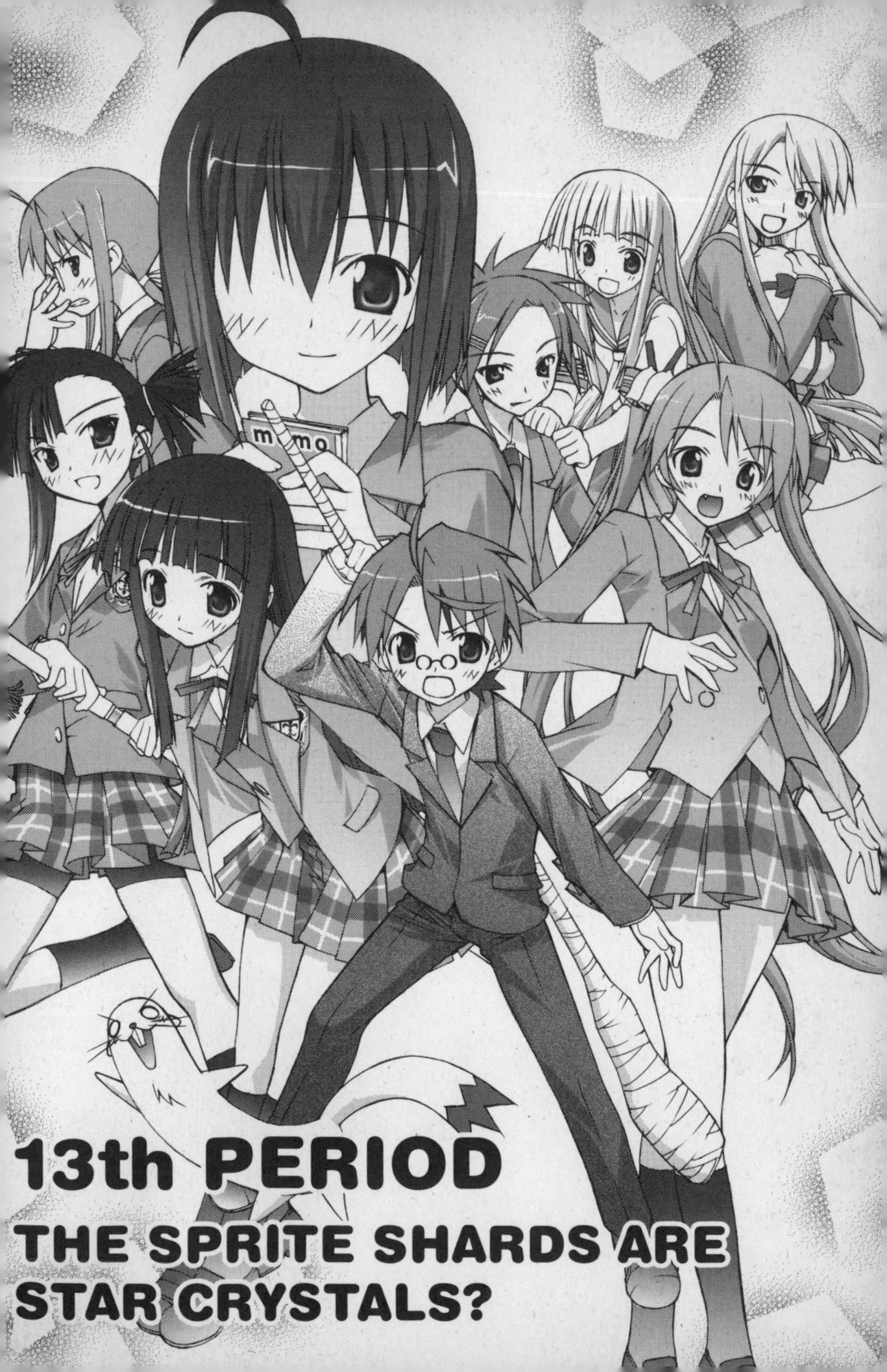
momo
13th PERIOD
THE SPRITE SHARDS ARE STAR CRYSTALS?

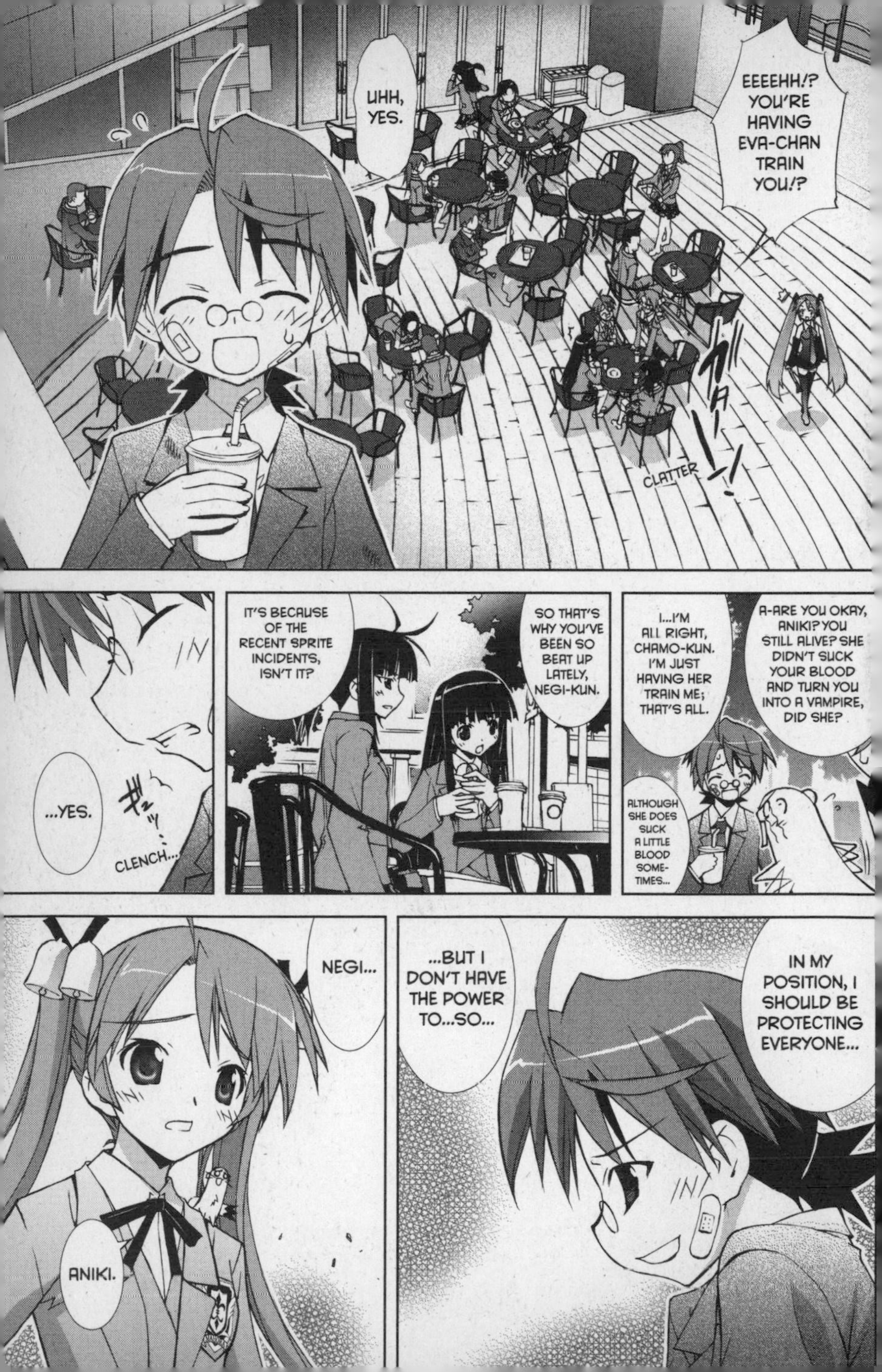
EEEEHH!? YOU'RE HAVING EVA-CHAN TRAIN YOU!?
UHH, YES.
CLATTER
A-ARE YOU OKAY, ANIKI? YOU STILL ALIVE? SHE DIDN'T SUCK YOUR BLOOD AND TURN YOU INTO A VAMPIRE, DID SHE?
I...I'M ALL RIGHT, CHAMO-KUN. I'M JUST HAVING HER TRAIN ME; THAT'S ALL.
ALTHOUGH SHE DOES SUCK A LITTLE BLOOD SOME-TIMES...
SO THAT'S WHY YOU'VE BEEN SO BEAT UP LATELY, NEGI-KUN.
IT'S BECAUSE OF THE RECENT SPRITE INCIDENTS, ISN'T IT?
...YES.
CLENCH...
IN MY POSITION, I SHOULD BE PROTECTING EVERYONE...
...BUT I DON'T HAVE THE POWER TO...SO...
NEGI...
ANIKI.

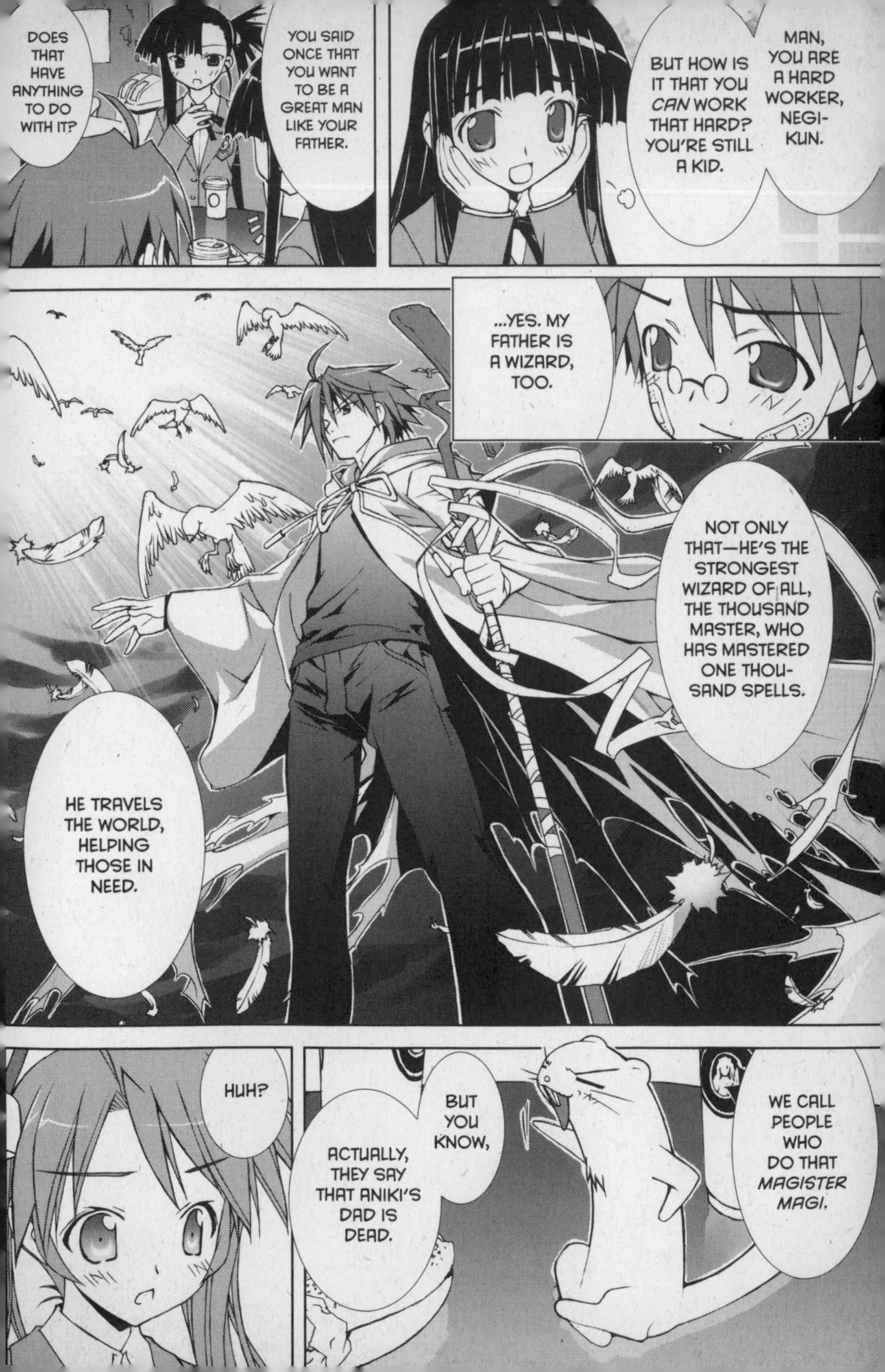
MAN, YOU ARE A HARD WORKER, NEGI-KUN.
BUT HOW IS IT THAT YOU *CAN* WORK THAT HARD? YOU'RE STILL A KID.
YOU SAID ONCE THAT YOU WANT TO BE A GREAT MAN LIKE YOUR FATHER.
DOES THAT HAVE ANYTHING TO DO WITH IT?
...YES. MY FATHER IS A WIZARD, TOO.
NOT ONLY THAT—HE'S THE STRONGEST WIZARD OF ALL, THE THOUSAND MASTER, WHO HAS MASTERED ONE THOUSAND SPELLS.
HE TRAVELS THE WORLD, HELPING THOSE IN NEED.
WE CALL PEOPLE WHO DO THAT *MAGISTER MAGI.*
BUT YOU KNOW,
ACTUALLY, THEY SAY THAT ANIKI'S DAD IS DEAD.
HUH?

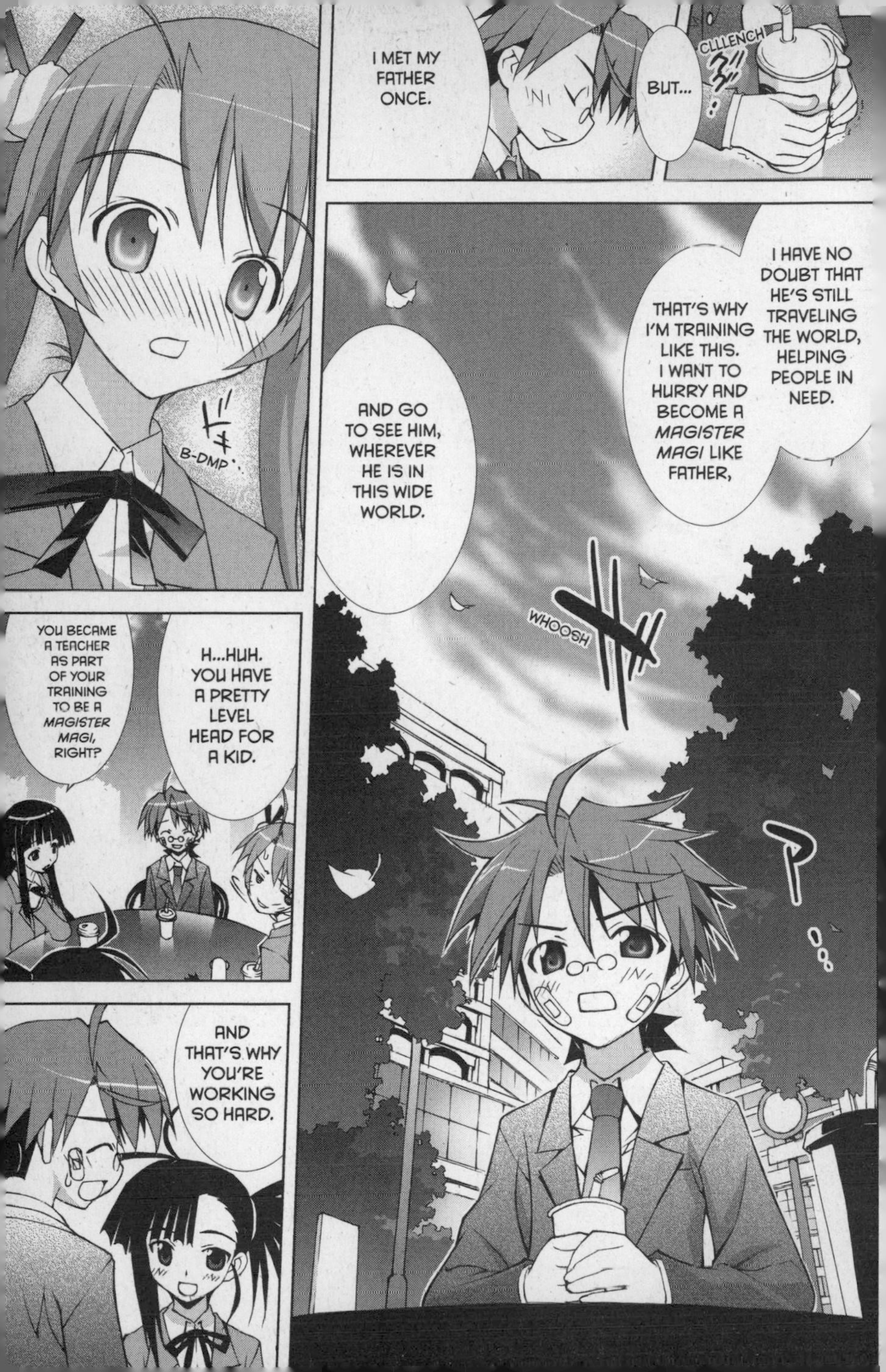
CLLLENCH
I MET MY FATHER ONCE.
BUT...
I HAVE NO DOUBT THAT HE'S STILL TRAVELING THE WORLD, HELPING PEOPLE IN NEED.
THAT'S WHY I'M TRAINING LIKE THIS. I WANT TO HURRY AND BECOME A *MAGISTER MAGI* LIKE FATHER,
AND GO TO SEE HIM, WHEREVER HE IS IN THIS WIDE WORLD.
WHOOSH
B-DMP
H...HUH. YOU HAVE A PRETTY LEVEL HEAD FOR A KID.
YOU BECAME A TEACHER AS PART OF YOUR TRAINING TO BE A *MAGISTER MAGI*, RIGHT?
AND THAT'S WHY YOU'RE WORKING SO HARD.

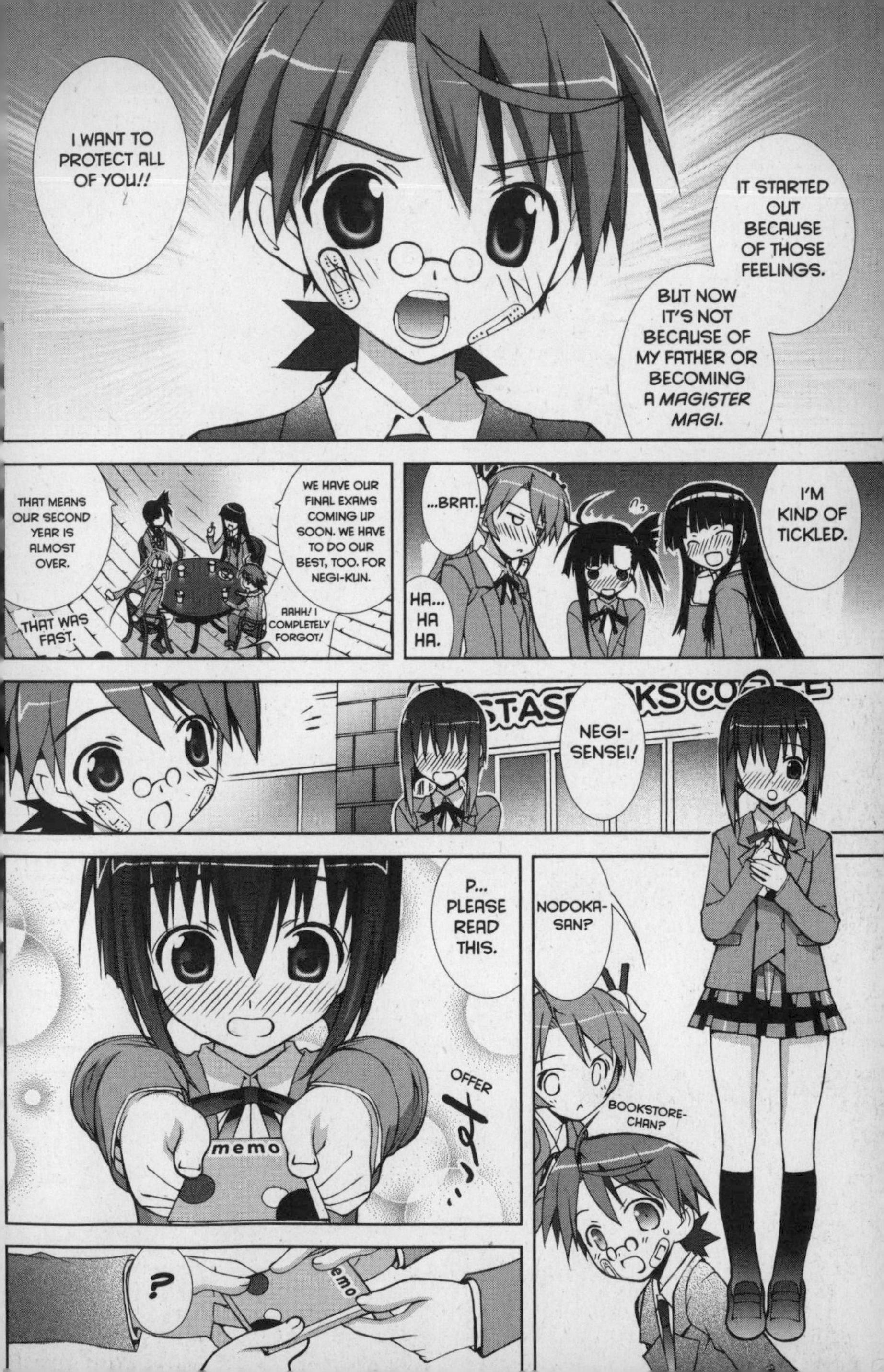
IT STARTED OUT BECAUSE OF THOSE FEELINGS.
BUT NOW IT'S NOT BECAUSE OF MY FATHER OR BECOMING A *MAGISTER MAGI*.
I WANT TO PROTECT ALL OF YOU!!
I'M KIND OF TICKLED.
...BRAT.
HA... HA HA.
WE HAVE OUR FINAL EXAMS COMING UP SOON. WE HAVE TO DO OUR BEST, TOO. FOR NEGI-KUN.
AAHH! I COMPLETELY FORGOT!
THAT MEANS OUR SECOND YEAR IS ALMOST OVER.
THAT WAS FAST.
NEGI-SENSEI!
NODOKA-SAN?
BOOKSTORE-CHAN?
P... PLEASE READ THIS.
OFFER
memo
?
memo

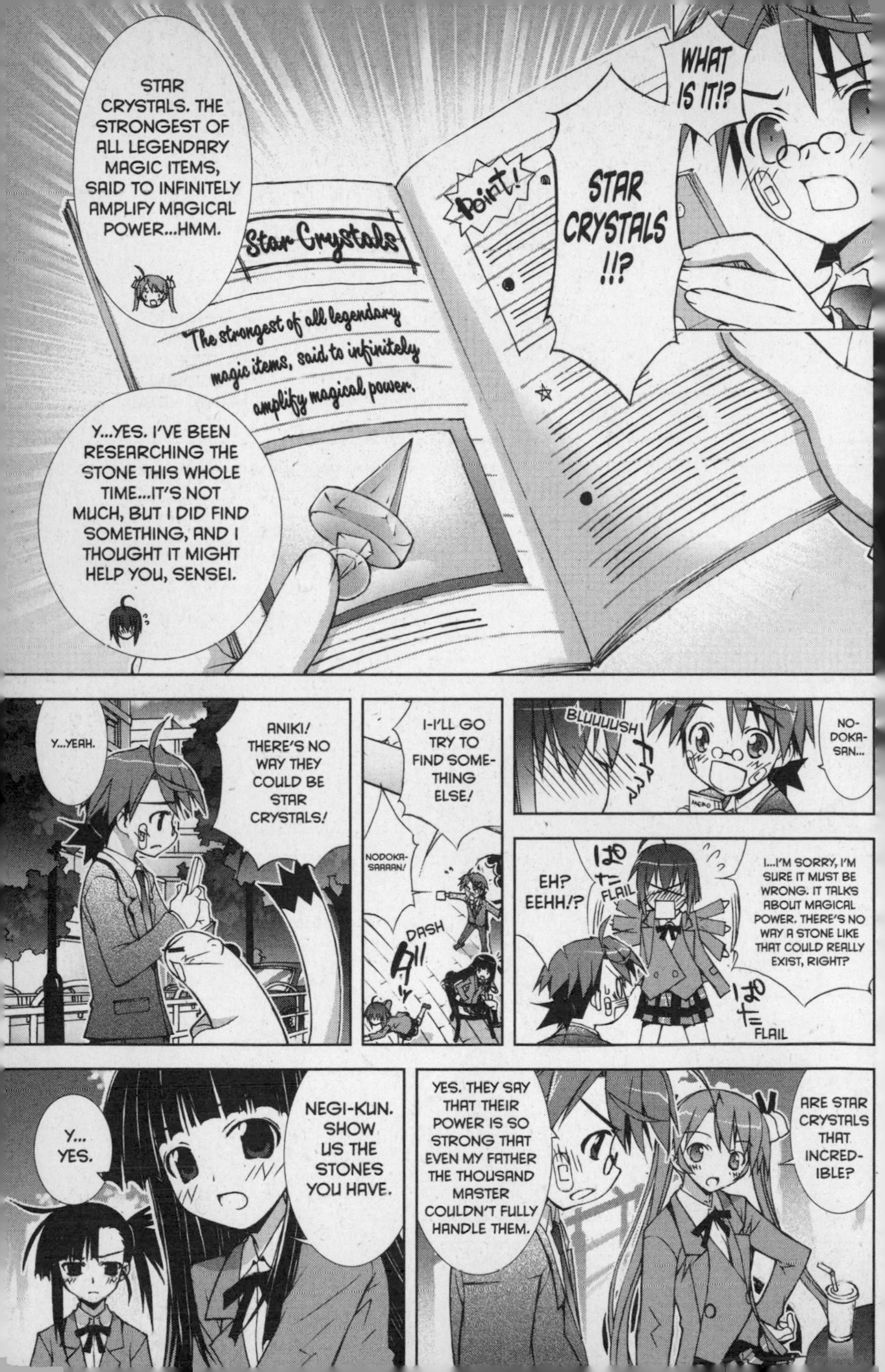
WHAT IS IT!?
STAR CRYSTALS !!?
Point!
STAR CRYSTALS. THE STRONGEST OF ALL LEGENDARY MAGIC ITEMS, SAID TO INFINITELY AMPLIFY MAGICAL POWER...HMM.
Star Crystals
The strongest of all legendary magic items, said to infinitely amplify magical power.
Y...YES. I'VE BEEN RESEARCHING THE STONE THIS WHOLE TIME...IT'S NOT MUCH, BUT I DID FIND SOMETHING, AND I THOUGHT IT MIGHT HELP YOU, SENSEI.
NO-DOKA-SAN...
BLUUUUSH
MEMO
I...I'M SORRY, I'M SURE IT MUST BE WRONG. IT TALKS ABOUT MAGICAL POWER. THERE'S NO WAY A STONE LIKE THAT COULD REALLY EXIST, RIGHT?
FLAIL
EH? EEHH!?
FLAIL
I-I'LL GO TRY TO FIND SOME-THING ELSE!
NODOKA-SAAAAN!
DASH
ANIKI! THERE'S NO WAY THEY COULD BE STAR CRYSTALS!
Y...YEAH.
ARE STAR CRYSTALS THAT INCRED-IBLE?
YES. THEY SAY THAT THEIR POWER IS SO STRONG THAT EVEN MY FATHER THE THOUSAND MASTER COULDN'T FULLY HANDLE THEM.
NEGI-KUN. SHOW US THE STONES YOU HAVE.
Y... YES.

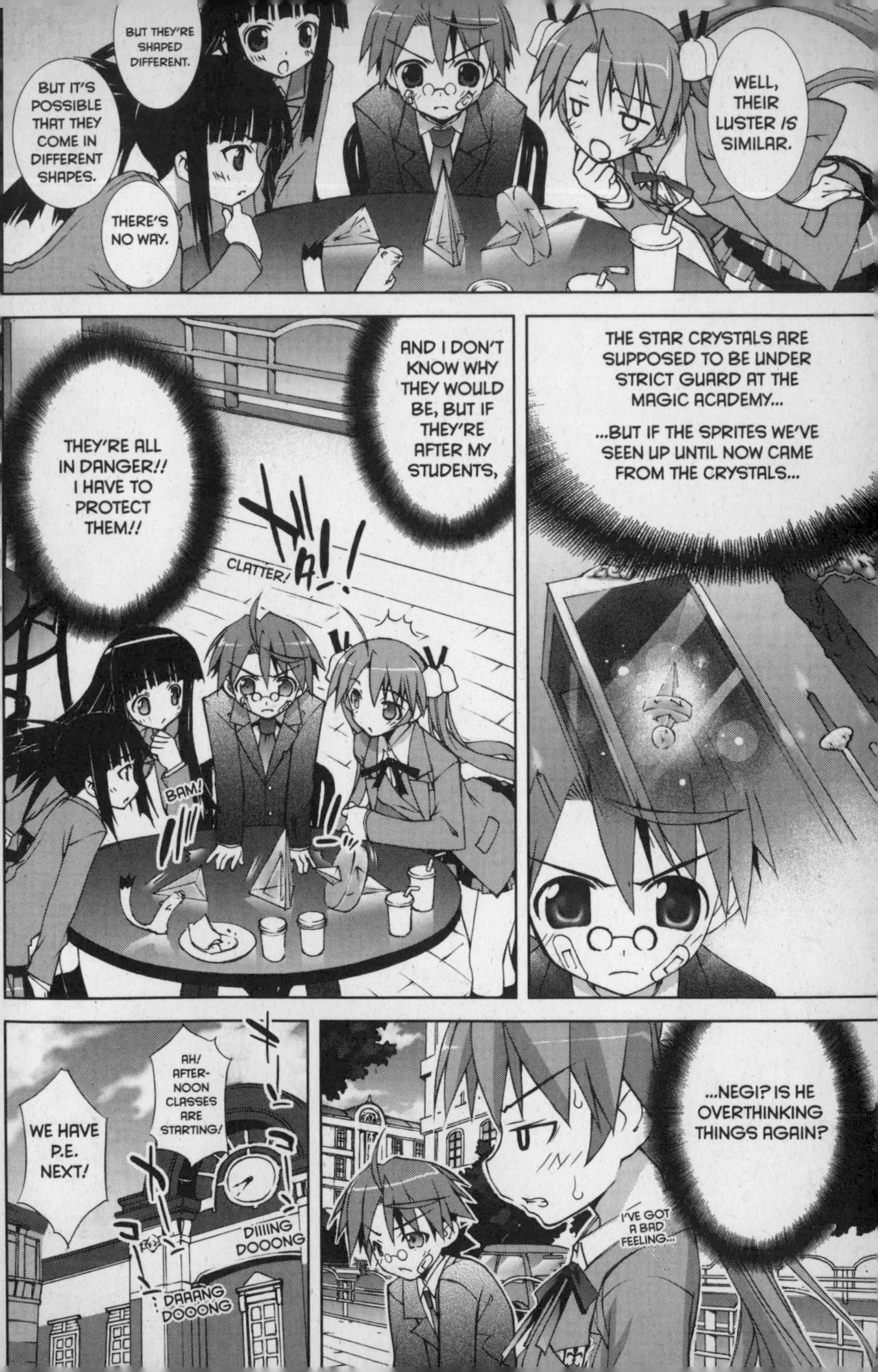
WELL, THEIR LUSTER IS SIMILAR.
BUT THEY'RE SHAPED DIFFERENT.
BUT IT'S POSSIBLE THAT THEY COME IN DIFFERENT SHAPES.
THERE'S NO WAY.
THE STAR CRYSTALS ARE SUPPOSED TO BE UNDER STRICT GUARD AT THE MAGIC ACADEMY...
...BUT IF THE SPRITES WE'VE SEEN UP UNTIL NOW CAME FROM THE CRYSTALS...
AND I DON'T KNOW WHY THEY WOULD BE, BUT IF THEY'RE AFTER MY STUDENTS,
THEY'RE ALL IN DANGER!! I HAVE TO PROTECT THEM!!
CLATTER!
BAM!
...NEGI? IS HE OVERTHINKING THINGS AGAIN?
I'VE GOT A BAD FEELING...
AH! AFTER-NOON CLASSES ARE STARTING!
WE HAVE P.E. NEXT!
DIIIING DOOONG
DAAAANG DOOONG

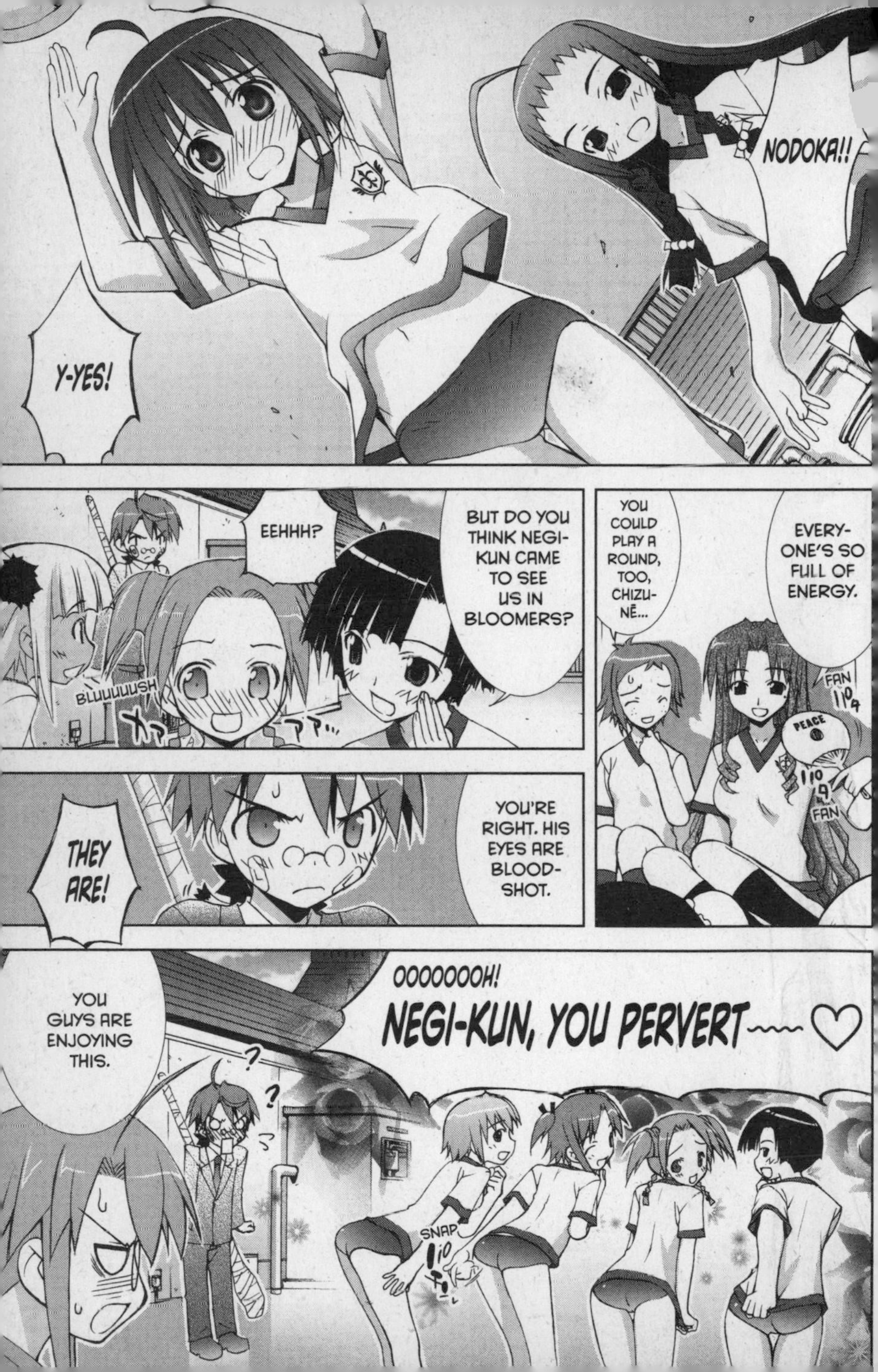
NODOKA!!
Y-YES!
EVERY-ONE'S SO FULL OF ENERGY.
YOU COULD PLAY A ROUND, TOO, CHIZU-NĒ...
FAN
PEACE
FAN
BUT DO YOU THINK NEGI-KUN CAME TO SEE US IN BLOOMERS?
EEHHH?
BLUUUUUSH
YOU'RE RIGHT. HIS EYES ARE BLOOD-SHOT.
THEY ARE!
OOOOOOOH!
NEGI-KUN, YOU PERVERT~~~ ♡
YOU GUYS ARE ENJOYING THIS.
SNAP

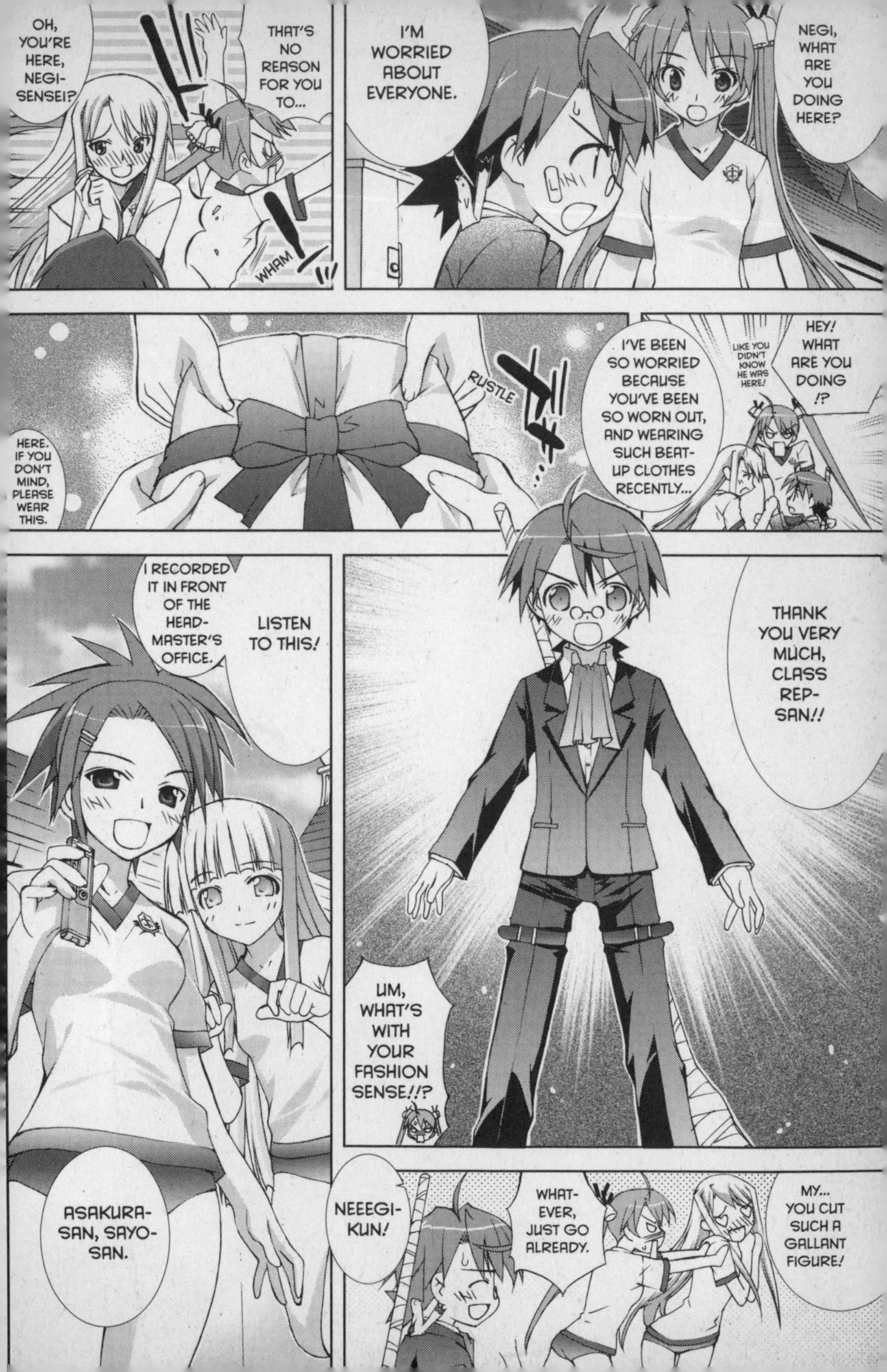
NEGI, WHAT ARE YOU DOING HERE?
I'M WORRIED ABOUT EVERYONE.
THAT'S NO REASON FOR YOU TO...
OH, YOU'RE HERE, NEGI-SENSEI?
WHAM
HEY! WHAT ARE YOU DOING !?
LIKE YOU DIDN'T KNOW HE WAS HERE!
I'VE BEEN SO WORRIED BECAUSE YOU'VE BEEN SO WORN OUT, AND WEARING SUCH BEAT-UP CLOTHES RECENTLY...
RUSTLE
HERE. IF YOU DON'T MIND, PLEASE WEAR THIS.
THANK YOU VERY MUCH, CLASS REP-SAN!!
UM, WHAT'S WITH YOUR FASHION SENSE!!?
MY... YOU CUT SUCH A GALLANT FIGURE!
WHAT-EVER, JUST GO ALREADY.
NEEEGI-KUN!
LISTEN TO THIS!
I RECORDED IT IN FRONT OF THE HEAD-MASTER'S OFFICE.
ASAKURA-SAN, SAYO-SAN.

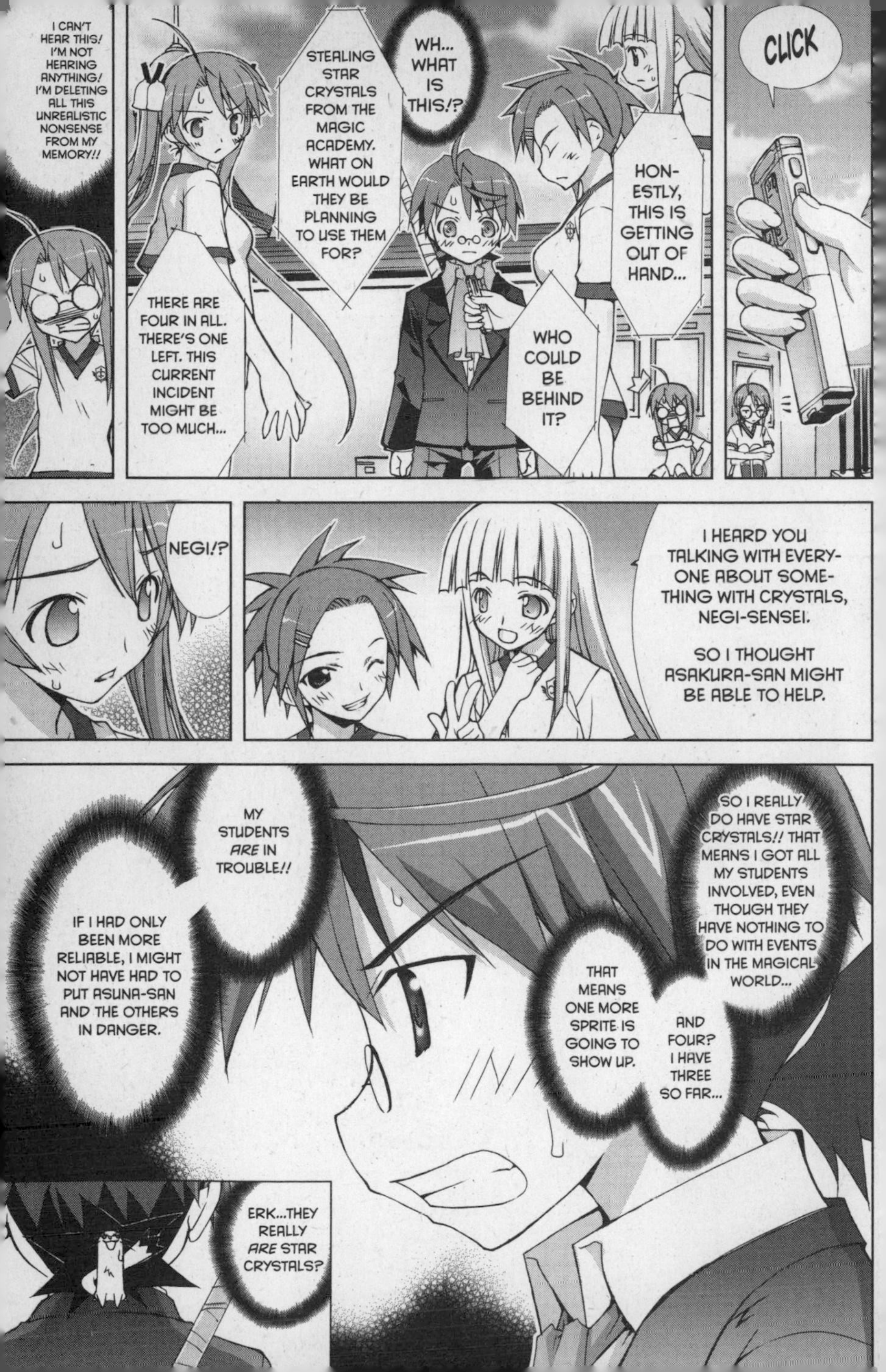
CLICK
WH... WHAT IS THIS!?
STEALING STAR CRYSTALS FROM THE MAGIC ACADEMY. WHAT ON EARTH WOULD THEY BE PLANNING TO USE THEM FOR?
HON-ESTLY, THIS IS GETTING OUT OF HAND...
WHO COULD BE BEHIND IT?
THERE ARE FOUR IN ALL. THERE'S ONE LEFT. THIS CURRENT INCIDENT MIGHT BE TOO MUCH...
I CAN'T HEAR THIS! I'M NOT HEARING ANYTHING! I'M DELETING ALL THIS UNREALISTIC NONSENSE FROM MY MEMORY!!
I HEARD YOU TALKING WITH EVERY-ONE ABOUT SOME-THING WITH CRYSTALS, NEGI-SENSEI.
SO I THOUGHT ASAKURA-SAN MIGHT BE ABLE TO HELP.
NEGI!?
SO I REALLY DO HAVE STAR CRYSTALS!! THAT MEANS I GOT ALL MY STUDENTS INVOLVED, EVEN THOUGH THEY HAVE NOTHING TO DO WITH EVENTS IN THE MAGICAL WORLD...
AND FOUR? I HAVE THREE SO FAR...
THAT MEANS ONE MORE SPRITE IS GOING TO SHOW UP.
MY STUDENTS *ARE* IN TROUBLE!!
IF I HAD ONLY BEEN MORE RELIABLE, I MIGHT NOT HAVE HAD TO PUT ASUNA-SAN AND THE OTHERS IN DANGER.
ERK...THEY REALLY *ARE* STAR CRYSTALS?

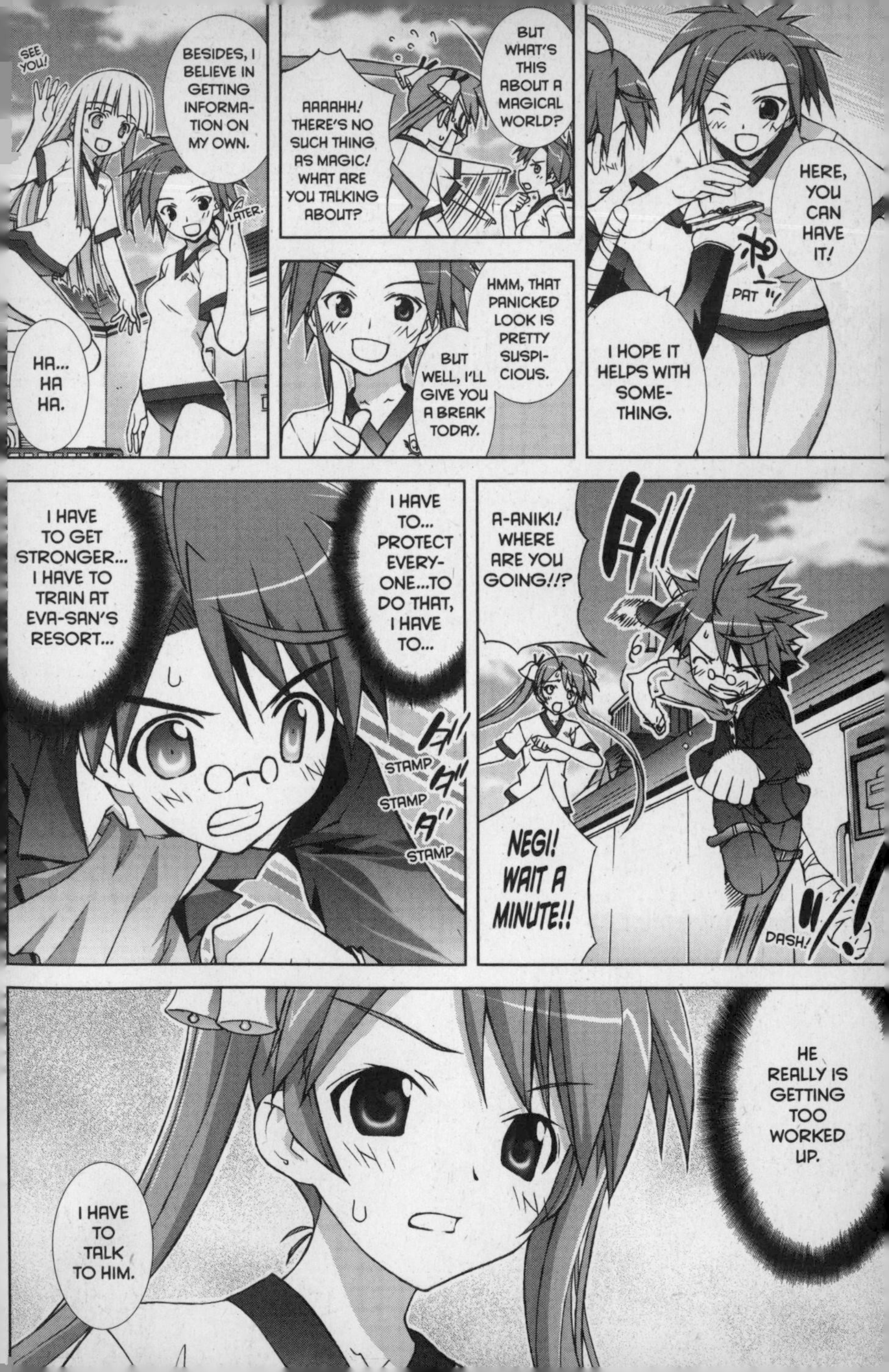
HERE, YOU CAN HAVE IT!
PAT
I HOPE IT HELPS WITH SOMETHING.
BUT WHAT'S THIS ABOUT A MAGICAL WORLD?
AAAAHH! THERE'S NO SUCH THING AS MAGIC! WHAT ARE YOU TALKING ABOUT?
HMM, THAT PANICKED LOOK IS PRETTY SUSPICIOUS.
BUT WELL, I'LL GIVE YOU A BREAK TODAY.
BESIDES, I BELIEVE IN GETTING INFORMATION ON MY OWN.
SEE YOU!
LATER.
HA... HA HA.
A-ANIKI! WHERE ARE YOU GOING!!?
NEGI! WAIT A MINUTE!!
DASH!
I HAVE TO... PROTECT EVERYONE...TO DO THAT, I HAVE TO...
I HAVE TO GET STRONGER... I HAVE TO TRAIN AT EVA-SAN'S RESORT...
STAMP
STAMP
STAMP
HE REALLY IS GETTING TOO WORKED UP.
I HAVE TO TALK TO HIM.

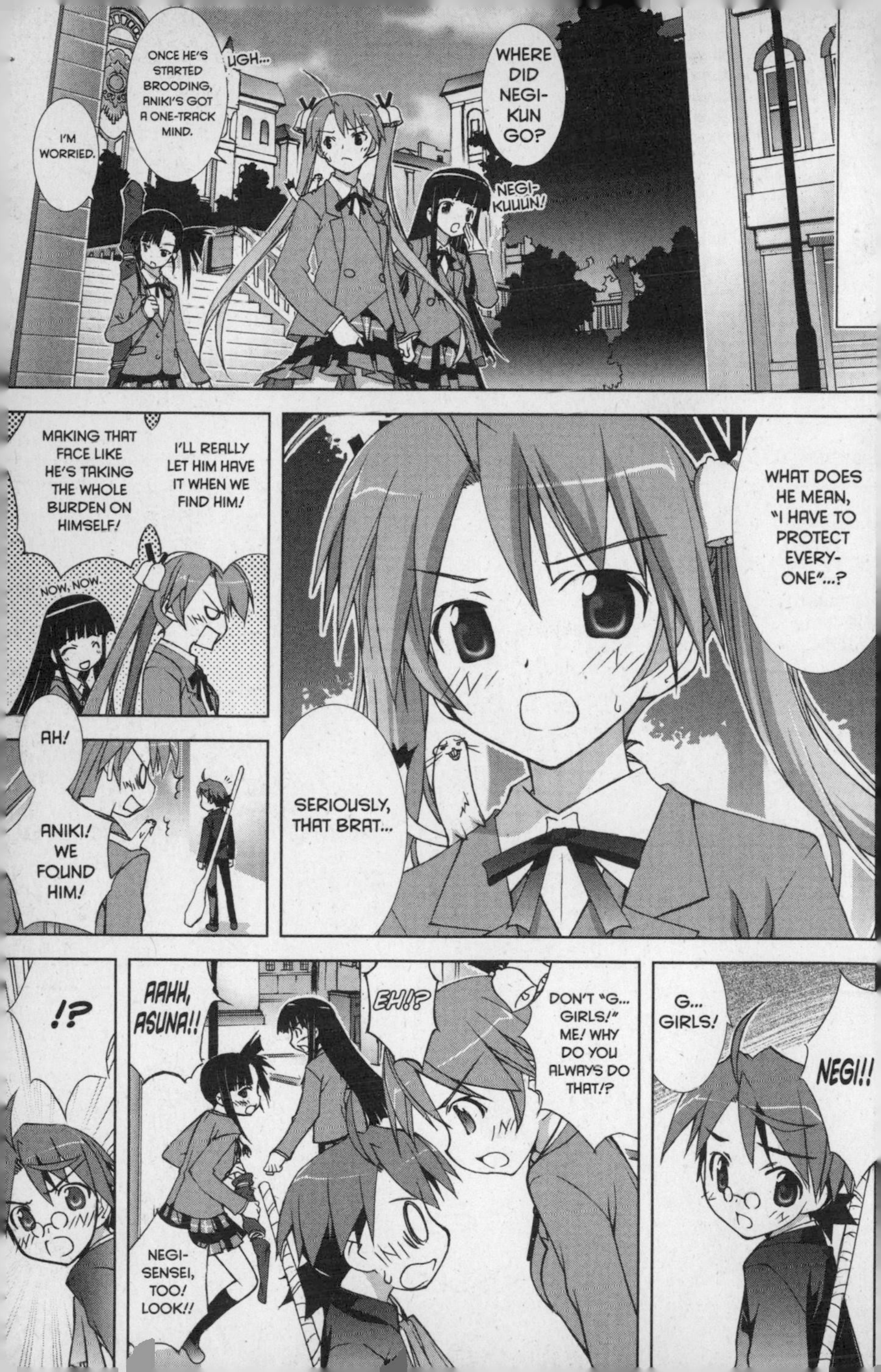
WHERE DID NEGI-KUN GO?
NEGI-KUUUN!
UGH...
ONCE HE'S STARTED BROODING, ANIKI'S GOT A ONE-TRACK MIND.
I'M WORRIED.
WHAT DOES HE MEAN, "I HAVE TO PROTECT EVERY-ONE"...?
SERIOUSLY, THAT BRAT...
I'LL REALLY LET HIM HAVE IT WHEN WE FIND HIM!
MAKING THAT FACE LIKE HE'S TAKING THE WHOLE BURDEN ON HIMSELF!
NOW, NOW.
AH!
ANIKI! WE FOUND HIM!
G... GIRLS!
NEGI!!
DON'T "G... GIRLS!" ME! WHY DO YOU ALWAYS DO THAT!?
EH!?
AAHH, ASUNA!!
NEGI-SENSEI, TOO! LOOK!!
!?

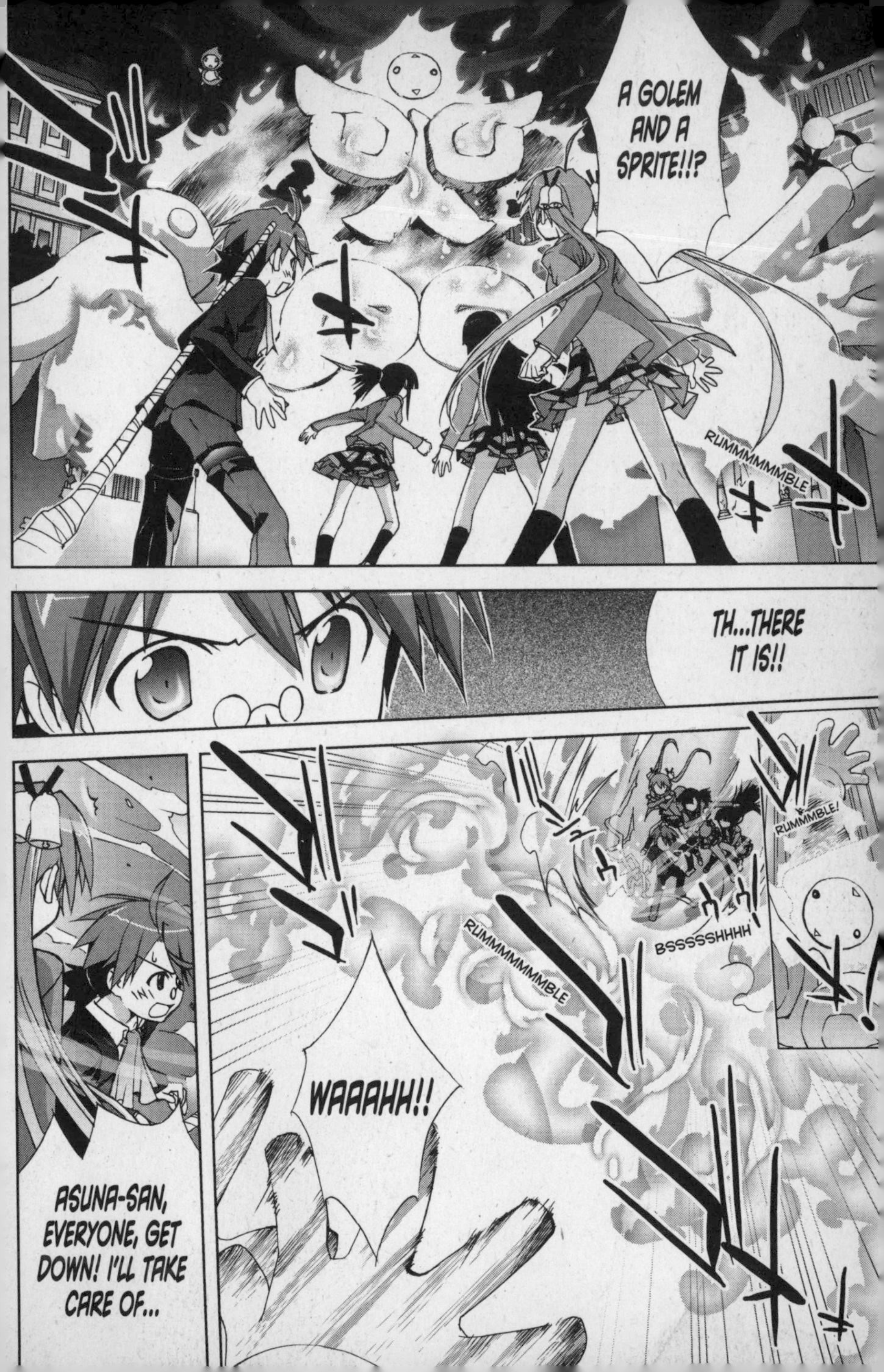
A GOLEM AND A SPRITE!!?
RUMMMMMMMBLE
TH...THERE IT IS!!
RUMMMBLE!
BSSSSSHHHH
RUMMMMMMMMBLE
WAAAHH!!
ASUNA-SAN, EVERYONE, GET DOWN! I'LL TAKE CARE OF...

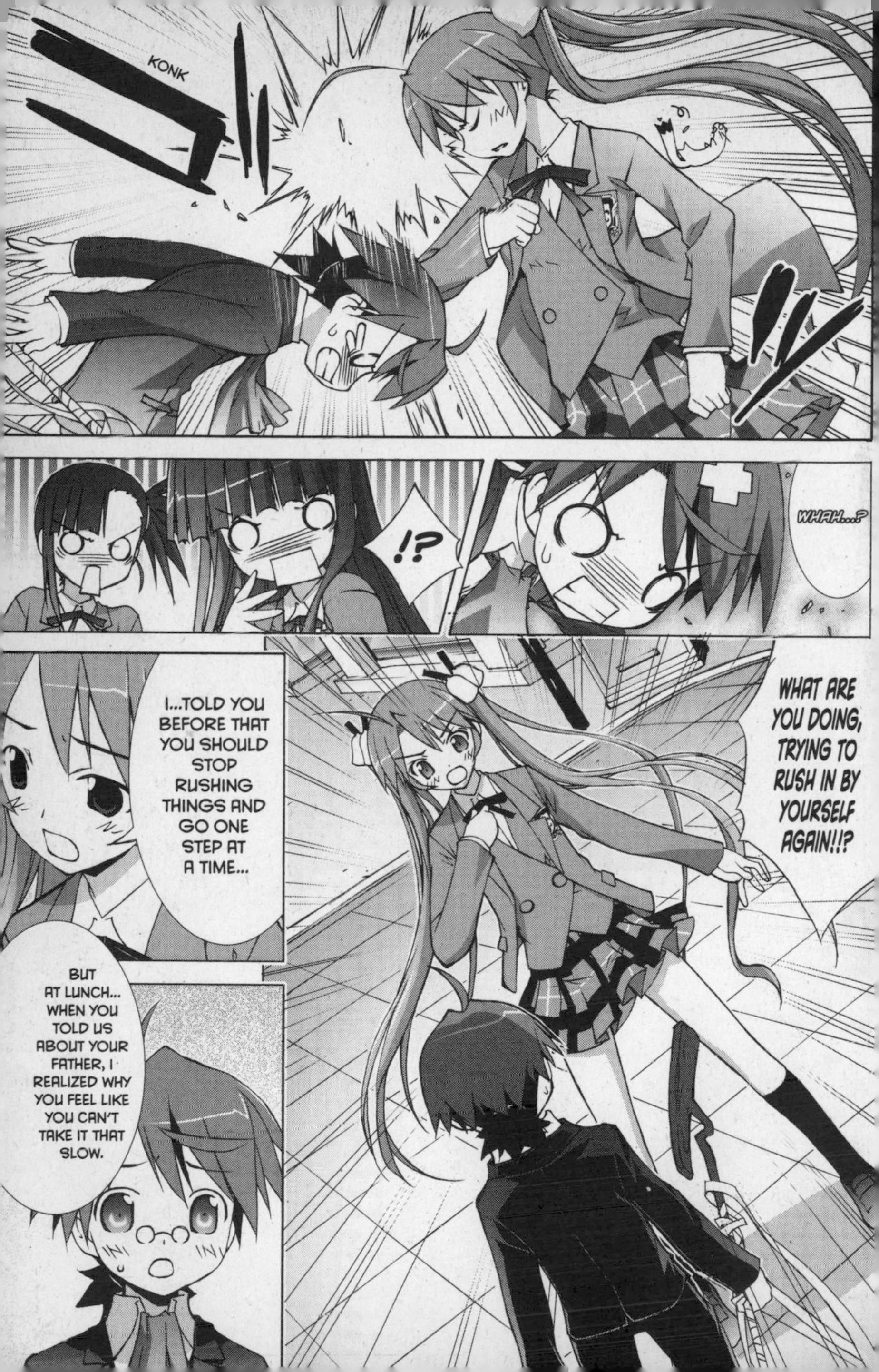
KONK
WHAH...?
!?
WHAT ARE YOU DOING, TRYING TO RUSH IN BY YOURSELF AGAIN!!?
I...TOLD YOU BEFORE THAT YOU SHOULD STOP RUSHING THINGS AND GO ONE STEP AT A TIME...
BUT AT LUNCH... WHEN YOU TOLD US ABOUT YOUR FATHER, I REALIZED WHY YOU FEEL LIKE YOU CAN'T TAKE IT THAT SLOW.

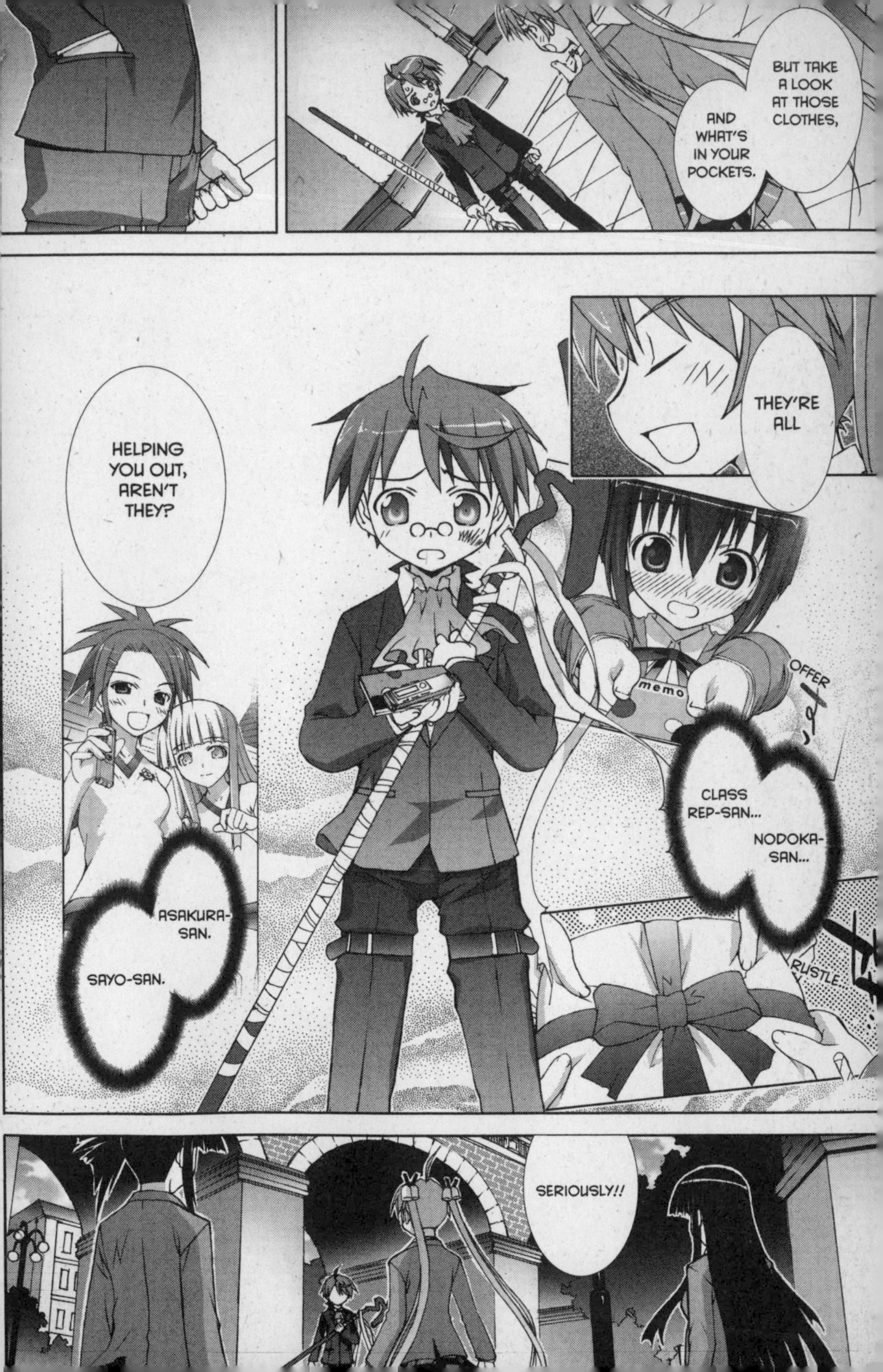
BUT TAKE A LOOK AT THOSE CLOTHES,
AND WHAT'S IN YOUR POCKETS.
THEY'RE ALL
memo
OFFER
CLASS REP-SAN...
NODOKA-SAN...
RUSTLE
HELPING YOU OUT, AREN'T THEY?
ASAKURA-SAN.
SAYO-SAN.
SERIOUSLY!!

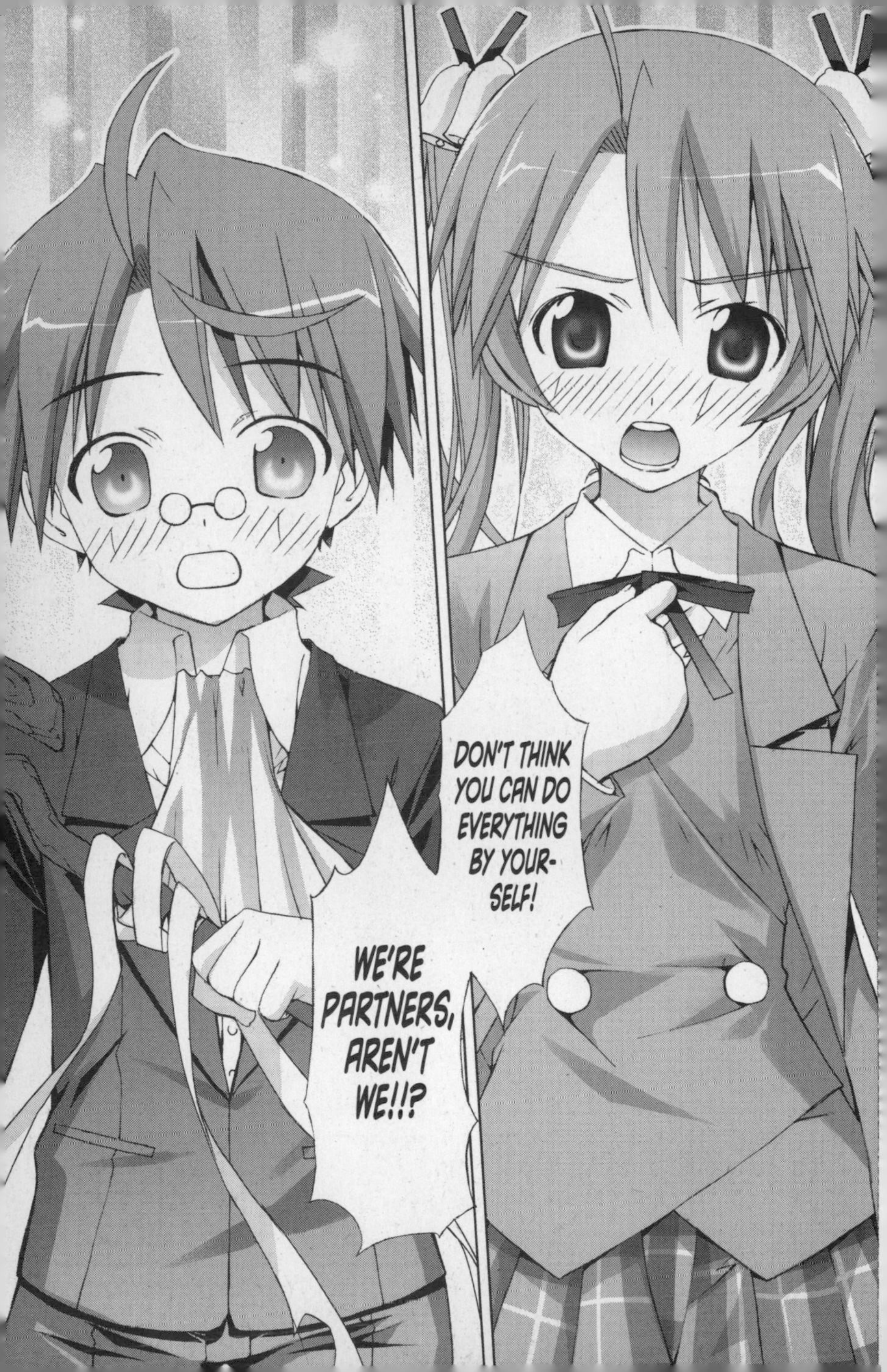
DON'T THINK YOU CAN DO EVERYTHING BY YOUR-SELF!
WE'RE PARTNERS, AREN'T WE!!?

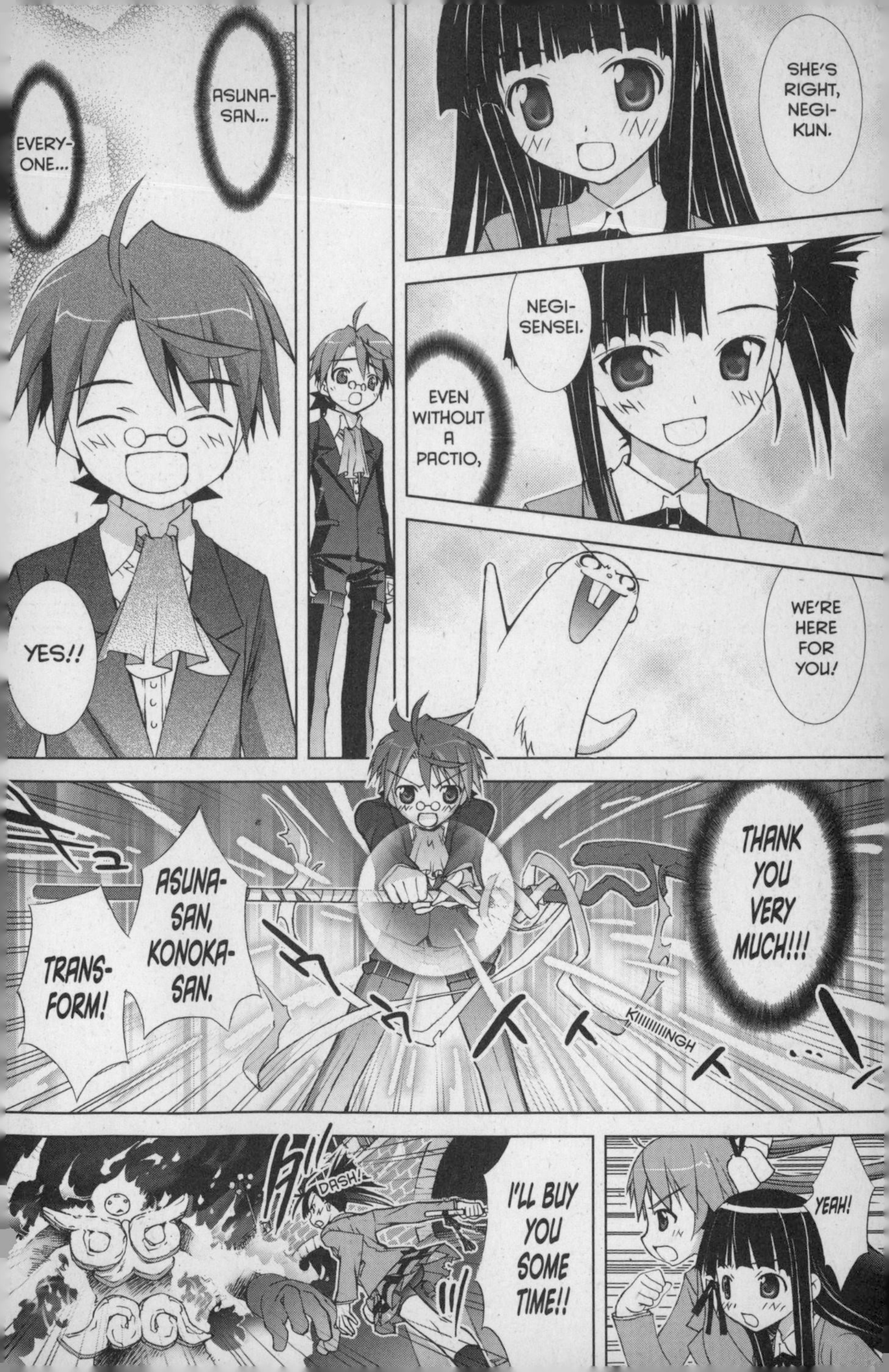
SHE'S RIGHT, NEGI-KUN.
NEGI-SENSEI.
EVEN WITHOUT A PACTIO,
WE'RE HERE FOR YOU!
ASUNA-SAN...
EVERY-ONE...
YES!!
THANK YOU VERY MUCH!!!
KIIIIIIIIINGH
ASUNA-SAN, KONOKA-SAN.
TRANS-FORM!
YEAH!
I'LL BUY YOU SOME TIME!!
DASH!

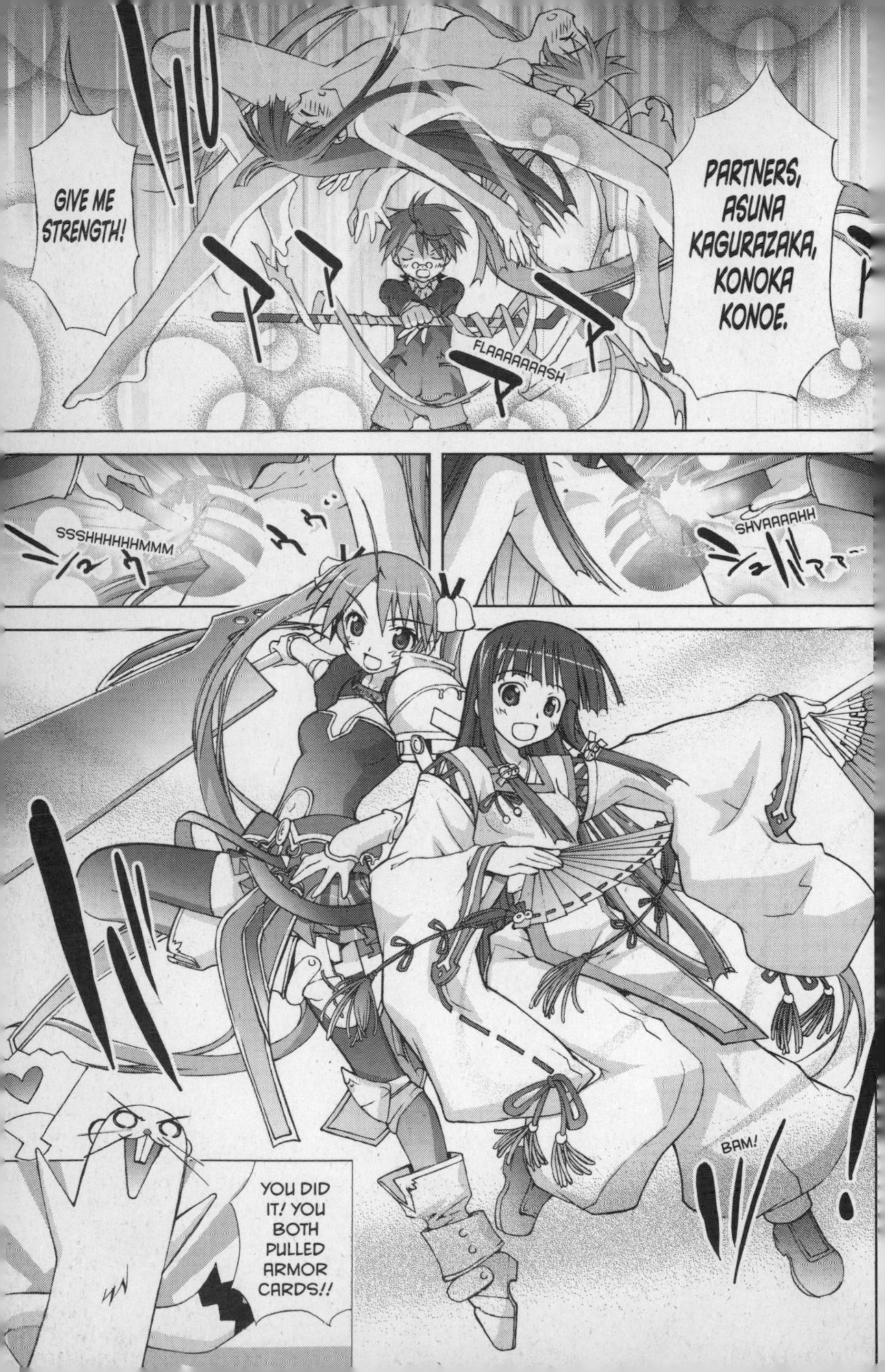
PARTNERS, ASUNA KAGURAZAKA, KONOKA KONOE.
FLAAAAAAASH
GIVE ME STRENGTH!
SHVAAAAHH
SSSHHHHHHHMMM
BAM!
YOU DID IT! YOU BOTH PULLED ARMOR CARDS!!

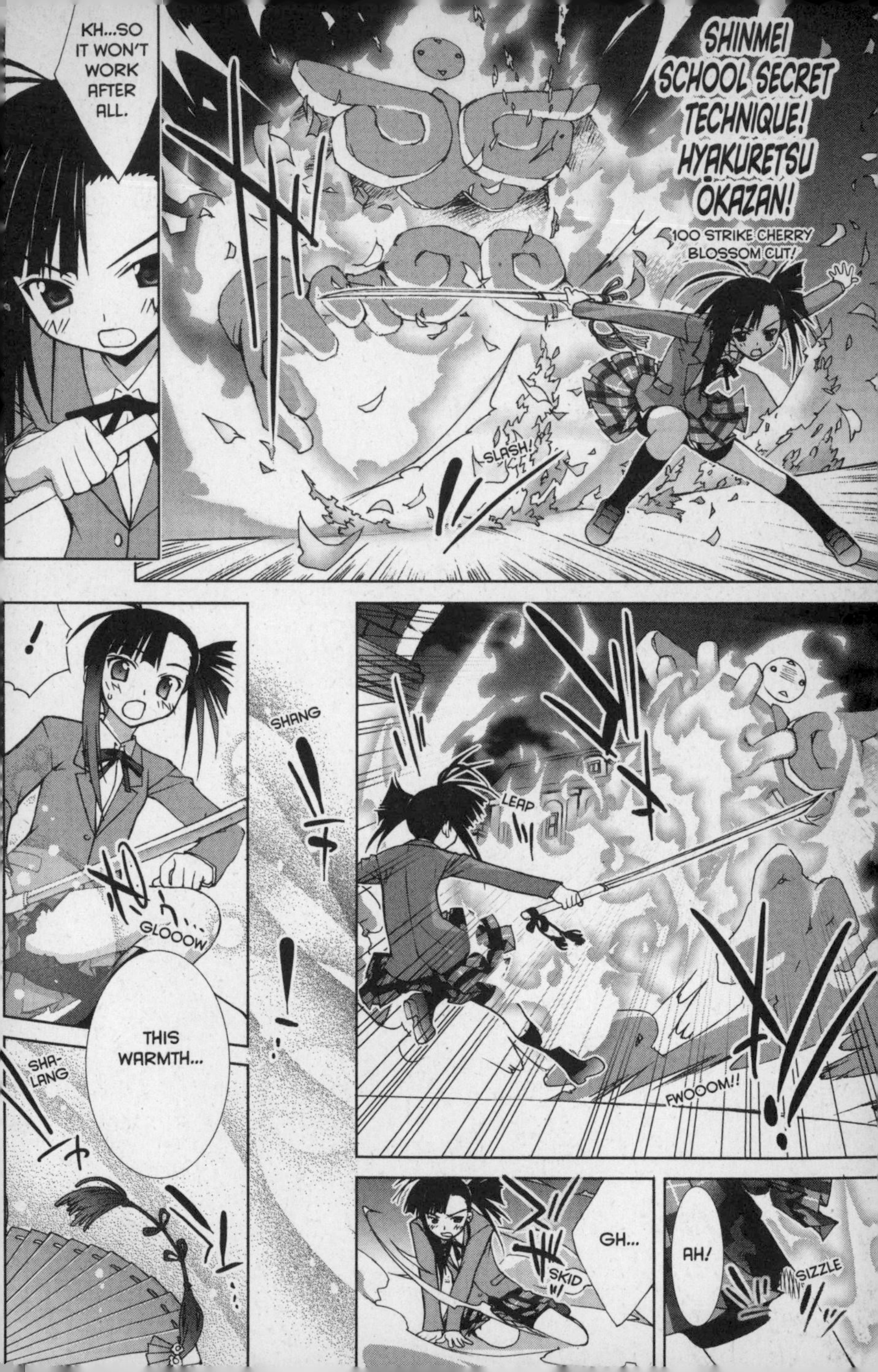
SHINMEI SCHOOL SECRET TECHNIQUE! HYAKURETSU ŌKAZAN!
100 STRIKE CHERRY BLOSSOM CUT!
SLASH!
KH...SO IT WON'T WORK AFTER ALL.
LEAP
FWOOOM!!
SIZZLE
AH!
GH...
SKID
!
SHANG
GLOOOW
THIS WARMTH...
SHA-LANG

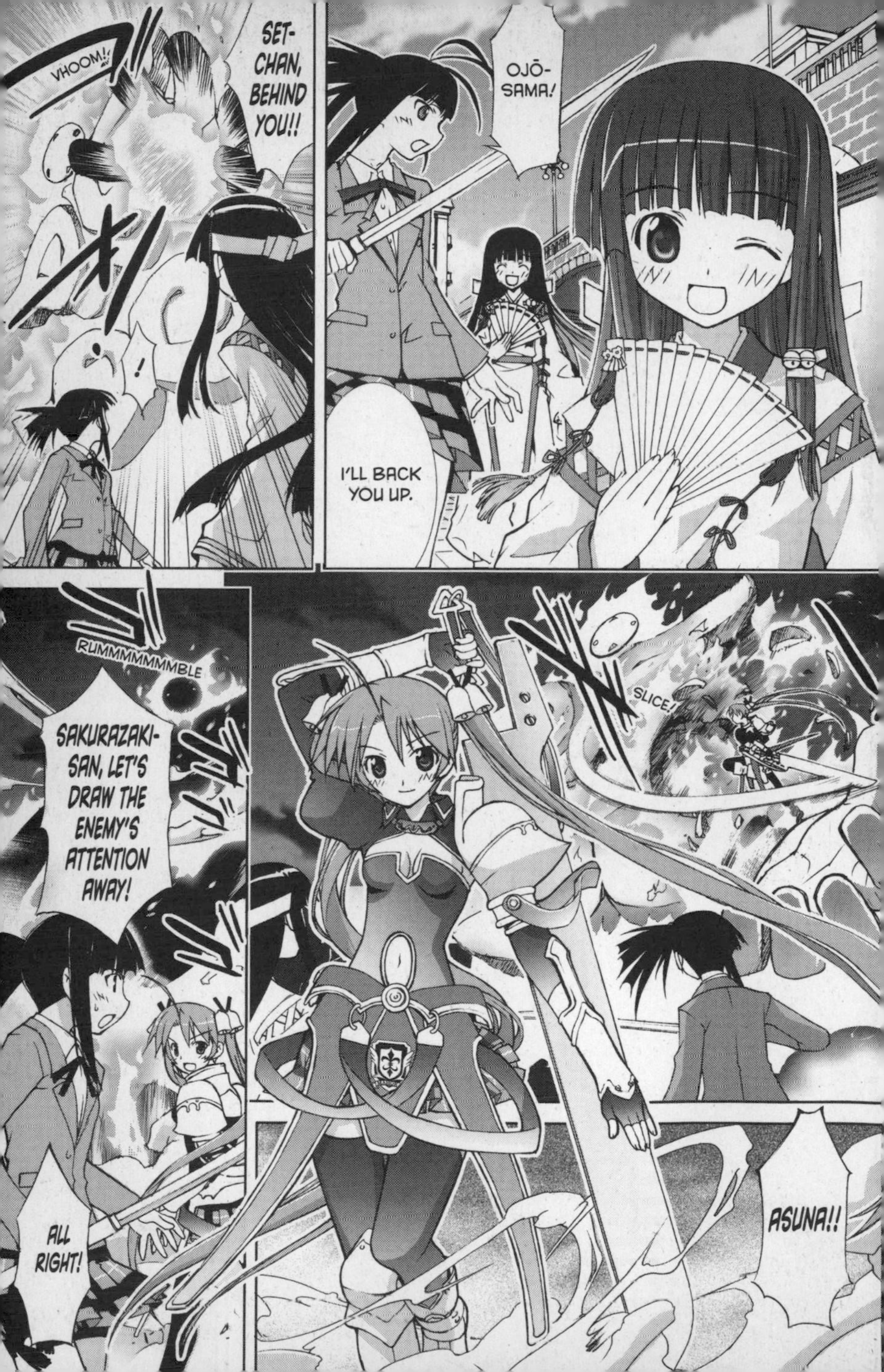
OJŌ-SAMA!
I'LL BACK YOU UP.
SET-CHAN, BEHIND YOU!!
VHOOM!!
SLICE!
ASUNA!!
RUMMMMMMMBLE
SAKURAZAKI-SAN, LET'S DRAW THE ENEMY'S ATTENTION AWAY!
ALL RIGHT!

HERE IT COMES!!

BWAH!

RASTEL MASKIL MAGISTER.

BOOOOOOOOOM

NEGI! NOW!!

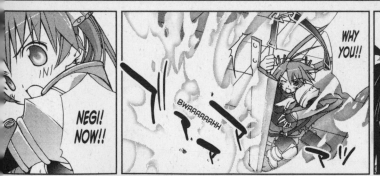

BWAAAAAAHH

WHY YOU!!

ASUNA-SAN! IT'S COMING BACK!

FLET UNA VENTE!

BLOW, GUST OF WIND!

GHINNNNNNGH

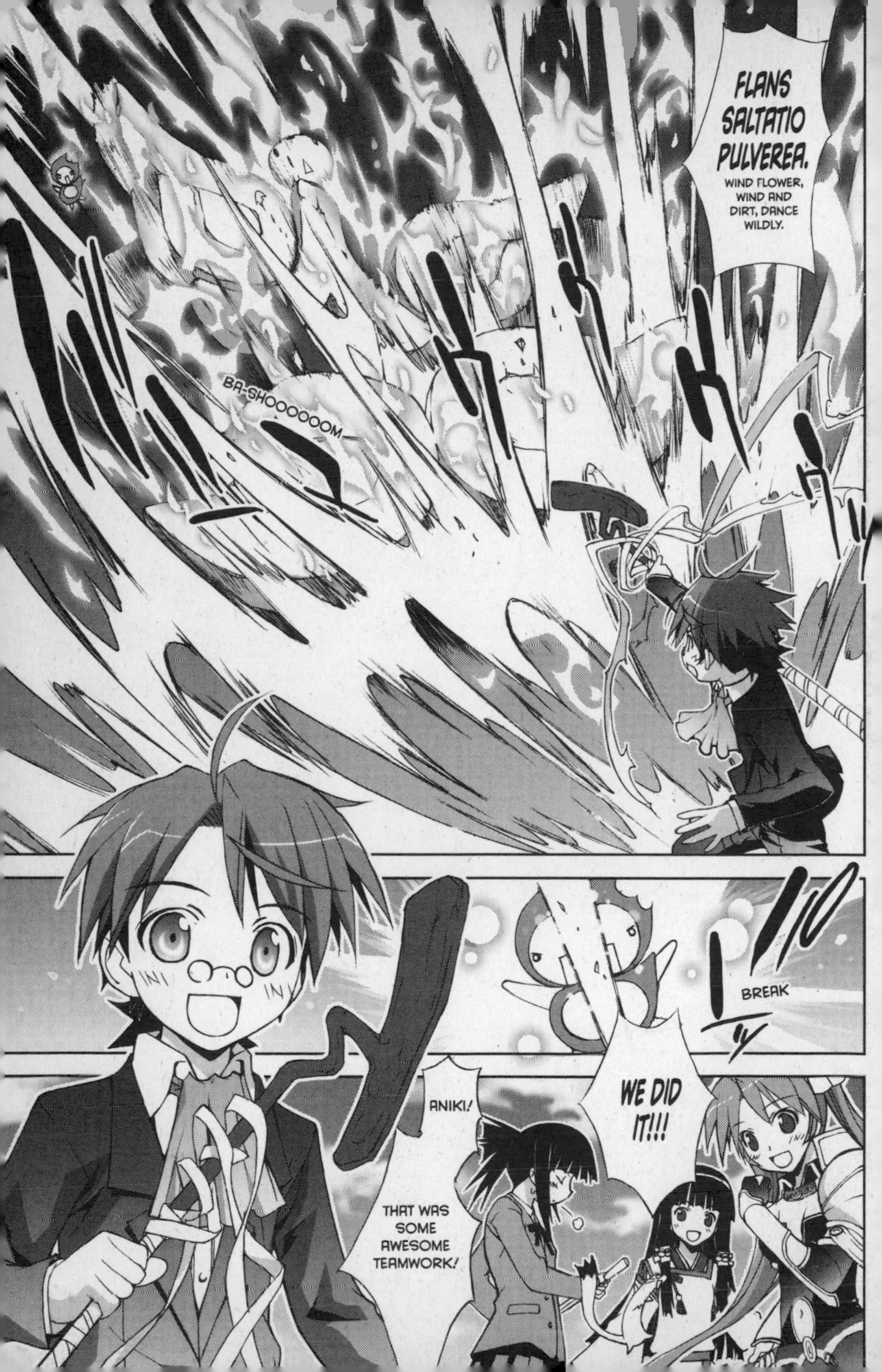
FLANS SALTATIO PULVEREA.
WIND FLOWER, WIND AND DIRT, DANCE WILDLY.
BA-SHOOOOOOM
BREAK
WE DID IT!!!
ANIKI!
THAT WAS SOME AWESOME TEAMWORK!

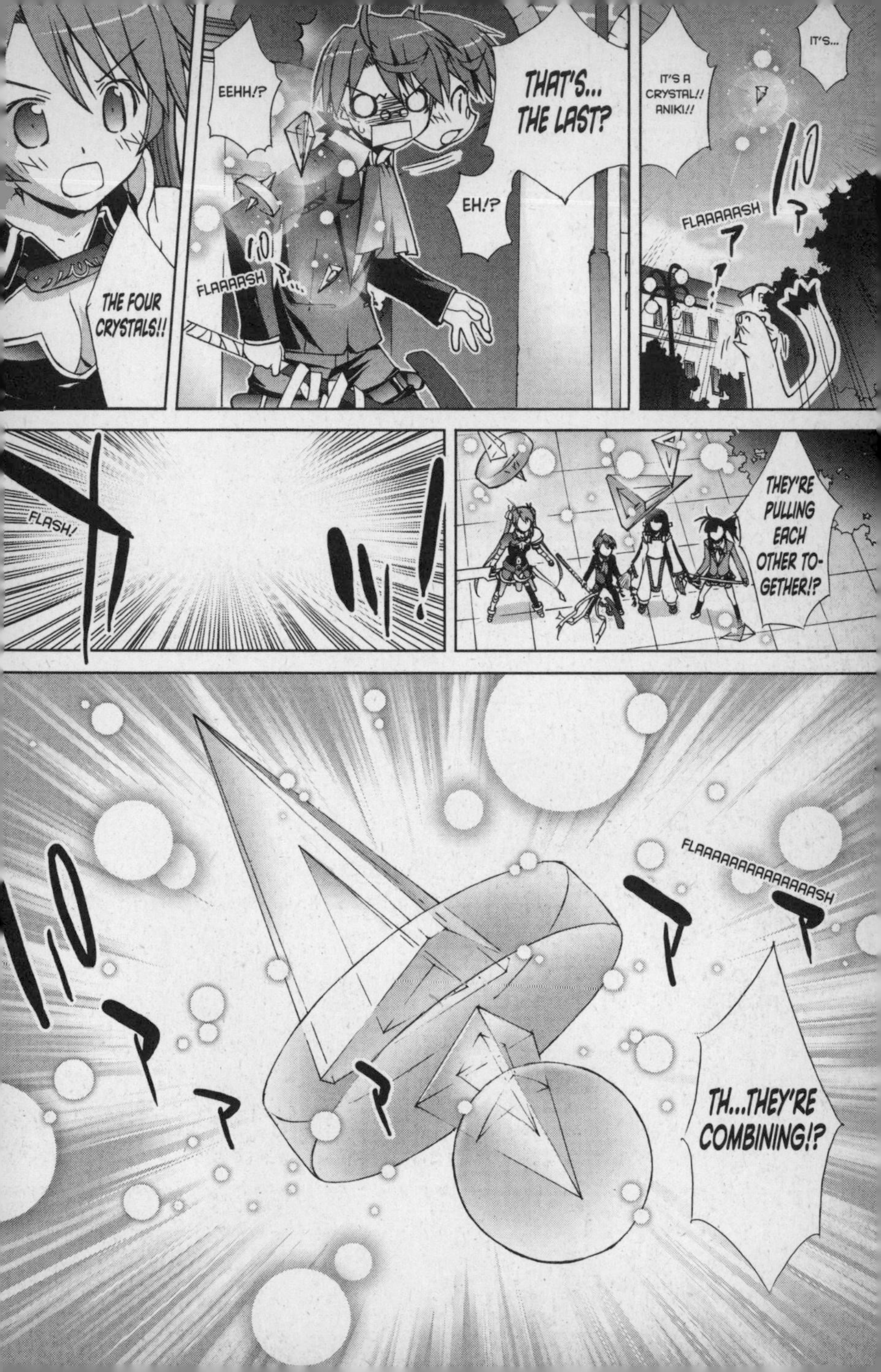
IT'S...
IT'S A CRYSTAL!! ANIKI!!
FLAAAAAASH
THAT'S... THE LAST?
EH!?
EEHH!?
FLAAAAASH
THE FOUR CRYSTALS!!
THEY'RE PULLING EACH OTHER TO-GETHER!?
FLASH!
FLAAAAAAAAAAAAAAAASH
TH...THEY'RE COMBINING!?

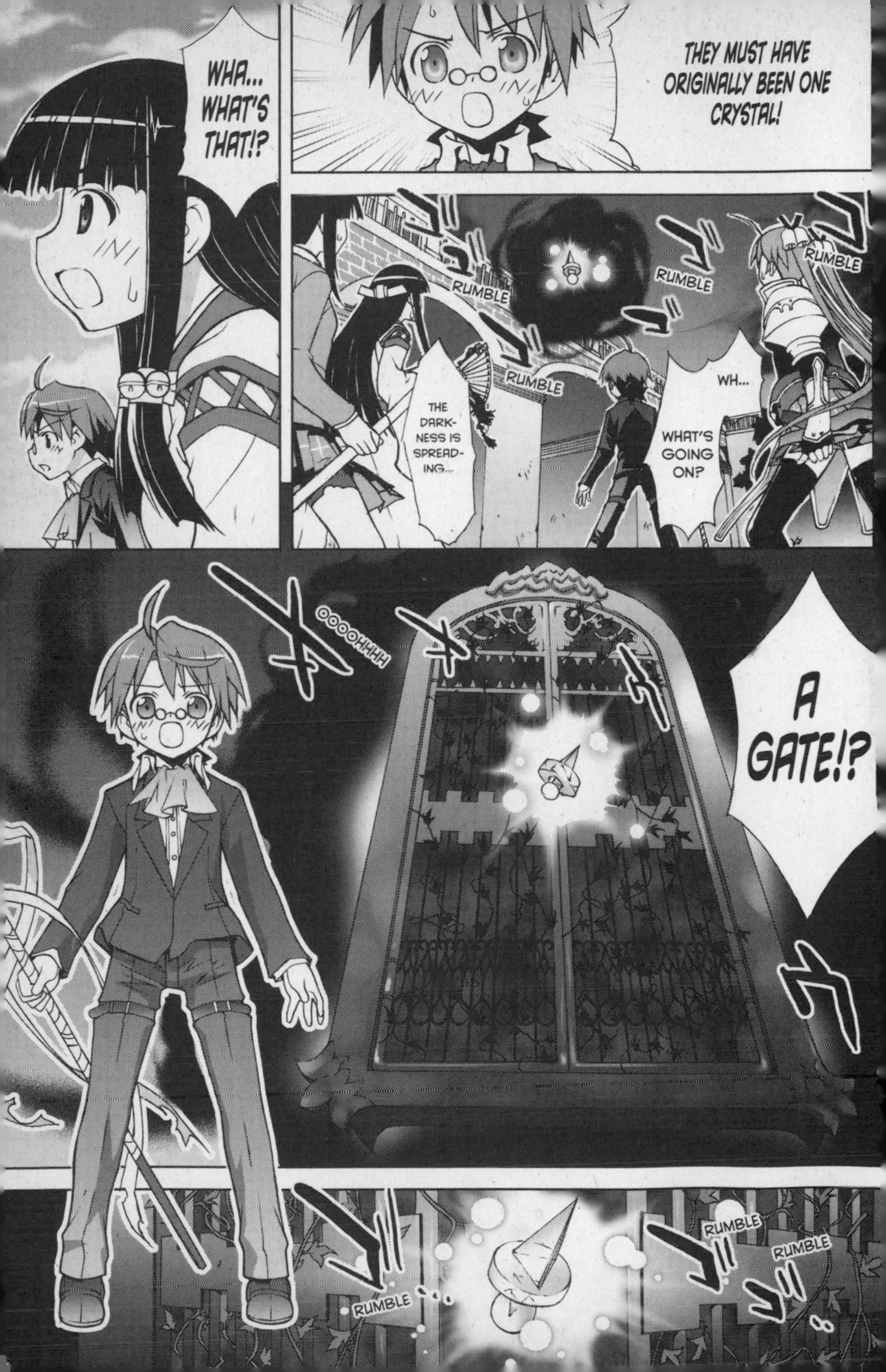
THEY MUST HAVE ORIGINALLY BEEN ONE CRYSTAL!
RUMBLE
RUMBLE
WH...
WHAT'S GOING ON?
RUMBLE
RUMBLE
THE DARK-NESS IS SPREAD-ING...
WHA... WHAT'S THAT!?
A GATE!?
OOOOOHHHH
RUMBLE
RUMBLE
RUMBLE

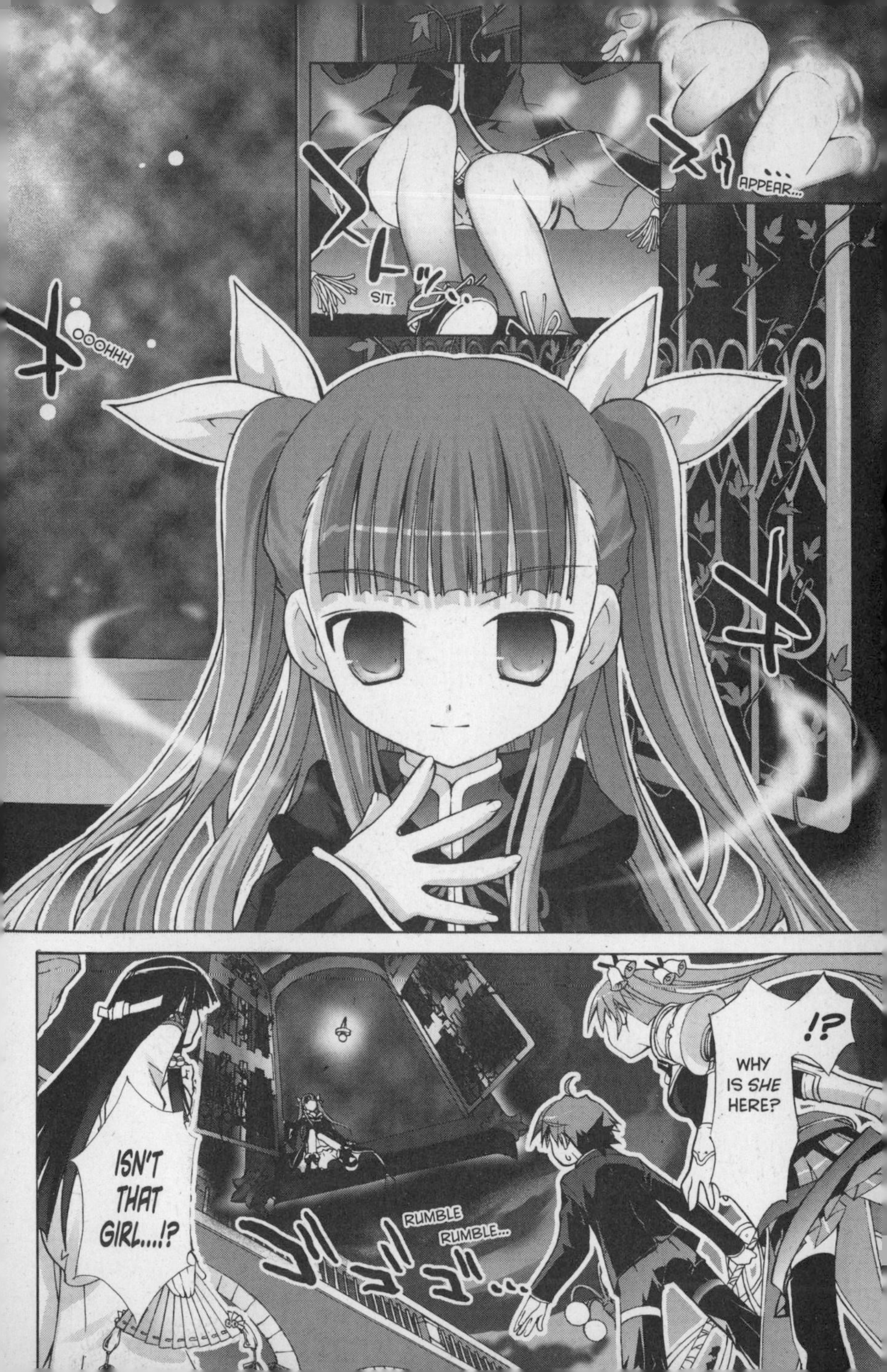

...APPEAR...
SIT.
OOOHHH
!?
WHY IS SHE HERE?
RUMBLE RUMBLE...
ISN'T THAT GIRL...!?

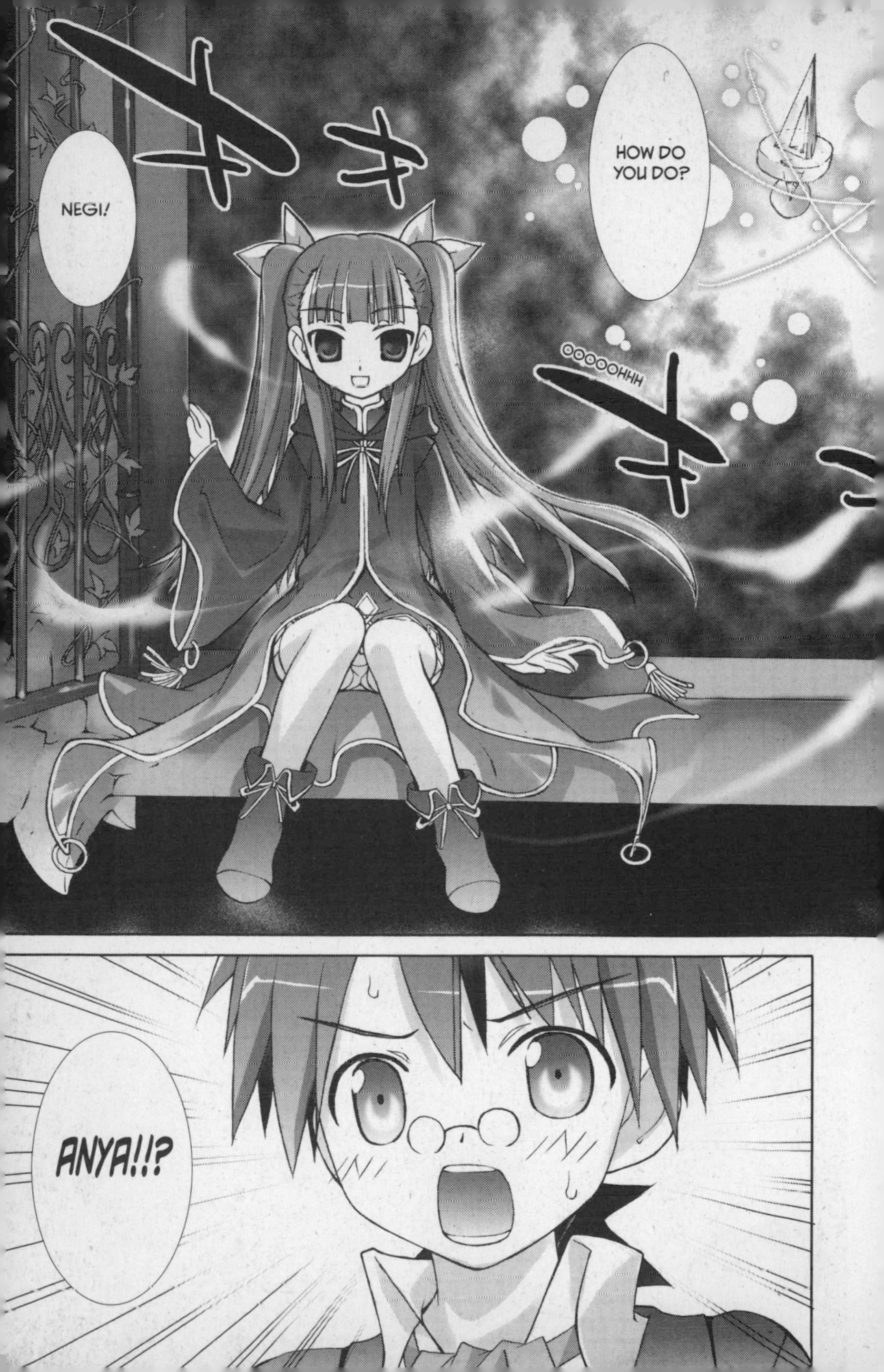
HOW DO YOU DO?
NEGI!
OOOOOHHH
ANYA!!?

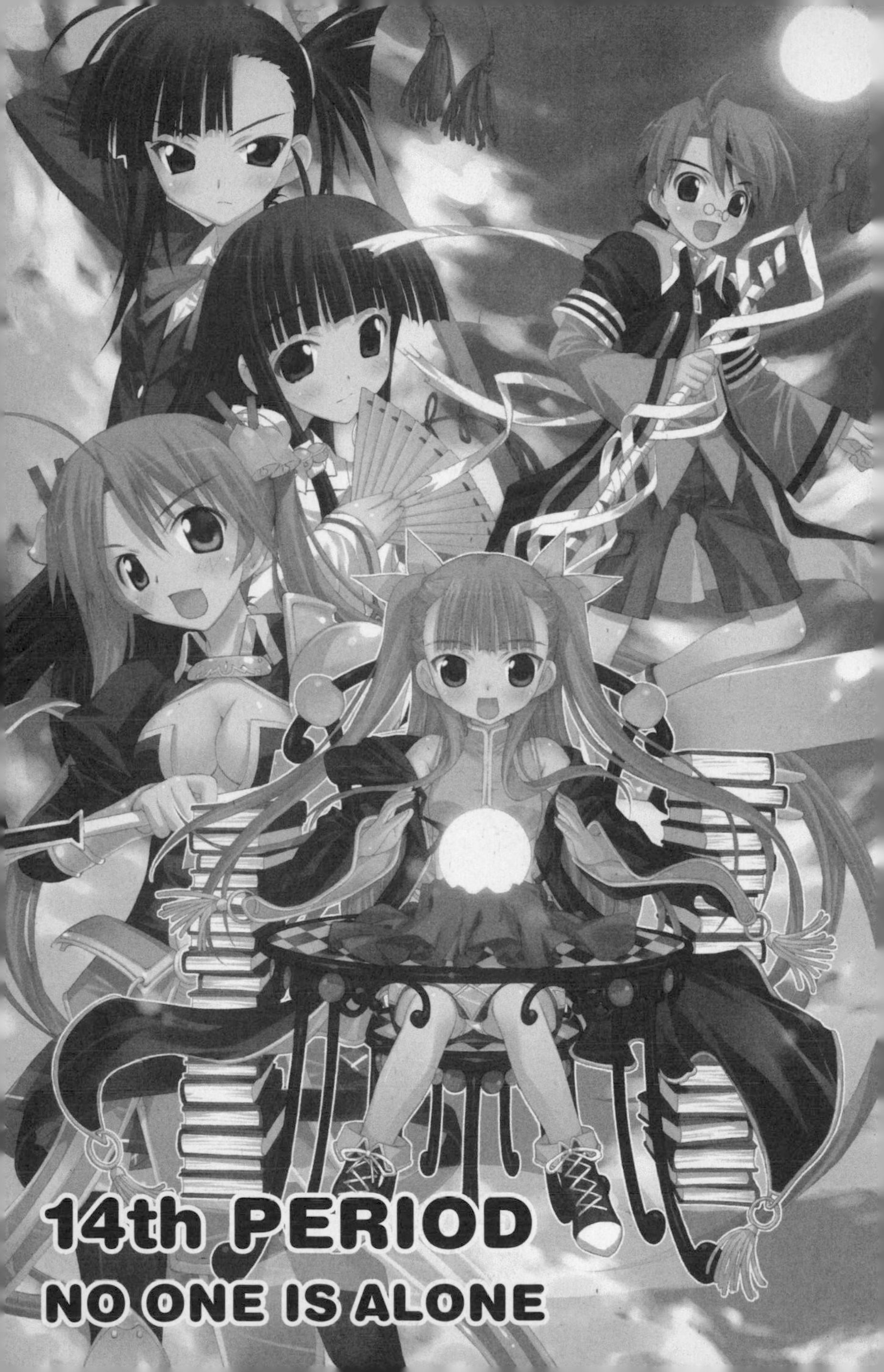
14th PERIOD
NO ONE IS ALONE

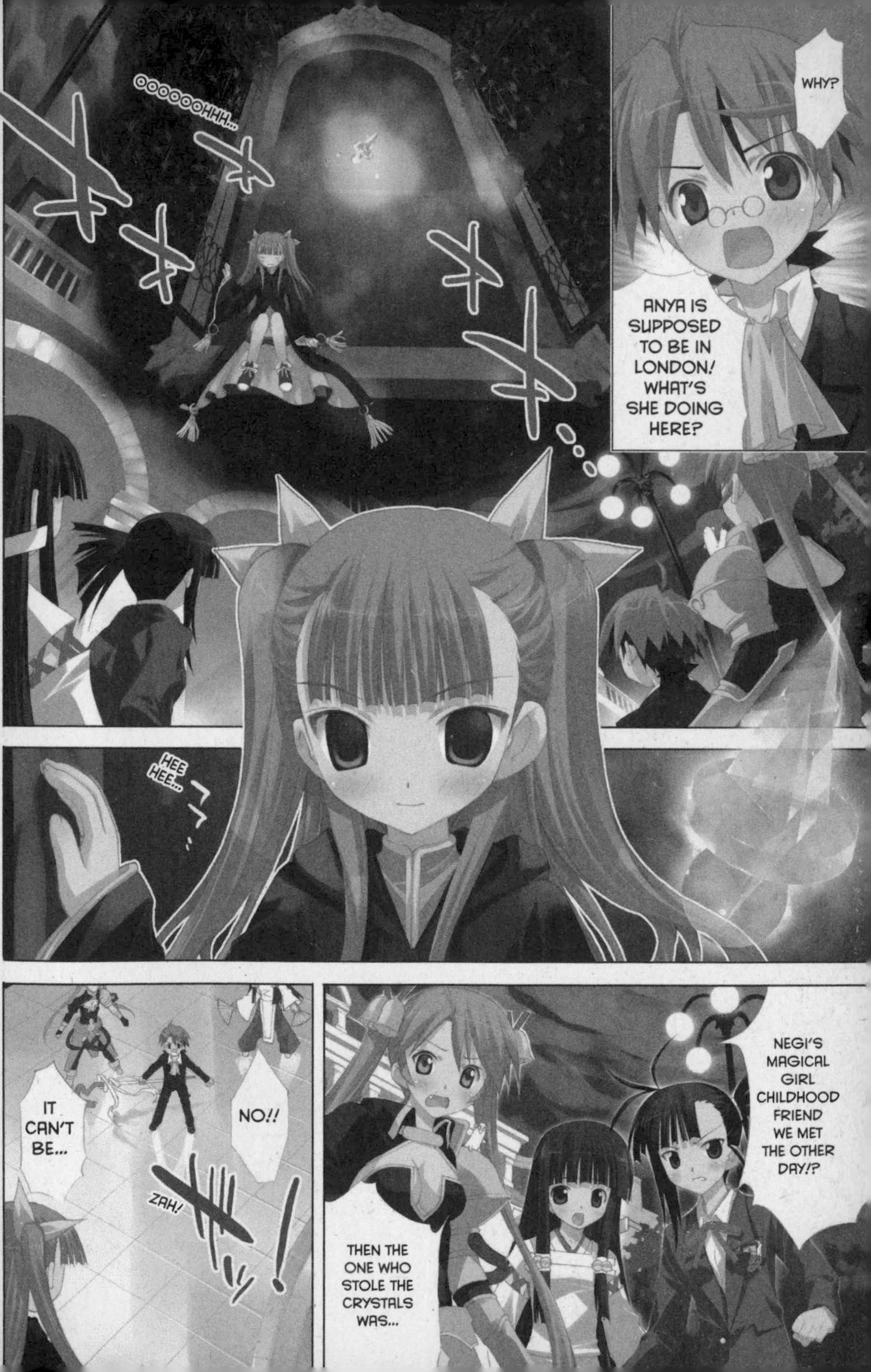
WHY?
ANYA IS SUPPOSED TO BE IN LONDON! WHAT'S SHE DOING HERE?
OOOOOOOHHH...
HEE HEE...
NEGI'S MAGICAL GIRL CHILDHOOD FRIEND WE MET THE OTHER DAY!?
THEN THE ONE WHO STOLE THE CRYSTALS WAS...
NO!!
IT CAN'T BE...
ZAH!

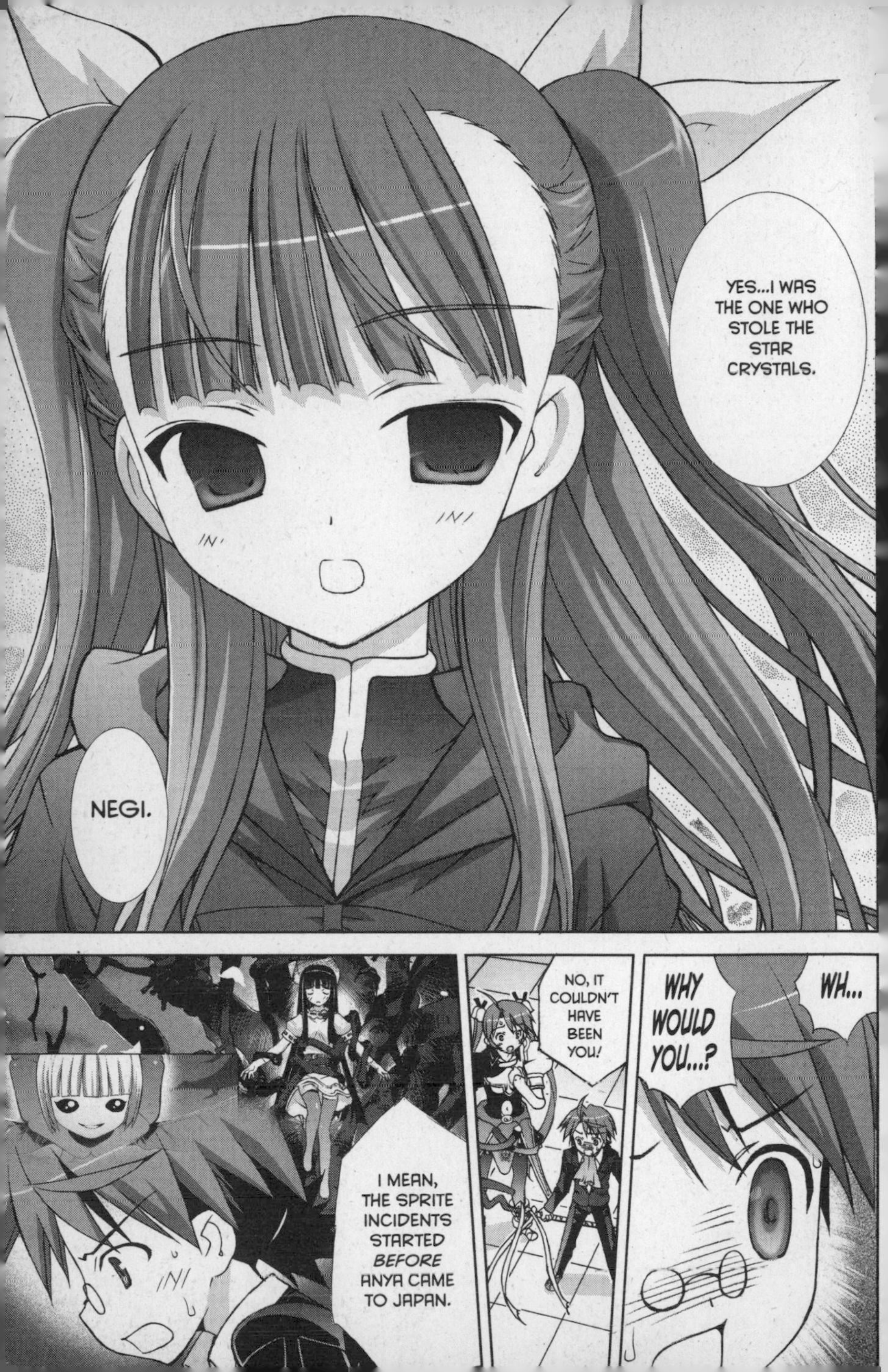
YES...I WAS THE ONE WHO STOLE THE STAR CRYSTALS.
NEGI.
WH...
WHY WOULD YOU...?
NO, IT COULDN'T HAVE BEEN YOU!
I MEAN, THE SPRITE INCIDENTS STARTED *BEFORE* ANYA CAME TO JAPAN.

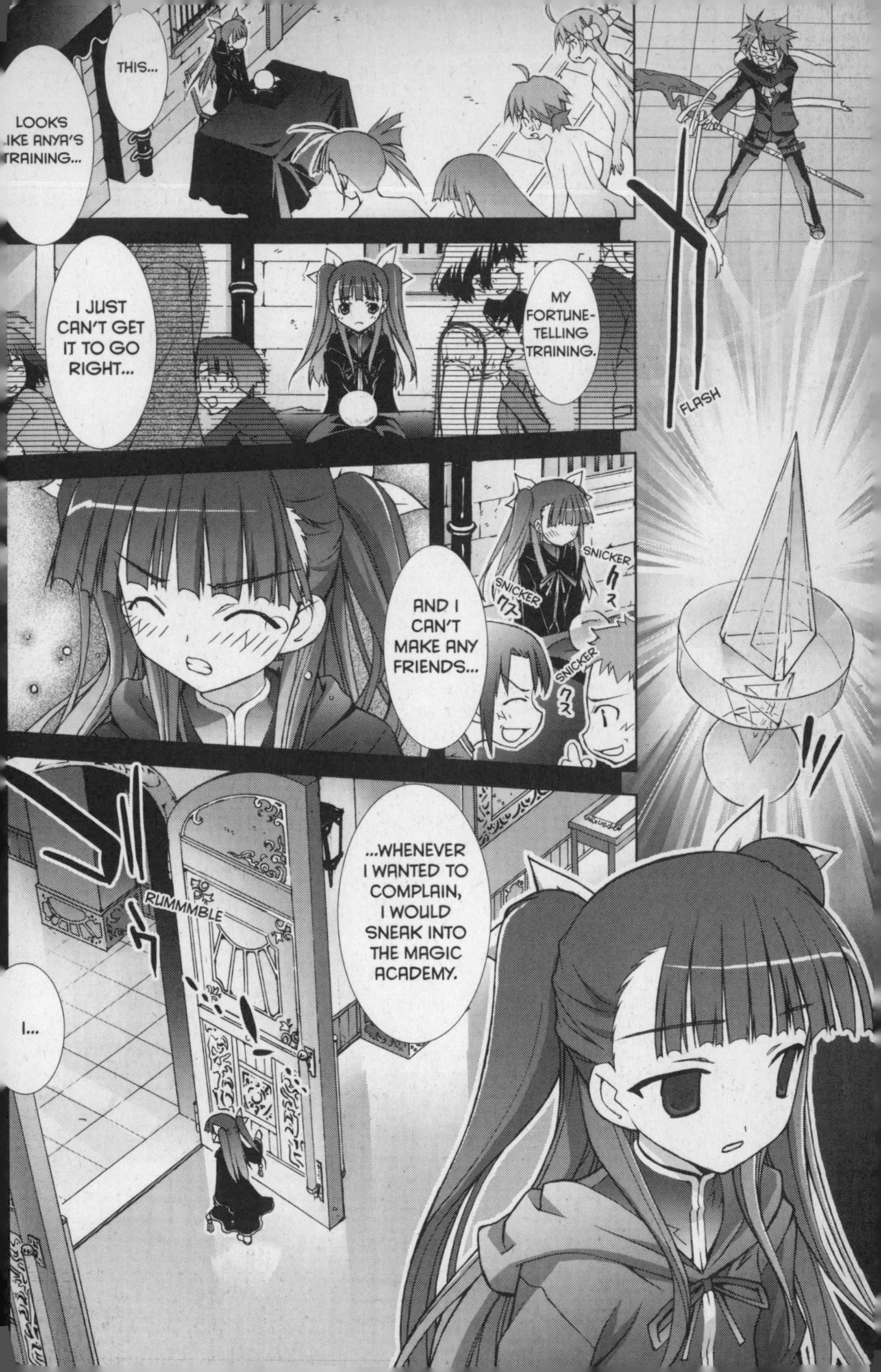
FLASH
THIS...
LOOKS LIKE ANYA'S TRAINING...
MY FORTUNE-TELLING TRAINING.
I JUST CAN'T GET IT TO GO RIGHT...
SNICKER クス
SNICKER クス
SNICKER クス
AND I CAN'T MAKE ANY FRIENDS...
...WHENEVER I WANTED TO COMPLAIN, I WOULD SNEAK INTO THE MAGIC ACADEMY.
RUMMMBLE
I...

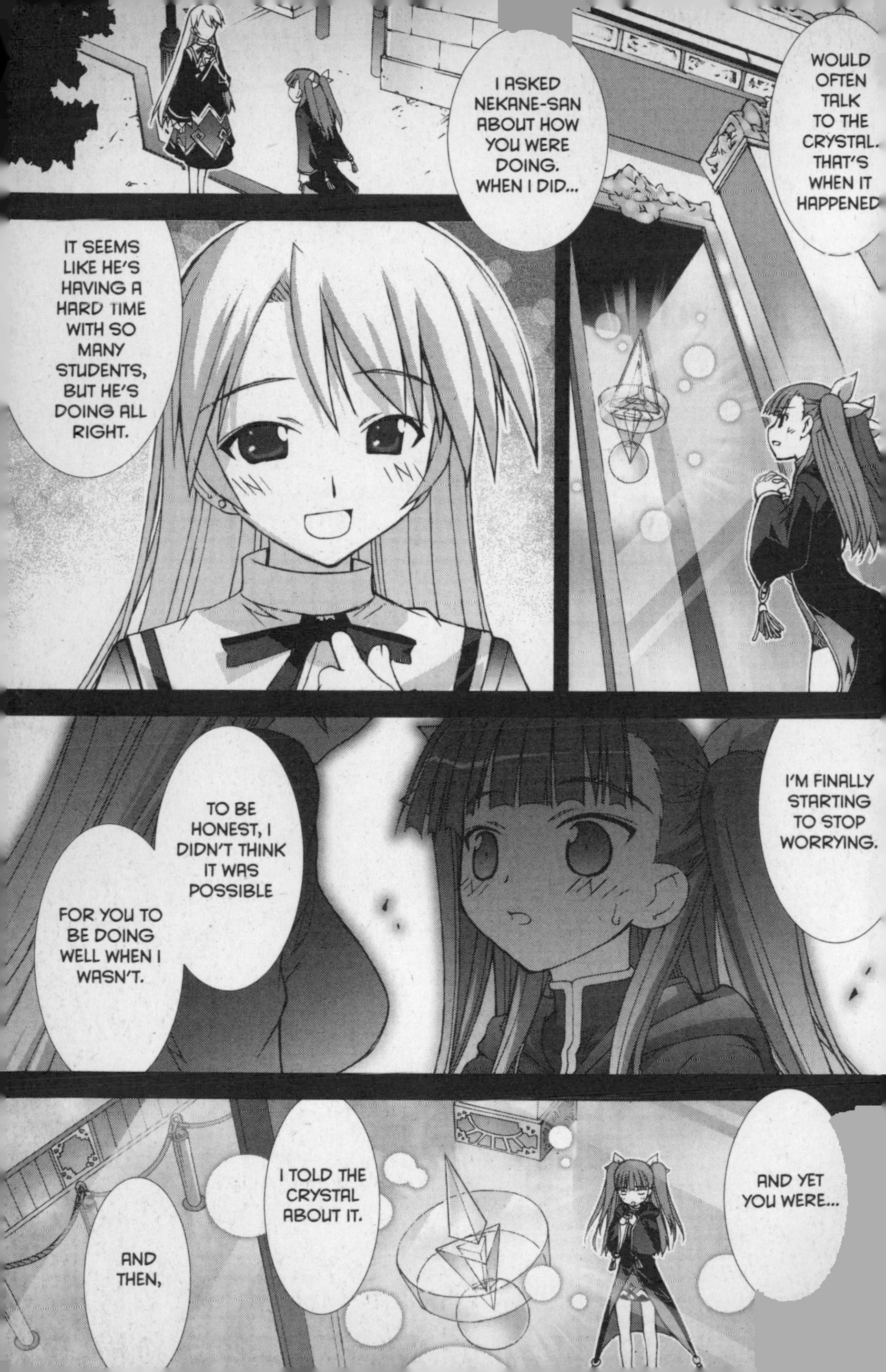
WOULD OFTEN TALK TO THE CRYSTAL. THAT'S WHEN IT HAPPENED
I ASKED NEKANE-SAN ABOUT HOW YOU WERE DOING. WHEN I DID...
IT SEEMS LIKE HE'S HAVING A HARD TIME WITH SO MANY STUDENTS, BUT HE'S DOING ALL RIGHT.
I'M FINALLY STARTING TO STOP WORRYING.
TO BE HONEST, I DIDN'T THINK IT WAS POSSIBLE
FOR YOU TO BE DOING WELL WHEN I WASN'T.
AND YET YOU WERE...
I TOLD THE CRYSTAL ABOUT IT.
AND THEN,

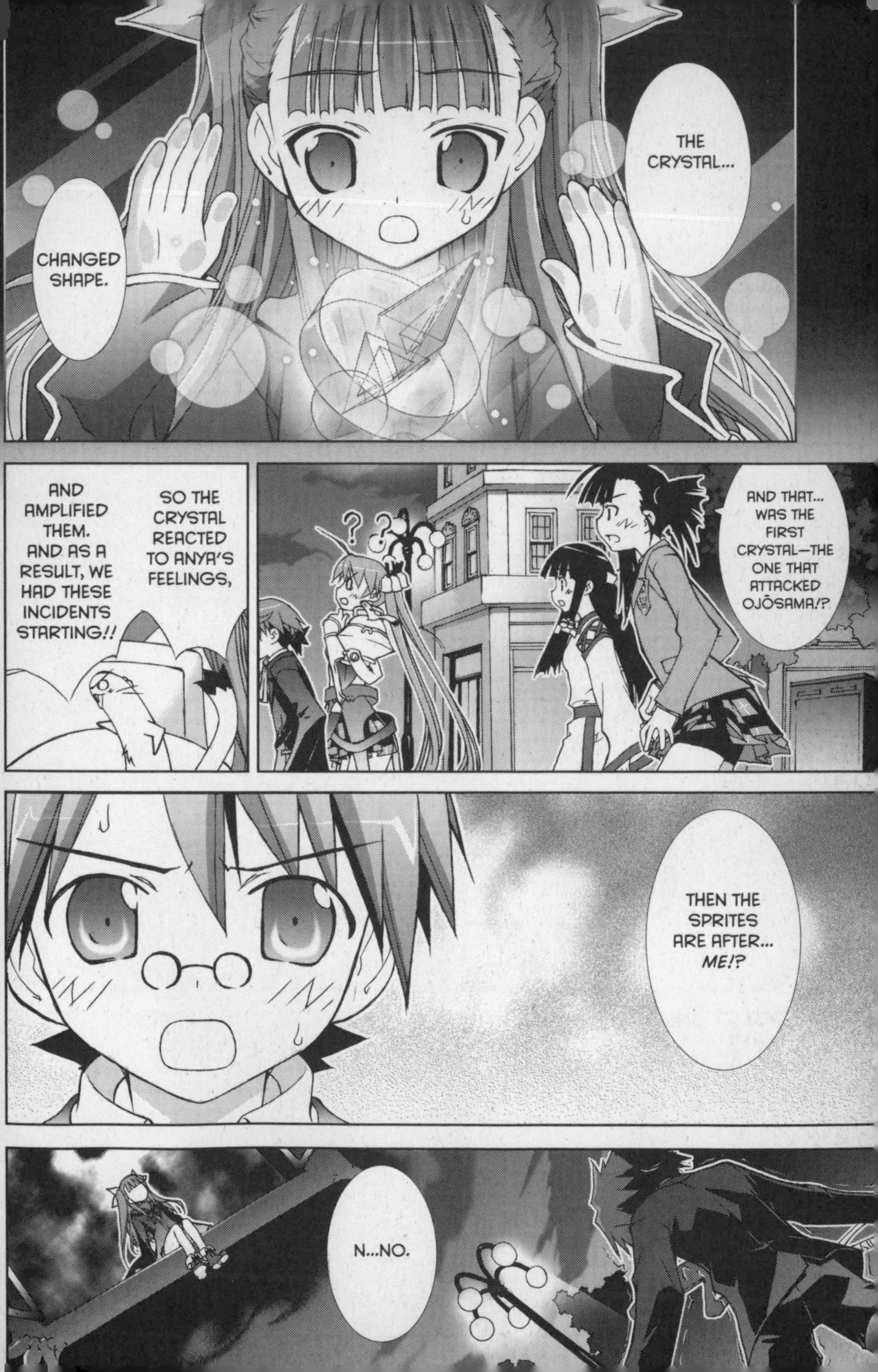
THE CRYSTAL...
CHANGED SHAPE.
AND THAT... WAS THE FIRST CRYSTAL—THE ONE THAT ATTACKED OJŌSAMA!?
SO THE CRYSTAL REACTED TO ANYA'S FEELINGS,
AND AMPLIFIED THEM. AND AS A RESULT, WE HAD THESE INCIDENTS STARTING!!
THEN THE SPRITES ARE AFTER... *ME!?*
N...NO.

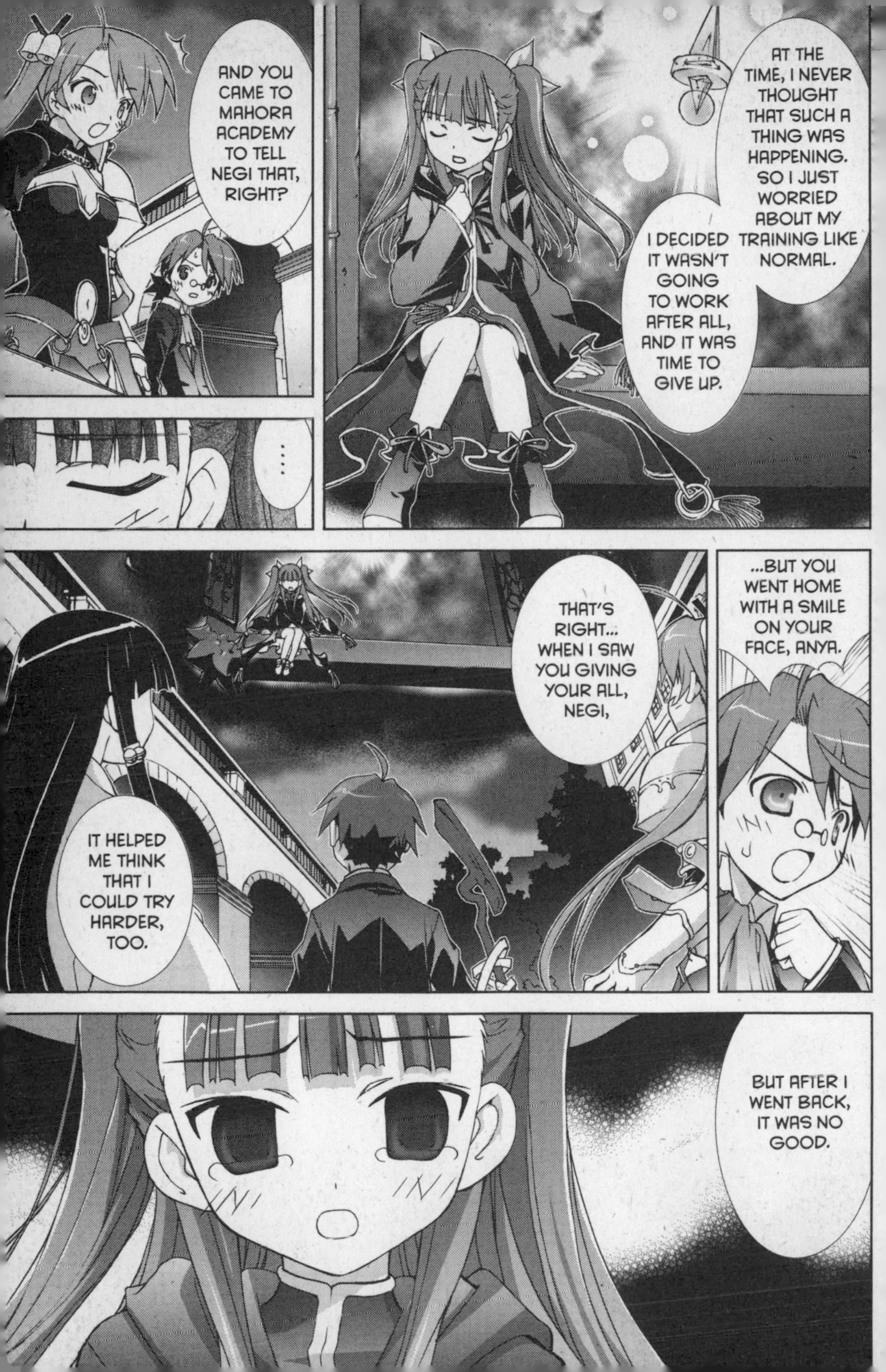
AT THE TIME, I NEVER THOUGHT THAT SUCH A THING WAS HAPPENING. SO I JUST WORRIED ABOUT MY TRAINING LIKE NORMAL.
I DECIDED IT WASN'T GOING TO WORK AFTER ALL, AND IT WAS TIME TO GIVE UP.
AND YOU CAME TO MAHORA ACADEMY TO TELL NEGI THAT, RIGHT?
....
...BUT YOU WENT HOME WITH A SMILE ON YOUR FACE, ANYA.
THAT'S RIGHT... WHEN I SAW YOU GIVING YOUR ALL, NEGI,
IT HELPED ME THINK THAT I COULD TRY HARDER, TOO.
BUT AFTER I WENT BACK, IT WAS NO GOOD.

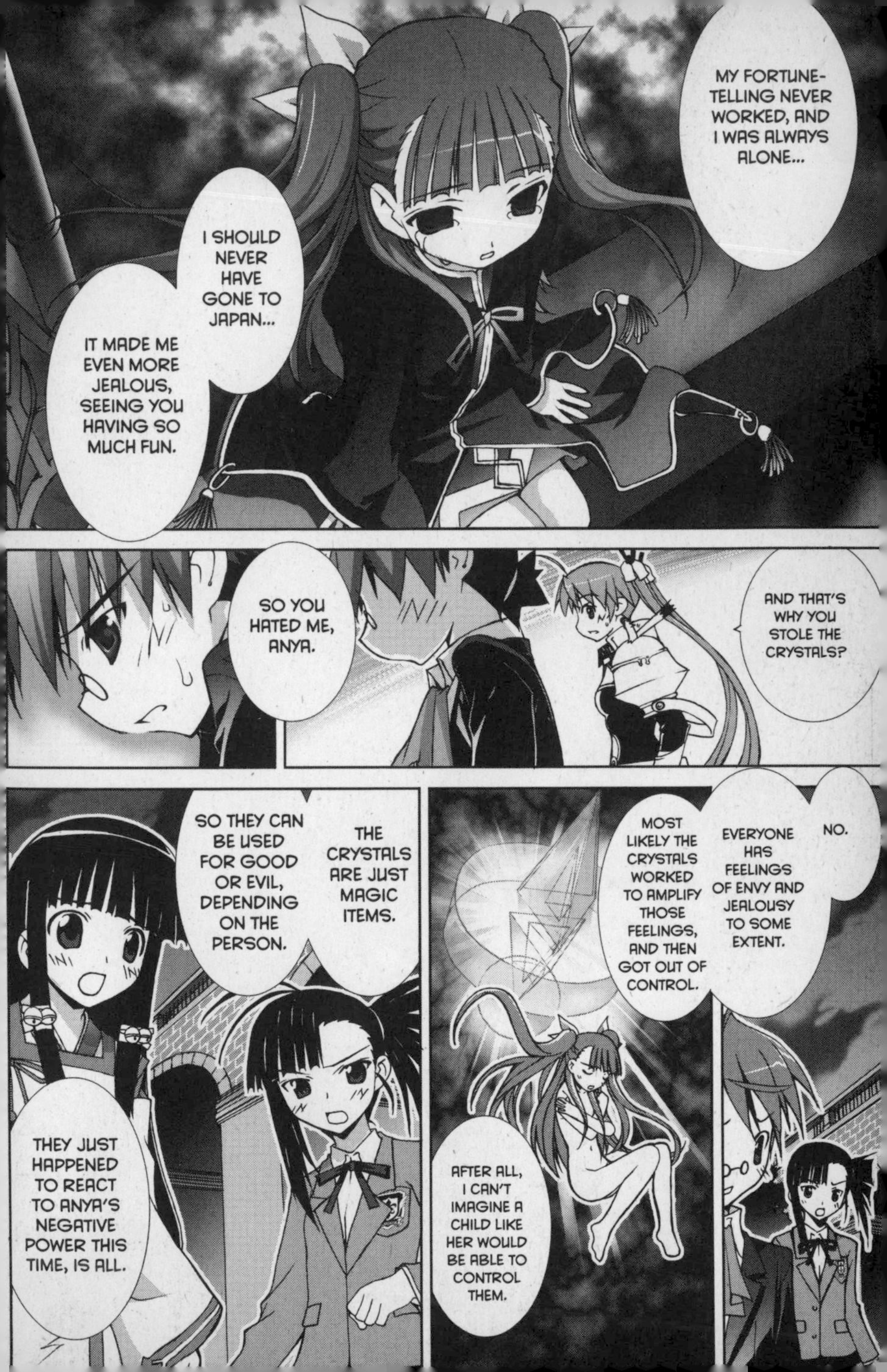
MY FORTUNE-TELLING NEVER WORKED, AND I WAS ALWAYS ALONE...
I SHOULD NEVER HAVE GONE TO JAPAN...
IT MADE ME EVEN MORE JEALOUS, SEEING YOU HAVING SO MUCH FUN.
AND THAT'S WHY YOU STOLE THE CRYSTALS?
SO YOU HATED ME, ANYA.
NO.
EVERYONE HAS FEELINGS OF ENVY AND JEALOUSY TO SOME EXTENT.
MOST LIKELY THE CRYSTALS WORKED TO AMPLIFY THOSE FEELINGS, AND THEN GOT OUT OF CONTROL.
AFTER ALL, I CAN'T IMAGINE A CHILD LIKE HER WOULD BE ABLE TO CONTROL THEM.
THE CRYSTALS ARE JUST MAGIC ITEMS.
SO THEY CAN BE USED FOR GOOD OR EVIL, DEPENDING ON THE PERSON.
THEY JUST HAPPENED TO REACT TO ANYA'S NEGATIVE POWER THIS TIME, IS ALL.

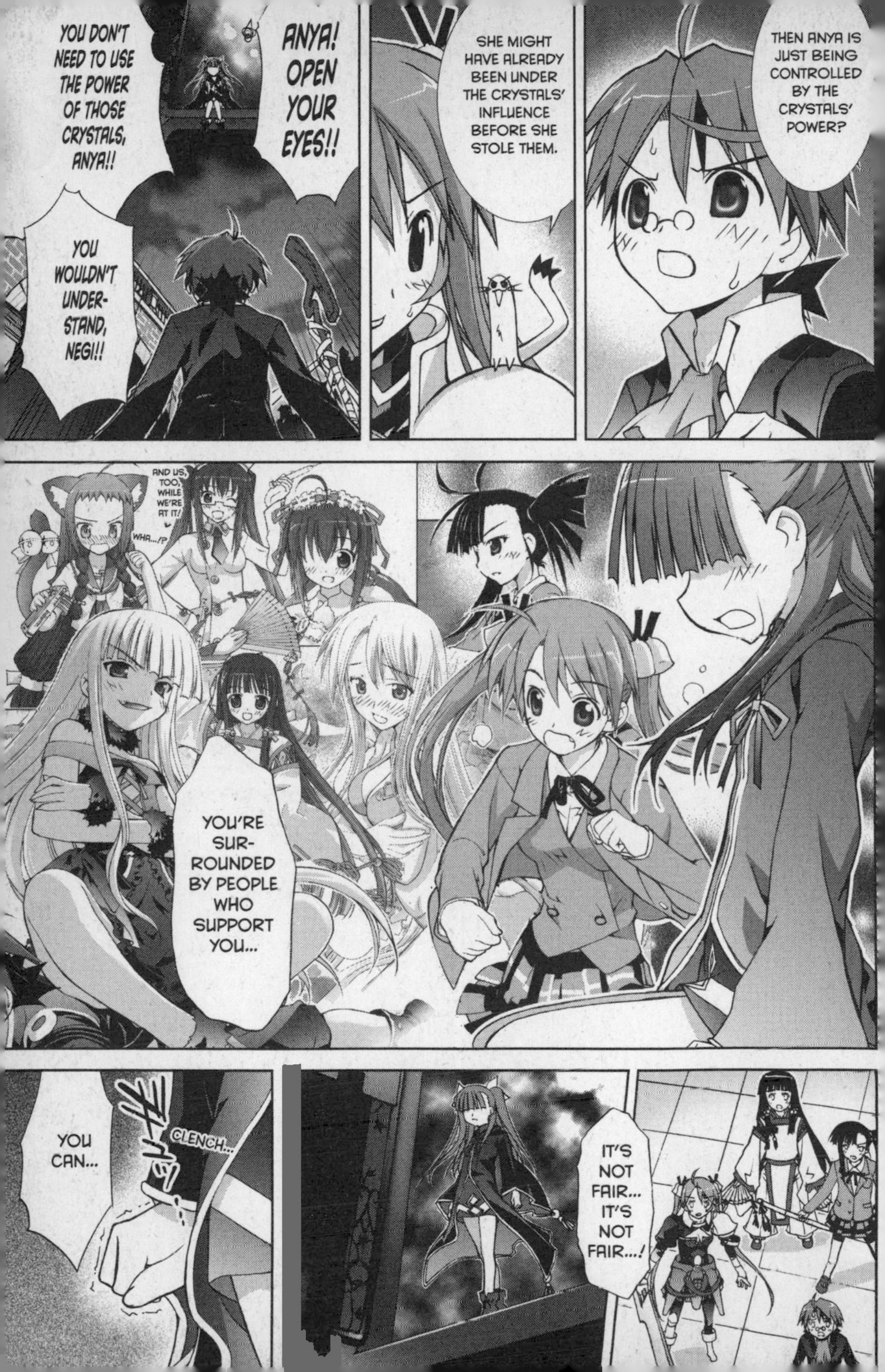
THEN ANYA IS JUST BEING CONTROLLED BY THE CRYSTALS' POWER?
SHE MIGHT HAVE ALREADY BEEN UNDER THE CRYSTALS' INFLUENCE BEFORE SHE STOLE THEM.
ANYA! OPEN YOUR EYES!!
YOU DON'T NEED TO USE THE POWER OF THOSE CRYSTALS, ANYA!!
YOU WOULDN'T UNDER-STAND, NEGI!!
AND US, TOO, WHILE WE'RE AT IT!
WHA...!?
YOU'RE SUR-ROUNDED BY PEOPLE WHO SUPPORT YOU...
IT'S NOT FAIR... IT'S NOT FAIR...!
CLENCH...
YOU CAN...

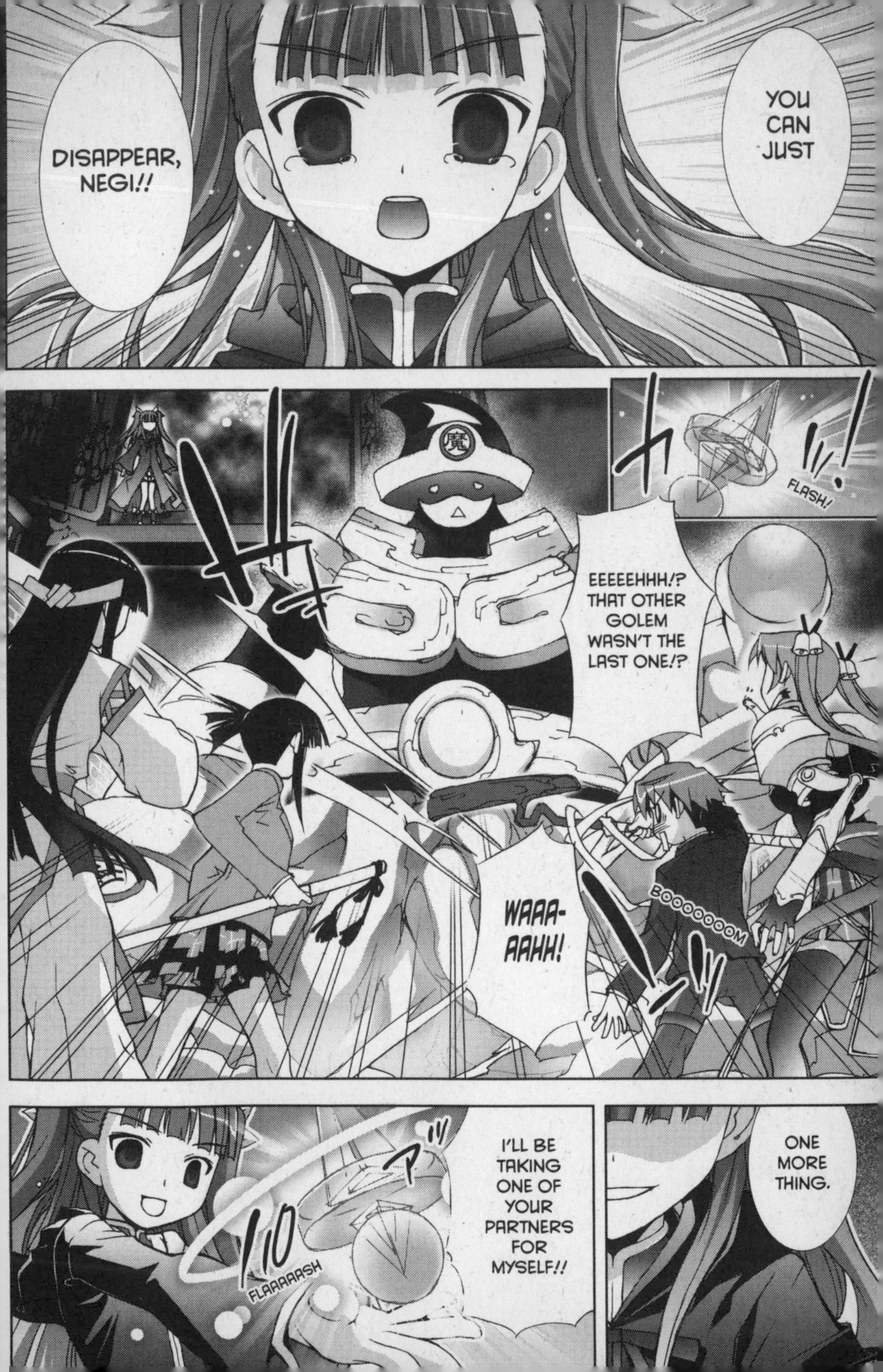

YOU CAN JUST
DISAPPEAR, NEGI!!
FLASH!
EEEEEHHH!? THAT OTHER GOLEM WASN'T THE LAST ONE!?
BOOOOOOOOM
WAAA-AAHH!
ONE MORE THING.
I'LL BE TAKING ONE OF YOUR PARTNERS FOR MYSELF!!
FLAAAAASH

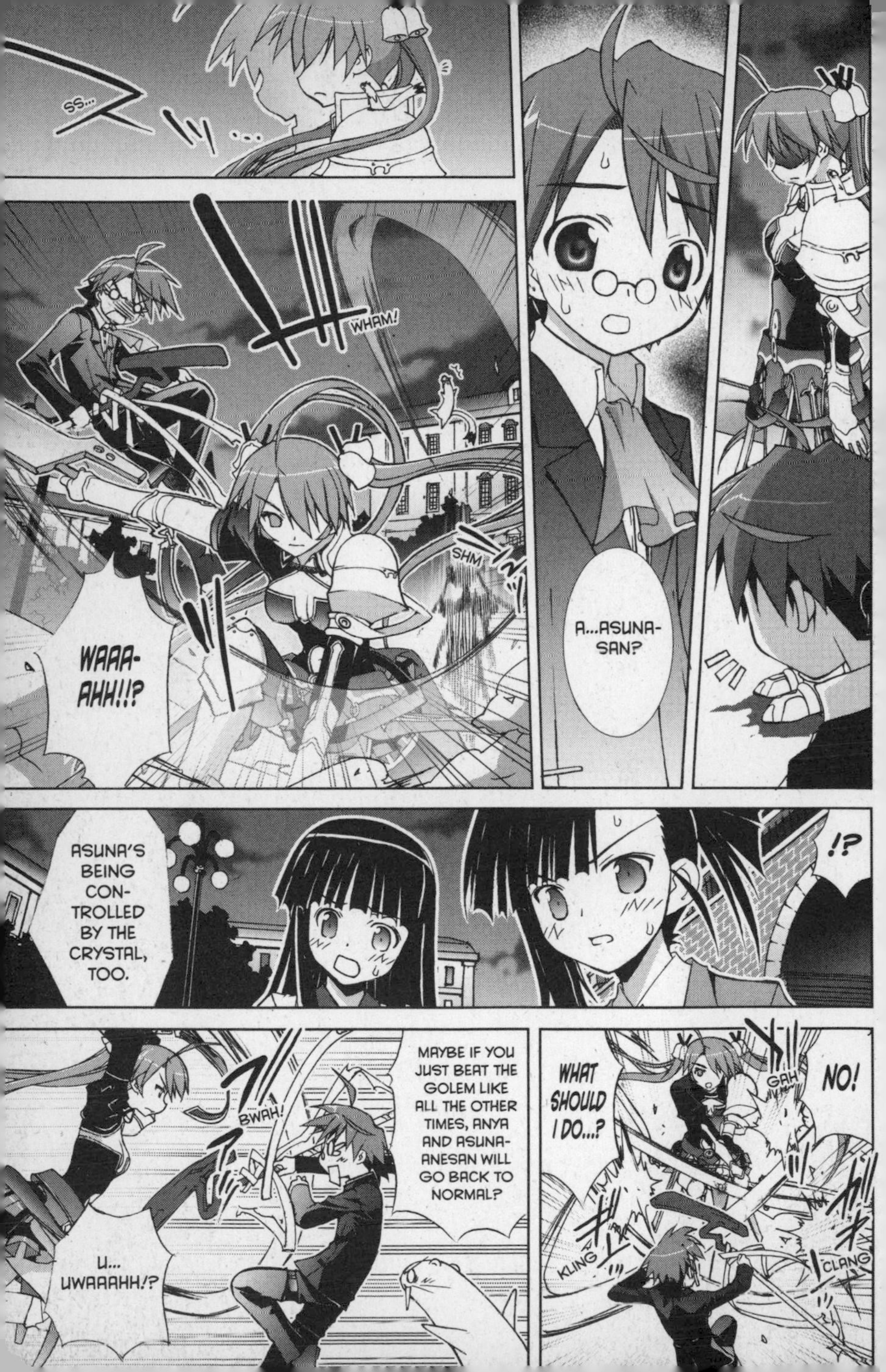
A...ASUNA-SAN?
SS...
WHAM!
SHM
WAAA-AHH!!?
!?
ASUNA'S BEING CON-TROLLED BY THE CRYSTAL, TOO.
NO!
GAH
WHAT SHOULD I DO...?
CLANG
KLING
MAYBE IF YOU JUST BEAT THE GOLEM LIKE ALL THE OTHER TIMES, ANYA AND ASUNA-ANESAN WILL GO BACK TO NORMAL?
BWAH!
U... UWAAAHH!?

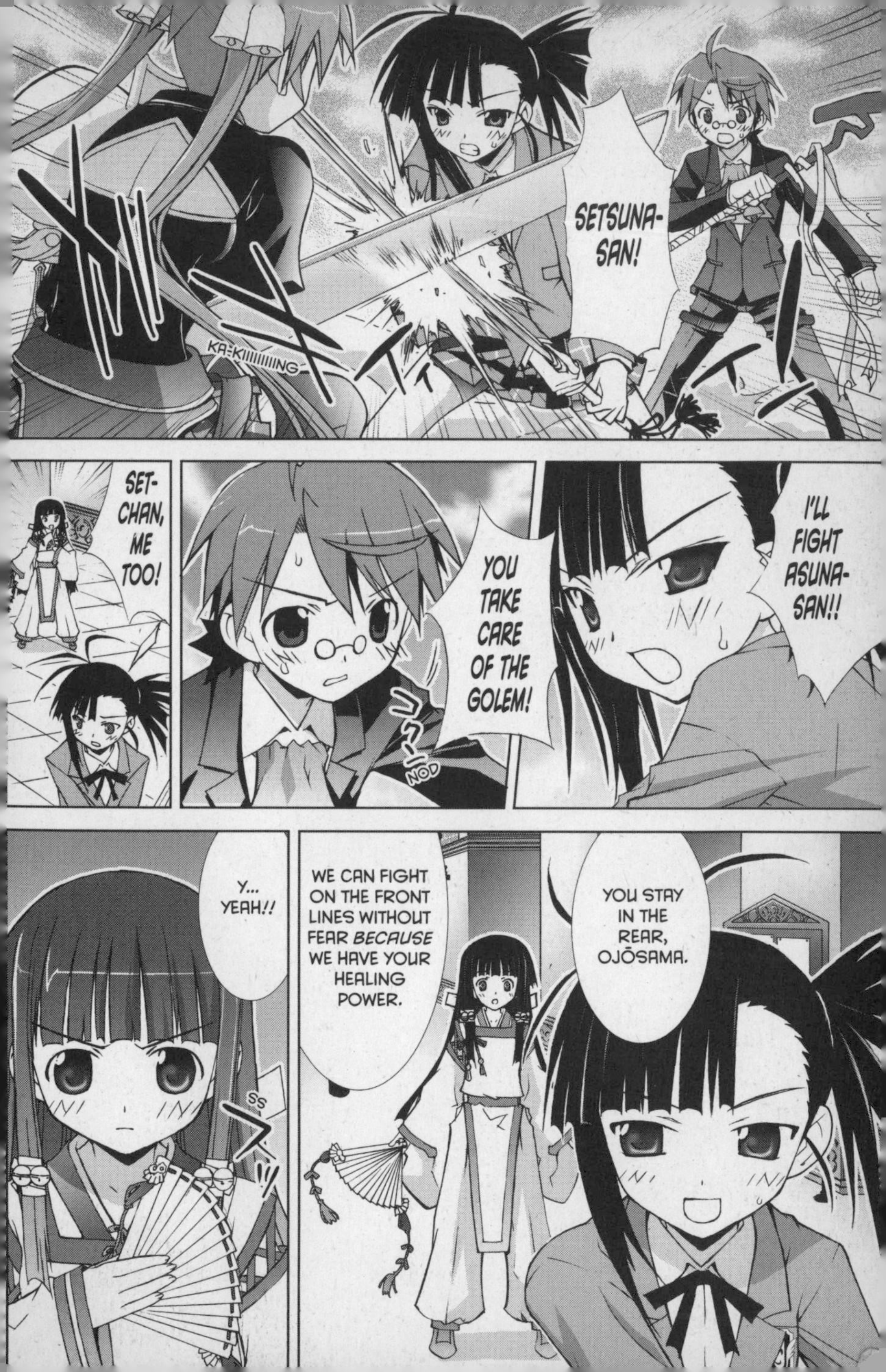
SETSUNA-SAN!
KA-KIIIIIIIIING
I'LL FIGHT ASUNA-SAN!!
YOU TAKE CARE OF THE GOLEM!
NOD
SET-CHAN, ME TOO!
YOU STAY IN THE REAR, OJŌSAMA.
WE CAN FIGHT ON THE FRONT LINES WITHOUT FEAR *BECAUSE* WE HAVE YOUR HEALING POWER.
Y... YEAH!!
SS

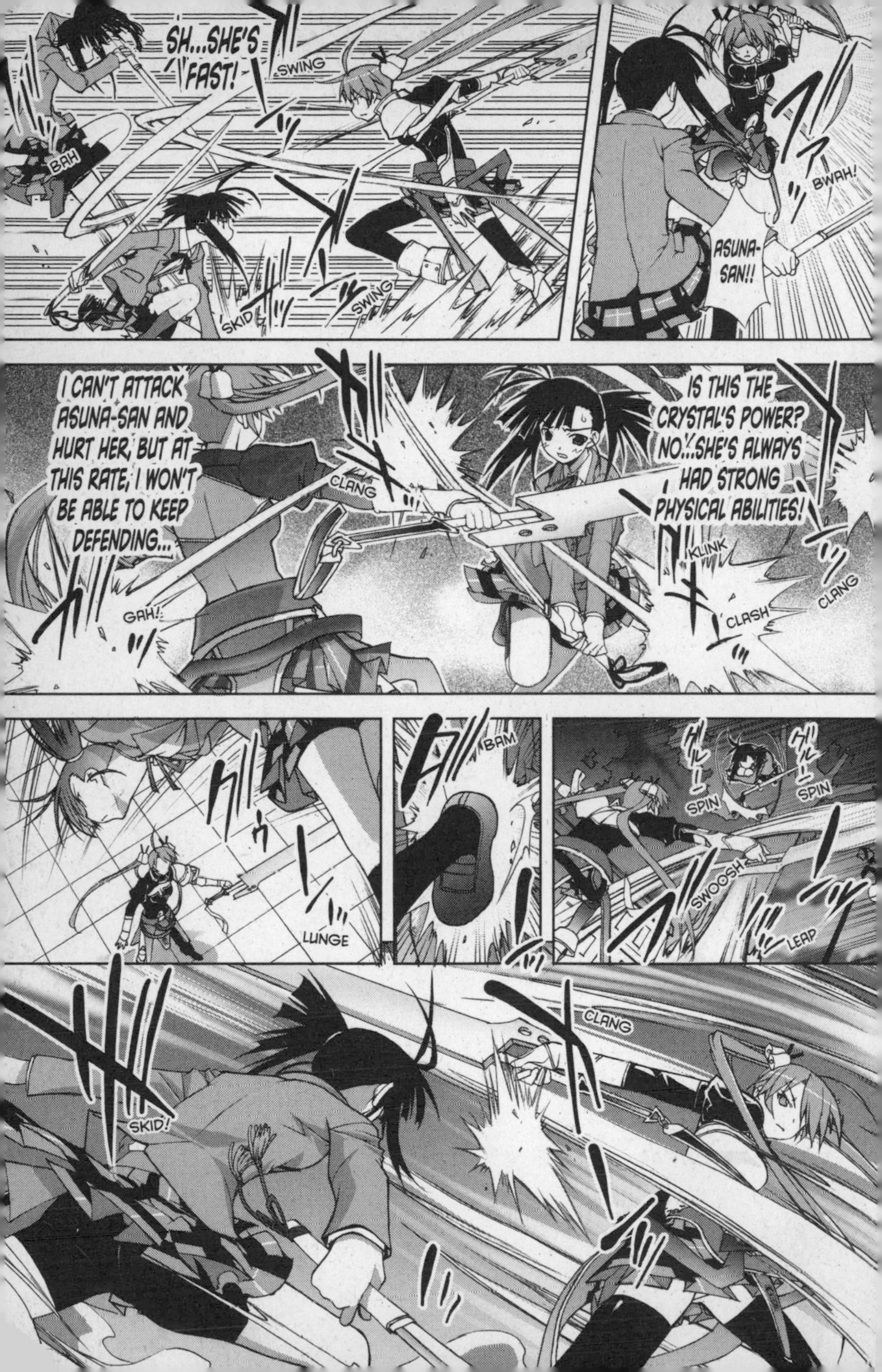
BWAH!
ASUNA-SAN!!
SWING
SH...SHE'S FAST!
BAH
SWING
SKID
IS THIS THE CRYSTAL'S POWER? NO...SHE'S ALWAYS HAD STRONG PHYSICAL ABILITIES!
CLANG
KLINK
CLASH
CLANG
I CAN'T ATTACK ASUNA-SAN AND HURT HER, BUT AT THIS RATE, I WON'T BE ABLE TO KEEP DEFENDING...
GAH!
SPIN
SPIN
SWOOSH
LEAP
BAM
LUNGE
CLANG
SKID!

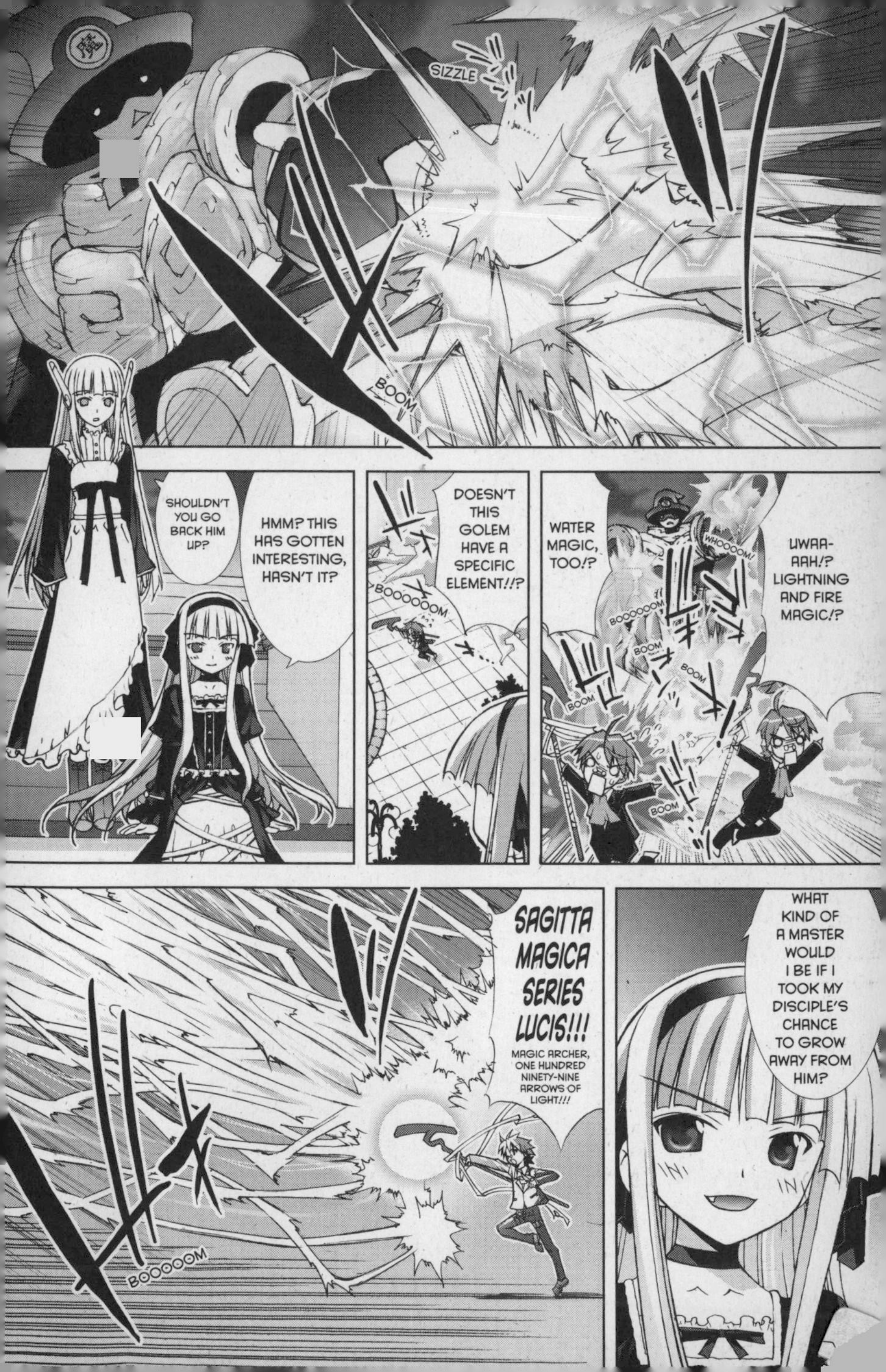
SIZZLE
BOOM
UWAA-AAH!? LIGHTNING AND FIRE MAGIC!?
WATER MAGIC, TOO!?
WHOOOOM!
BOOOOOOM
BOOM
BOOM
BOOM
BOOM
DOESN'T THIS GOLEM HAVE A SPECIFIC ELEMENT!!?
BOOOOOOM
HMM? THIS HAS GOTTEN INTERESTING, HASN'T IT?
SHOULDN'T YOU GO BACK HIM UP?
WHAT KIND OF A MASTER WOULD I BE IF I TOOK MY DISCIPLE'S CHANCE TO GROW AWAY FROM HIM?
SAGITTA MAGICA SERIES LUCIS!!!
MAGIC ARCHER, ONE HUNDRED NINETY-NINE ARROWS OF LIGHT!!!
BOOOOOM

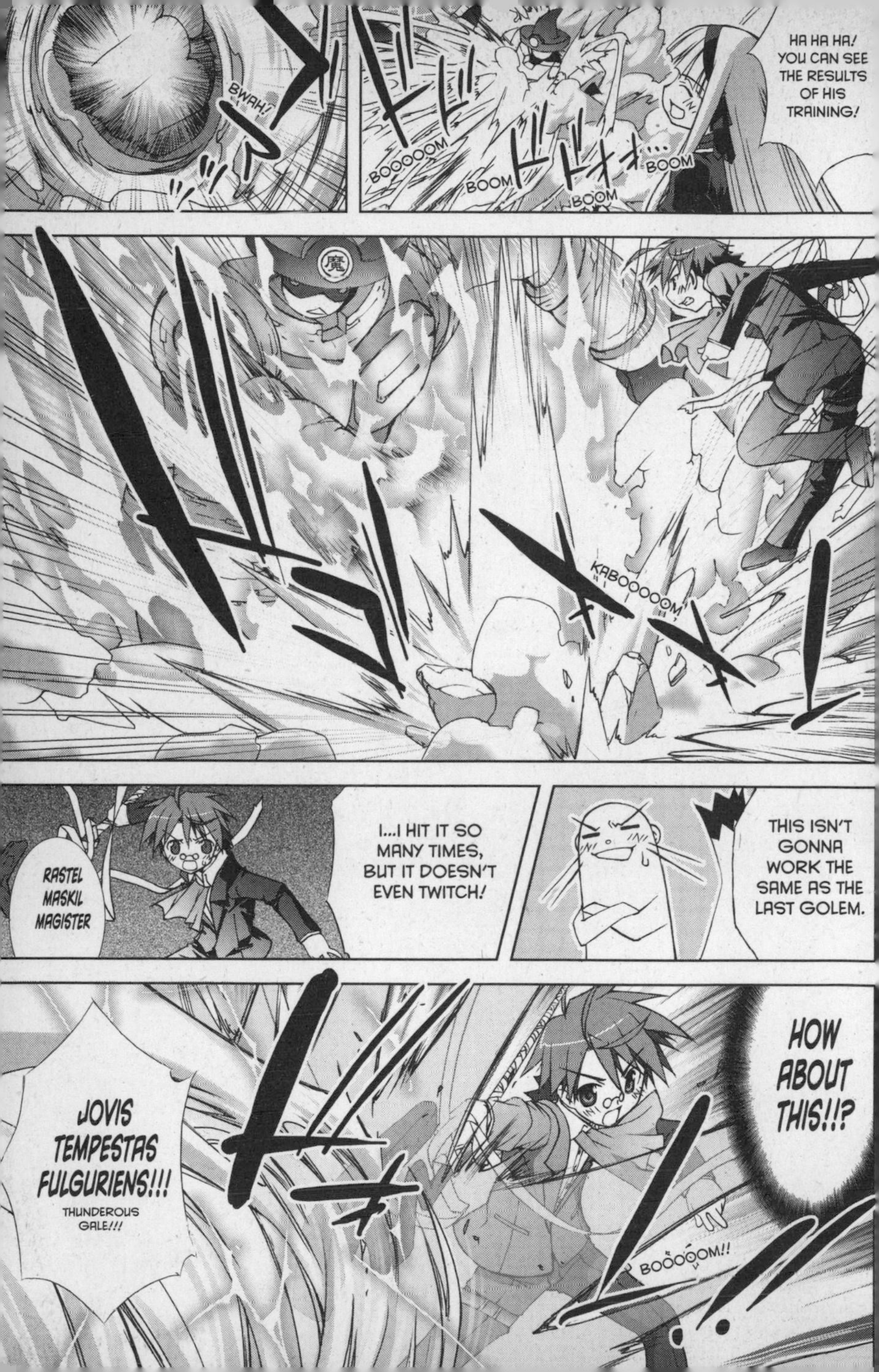
HA HA HA! YOU CAN SEE THE RESULTS OF HIS TRAINING!
BOOOOOM
BOOM
BOOM
...BOOM
BWAH!
KABOOOOOM
THIS ISN'T GONNA WORK THE SAME AS THE LAST GOLEM.
I...I HIT IT SO MANY TIMES, BUT IT DOESN'T EVEN TWITCH!
RASTEL MASKIL MAGISTER
HOW ABOUT THIS!!?
JOVIS TEMPESTAS FULGURIENS!!!
THUNDEROUS GALE!!!
BOOOOOM!!

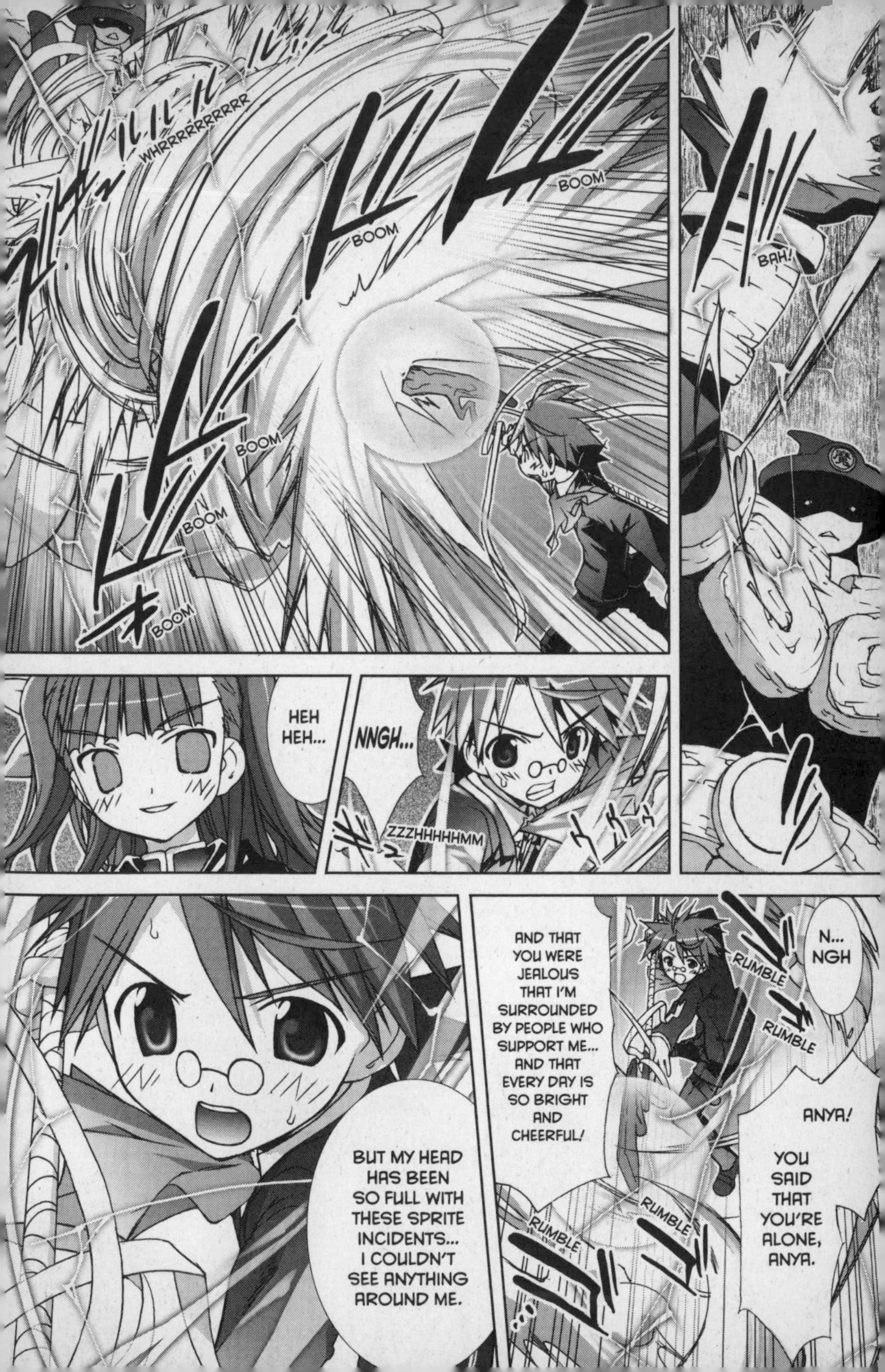
BAH!
BOOM
BOOM
WHRRRRRRRRRR
BOOM
BOOM
BOOM
NNGH...
ZZZHHHHHMM
HEH HEH...
N... NGH
RUMBLE
RUMBLE
ANYA!
YOU SAID THAT YOU'RE ALONE, ANYA.
AND THAT YOU WERE JEALOUS THAT I'M SURROUNDED BY PEOPLE WHO SUPPORT ME... AND THAT EVERY DAY IS SO BRIGHT AND CHEERFUL!
RUMBLE
RUMBLE
BUT MY HEAD HAS BEEN SO FULL WITH THESE SPRITE INCIDENTS... I COULDN'T SEE ANYTHING AROUND ME.

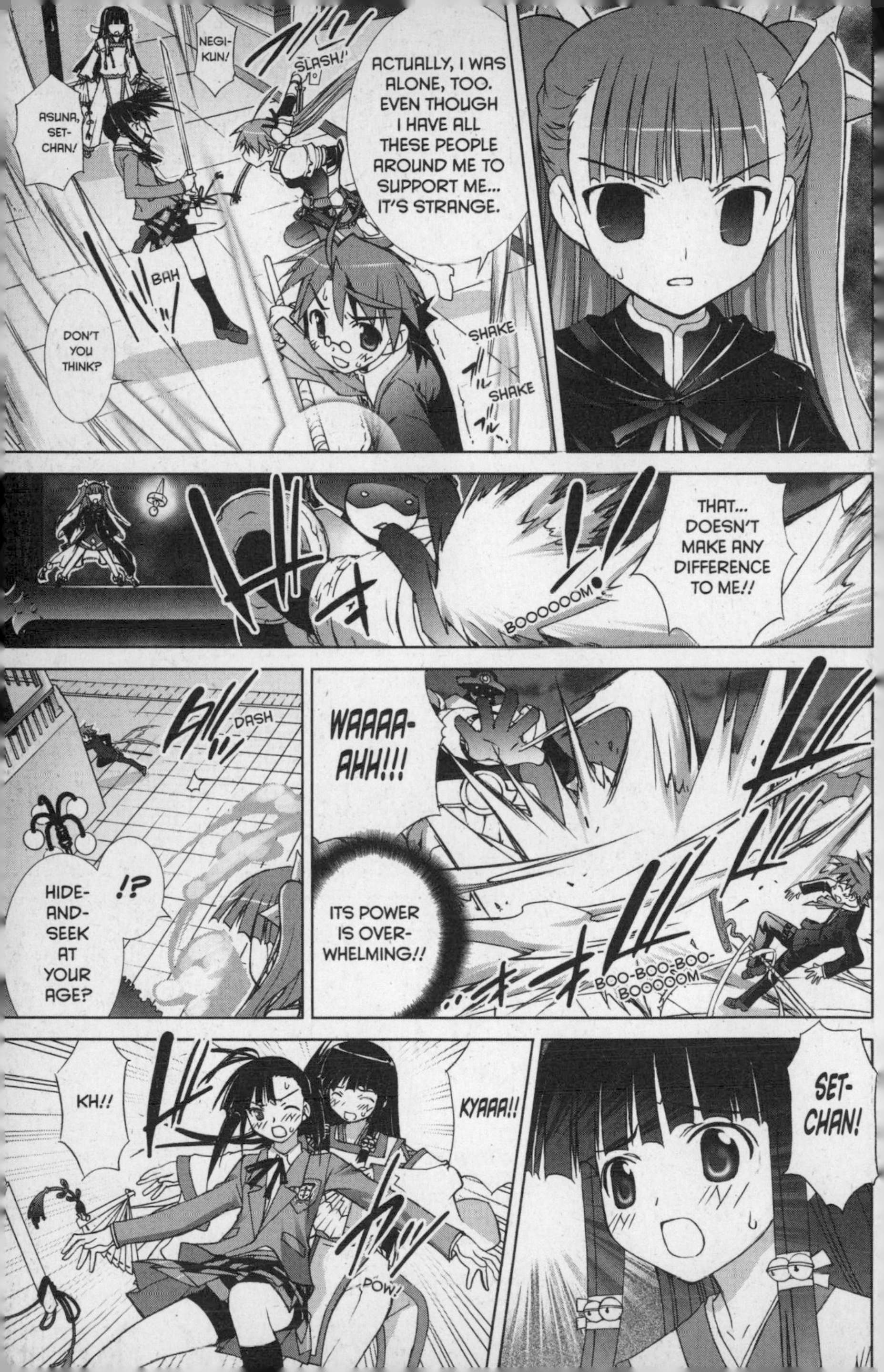
ACTUALLY, I WAS ALONE, TOO. EVEN THOUGH I HAVE ALL THESE PEOPLE AROUND ME TO SUPPORT ME... IT'S STRANGE.
SLASH!
NEGI-KUN!
ASUNA, SET-CHAN!
SHAKE
SHAKE
BAH
DON'T YOU THINK?
THAT... DOESN'T MAKE ANY DIFFERENCE TO ME!!
BOOOOOOM
WAAAA-AHH!!!
ITS POWER IS OVER-WHELMING!!
BOO-BOO-BOO-BOOOOOM
DASH
!?
HIDE-AND-SEEK AT YOUR AGE?
SET-CHAN!
KYAAA!!
KH!!
POW!

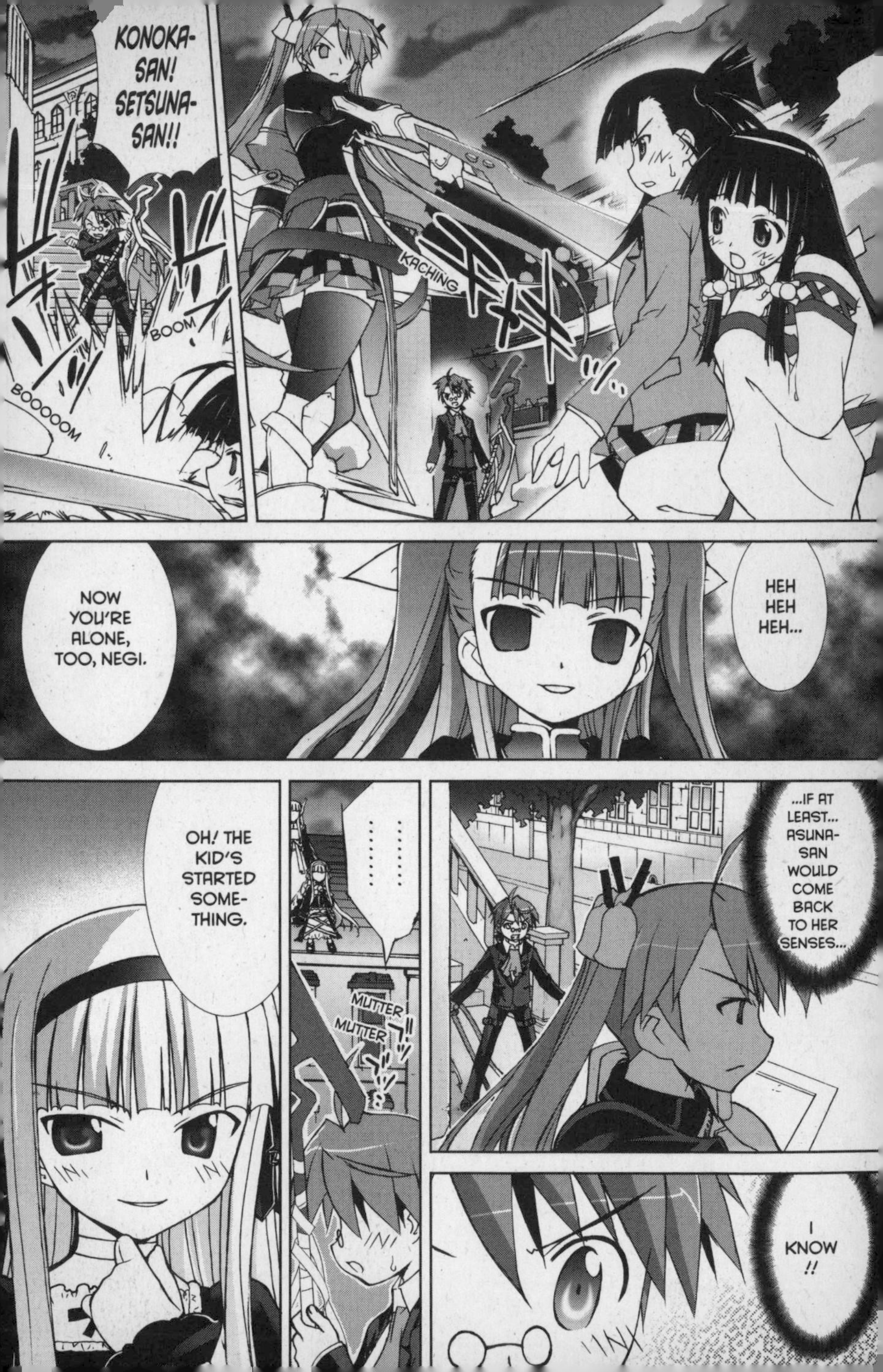
KACHING
KONOKA-SAN! SETSUNA-SAN!!
BOOM
BOOOOOM
HEH HEH HEH...
NOW YOU'RE ALONE, TOO, NEGI.
...IF AT LEAST... ASUNA-SAN WOULD COME BACK TO HER SENSES...
I KNOW!!
......
MUTTER MUTTER
OH! THE KID'S STARTED SOMETHING.

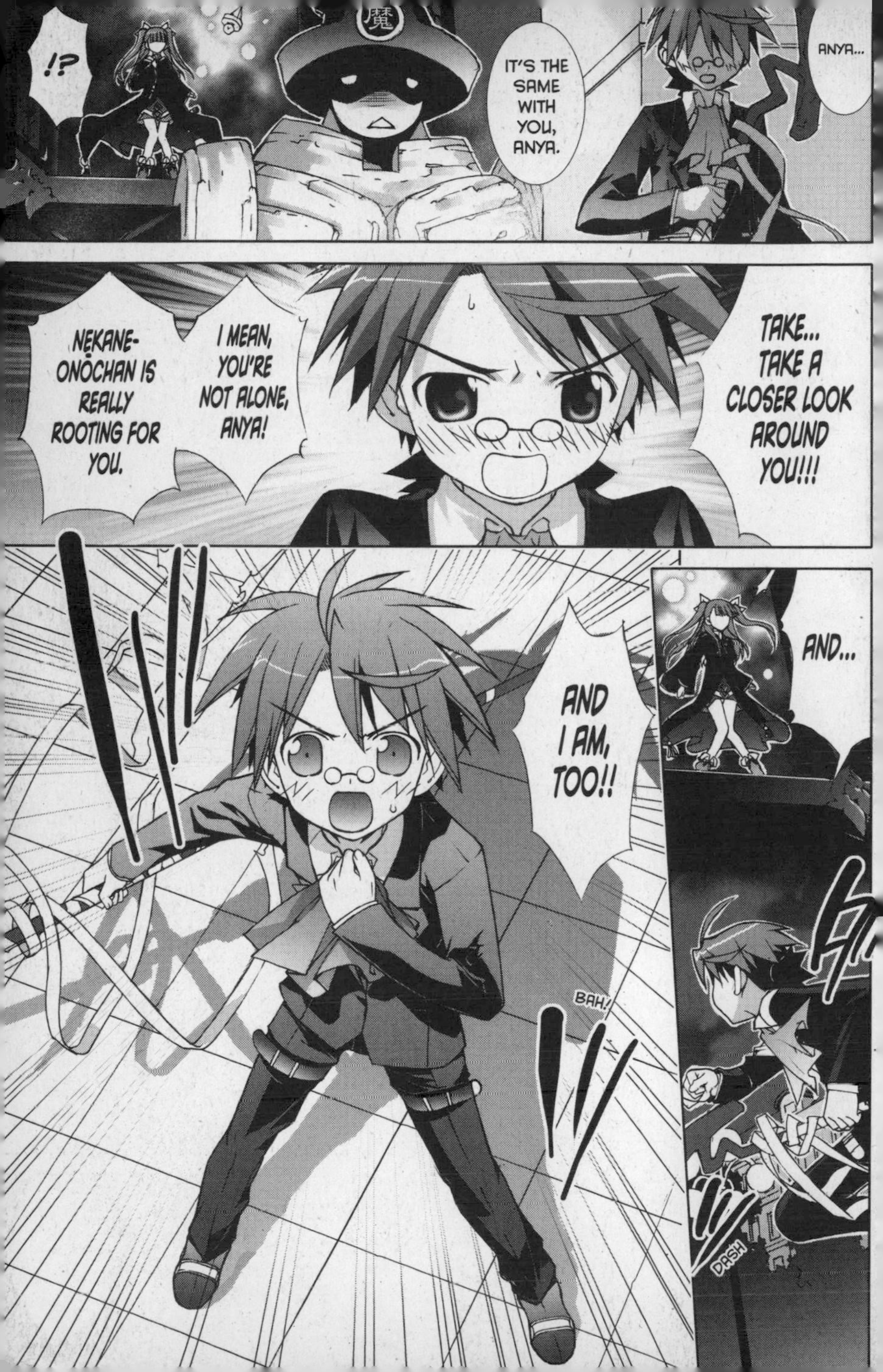
ANYA...
IT'S THE SAME WITH YOU, ANYA.
!?
TAKE... TAKE A CLOSER LOOK AROUND YOU!!!
I MEAN, YOU'RE NOT ALONE, ANYA!
NEKANE-ONŌCHAN IS REALLY ROOTING FOR YOU.
AND...
DASH
AND I AM, TOO!!
BAH!

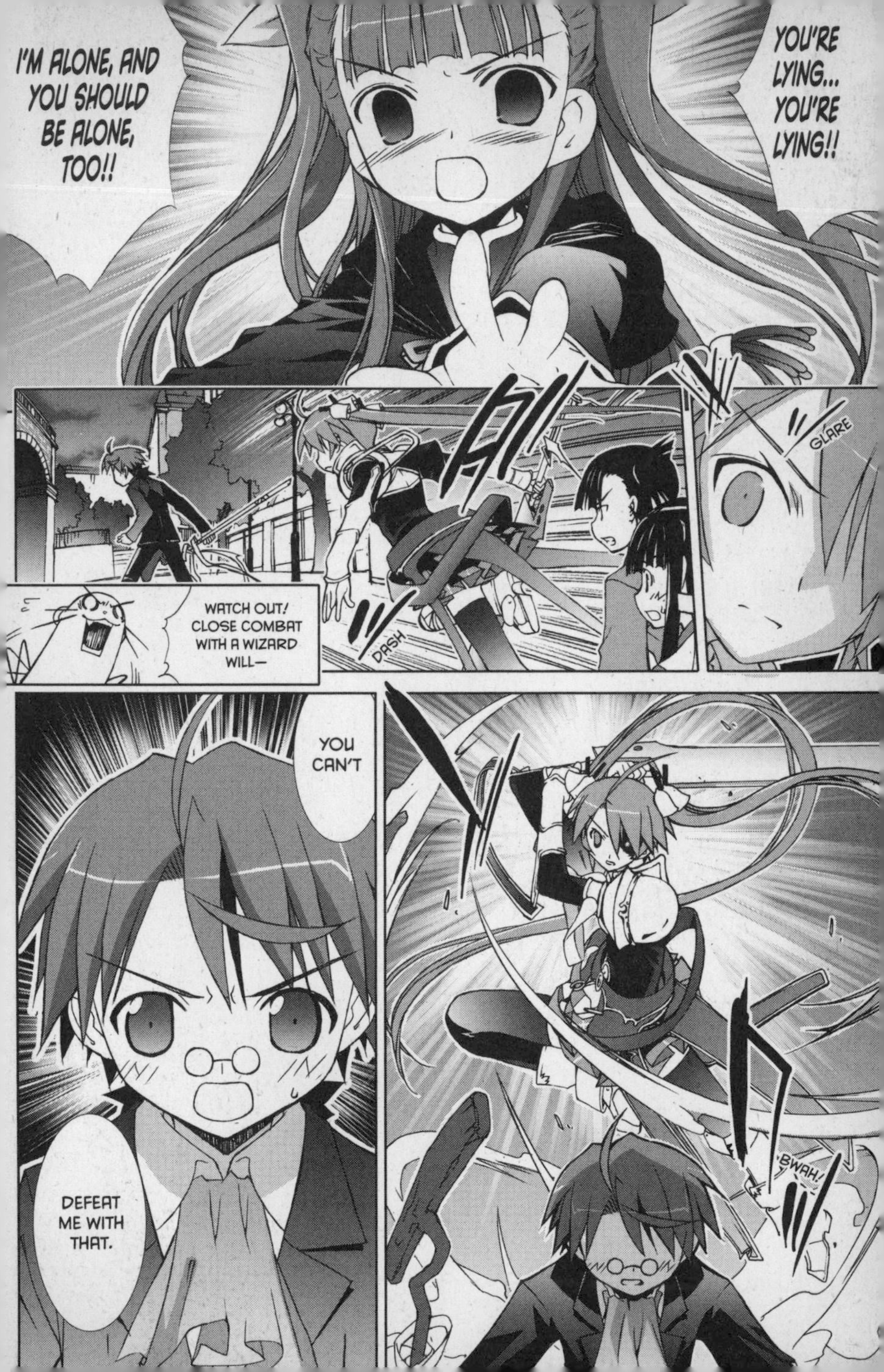
YOU'RE LYING... YOU'RE LYING!!
I'M ALONE, AND YOU SHOULD BE ALONE, TOO!!
GLARE
DASH
WATCH OUT! CLOSE COMBAT WITH A WIZARD WILL—
BWAH!
YOU CAN'T
DEFEAT ME WITH THAT.

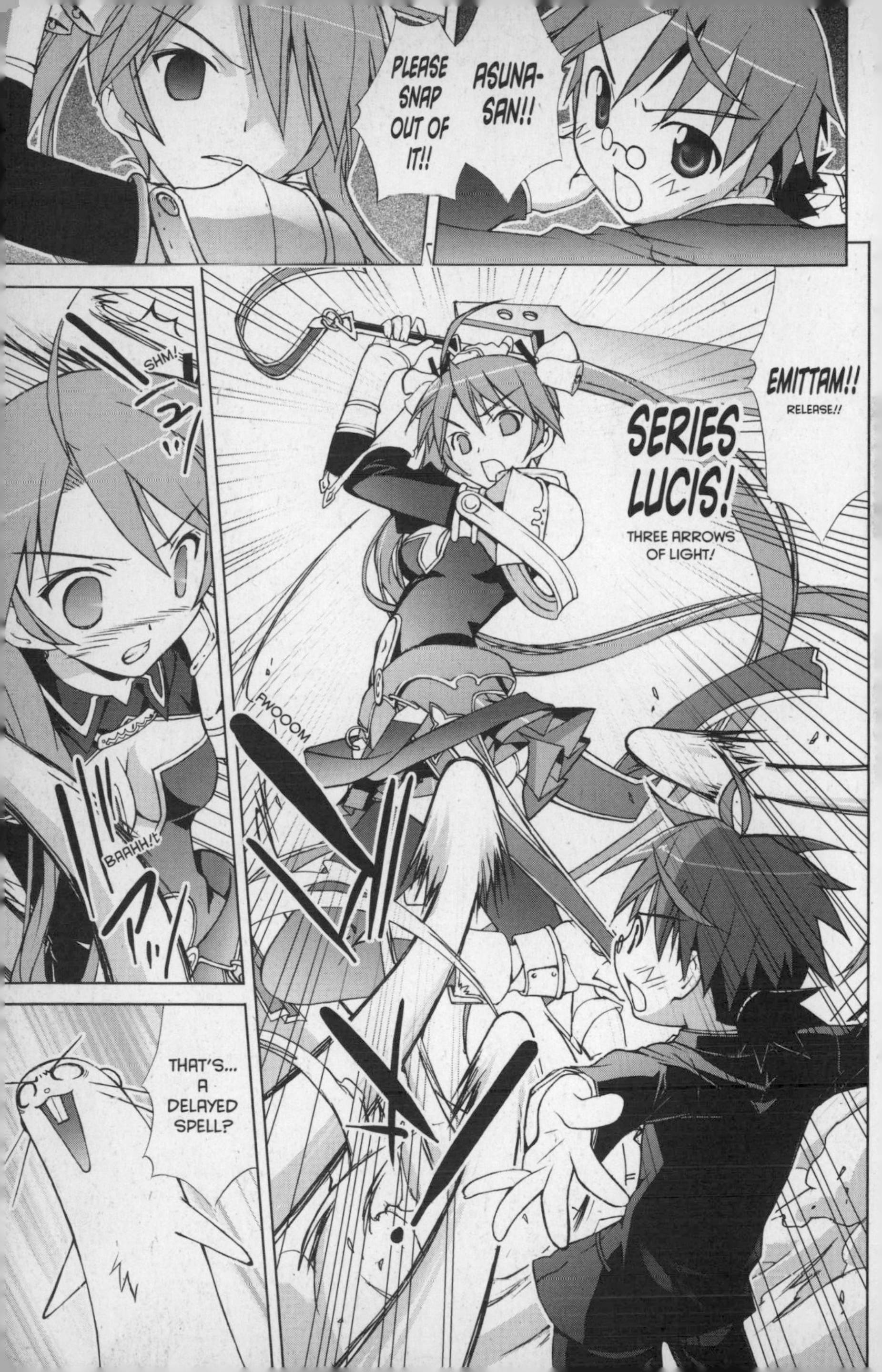
ASUNA-SAN!!
PLEASE SNAP OUT OF IT!!
EMITTAM!!
RELEASE!!
SERIES LUCIS!
THREE ARROWS OF LIGHT!
FWOOOM
SHM!
BAAHH!t
THAT'S... A DELAYED SPELL?

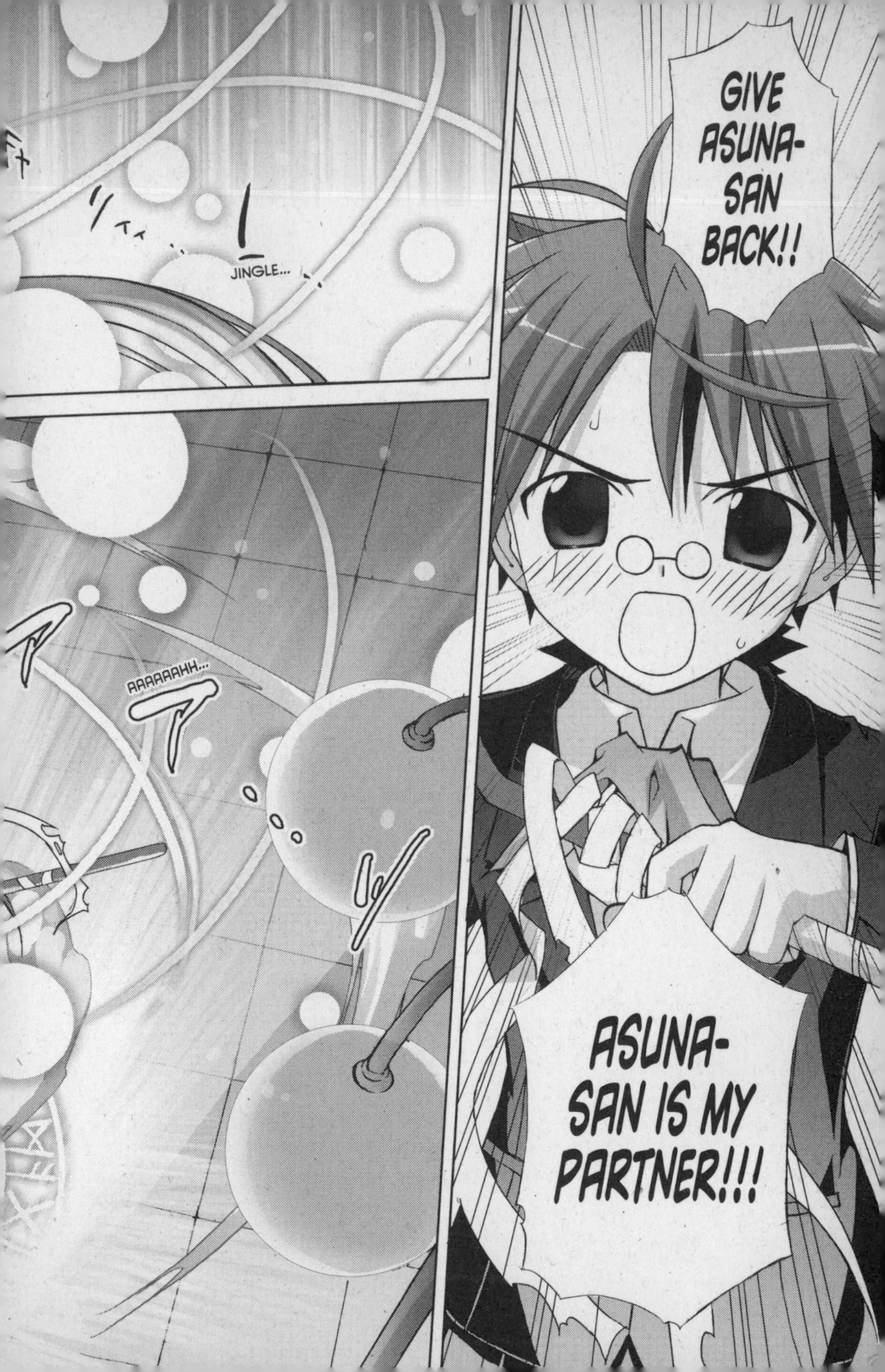
GIVE ASUNA-SAN BACK!!
ASUNA-SAN IS MY PARTNER!!!
JINGLE...
AAAAAAHH...

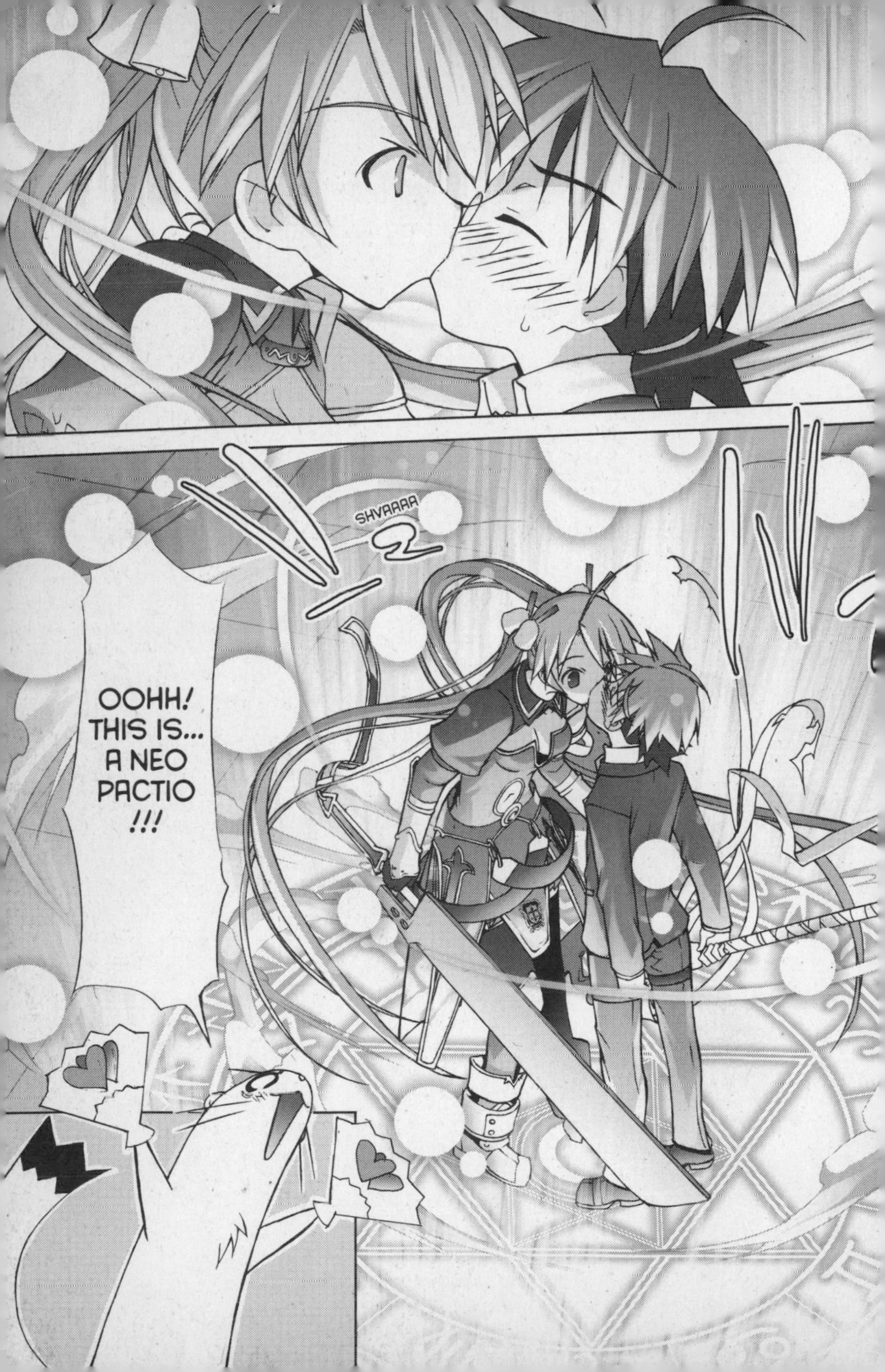
SHVAAAA
OOHH! THIS IS... A NEO PACTIO !!!

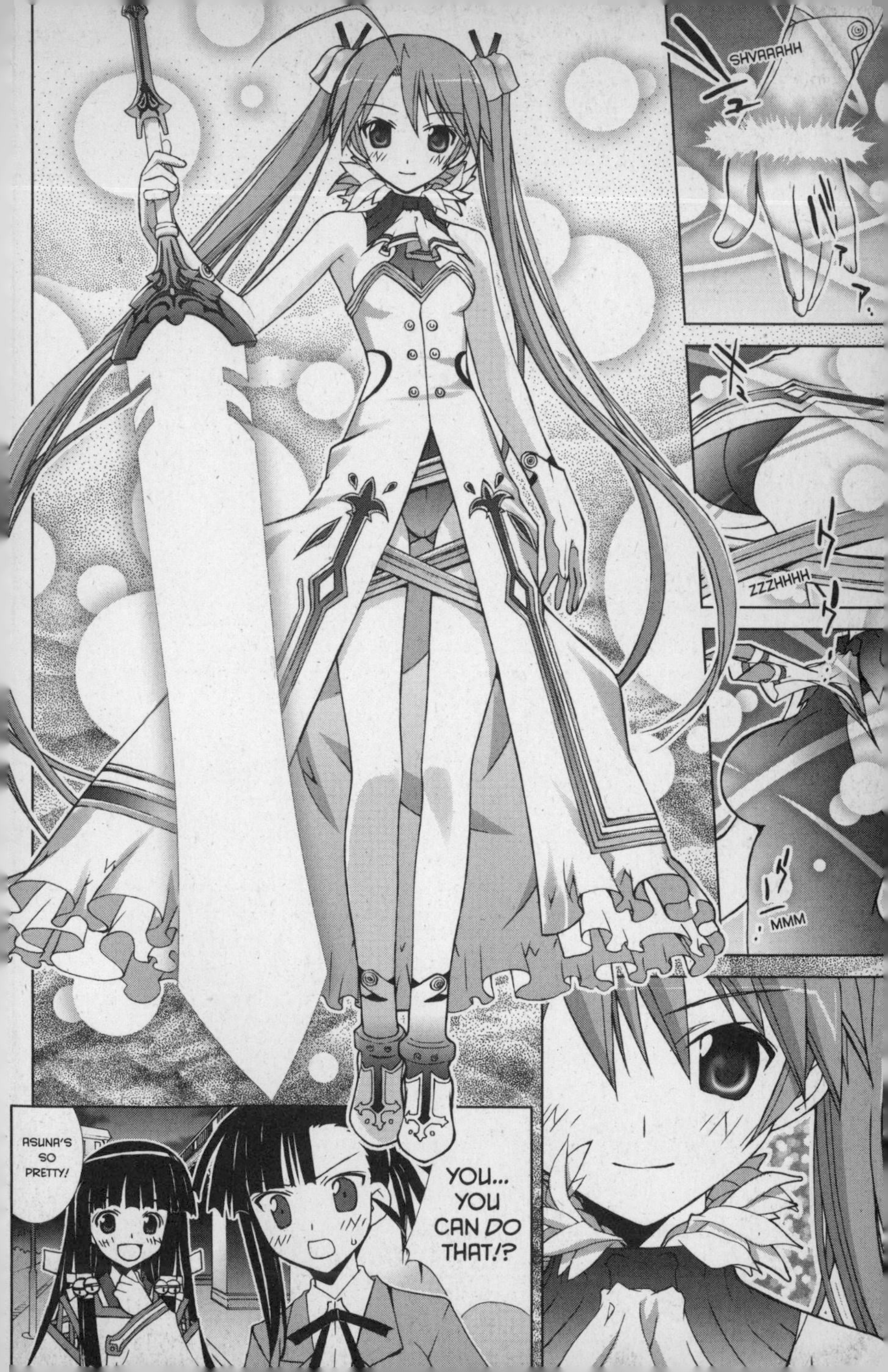
SHVAAAHH
ZZZHHHH
MMM
YOU... YOU CAN *DO* THAT!?
ASUNA'S SO PRETTY!

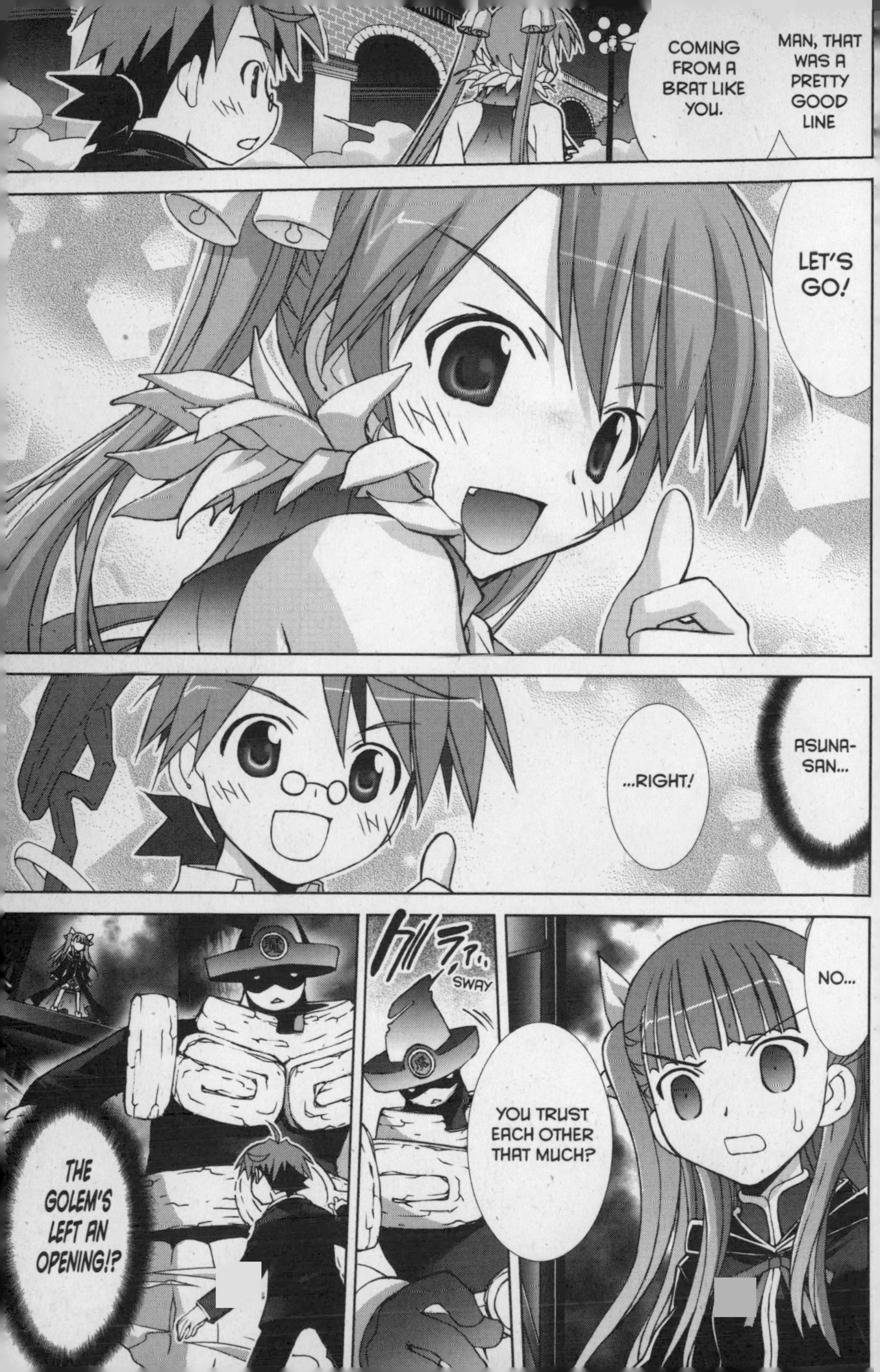
MAN, THAT WAS A PRETTY GOOD LINE
COMING FROM A BRAT LIKE YOU.
LET'S GO!
ASUNA-SAN...
...RIGHT!
NO...
YOU TRUST EACH OTHER THAT MUCH?
SWAY
THE GOLEM'S LEFT AN OPENING!?

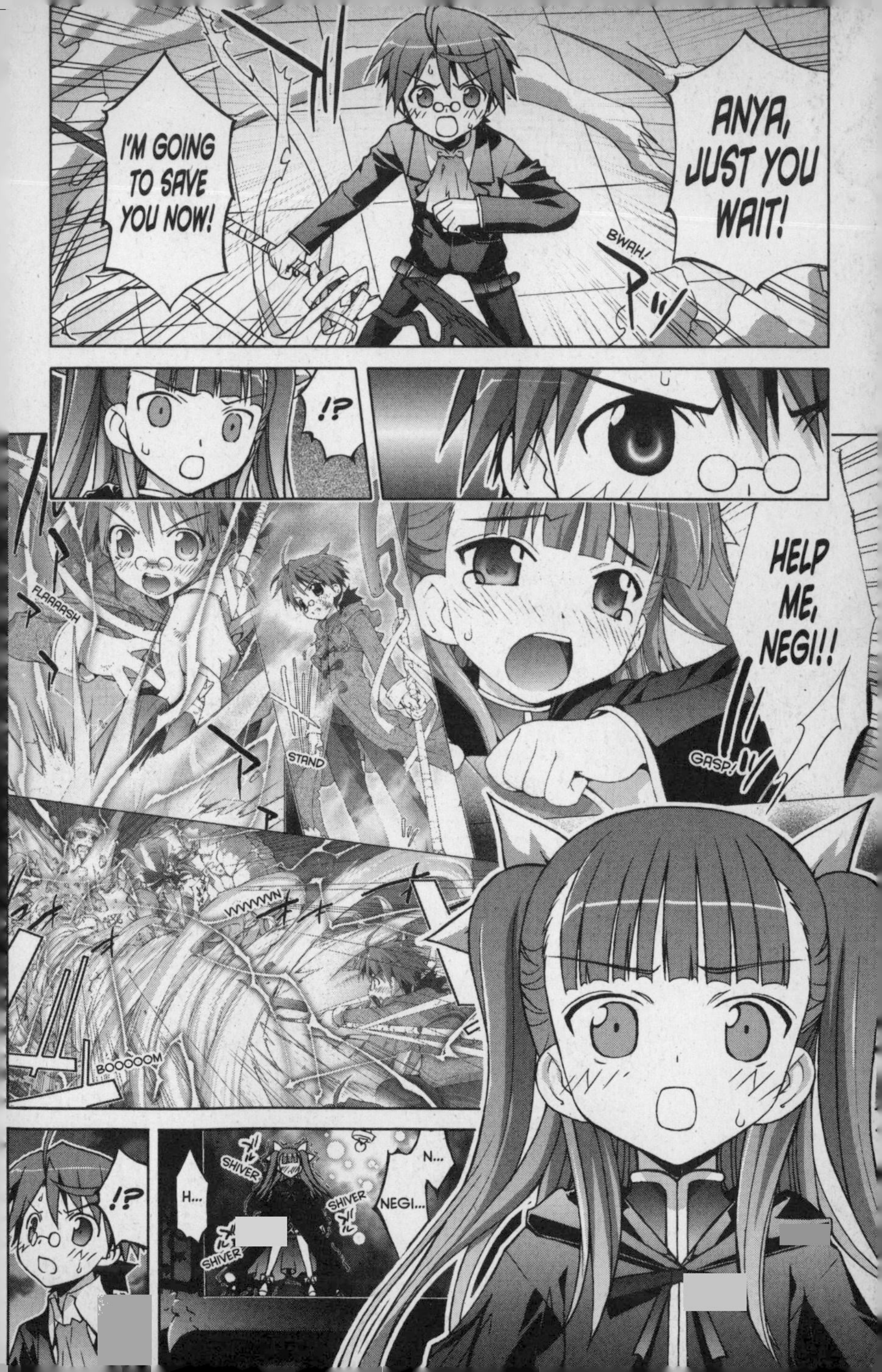
ANYA, JUST YOU WAIT!
BWAH!
I'M GOING TO SAVE YOU NOW!
!?
HELP ME, NEGI!!
GASP!
FLAAAASH
STAND
VVVVVVN
BOOOOOM
N...
NEGI...
SHIVER
SHIVER
H...
SHIVER
!?

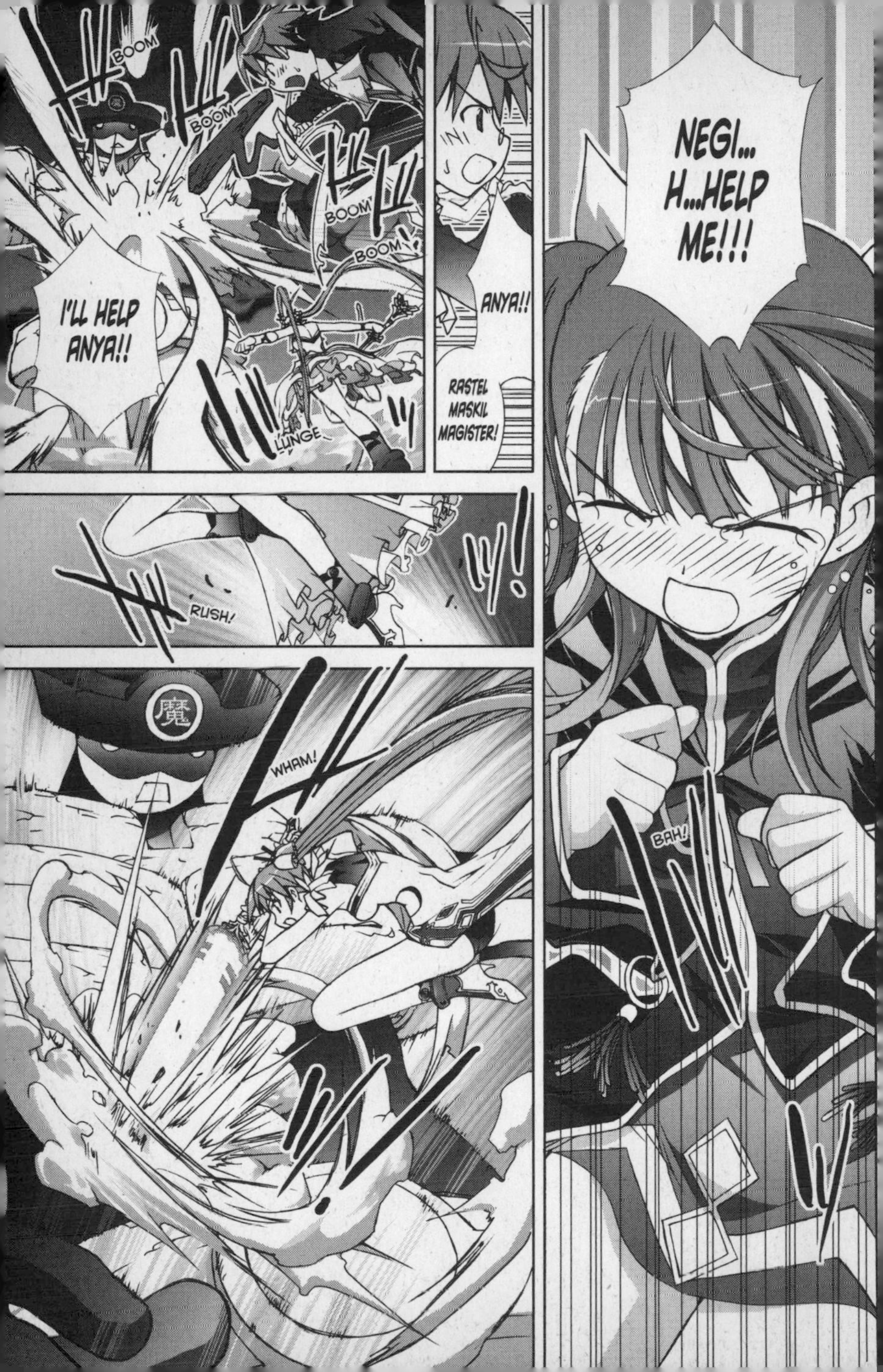
NEGI... H...HELP ME!!!
BAH!
ANYA!!
RASTEL MASKIL MAGISTER!
BOOM
BOOM
BOOM
BOOM
I'LL HELP ANYA!!
LUNGE
RUSH!
WHAM!

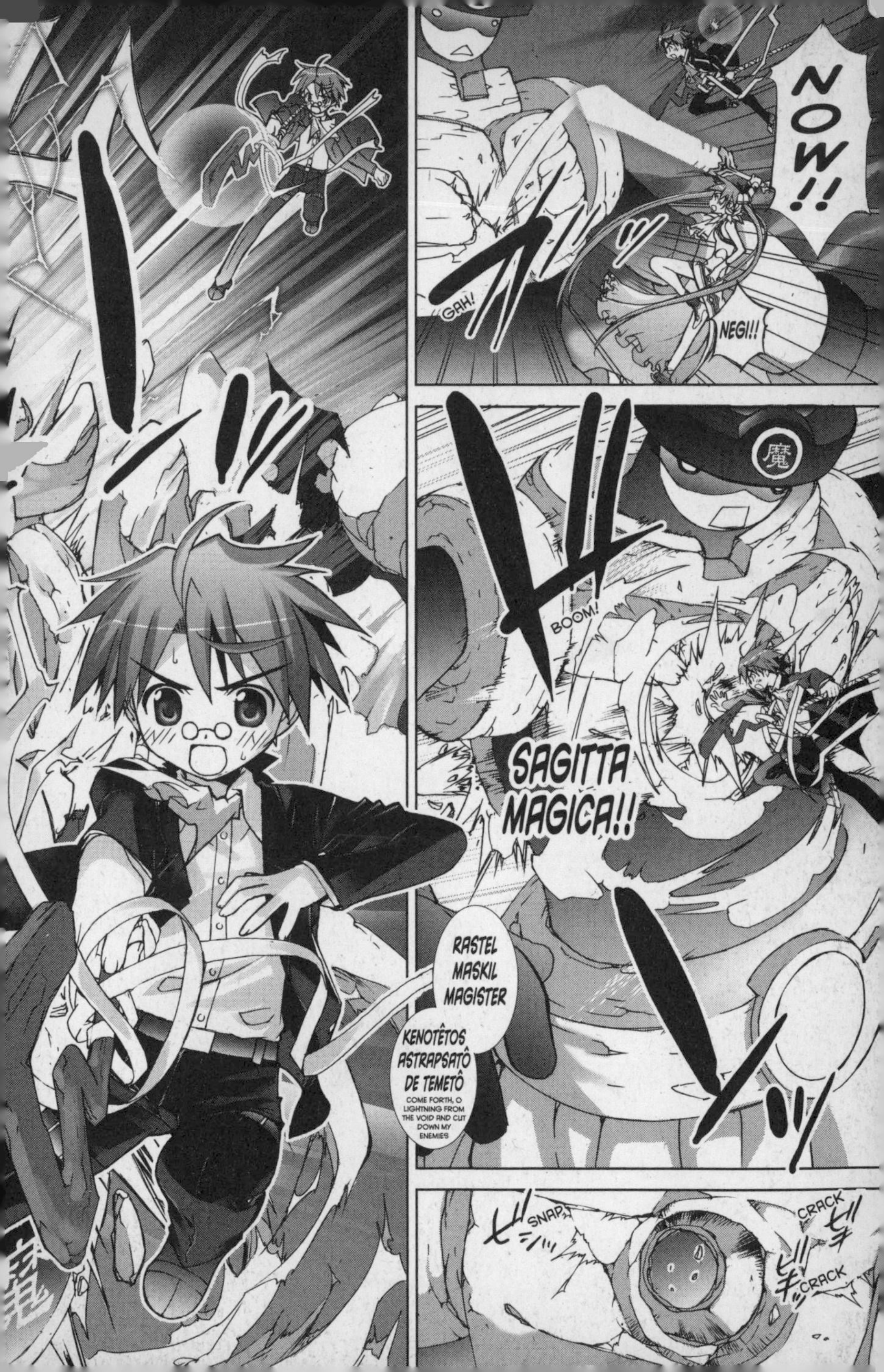
NOW!!
GAH!
NEGI!!
BOOM!
SAGITTA MAGICA!!
SNAP
CRACK
CRACK
RASTEL MASKIL MAGISTER
KENOTÊTOS ASTRAPSATÔ DE TEMETÔ
COME FORTH, O LIGHTNING FROM THE VOID AND CUT DOWN MY ENEMIES

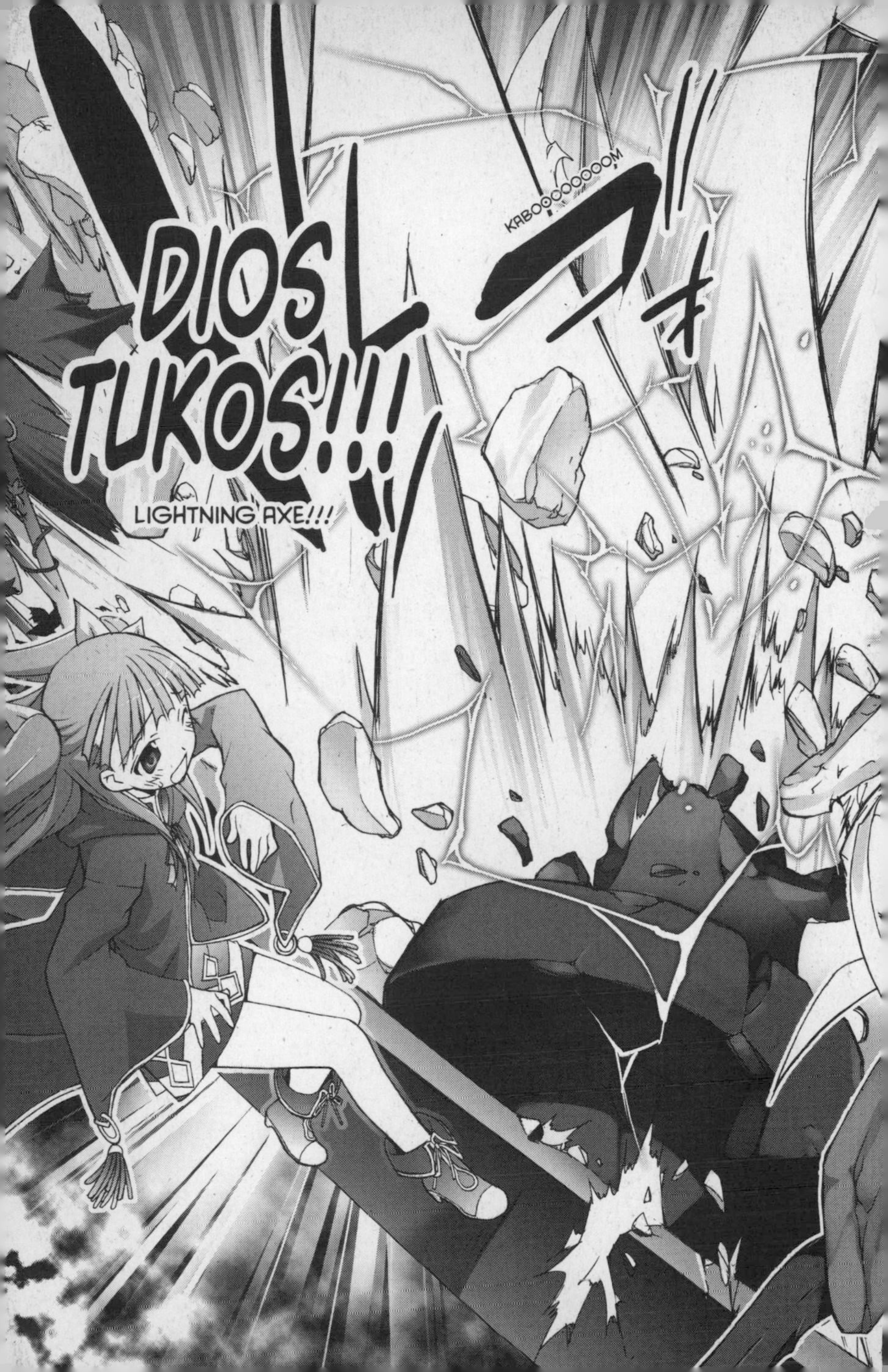
KABOOOOOOOOM
DIOS TUKOS!!!
LIGHTNING AXE!!!

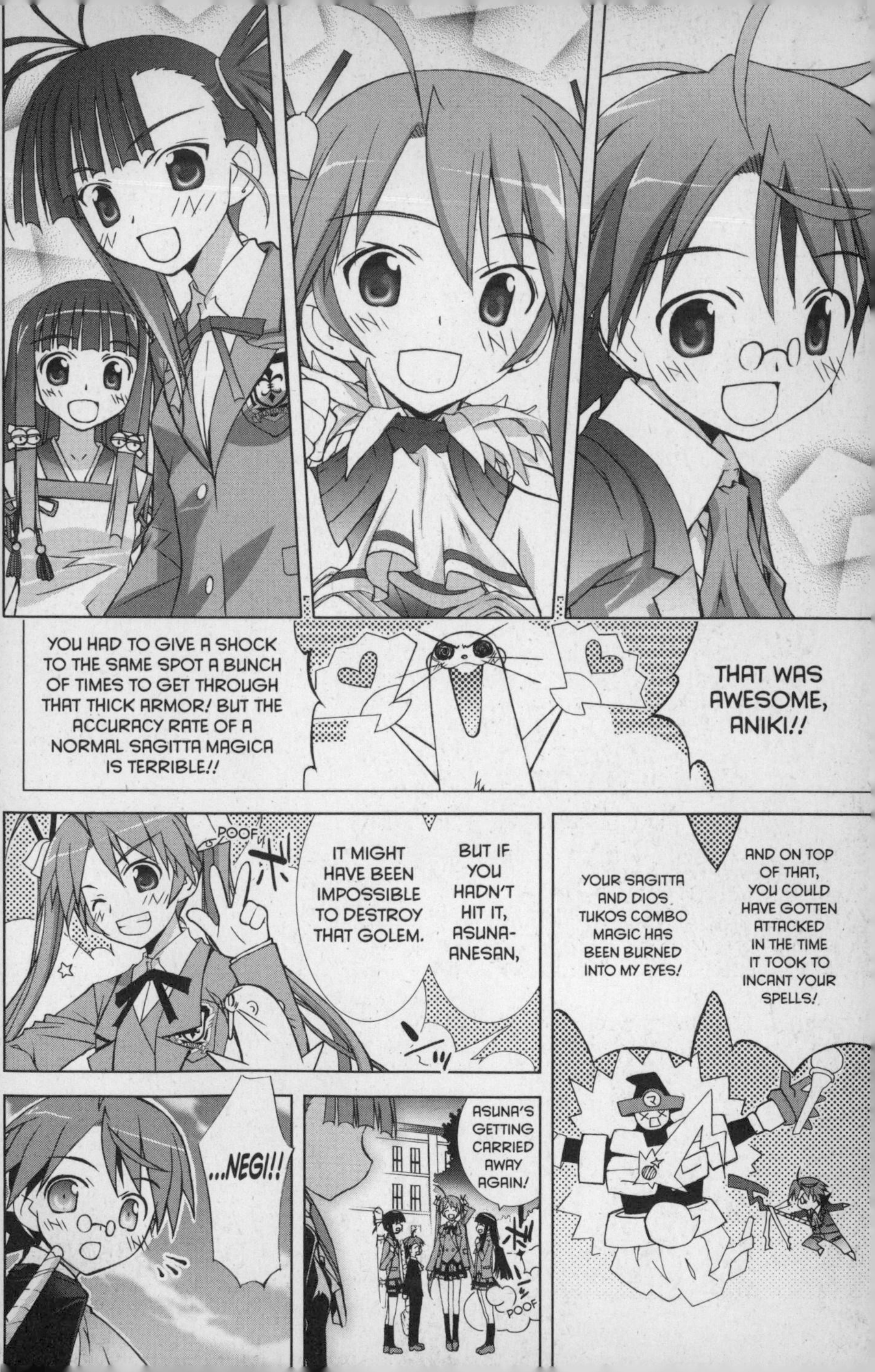
THAT WAS AWESOME, ANIKI!!
YOU HAD TO GIVE A SHOCK TO THE SAME SPOT A BUNCH OF TIMES TO GET THROUGH THAT THICK ARMOR! BUT THE ACCURACY RATE OF A NORMAL SAGITTA MAGICA IS TERRIBLE!!
AND ON TOP OF THAT, YOU COULD HAVE GOTTEN ATTACKED IN THE TIME IT TOOK TO INCANT YOUR SPELLS!
YOUR SAGITTA AND DIOS TUKOS COMBO MAGIC HAS BEEN BURNED INTO MY EYES!
BUT IF YOU HADN'T HIT IT, ASUNA-ANESAN,
IT MIGHT HAVE BEEN IMPOSSIBLE TO DESTROY THAT GOLEM.
POOF
ASUNA'S GETTING CARRIED AWAY AGAIN!
POOF
...NEGI!!

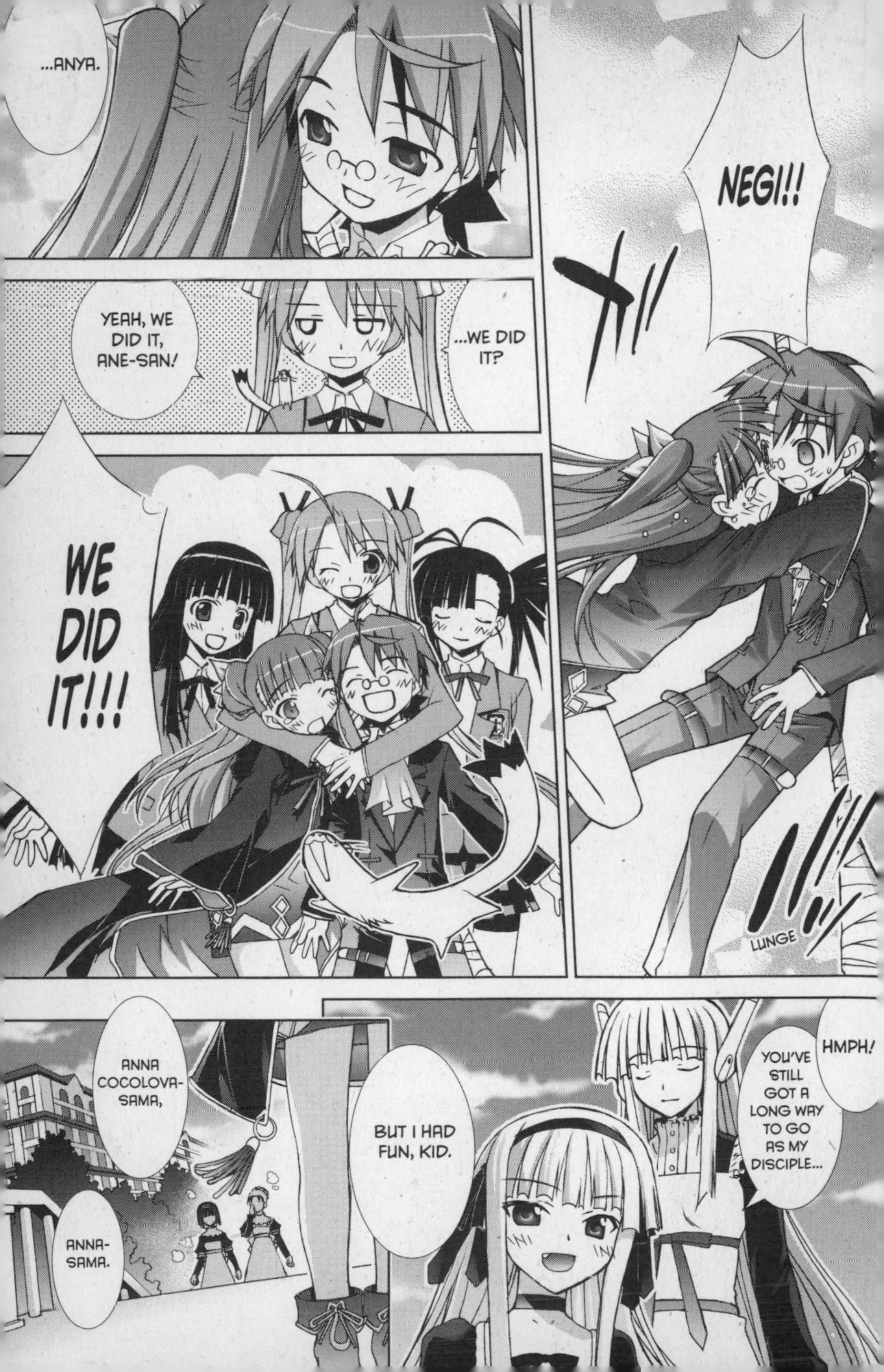

NEGI!!
LUNGE
...ANYA.
...WE DID IT?
YEAH, WE DID IT, ANE-SAN!
WE DID IT!!!
HMPH!
YOU'VE STILL GOT A LONG WAY TO GO AS MY DISCIPLE...
BUT I HAD FUN, KID.
ANNA COCOLOVA-SAMA,
ANNA-SAMA.

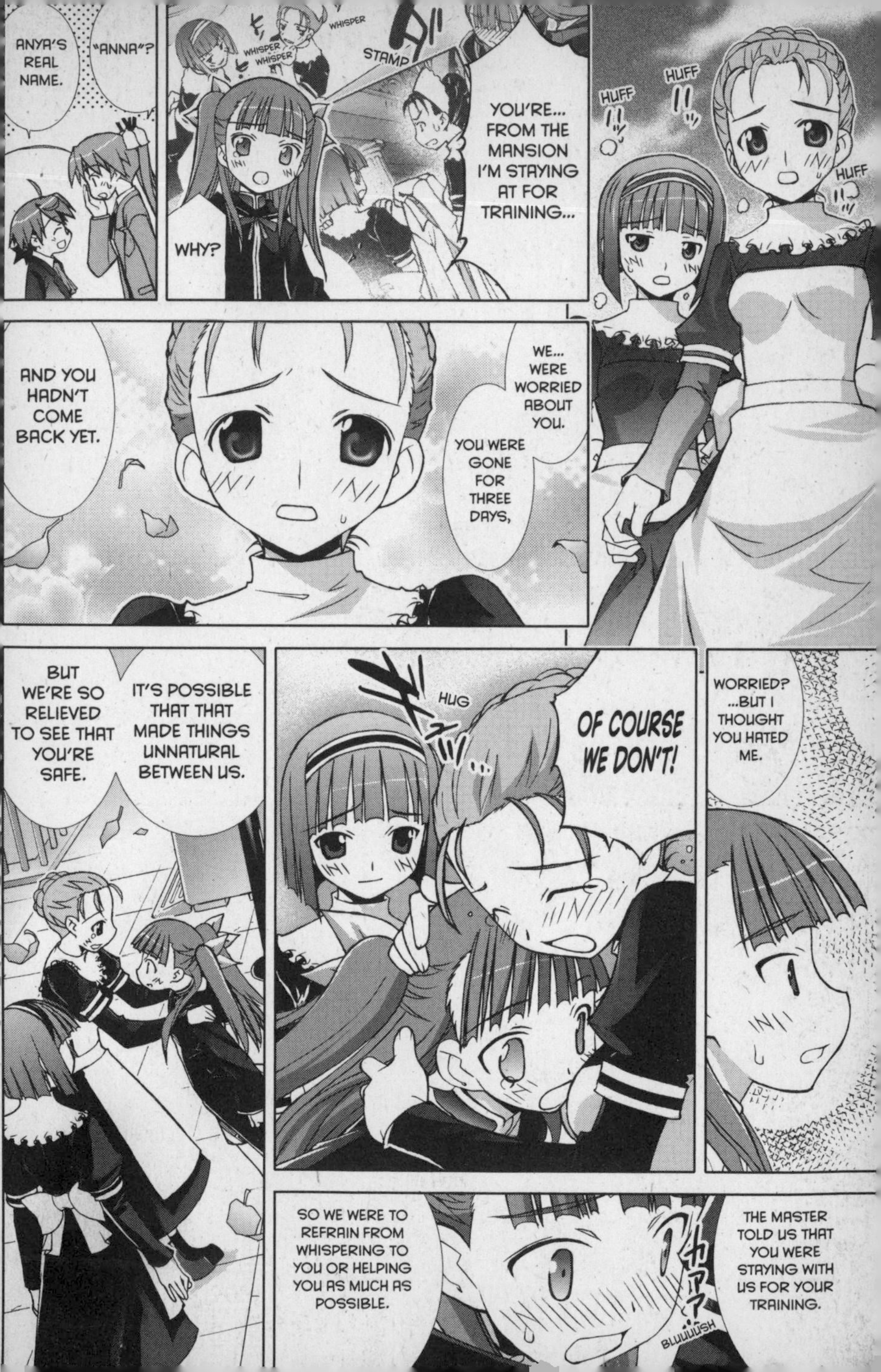

HUFF
HUFF
HUFF
WHISPER
STAMP
WHISPER WHISPER
YOU'RE... FROM THE MANSION I'M STAYING AT FOR TRAINING...
WHY?
"ANNA"?
ANYA'S REAL NAME.
WE... WERE WORRIED ABOUT YOU.
YOU WERE GONE FOR THREE DAYS,
AND YOU HADN'T COME BACK YET.
WORRIED? ...BUT I THOUGHT YOU HATED ME.
OF COURSE WE DON'T!
HUG
THE MASTER TOLD US THAT YOU WERE STAYING WITH US FOR YOUR TRAINING.
BLUUUUSH
SO WE WERE TO REFRAIN FROM WHISPERING TO YOU OR HELPING YOU AS MUCH AS POSSIBLE.
IT'S POSSIBLE THAT THAT MADE THINGS UNNATURAL BETWEEN US.
BUT WE'RE SO RELIEVED TO SEE THAT YOU'RE SAFE.

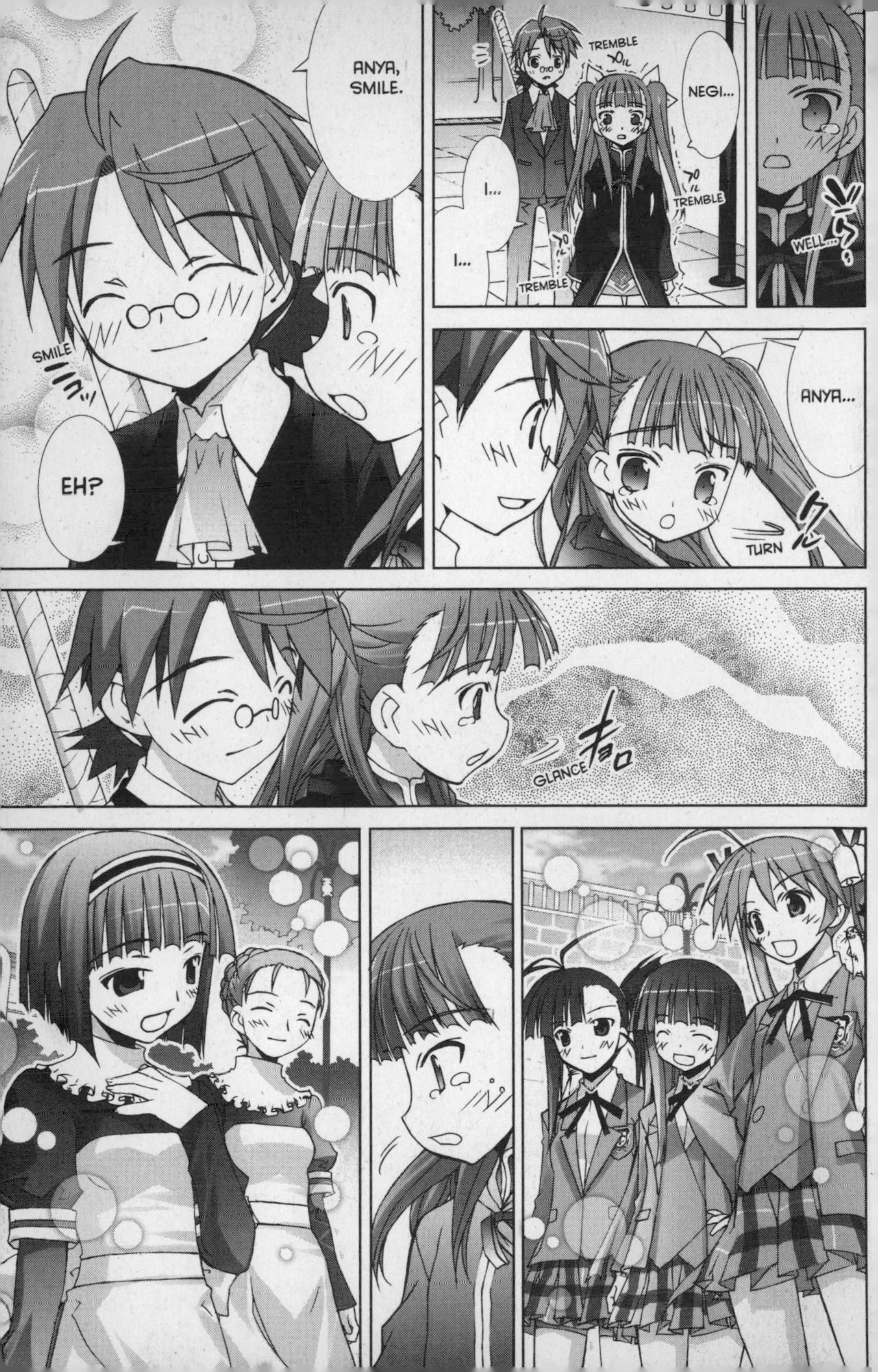
WELL...
NEGI...
TREMBLE
I...
I...
TREMBLE
TREMBLE
ANYA...
TURN
ANYA, SMILE.
SMILE
EH?
GLANCE

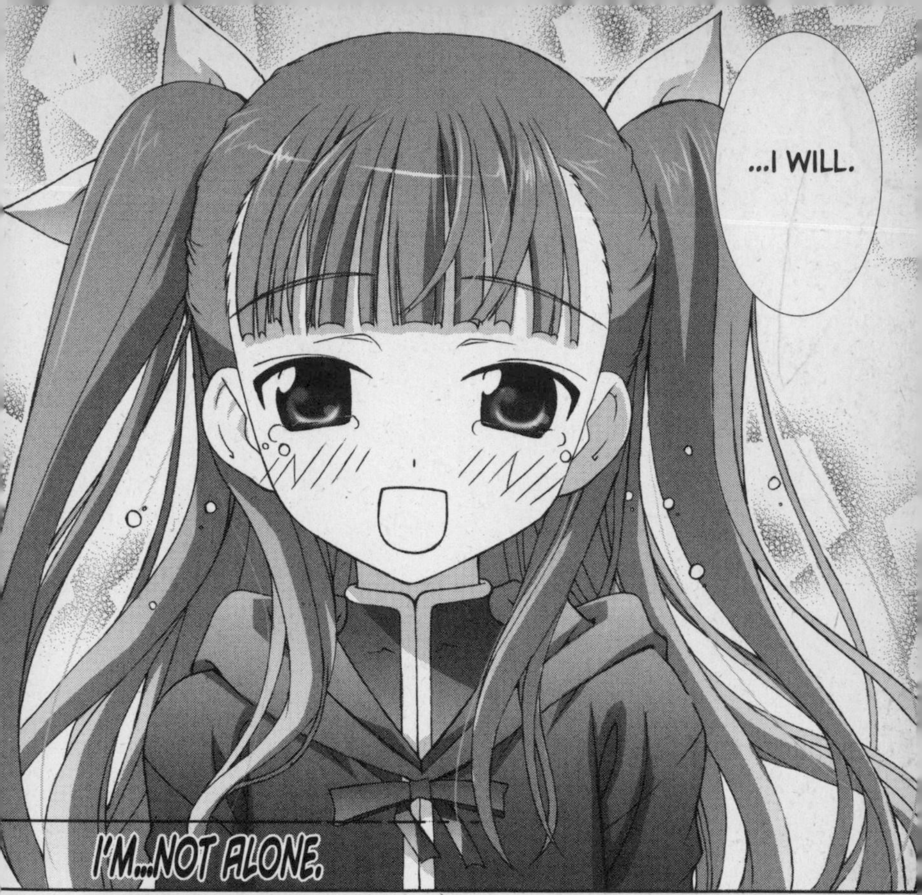
...I WILL.
I'M...NOT ALONE.
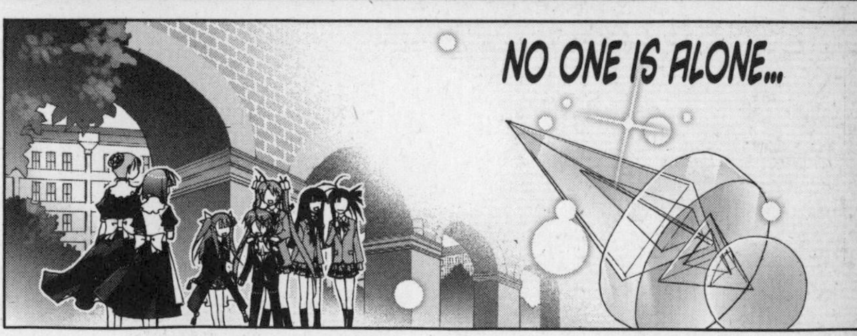
NO ONE IS ALONE...

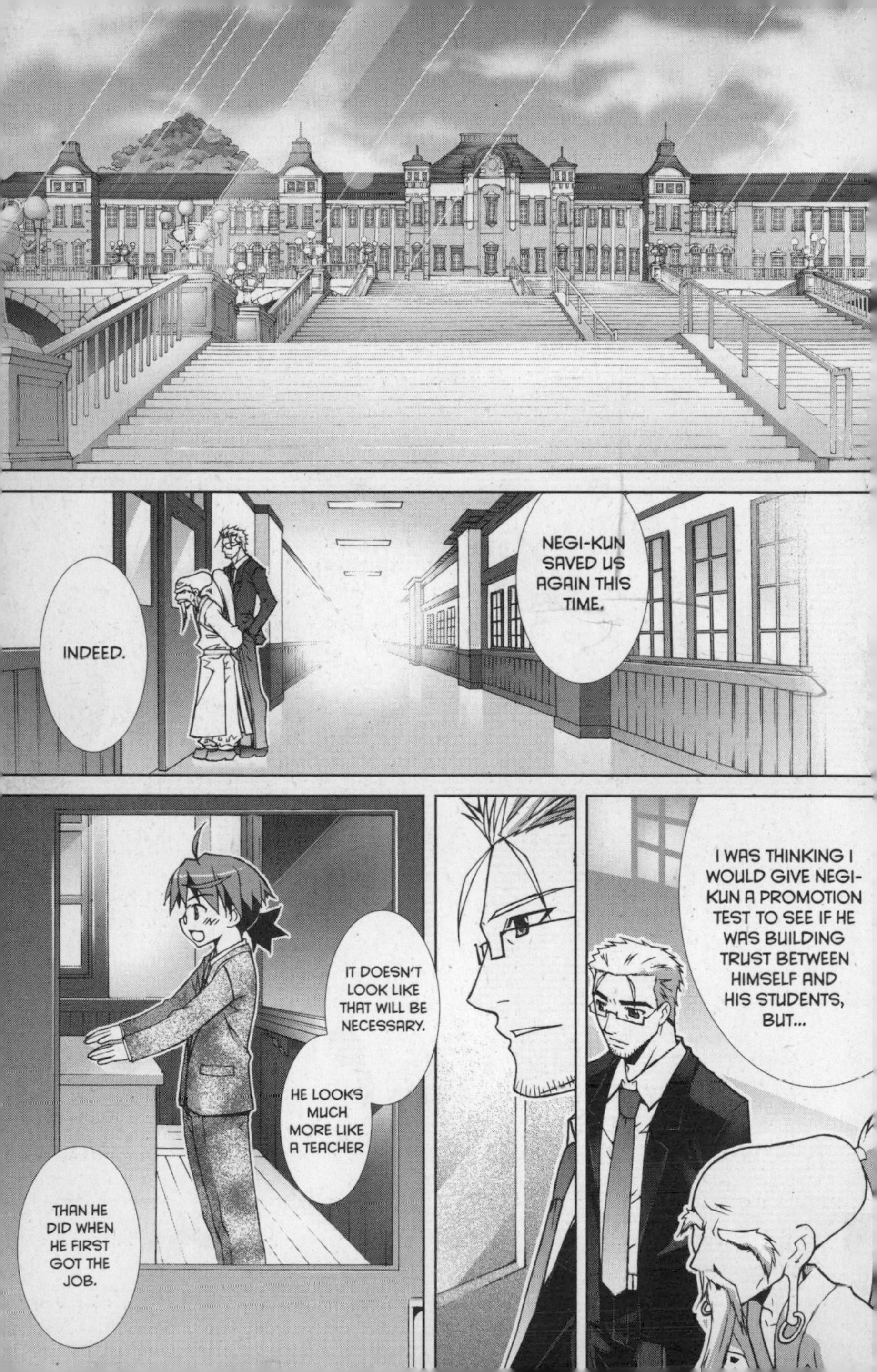
NEGI-KUN SAVED US AGAIN THIS TIME.
INDEED.
I WAS THINKING I WOULD GIVE NEGI-KUN A PROMOTION TEST TO SEE IF HE WAS BUILDING TRUST BETWEEN HIMSELF AND HIS STUDENTS, BUT...
IT DOESN'T LOOK LIKE THAT WILL BE NECESSARY.
HE LOOKS MUCH MORE LIKE A TEACHER
THAN HE DID WHEN HE FIRST GOT THE JOB.

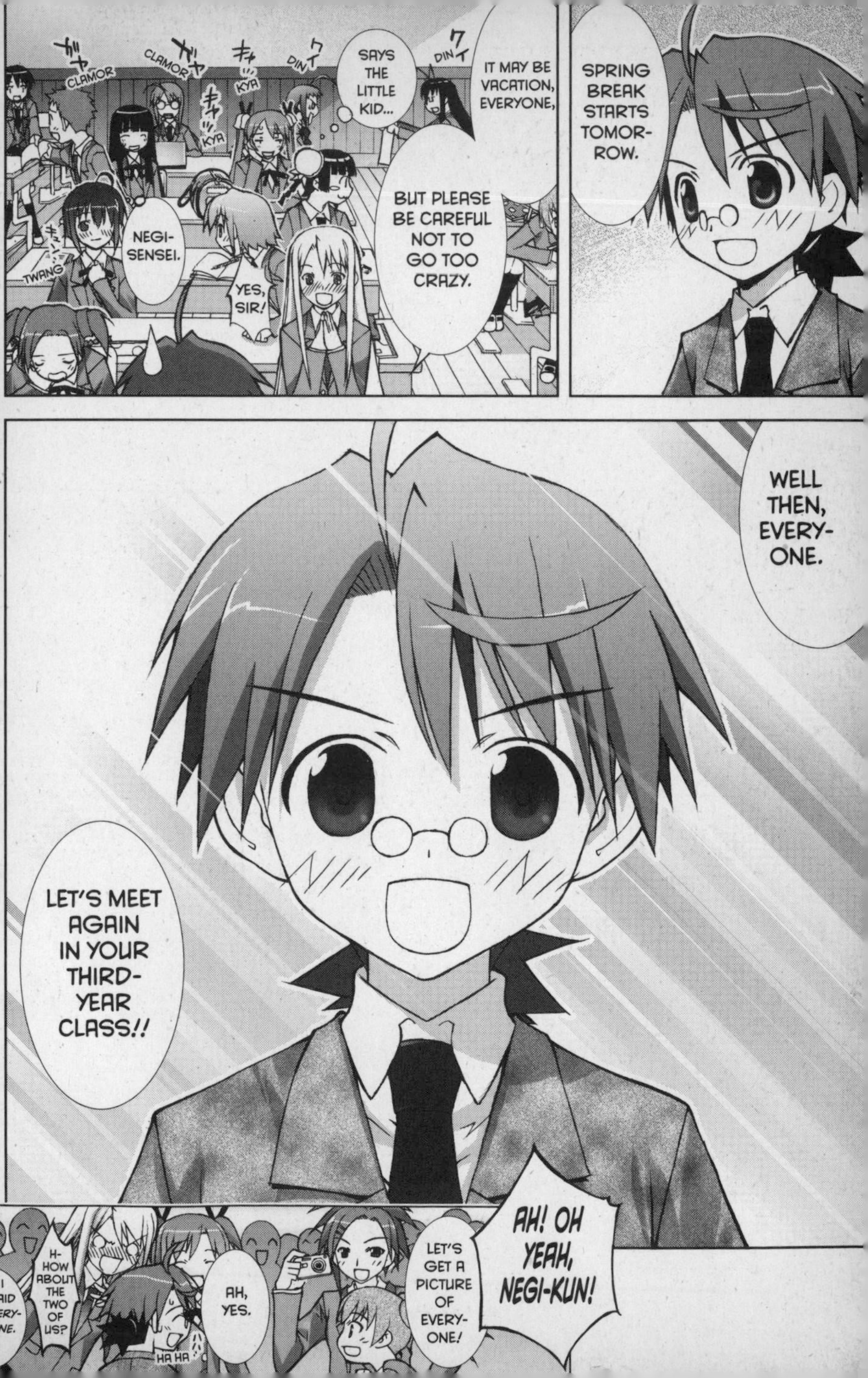
SPRING BREAK STARTS TOMORROW.
IT MAY BE VACATION, EVERYONE,
DIN
DIN
SAYS THE LITTLE KID...
KYA
KYA
CLAMOR
CLAMOR
BUT PLEASE BE CAREFUL NOT TO GO TOO CRAZY.
YES, SIR!
NEGI-SENSEI.
TWANG
WELL THEN, EVERYONE.
LET'S MEET AGAIN IN YOUR THIRD-YEAR CLASS!!
AH! OH YEAH, NEGI-KUN!
LET'S GET A PICTURE OF EVERYONE!
AH, YES.
H-HOW ABOUT THE TWO OF US?
HA HA
I SAID EVERYONE.

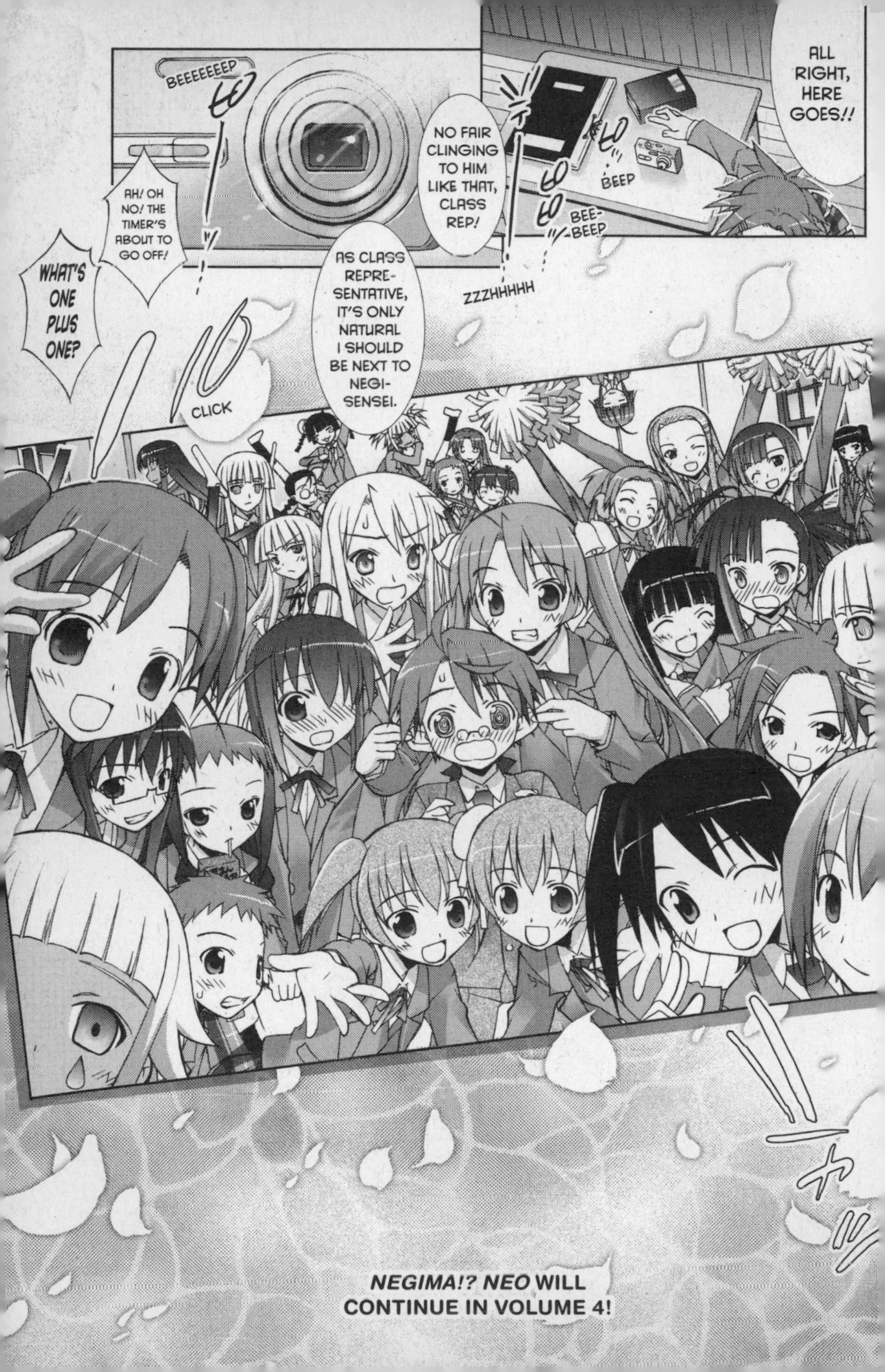
ALL RIGHT, HERE GOES!!
BEEP
BEE-BEEP
NO FAIR CLINGING TO HIM LIKE THAT, CLASS REP!
BEEEEEEEP
AH! OH NO! THE TIMER'S ABOUT TO GO OFF!
ZZZHHHHH
AS CLASS REPRESENTATIVE, IT'S ONLY NATURAL I SHOULD BE NEXT TO NEGI-SENSEI.
WHAT'S ONE PLUS ONE?
CLICK
NEGIMA!? NEO WILL CONTINUE IN VOLUME 4!

SPECIAL PERIOD / BONUS FOUR-PANEL MANGA

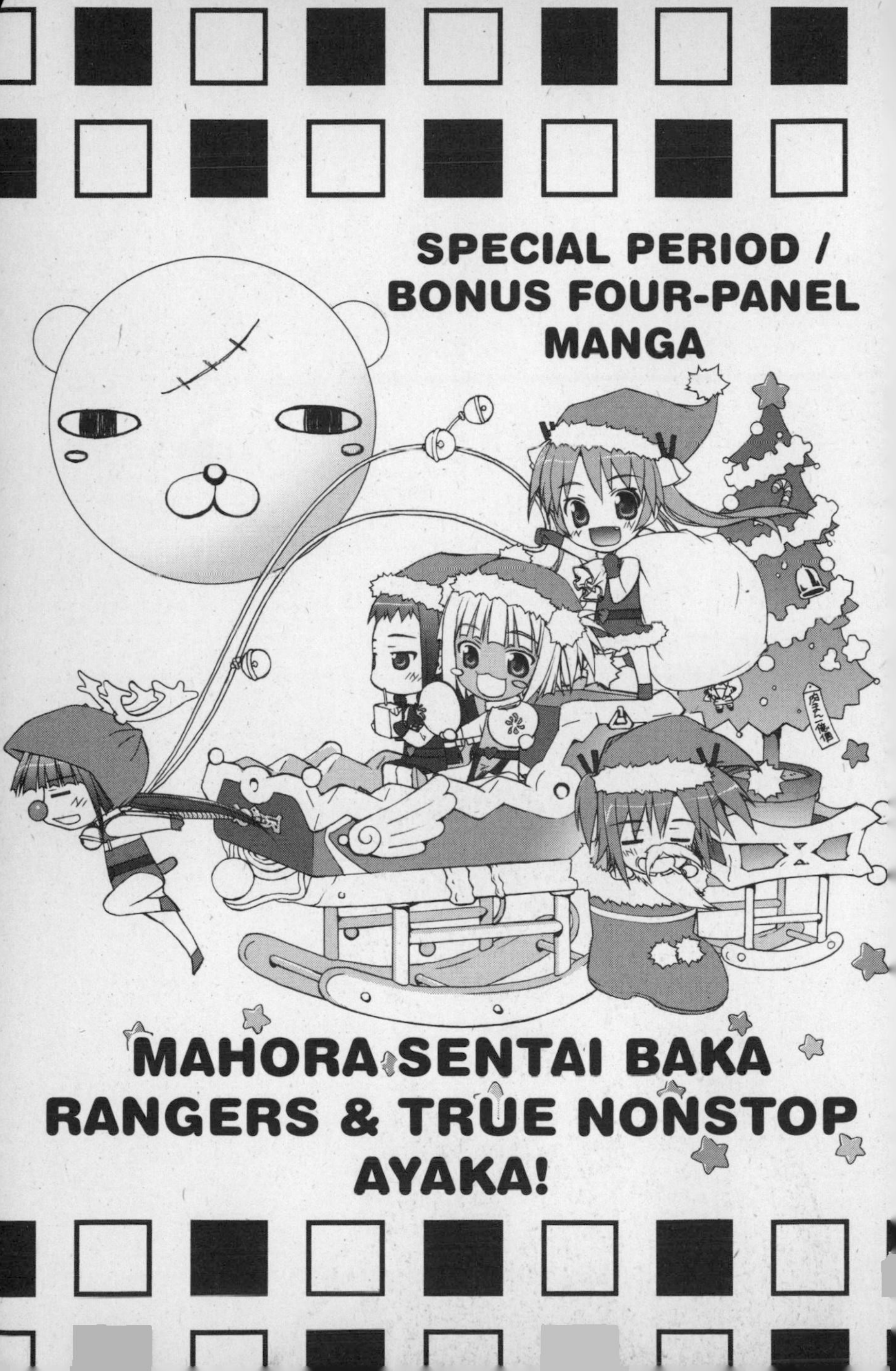

MAHORA SENTAI BAKA RANGERS & TRUE NONSTOP AYAKA!

ENTER THE SEA MONSTER!

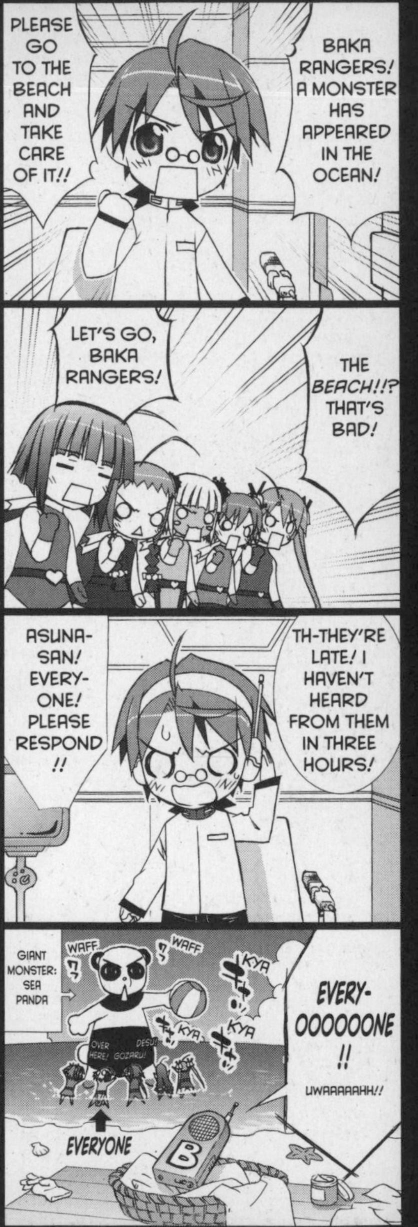

BAKA PINK-CHAN

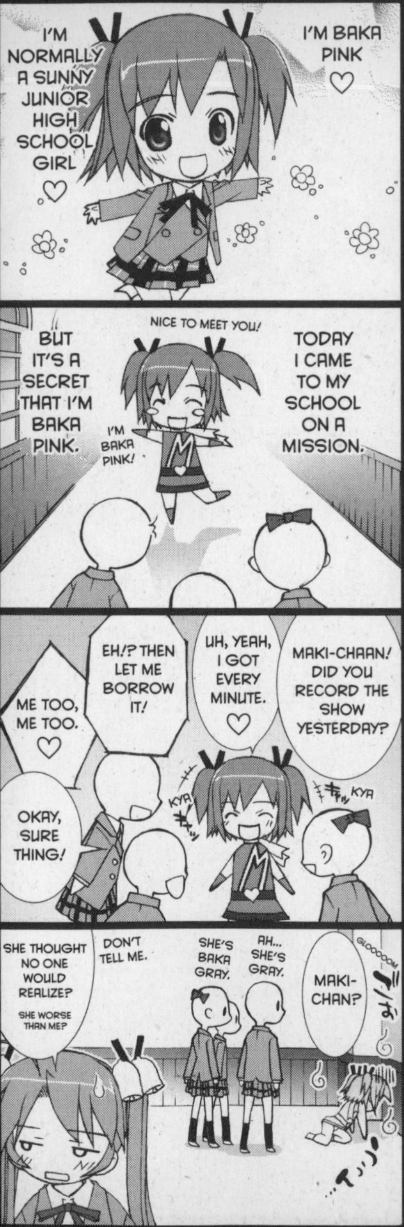

ARRANGING OUR STRAY HAIRS

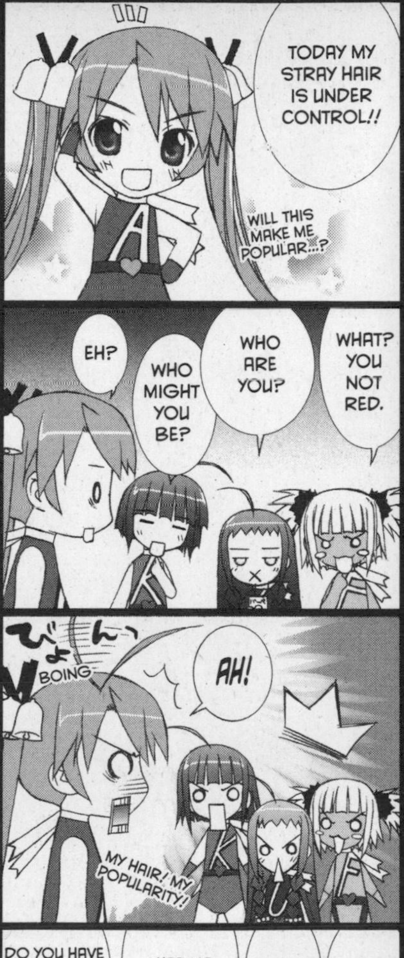
TODAY MY STRAY HAIR IS UNDER CONTROL!!
WILL THIS MAKE ME POPULAR...?
WHAT? YOU NOT RED.
WHO ARE YOU?
WHO MIGHT YOU BE?
EH?
AH!
BOING
MY HAIR! MY POPULARITY!
IT RED!
BRILLIANT DISGUISE.
I HAD NO IDEA IT WAS YOU.
DO YOU HAVE POWER OF RECOGNITION...?

BIBLION INTRODUCTIONS 1

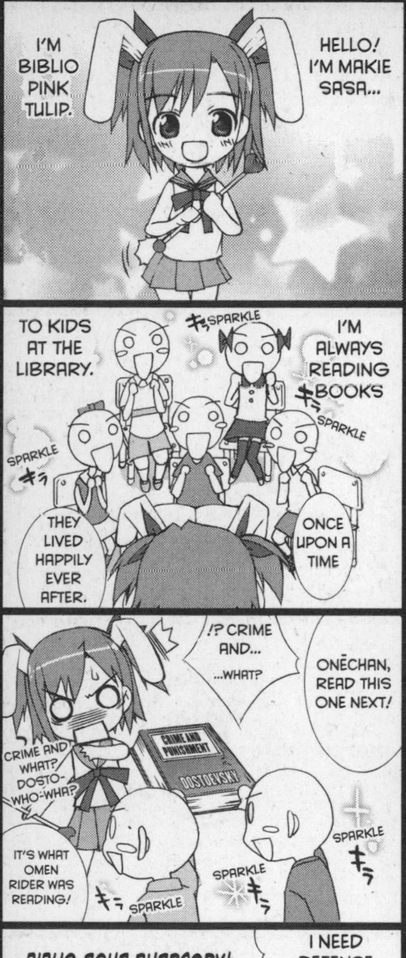
HELLO! I'M MAKIE SASA...
I'M BIBLIO PINK TULIP.
I'M ALWAYS READING BOOKS
SPARKLE
TO KIDS AT THE LIBRARY.
SPARKLE
SPARKLE
ONCE UPON A TIME
THEY LIVED HAPPILY EVER AFTER.
ONĒCHAN, READ THIS ONE NEXT!
!? CRIME AND... ...WHAT?
CRIME AND PUNISHMENT
DOSTOEVSKY
CRIME AND WHAT? DOSTO-WHO-WHA?
SPARKLE
SPARKLE
IT'S WHAT OMEN RIDER WAS READING!
SPARKLE
I NEED DEFENSE MOVES IN UNEXPECTED PLACES.
BIBLIO AQUA RHAPSODY!
POOF
NĒCHAN, THAT'S COOL!!
TEACH US HOW TO DO IT!!

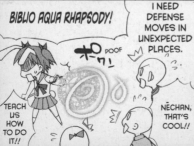

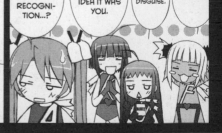

BIBLION INTRODUCTIONS 2

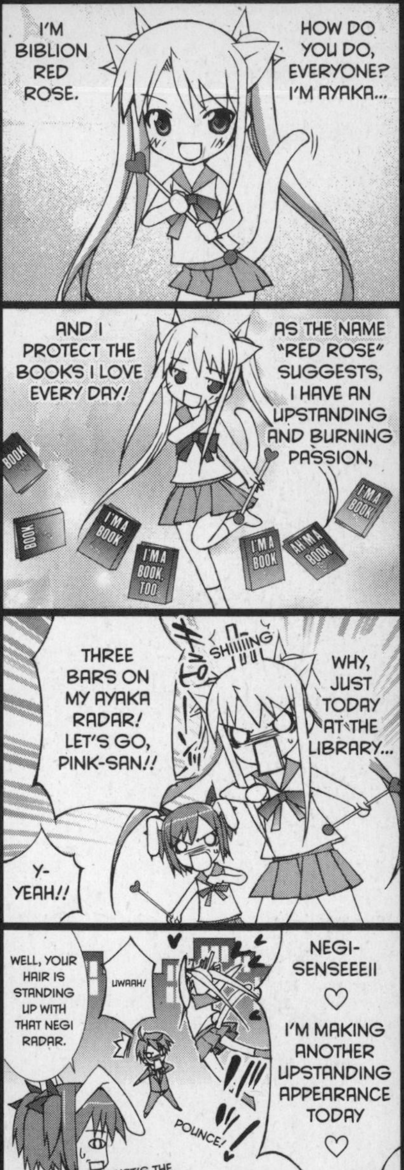
HOW DO YOU DO, EVERYONE? I'M AYAKA...
I'M BIBLION RED ROSE.
AS THE NAME "RED ROSE" SUGGESTS, I HAVE AN UPSTANDING AND BURNING PASSION,
AND I PROTECT THE BOOKS I LOVE EVERY DAY!
BOOK
BOOK
I'M A BOOK
I'M A BOOK, TOO
I'M A BOOK
AH'M A BOOK
I'M A BOOK
WHY, JUST TODAY AT THE LIBRARY...
SHIIIING
THREE BARS ON MY AYAKA RADAR! LET'S GO, PINK-SAN!!
Y- YEAH!!
NEGI-SENSEEII ♡ I'M MAKING ANOTHER UPSTANDING APPEARANCE TODAY ♡
POUNCE!
UWAAH!
WELL, YOUR HAIR IS STANDING UP WITH THAT NEGI RADAR.
WHAT'S THE POINT OF TRACKING SENSEI?

ROCKIN' ROULIN ROUGE

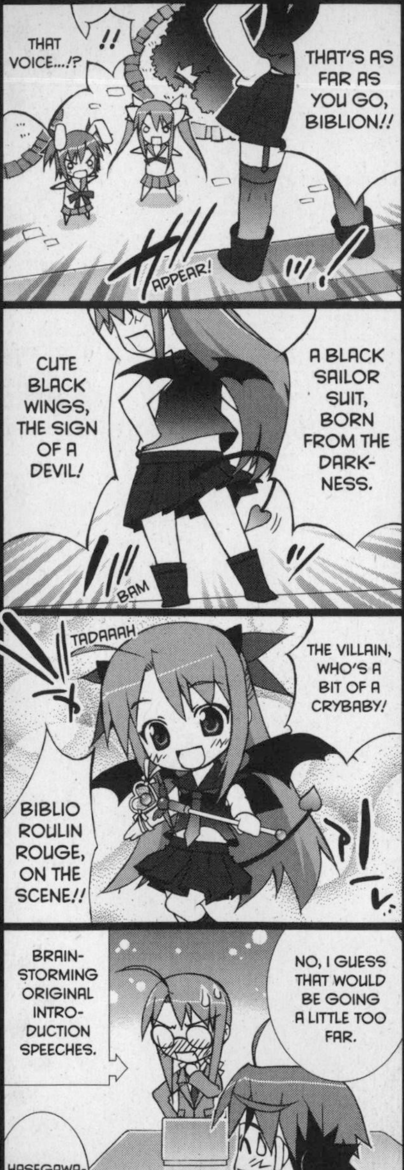
THAT'S AS FAR AS YOU GO, BIBLION!!
!!
THAT VOICE...!?
APPEAR!
A BLACK SAILOR SUIT, BORN FROM THE DARK-NESS.
CUTE BLACK WINGS, THE SIGN OF A DEVIL!
BAM
THE VILLAIN, WHO'S A BIT OF A CRYBABY!
TADAAAH
BIBLIO ROULIN ROUGE, ON THE SCENE!!
NO, I GUESS THAT WOULD BE GOING A LITTLE TOO FAR.
BRAIN-STORMING ORIGINAL INTRO-DUCTION SPEECHES.
HASEGAWA-SAN?

TRUE NONSTOP AYAKA! 1

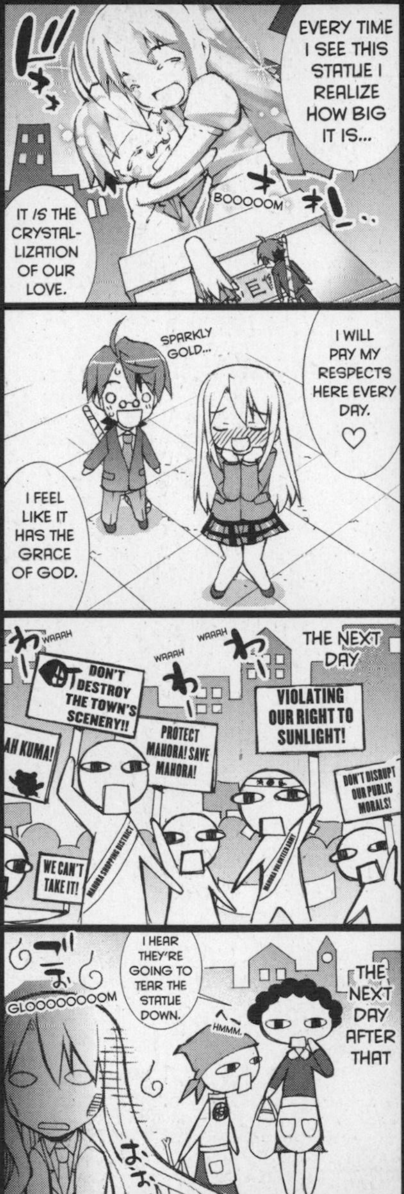
EVERY TIME I SEE THIS STATUE I REALIZE HOW BIG IT IS...
BOOOOOM
IT IS THE CRYSTALLIZATION OF OUR LOVE.
I WILL PAY MY RESPECTS HERE EVERY DAY. ♡
SPARKLY GOLD...
I FEEL LIKE IT HAS THE GRACE OF GOD.
THE NEXT DAY
WAAAH
WAAAH
WAAAH
VIOLATING OUR RIGHT TO SUNLIGHT!
DON'T DISRUPT OUR PUBLIC MORALS!
PROTECT MAHORA! SAVE MAHORA!
DON'T DESTROY THE TOWN'S SCENERY!!
AH KUMA!
MAHORA SHOPPING DISTRICT
WE CAN'T TAKE IT!
THE NEXT DAY AFTER THAT
I HEAR THEY'RE GOING TO TEAR THE STATUE DOWN.
HMMM.
GLOOOOOOOOM

TRUE NONSTOP AYAKA! 2

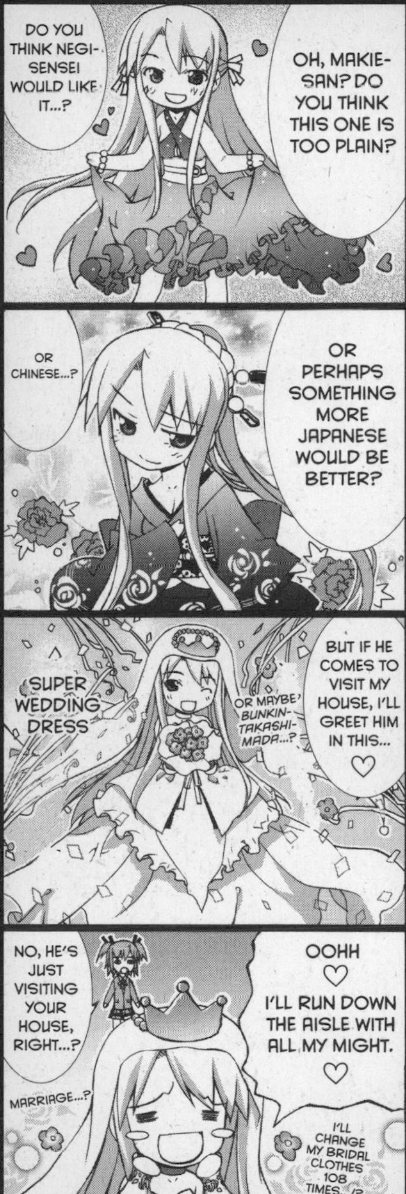
OH, MAKIE-SAN? DO YOU THINK THIS ONE IS TOO PLAIN?
DO YOU THINK NEGI-SENSEI WOULD LIKE IT...?
OR PERHAPS SOMETHING MORE JAPANESE WOULD BE BETTER?
OR CHINESE...?
BUT IF HE COMES TO VISIT MY HOUSE, I'LL GREET HIM IN THIS... ♡
OR MAYBE BUNKIN-TAKASHIMADA...?
SUPER WEDDING DRESS
OOHH ♡ I'LL RUN DOWN THE AISLE WITH ALL MY MIGHT. ♡
I'LL CHANGE MY BRIDAL CLOTHES 108 TIMES...!?
NO, HE'S JUST VISITING YOUR HOUSE, RIGHT...?
MARRIAGE...?

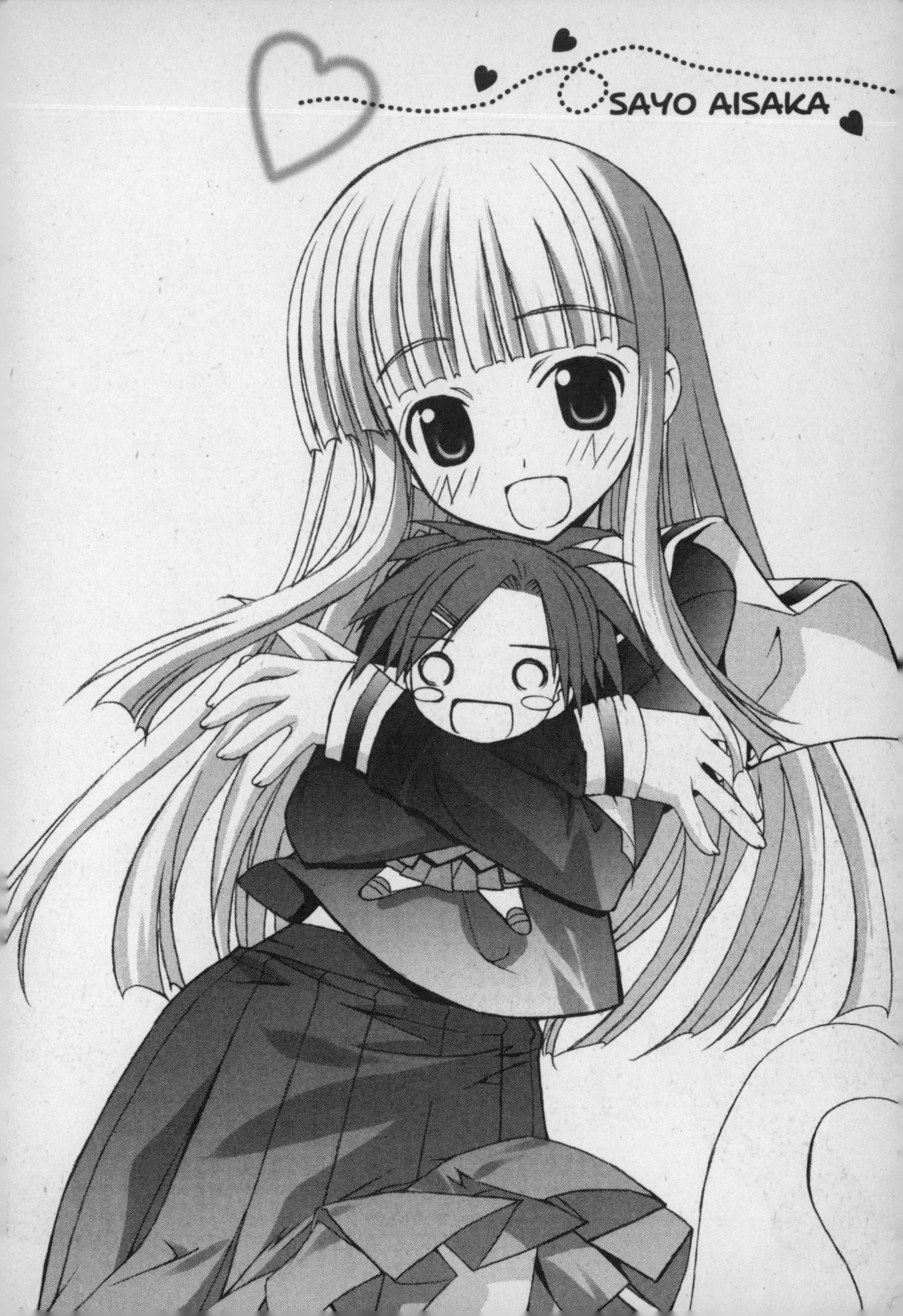
SAYO AISAKA

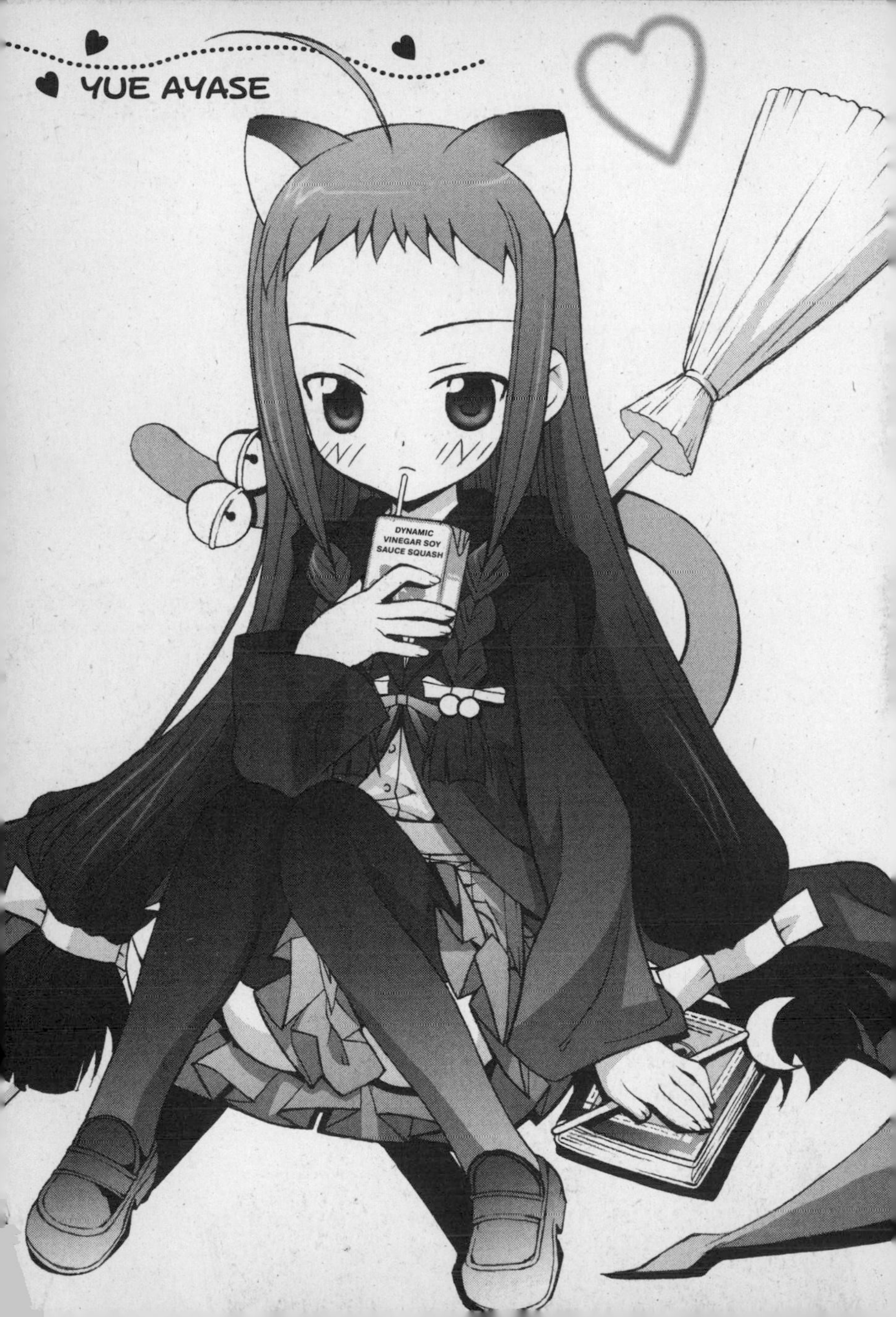
YUE AYASE
DYNAMIC
VINEGAR SOY
SAUCE SQUASH

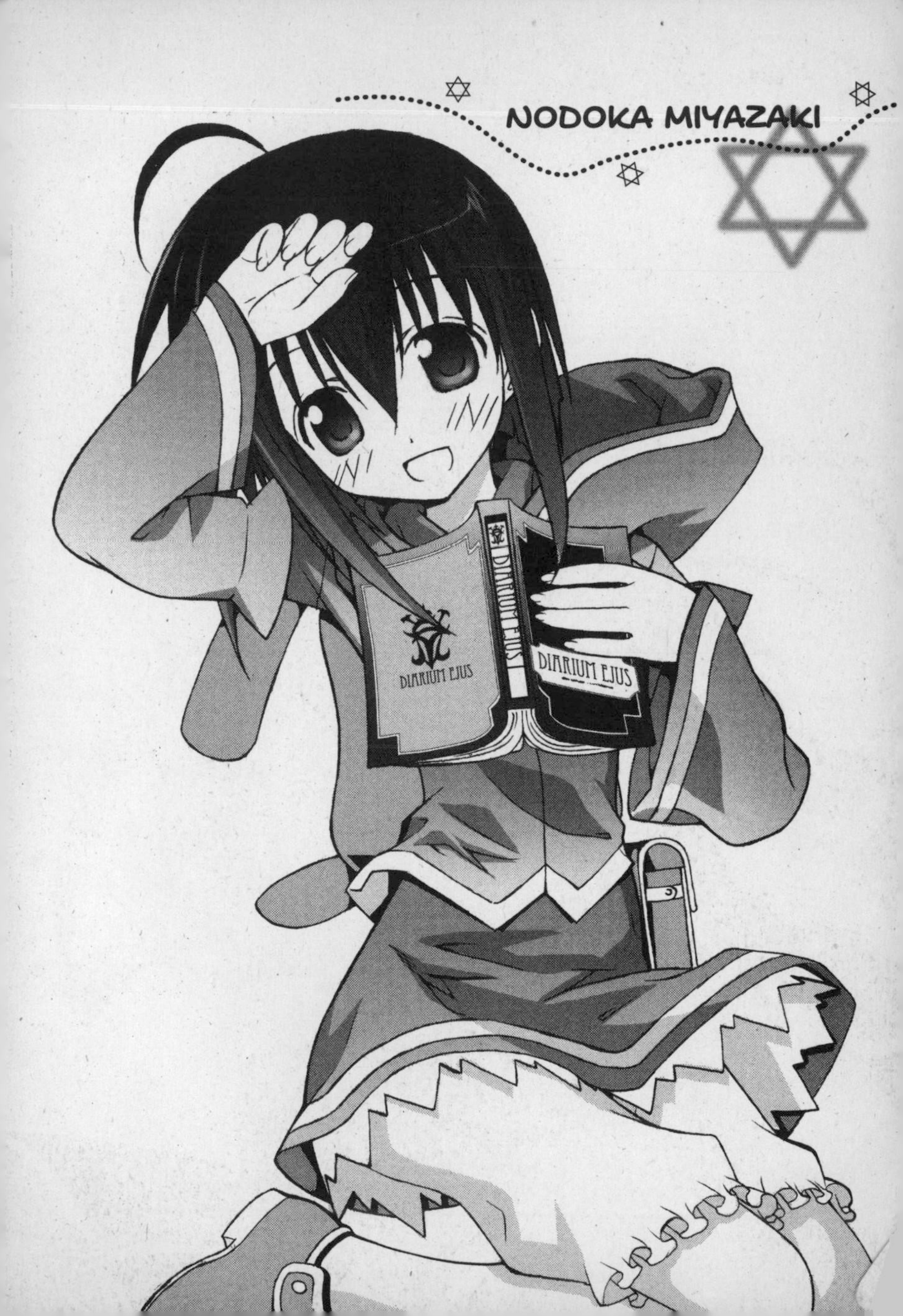
NODOKA MIYAZAKI
DIARIUM EJUS
DIARIUM EJUS
DIARIUM EJUS

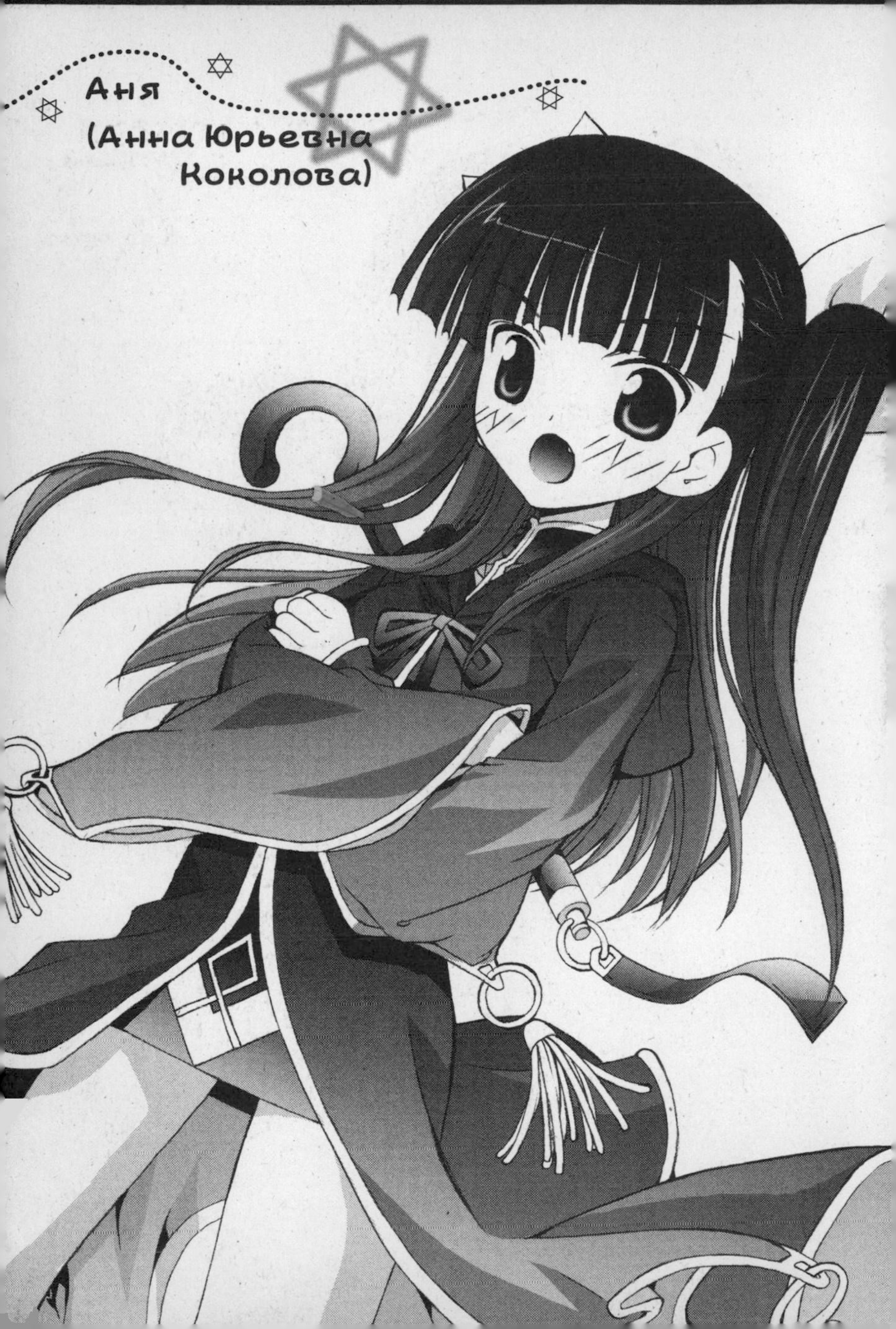
Аня
(Анна Юрьевна
Коколова)

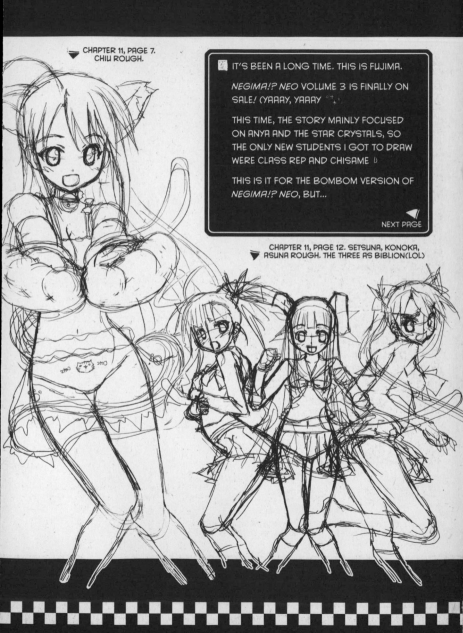

CHAPTER 11, PAGE 7.
CHIU ROUGH.

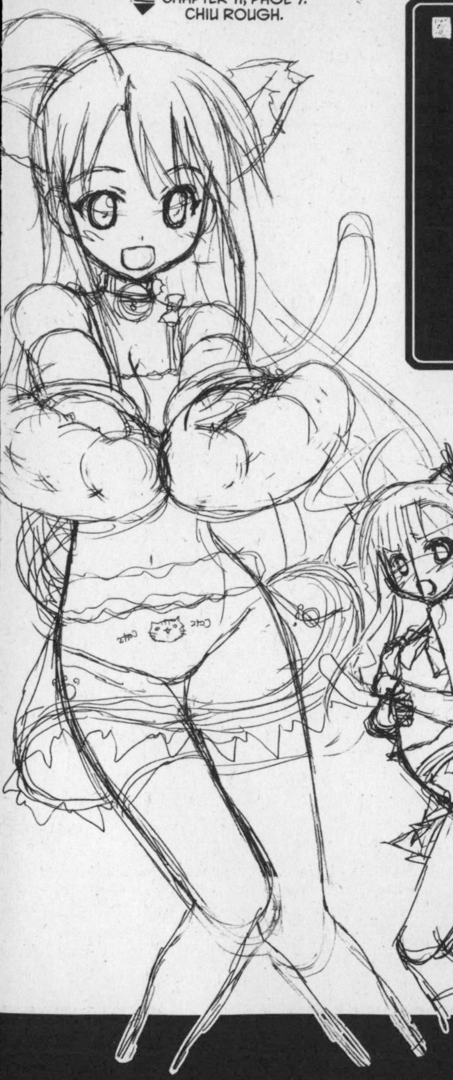

IT'S BEEN A LONG TIME. THIS IS FUJIMA.

NEGIMA!? NEO VOLUME 3 IS FINALLY ON SALE! (YAAAY, YAAAY

THIS TIME, THE STORY MAINLY FOCUSED ON ANYA AND THE STAR CRYSTALS, SO THE ONLY NEW STUDENTS I GOT TO DRAW WERE CLASS REP AND CHISAME

THIS IS IT FOR THE BOMBOM VERSION OF *NEGIMA!? NEO*, BUT...

NEXT PAGE

CHAPTER 11, PAGE 12. SETSUNA, KONOKA, ASUNA ROUGH. THE THREE AS BIBLION(LOL)

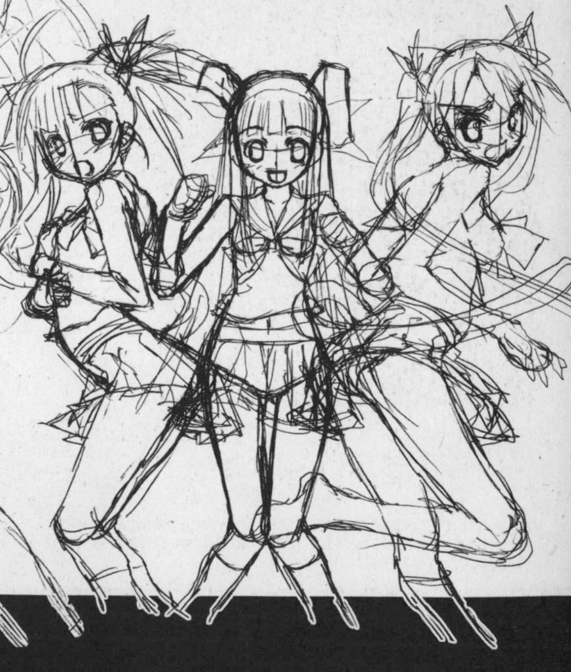

AFTERWORD!?

THE SERIES IS GOING TO CONTINUE IN MAGAZINE SPECIAL. M(__)M (DEEP BOW)

THIS IS ALL THANKS TO THE SUPPORT OF ALL OF YOU WHO HAVE THIS BOOK IN YOUR HAND AND ARE READING IT. TRULY, THANK YOU VERY MUCH!! I PLAN ON DRAWING ALL THE CHARACTERS I COULDN'T DRAW BEFORE, SO PLEASE CONTINUE TO ENJOY *NEGIMA!? NEO* ☆

CHANGING THE SUBJECT, ABOUT THE BONUSES FOR THIS COMIC—THE NONSTOP AYAKA IN VOLUME 2 WAS EXTREMELY POPULAR, SO I DID IT AGAIN FOR THIS VOLUME (LAUGH). I HOPE YOU WILL ENJOY IT AGAIN!

WELL THEN, LET'S MEET AGAIN IN VOLUME 4!!

NOVEMBER 2007,
TAKUYA FUJIMA

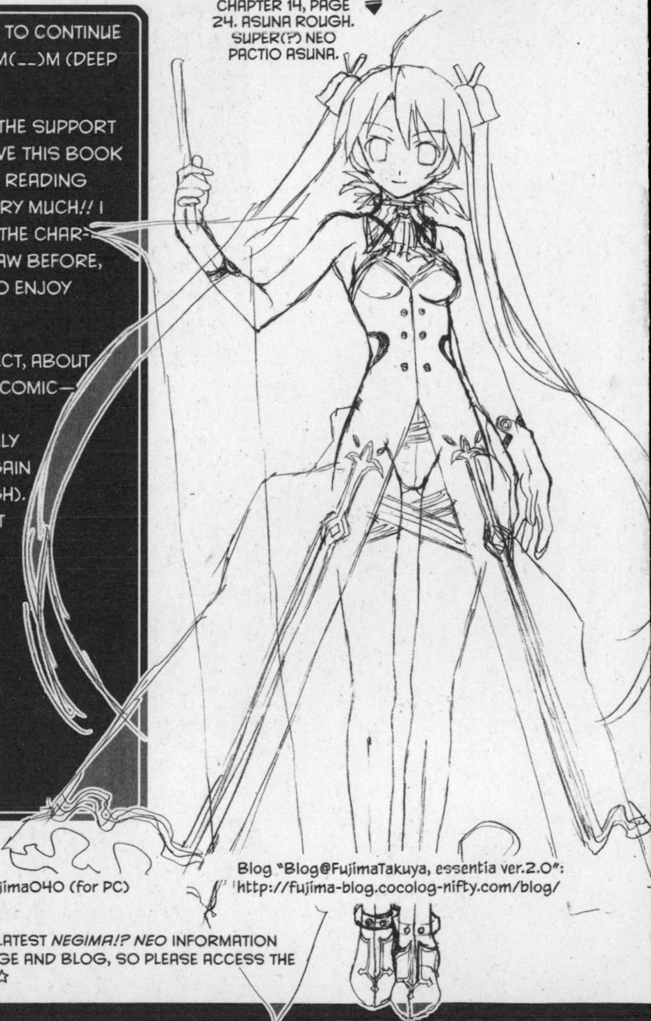

CHAPTER 14, PAGE 24. ASUNA ROUGH. SUPER(?) NEO PACTIO ASUNA.

HP "ESSENTIA.web":
http://www.geocities.co.jp/fujima040 (for PC)

Blog "Blog@FujimaTakuya, essentia ver.2.0":
http://fujima-blog.cocolog-nifty.com/blog/

I WANT TO ANNOUNCE THE LATEST *NEGIMA!? NEO* INFORMATION AS IT COMES ON MY HOMEPAGE AND BLOG, SO PLEASE ACCESS THE SITES AND CHECK THEM OUT ☆

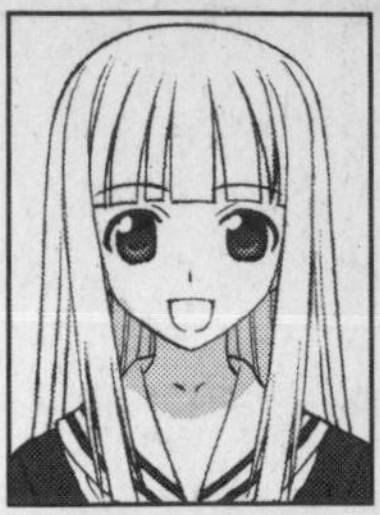

1. SAYO AISAKA

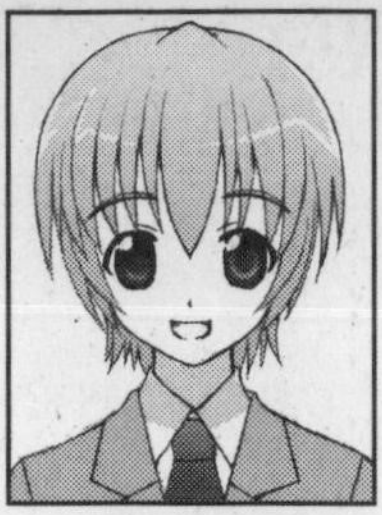

5. AKO IZUMI
NURSE'S OFFICE AIDE, SOCCER TEAM (NON-SCHOOL ACTIVITY)

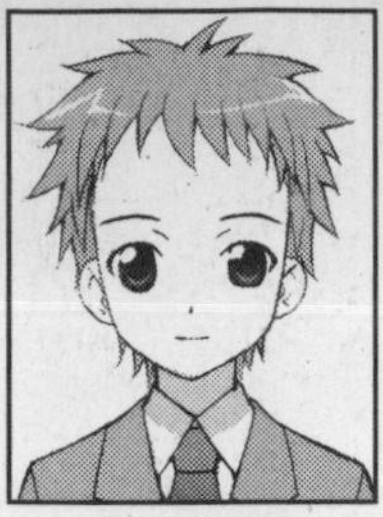

9. MISORA KASUGA
TRACK AND FIELD

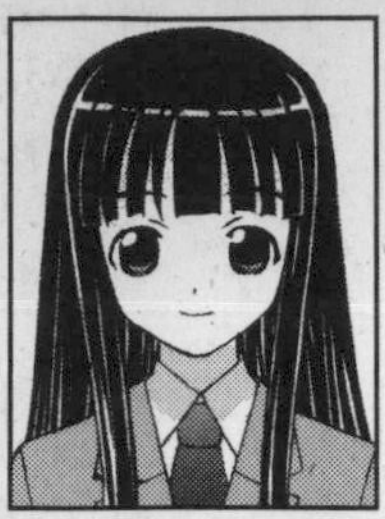

13. KONOKA KONOE
SECRETARY, FORTUNE-TELLING CLUB, LIBRARY EXPLORATION CLUB

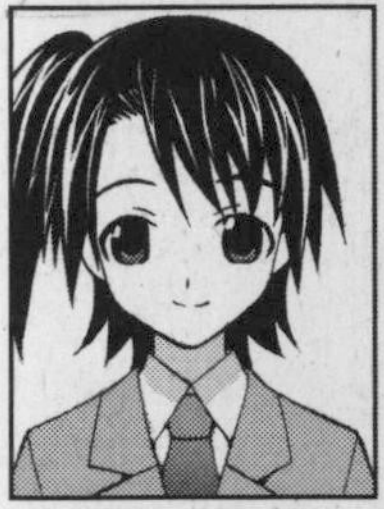

2. YUNA AKASHI
BASKETBALL TEAM

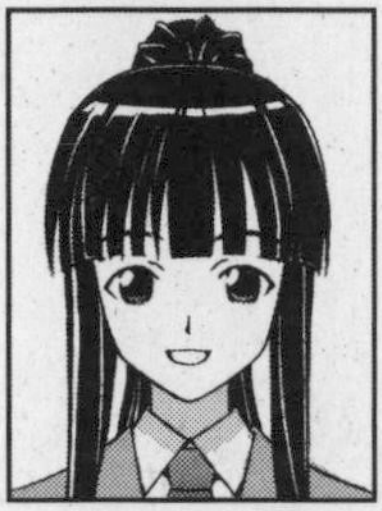

6. AKIRA OKOCHI
SWIM TEAM

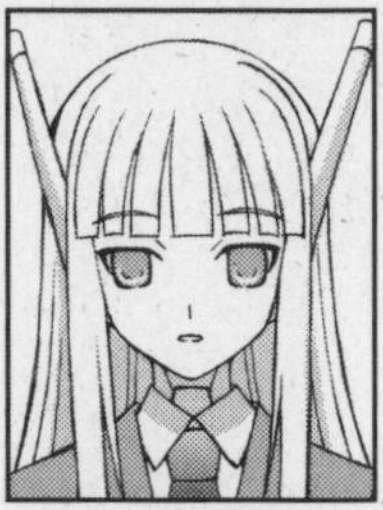

10. CHACHAMARU KARAKUI
TEA CEREMONY CLUB, GO CLUB

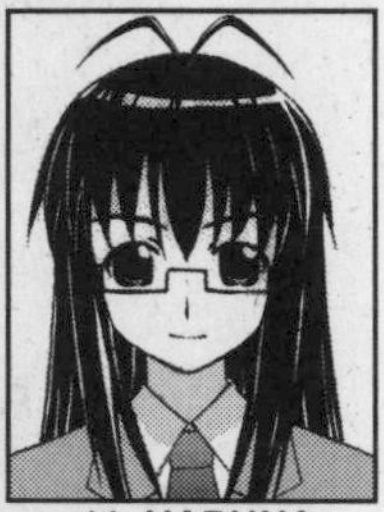

14. HARUNA SAOTOME
MANGA CLUB, LIBRARY EXPLORATION CLUB

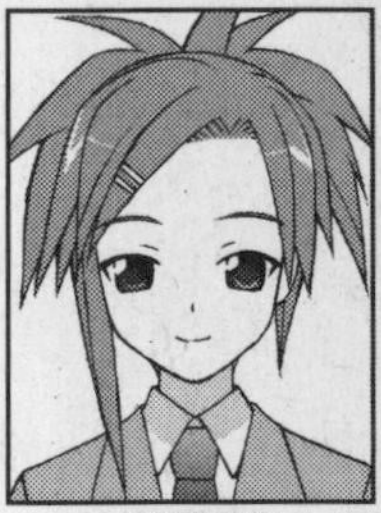

3. KAZUMI ASAKURA
SCHOOL NEWSPAPER

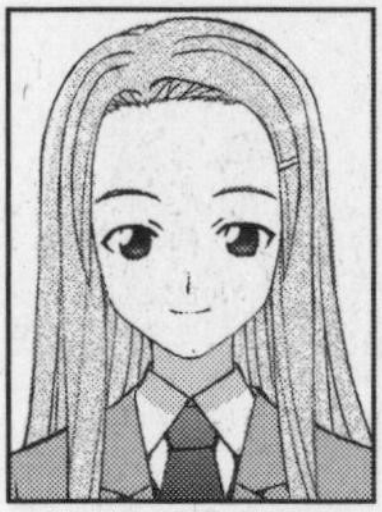

7. MISA KAKIZAKI
CHEERLEADER, CHORUS

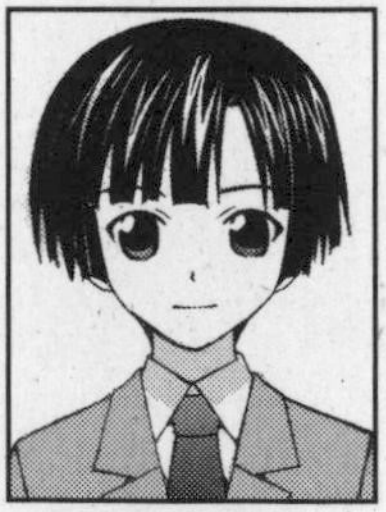

11. MADOKA KUGIMIYA
CHEERLEADER

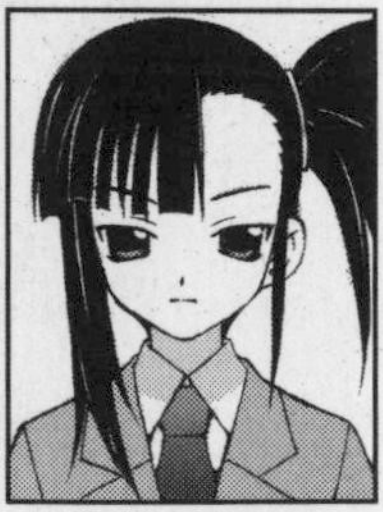

15. SETSUNA SAKURAZAKI
KENDO CLUB

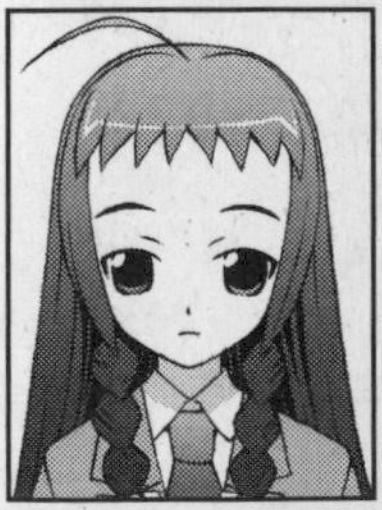

4. YUE AYASE
KIDS' LIT CLUB, PHILOSOPHY CLUB, LIBRARY EXPLORATION CLUB

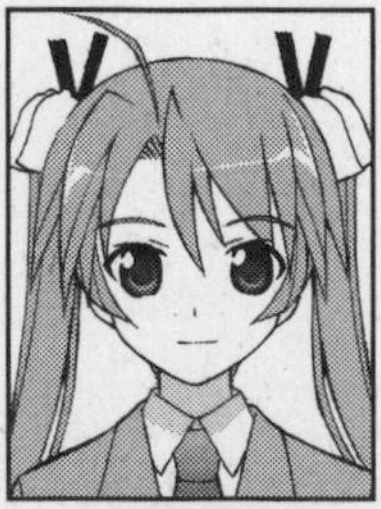

8. ASUNA KAGURAZAKA
ART CLUB

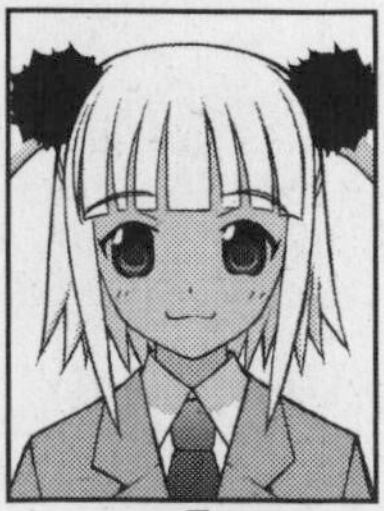

12. KŪ FEI
CHINESE MARTIAL ARTS CLUB

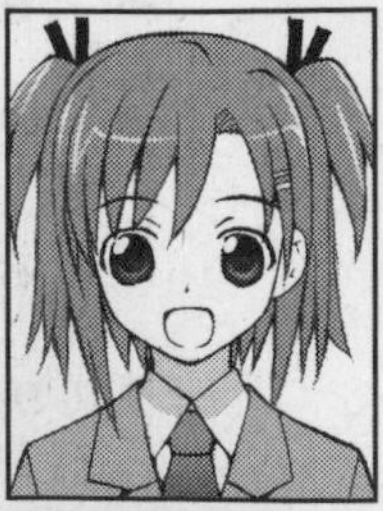

16. MAKIE SASAKI
GYMNASTICS

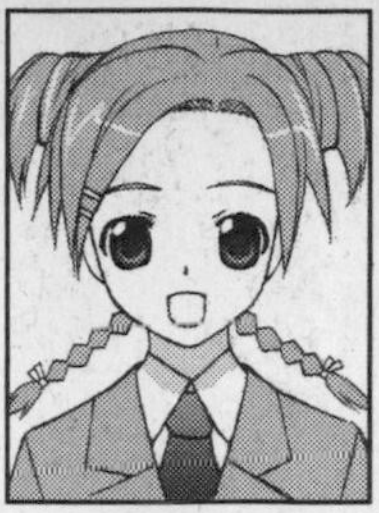

17. SAKURAKO SHIINA
LACROSSE TEAM, CHEERLEADER

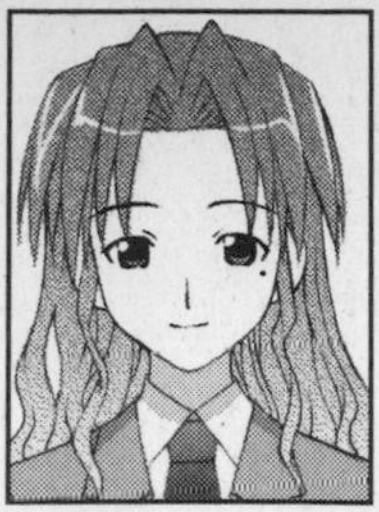

21. CHIZURU NABA
ASTRONOMY CLUB

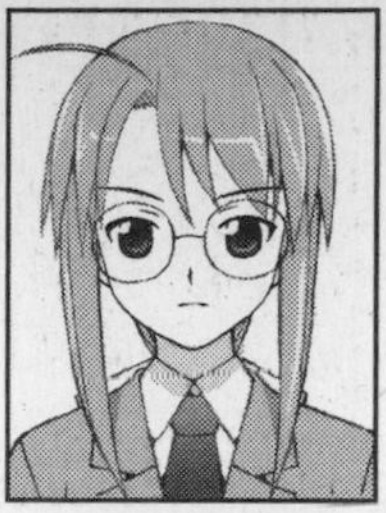

25. CHISAME HASEGAWA

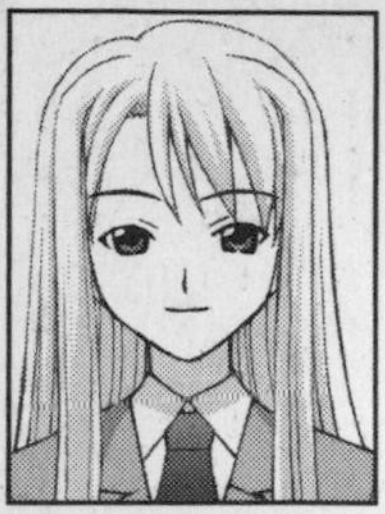

29. AYAKA YUKIHIRO
CLASS REPRESENTATIVE, EQUESTRIAN CLUB, FLOWER ARRANGEMENT CLUB

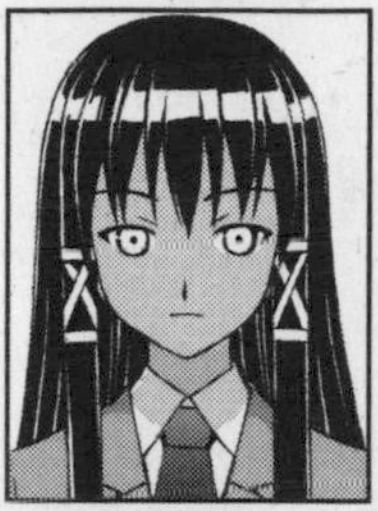

18. MANA TATSUMIYA
BIATHLON (NON-SCHOOL ACTIVITY)

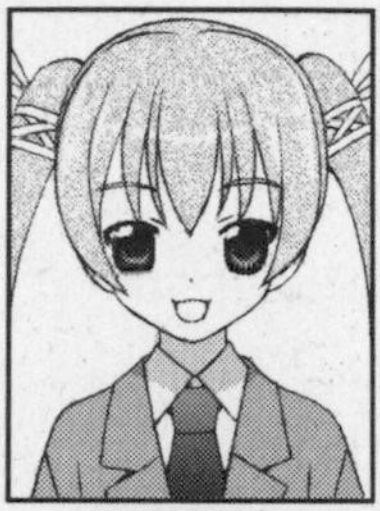

22. FUKA NARUTAKI
WALKING CLUB

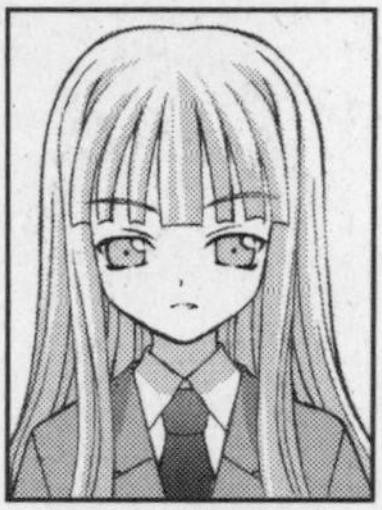

26. EVANGELINE A.K. MCDOWELL
GO CLUB, TEA CEREMONY CLUB

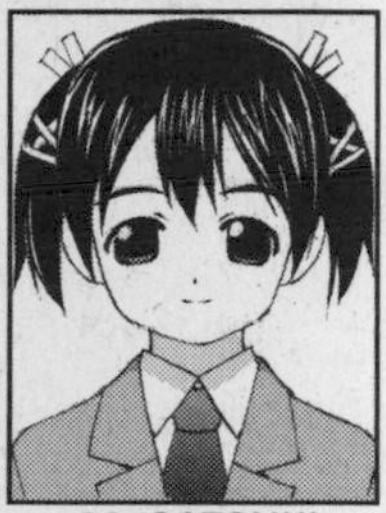

30. SATSUKI YOTSUBA
LUNCH REPRESENTATIVE, COOKING CLUB

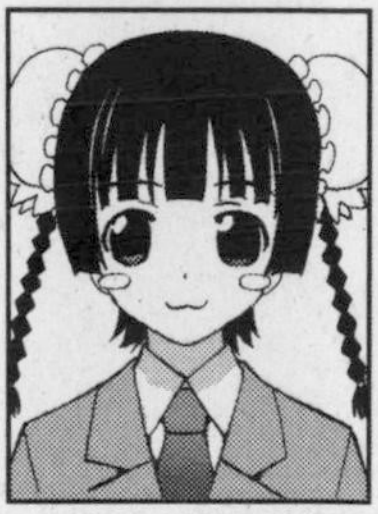

19. CHAO LINGSHEN
COOKING CLUB, CHINESE MARTIAL ARTS CLUB, ROBOTICS CLUB, CHINESE MEDICINE CLUB, BIO-ENGINEERING CLUB, QUANTUM PHYSICS CLUB (UNIVERSITY)

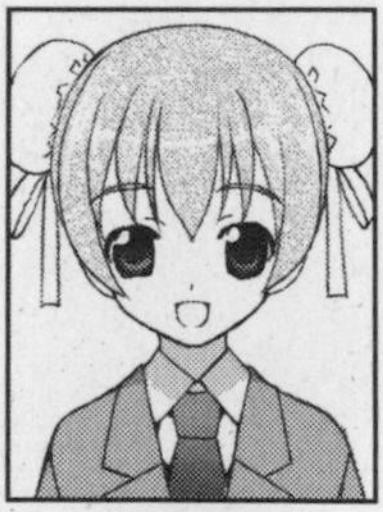

23. FUMIKA NARUTAKI
SCHOOL BEAUTIFICATION COMMITTEE, WALKING CLUB

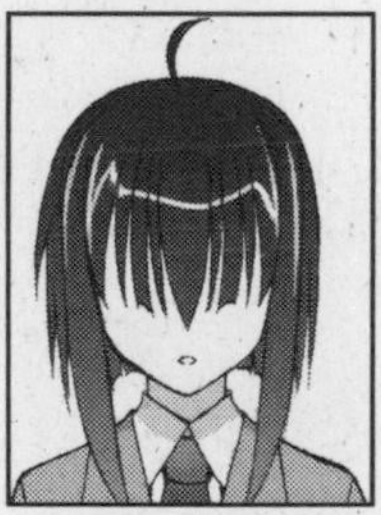

27. NODOKA MIYAZAKI
GENERAL LIBRARY COMMITTEE MEMBER, LIBRARIAN, LIBRARY EXPLORATION CLUB

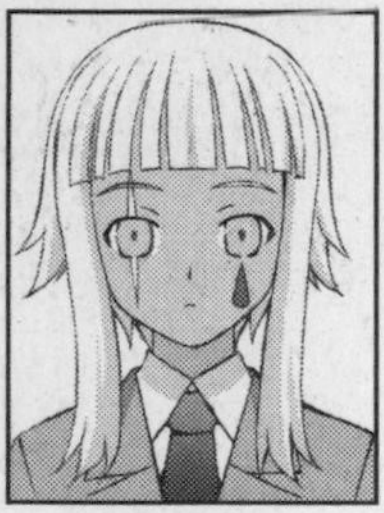

31. ZAZIE RAINYDAY
MAGIC AND ACROBATICS CLUB (NON-SCHOOL ACTIVITY)

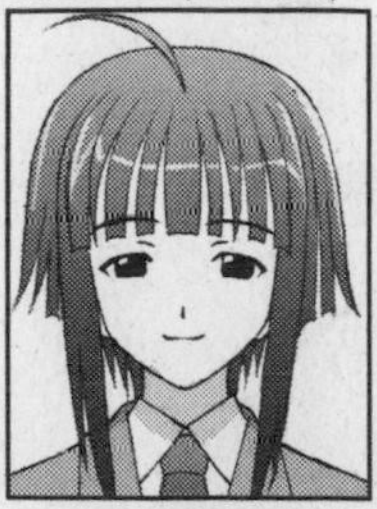

20. KAEDE NAGASE
WALKING CLUB

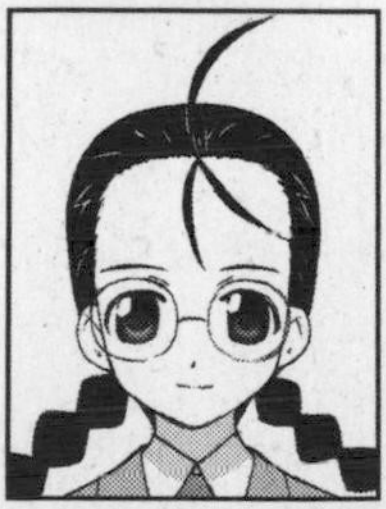

24. SATOMI HAKASE
ROBOTICS CLUB (UNIVERSITY), JET PROPULSION CLUB (UNIVERSITY)

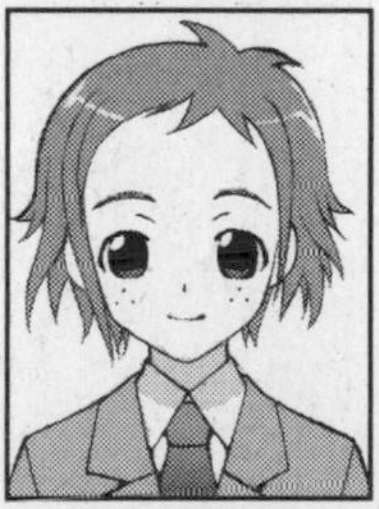

28. NATSUMI MURAKAMI
DRAMA CLUB

Translation Notes

Japanese is a tricky language for most Westerners, and translation is often more art than science. For your edification and reading pleasure, here are notes on some of the places where we could have gone in a different direction with our translation of the work, or where a Japanese cultural reference is used.

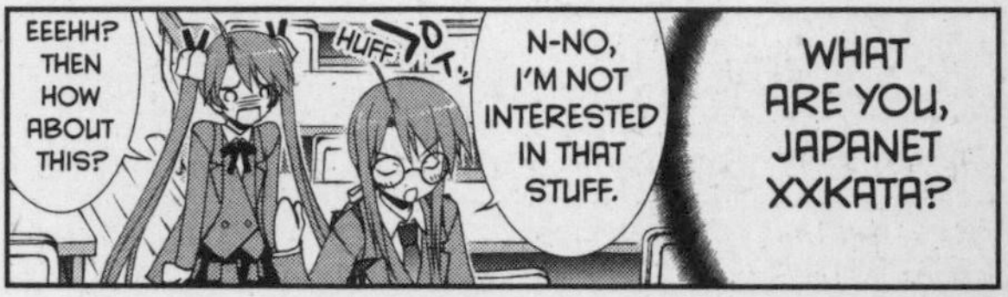
WHAT ARE YOU, JAPANET XXKATA?
N-NO, I'M NOT INTERESTED IN THAT STUFF.
HUFF
EEEHH? THEN HOW ABOUT THIS?

Japanet Takata, page 42

Japanet Takata is a big home-shopping company in Japan, much like QVC here in America. They advertise their products over TV and radio, and of course they have a website. The name was X-ed out when Chisame thought it, because it's copyrighted and she didn't want to get Fujima-sensei in trouble.

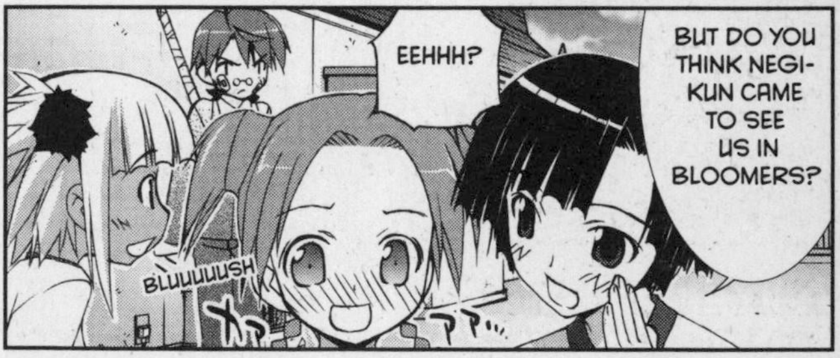
BUT DO YOU THINK NEGI-KUN CAME TO SEE US IN BLOOMERS?
EEHHH?
BLUUUUUSH

Bloomers, page 117

Here, "bloomers" refers to the shorts the girls are wearing as part of their P.E. uniform.

One plus one, page 173

As we all know, one plus one is two, or in Japanese, "*ni*." "Ni" also happens to be the sound of a smile, so saying it is kind of like saying "cheese" for a picture.

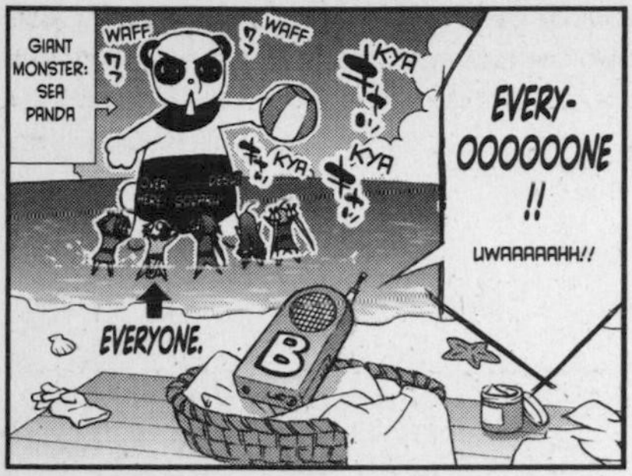
EVERY-
OOOOOONE
!!
UWAAAAAHH!!
WAFF
WAFF
KYA
KYA
KYA
KYA
GIANT MONSTER: SEA PANDA
EVERYONE.

Desu and *gozaru*, page 176

Just as a reminder, Yue usually ends her sentences with *desu* to make them polite, whether it's grammatically correct or not, and Kaede ends many of her sentences in *gozaru* to make them more polite and ninja-esque.

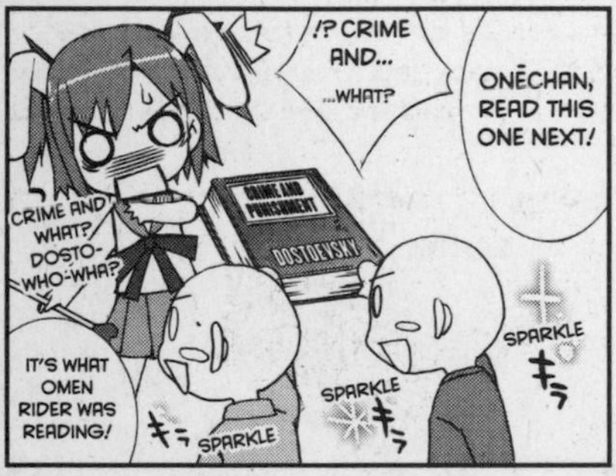
ONĒCHAN, READ THIS ONE NEXT!
!? CRIME AND...
...WHAT?
CRIME AND WHAT? DOSTO-WHO-WHA?
CRIME AND PUNISHMENT
DOSTOEVSKY
SPARKLE
SPARKLE
IT'S WHAT OMEN RIDER WAS READING!
SPARKLE

Omen Rider, page 177

Omen Rider is a superhero, much like Kamen Rider. Both *omen* and *kamen* mean mask, so they're both Masked Riders. They work a lot like the Power Rangers, so it would make sense that Omen Rider would also be reading books to kids at the library.

Ah kuma, page 179

This protestor's sign says "Ah kuma," which could mean one of two things. As one word, *akuma*, it means devil, something you might call someone you're protesting against. But separate, it can mean, "Oh, a bear!" which might explain the silhouette of what looks like a flying bear on the sign.

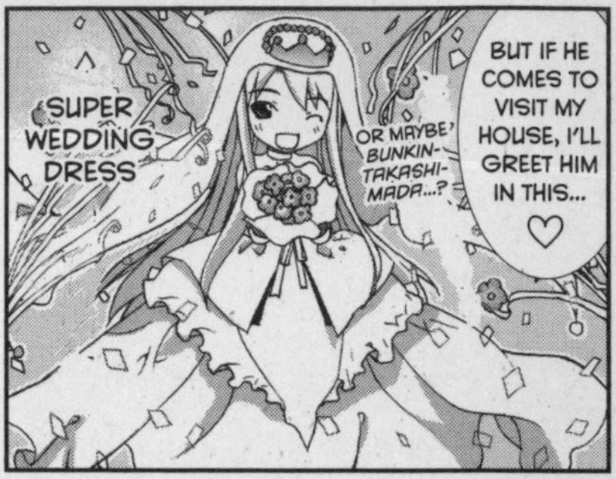
BUT IF HE COMES TO VISIT MY HOUSE, I'LL GREET HIM IN THIS... ♡
OR MAYBE BUNKIN-TAKASHIMADA...?
SUPER WEDDING DRESS

Bunkin-takashimada, page 179

Bunkin-takashimada is a traditional Japanese hair style worn by brides at traditional Japanese weddings.

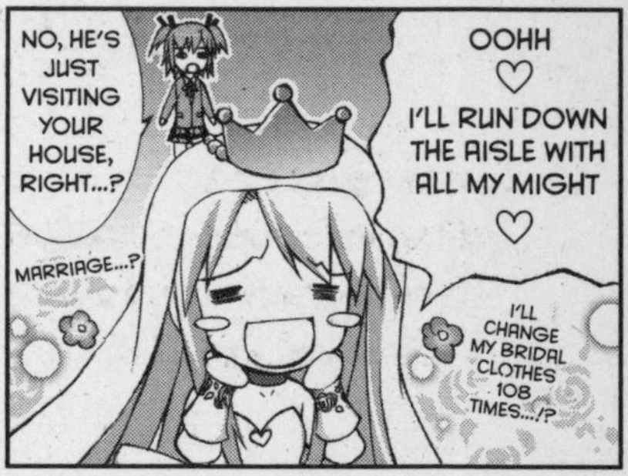
OOHH ♡ I'LL RUN DOWN THE AISLE WITH ALL MY MIGHT ♡
NO, HE'S JUST VISITING YOUR HOUSE, RIGHT...?
I'LL CHANGE MY BRIDAL CLOTHES 108 TIMES...!?
MARRIAGE...?

Changing her bridal clothes, page 179

At Japanese wedding receptions, sometimes the bride and groom change out of the clothes they wore for the ceremony and into something a little more colorful. Also, in the case of traditional Japanese weddings, sometimes they will change from their traditional Japanese clothing into something more Western (in the case of a bride, from a kimono into a gown). This is called *ironaoshi* (or *o-ironaoshi*, to be more polite), and only someone as rich as Ayaka would be able to afford 108 wedding outfits.

Preview of
Negima!? neo
Volume 4

**We're pleased to present you a preview from volume 4.
Please check our website (www.delreymanga.com)
to see when this volume will be available in English.
For now you'll have to make do with Japanese!**

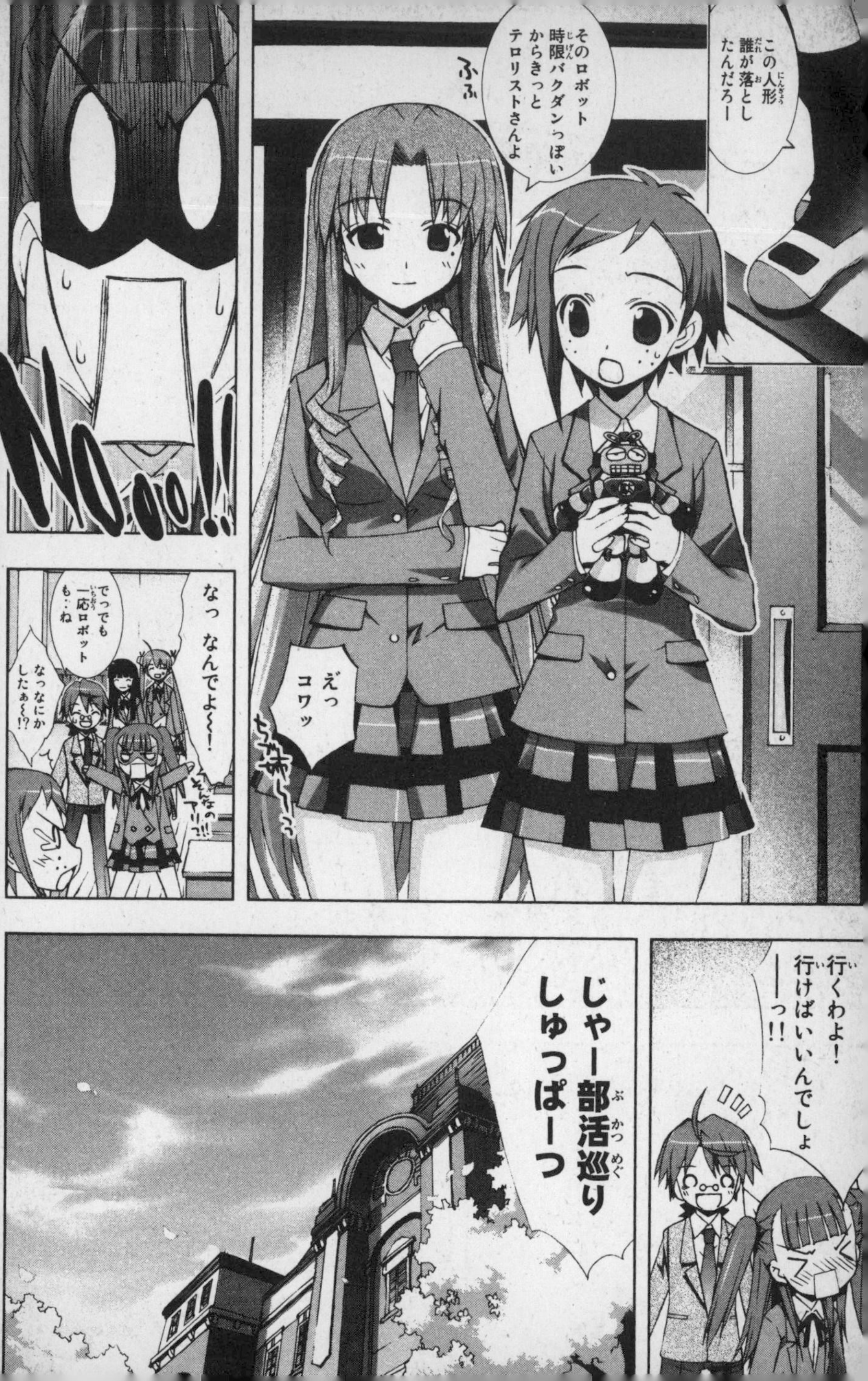
この人形誰が落としたんだろー
そのロボット時限バクダンっぽいからきっとテロリストさんよ
ふふ
えっ コワッ
NOooo!!
なっ なんでよ〜!
でっでも一応ロボットも…ね
なっなにかしたぁ〜!?
そんなのアリっ!!
行くわよ! 行けばいいんでしょーーっ!!
じゃー部活巡りしゅっぱーつ

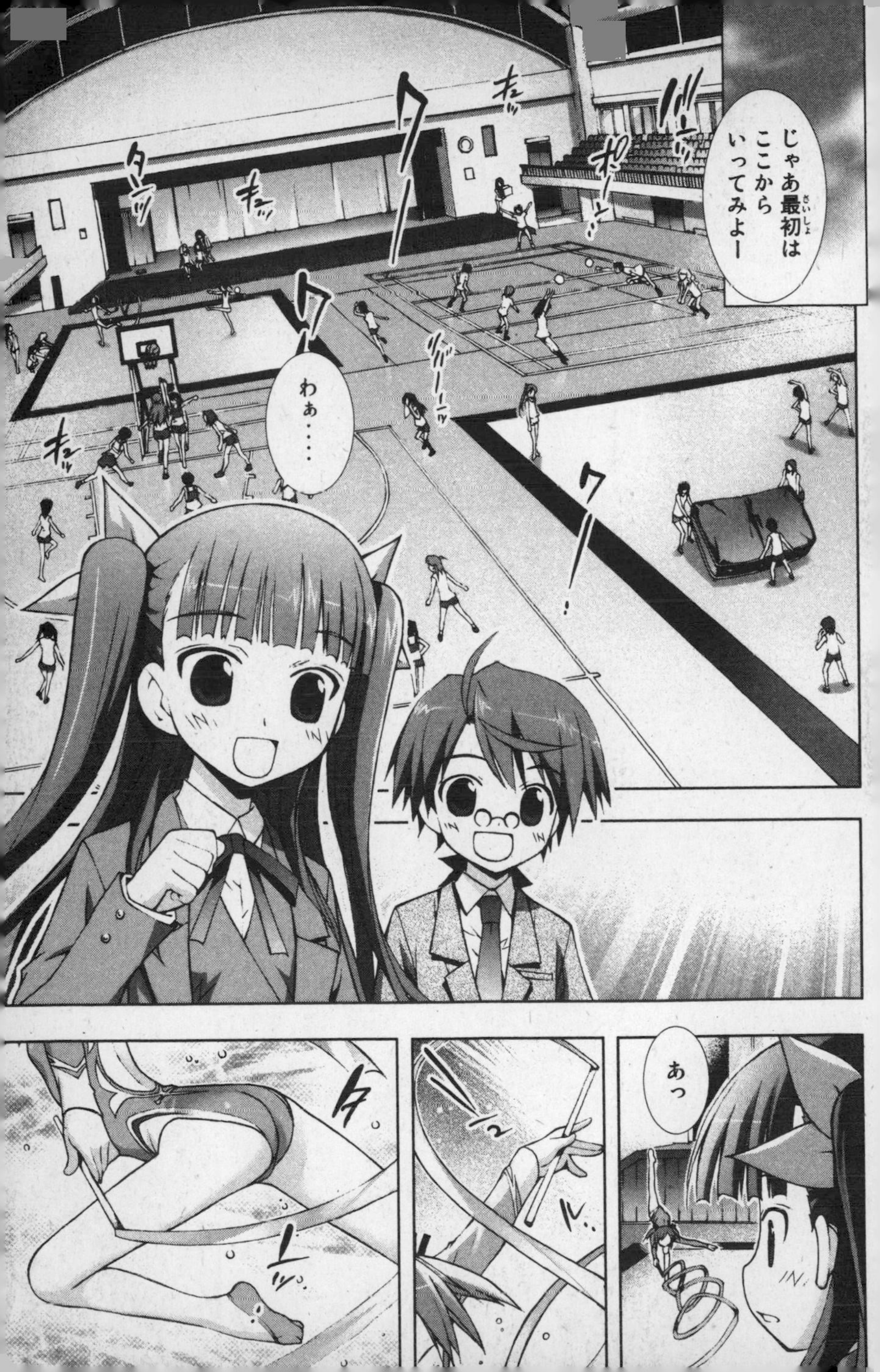
じゃあ最初はここからいってみよー
わぁ・・・・
あっ

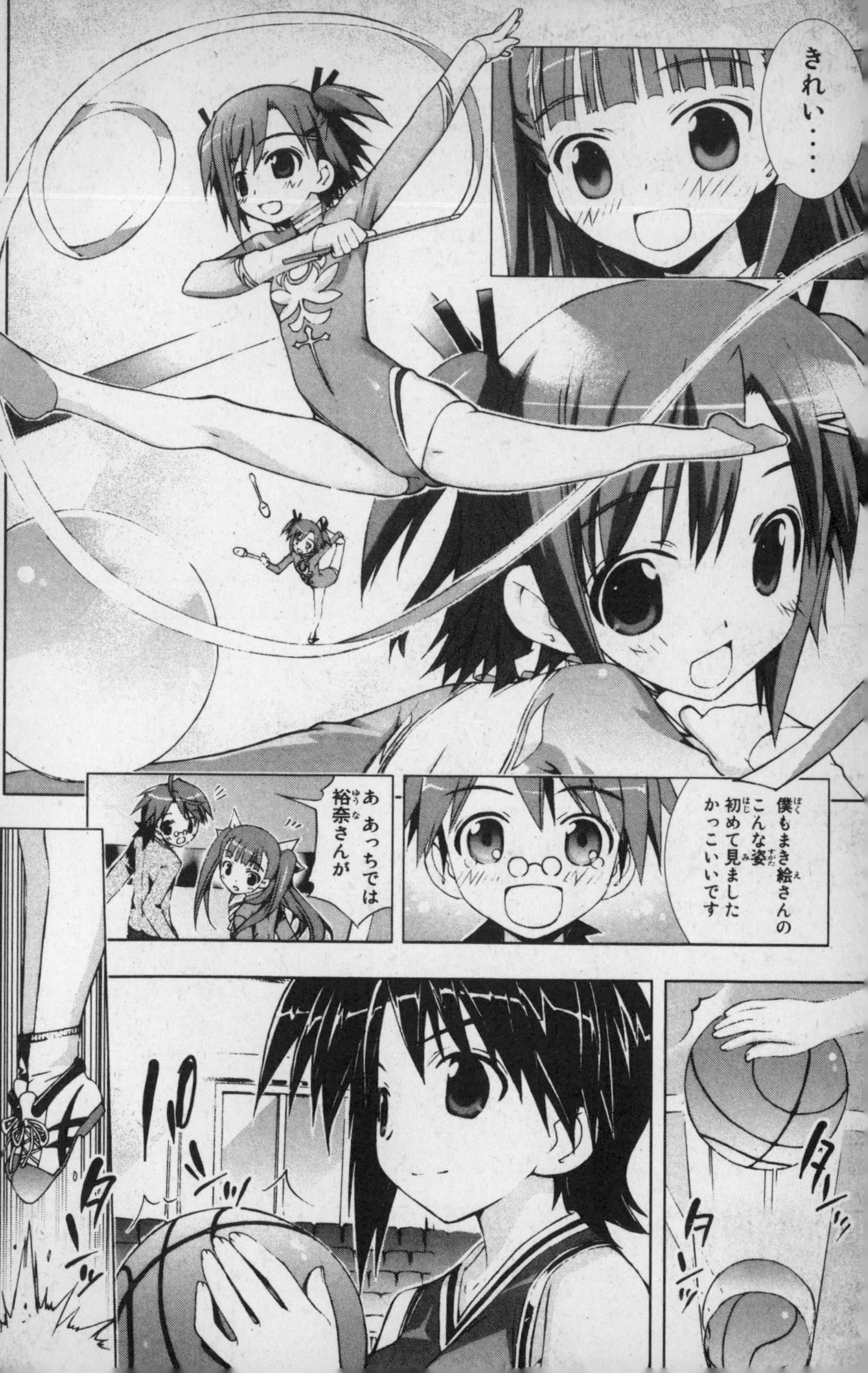
きれい……
僕もまき絵さんのこんな姿初めて見ましたかっこいいです
あ あっちでは裕奈さんが

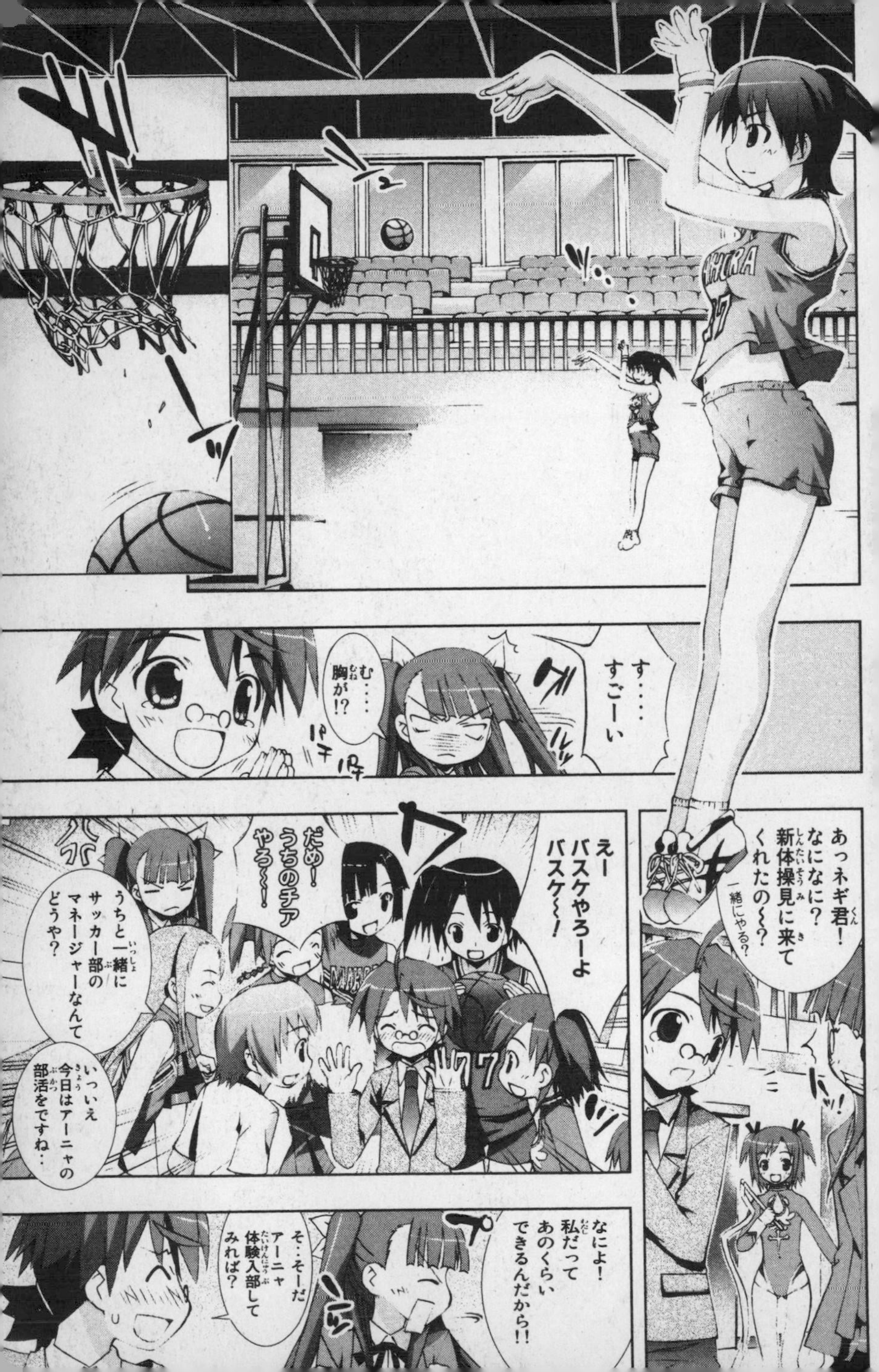
す……
すごーい
む……
胸が!?
あっネギ君!
なになに?
新体操見に来てくれたの~?
一緒にやる?
えー
バスケやろーよ
バスケ~!
だめ!
うちのチア
やろ~~!
うちと一緒に
サッカー部の
マネージャーなんて
どうや?
いっいえ
今日はアーニャの
部活をですね‥
なによ!
私だって
あのくらい
できるんだから!!
そ‥そーだ
アーニャ
体験入部して
みれば?

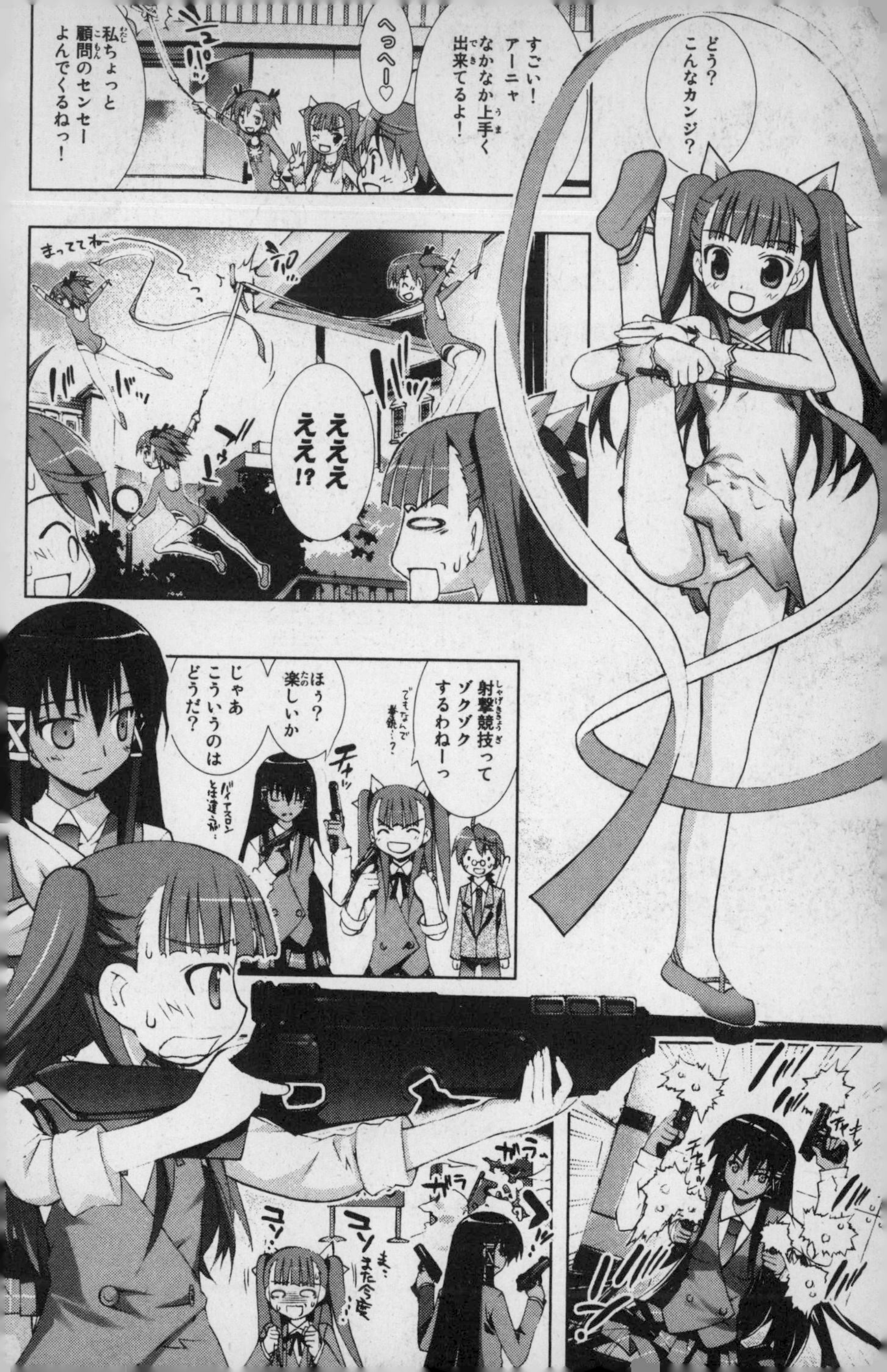
どう？こんなカンジ？
すごい！アーニャなかなか上手く出来てるよ！
へっへー♡
シュパッ
私ちょっと顧問のセンセーよんでくるねっ！
まっててね～
ええええええ!?
射撃競技ってゾクゾクするわねーっ
でもなんで拳銃…？
チャッ
ほぅ？楽しいか
じゃあこういうのは
どうだ？
バイアスロンとは違う…
チャキッ
ガラ
ガラ
ゴツ
ゴツ…
ま、また今度…

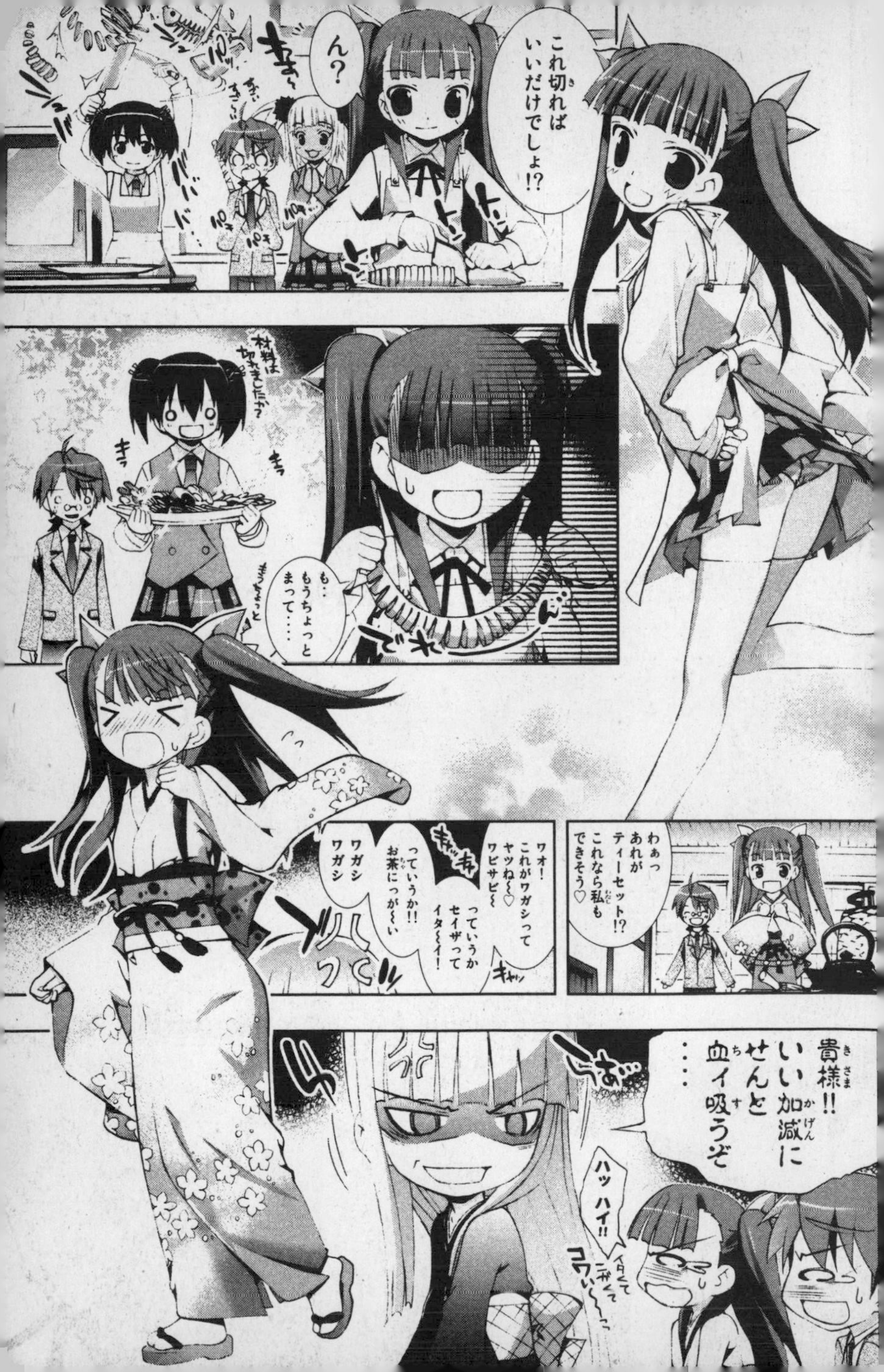
これ切ればいいだけでしょ!?
ん?
トン トン
バババ
材料は切れましたか?
も…もうちょっとまって……
もうちょっと
わぁっ あれがティーセット!? これなら私もできそう♡
ワオ! これがワガシってヤツね~♡ ワビサビ~
っていうかセイザってイタ~イ!
っていうか!! お茶にっが~い
ワガシ ワガシ
貴様!! いい加減にせんと血イ吸うぞ……
ハッ ハイ!!
イタくてニガくてコワい~~

PHOENIX WRIGHT
ACE ATTORNEY:
OFFICIAL CASEBOOK

BASED ON THE HIT VIDEO GAME FROM CAPCOM!

VOLUME ONE: THE PHOENIX WRIGHT FILES
VOLUME TWO: THE MILES EDGEWORTH FILES

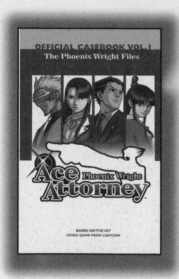

Available anywhere books or comics are sold!

IT'S HERO TIME!

BASED ON THE HIT CARTOON NETWORK SERIES

BEN 10: ALIEN FORCE

Ben Tennyson chose to lead a normal life, setting aside the awesome power of the Omnitrix.

Now, five years later, Grandpa Max has been kidnapped, strange aliens threaten Earth, and only Ben and his superpowered friends Gwen and Kevin can save the day!

Available anywhere books or comics are sold!

TOMARE!
STOP

You're going the wrong way!

MANGA IS A COMPLETELY DIFFERENT TYPE OF READING EXPERIENCE.

TO START AT THE BEGINNING, GO TO THE END!

That's right!

Authentic manga is read the traditional Japanese way—from right to left—exactly the opposite of how American books are read. It's easy to follow: Just go to the other end of the book, and read each page—and each panel—from right side to left side, starting at the top right. Now you're experiencing manga as it was meant to be!

NOV 09

CH